# Architecting Solutions with SAP Business Technology Platform

An architectural guide to integrating, extending, and innovating enterprise solutions using SAP BTP

**Serdar Simsekler**

**Eric Du**

BIRMINGHAM—MUMBAI

# Architecting Solutions with SAP Business Technology Platform

**Associate Group Product Manager**: Alok Dhuri
**Publishing Product Manager**: Alok Dhuri
**Project Manager**: Prajakta Naik
**Senior Editor**: Rounak Kulkarni
**Technical Editor**: Maran Fernandes
**Copy Editor**: Safis Editing
**Project Coordinator**: Manisha Singh
**Proofreader**: Safis Editing
**Indexer**: Pratik Shirodkar
**Production Designer**: Shankar Kalbhor
**Developer Relations Marketing Executives**: Deepak Kumar and Rayyan Khan
**Business Development Executive**: Puneet Kaur

First published: October 2022
Production reference: 1141022

Published by Packt Publishing Ltd.
Livery Place
35 Livery Street
Birmingham
B3 2PB, UK.

ISBN 978-1-80107-567-1
www.packt.com

*To my wife Busra, (the Muse), and my children, Daniel Kerim (the Pioneer) and Isaac Faruk (the Integrator), for being my source of happiness. And, to my parents Mucefer and Ibrahim for their unconditional support throughout all my life.*

*– Serdar Simsekler*

*I am grateful to a large number of people who have taken the time to discuss various topics and share their knowledge with me. Thanks to the editors and team for their patience with my slow writing and unusual requests. Finally, my love goes to my family for their support through the writing process.*

*– Eric Du*

# Contributors

## About the authors

**Serdar Simsekler** is passionate about delivering innovative and robust technology solutions for business needs. His focus areas are enterprise architecture, IT strategy, innovation, cloud architecture, integration patterns, and software architecture. Currently working as an SAP Architect at Deloitte, he supports the digital transformation of several clients. He also leads Deloitte UK's SAP Cloud Architecture and BTP capability. In his previous Head of SAP Technology role at Centrica, he was responsible for developing the technology strategy for the entire SAP landscape of the enterprise. He likes reading philosophy and keeps self-nurturing his curiosity to learn new things. He lives with his wife and two sons in Surrey, United Kingdom.

**Eric Du** is a product and technology leader with a broad experience and expertise in the enterprise space. Currently working as VP of Technology & Architecture at SAP SuccessFactors, he leads the architectural efforts for the technology transformation by defining the target architecture, platform strategy, and culture transformation. Prior to this role, he focused on SAP's cross-product strategy and co-led SAP's overall North Star Architecture to shape the technology vision for SAP's Intelligent Enterprise strategy and define the architecture guardrails. Based in Silicon Valley, Eric is passionate about innovations; he serves the role of advisor and investor for multiple start-up companies. He lives with his family in Dublin, California.

## About the reviewer

As a lead solution architect at one of the world's leading technology companies, **Haishan Qian** designs, builds, and implements large-scale enterprise finance systems for global business operations, including digital media stores, subscription services, retail, and finished goods.

# Table of Contents

# Part 2 Foundations

## 3

## 4

5

# Non-Functional Design for Operability      99

# Part 3 Integration

6

# Defining Integration Strategy      129

# 7

## Cloud Integration                                                    151

# 8

## Data Integration                                                     187

# Part 4 Extensibility

9

## Application Development    209

# Part 5 Data to Value

## 13

# SAP Data Warehouse Cloud and SAP Analytics Cloud    323

## 14

# SAP Intelligent Technologies    365

# Preface

Digitalization has been a priority for all sizable companies to introduce efficiency, agility, and innovation. The world is changing so fast, and customers are becoming more demanding. Every company has its own digital transformation strategy to differentiate itself from the competition, and executives know that digitalization is vital for differentiation.

SAP BTP is the foundation of SAP's intelligent and sustainable enterprise vision for its customers. It's efficient, agile, and an enabler for innovation. It's technically robust, yet its superpower is its business centricity.

If you are involved in building IT and business strategies, it's essential to get yourself familiar with SAP BTP to see the big picture for digitalization with SAP solutions. Similarly, if you have design responsibilities for enterprise solutions, learning SAP BTP is crucial to produce effective and complete architecture designs.

Before reading a technical book, it's important to align your objectives with what the book offers. *Architecting Solutions with SAP Business Technology Platform* aims to provide a generalist view of SAP BTP capabilities. We were careful to provide design examples so that you can see in action the SAP BTP features we discussed.

There may be parts where we delve into more detail than usual or topics that we cover with briefer content than others. At the end of the day, we wanted to cover the end-to-end spectrum of SAP BTP services and provide as many primers as we could. This way, we hope you can see the complete picture of what SAP BTP caters to and get the right direction for further studying.

With this book, you'll learn SAP BTP in five parts. First, you'll see how SAP BTP is positioned in the intelligent enterprise. In the second part, you will learn the foundational elements of SAP BTP and how it operates. The next part covers integration architecture guidelines, integration strategy considerations, and integration styles with SAP's integration technologies. Later, you'll learn how to use application development capabilities to extend enterprise solutions for innovation and agility. This part also includes digital experience and process automation capabilities. The last part covers how SAP BTP can facilitate data-to-value and business intelligence use cases to produce actionable insights.

By the end of this book, you'll be able to architect solutions using SAP BTP to deliver high business value. Now, there is a lot to learn and time is precious. Happy reading!

**Disclaimer:**

Some diagrams in this book contain materials from *SAP Business Technology Platform Solution Diagrams, Design Elements & Icons*, used with the permission of SAP SE.

# Who this book is for

This SAP guide is for technical architects, solution architects, and enterprise architects working with SAP solutions to drive digital transformation and innovation with SAP BTP. We assume our readers already have some IT background and an understanding of basic cloud concepts. Working knowledge of the SAP ecosystem will also be beneficial.

# What this book covers

*Chapter 1, The Intelligent Enterprise*, introduces you to SAP's Intelligent Enterprise, its value propositions, and the business processes it can enable.

*Chapter 2, SAP Business Technology Platform Overview*, introduces the key pillars of **SAP Business Technology Platform (BTP)**.

*Chapter 3, Establishing a Foundation for SAP Business Technology Platform*, contains information on the foundational concepts of SAP BTP so that you understand the terminology and fundamental information before delving into the details in subsequent chapters.

*Chapter 4, Security and Connectivity*, contains information about the security elements of SAP BTP, which will help you understand the platform foundation that provides services for IAM and other security requirements.

*Chapter 5, Non-Functional Design for Operability*, provides information on how to design for operability considering non-functional requirements. This chapter will cover the NFD elements collectively and refer to further details that will be discussed in later chapters. This chapter will also discuss how SAP BTP is supported by SAP, SLA arrangements, Trust Center, engagements, and more.

*Chapter 6, Defining Integration Strategy*, teaches you about structured elements for building an integration methodology and defining an integration strategy.

*Chapter 7, Cloud Integration*, helps you understand process integration better by explaining the available options in SAP Integration Suite and elaborating on various use cases. As cross use cases, the API-based and event-driven integration topics will be explained by focusing on APIM and Event Mesh. Finally, the Open Connectors capability will be explained to illustrate how streamlined third-party application connectivity works.

*Chapter 8, Data Integration*, helps you understand data integration better by elaborating on various data integration use cases, mainly introducing the capabilities of SAP Data Intelligence and briefly touching upon other data integration solutions.

*Chapter 9, Application Development*, provides information on the application development options that you can incorporate in architecture designs. This chapter will introduce the Extension Suite capabilities and other SAP BTP services for digital experience.

*Chapter 10, Digital Process Automation*, explains what SAP BTP offers for process automation.

*Chapter 11, Containers and Kubernetes*, introduces the cloud-native programming model in SAP BTP. This chapter also explores how to use open-source projects and the capabilities of SAP using Gardener and Kyma.

*Chapter 12, SAP HANA Cloud*, introduces SAP HANA Cloud for storing and processing data.

*Chapter 13, SAP Data Warehouse Cloud and SAP Analytics Cloud*, introduces SAP Data Warehouse Cloud for modeling business semantics and SAP Analytics Cloud for advanced analytics, looking at how to use them to gain insights and support business decisions with confidence.

*Chapter 14, SAP Intelligent Technologies*, introduces SAP's ML/AI offerings to embed intelligence into your business processes.

# Download the color images

We also provide a PDF file that has color images of the screenshots and diagrams used in this book. You can download it here: `https://packt.link/K9xmW`.

# Conventions used

There are a number of text conventions used throughout this book.

`Code in text`: Indicates code words in text, database table names, folder names, filenames, file extensions, pathnames, dummy URLs, user input, and Twitter handles. Here is an example: "This means you can access these REST APIs with additional OData features, such as `$expand`, `$filter`, `$top`, and so on."

**Bold**: Indicates a new term, an important word, or words that you see onscreen. For instance, words in menus or dialog boxes appear in **bold**. Here is an example: "Select **System info** from the **Administration** panel."

> **Tips or important notes**
> Appear like this.

# Get in touch

Feedback from our readers is always welcome.

**General feedback**: If you have questions about any aspect of this book, email us at `customercare@packtpub.com` and mention the book title in the subject of your message.

**Errata**: Although we have taken every care to ensure the accuracy of our content, mistakes do happen. If you have found a mistake in this book, we would be grateful if you would report this to us. Please visit `www.packtpub.com/support/errata` and fill in the form.

**Piracy**: If you come across any illegal copies of our works in any form on the internet, we would be grateful if you would provide us with the location address or website name. Please contact us at `copyright@packt.com` with a link to the material.

**If you are interested in becoming an author**: If there is a topic that you have expertise in and you are interested in either writing or contributing to a book, please visit `authors.packtpub.com`.

# Share Your Thoughts

Once you've read *Architecting Solutions with SAP Business Technology Platform*, we'd love to hear your thoughts! Scan the QR code below to go straight to the Amazon review page for this book and share your feedback.

`https://packt.link/r/1801075670`

Your review is important to us and the tech community and will help us make sure we're delivering excellent quality content.

# Download a Free PDF copy of this book

Thanks for purchasing this book!

Do you like to read on the go but are unable to carry your print books everywhere?

Is your eBook purchase not compatible with the device of your choice?

Don't worry, now with every Packt book you get a DRM-free PDF version of that book at no cost.

Read anywhere, any place, on any device. Search, copy, and paste code from your favorite technical books directly into your application.

The perks don't stop there, you can get exclusive access to discounts, newsletters, and great free content in your inbox daily

Follow these simple steps to get the benefits:

1.  Scan the QR code or visit the link below

https://packt.link/free-ebook/978-1-80107-567-1

2.  Submit your proof of purchase
3.  That's it! We'll send your free PDF and other benefits to your email directly

# Part 1
# Introduction – What is SAP Business Technology Platform?

This part will introduce you to SAP **Business Technology Platform** (**BTP**) with an aim to highlight its importance and benefits. The first chapter will also help establish the role of SAP BTP as the platform of Intelligent Enterprise.

This part contains the following chapters:

- *Chapter 1, The Intelligent Enterprise*
- *Chapter 2, SAP Business Technology Platform Overview*

# 1
# The Intelligent Enterprise

In today's fast-moving world, businesses are constantly dealing with changes. What becomes clear is businesses with a digital strategy have been at an advantage to adapt to and navigate the crisis better. The COVID-19 crisis has made this imperative more urgent than ever. It has pushed companies over the technology tipping point and speeded up the adoption of digital technologies by several years.

Shifts during the crisis are most likely to stick through the recovery or have been transformed forever. To stay ahead, businesses need to adjust to evolving customer needs or expectations, increase remote working and online collaborations, build redundancy and full visibility in the supply chain with the qualification of additional suppliers, and use advanced technologies in operations and business decision-making. **SAP's** products and services address this need for agility by delivering software services to enable businesses to integrate and extend **end-to-end** (**E2E**) business processes, create new business models, and ultimately run as intelligent enterprises.

Even though this book is mainly about **SAP Business Technology Platform** (**SAP BTP**), it is important to understand the overall framework and how SAP BTP is fitting into the picture as the platform of Intelligent Enterprise. In this chapter, we are going to cover the following topics:

- What is Intelligent Enterprise?
- SAP offerings for Intelligent Enterprise

## What is Intelligent Enterprise?

To overcome challenges and stay ahead in their industry, businesses must be agile and resilient. Businesses should consistently apply advanced technologies and best practices to transform, innovate, and grow more profitable and sustainable. Intelligent Enterprise is the strategy and framework that represents what a modern enterprise looks like. SAP's strategy is enabled by an entire portfolio of products and services to help businesses to become intelligent enterprises—best-run businesses are intelligent enterprises.

So, what does an intelligent enterprise look like? An intelligent enterprise will run the most critical business processes with industry-leading applications that work together smoothly and with best practices.

These processes span different areas of business operations from lead generation to payment, recruiting to retirement, sourcing to managing different categories of spend, and product design to operate. Data is connected through all these processes to increase efficiency, gain better insights, and make decisions confidently.

The following screenshot provides an overview of the Intelligent Enterprise framework and its components. Through this chapter, we will introduce them and how they fit into the overall framework:

## Intelligent Enterprise

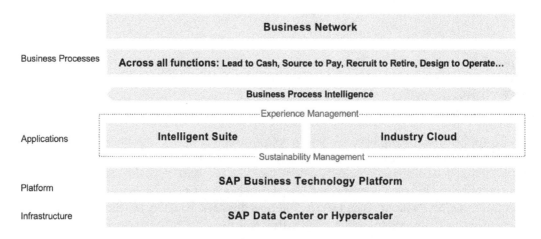

Figure 1.1: Intelligent Enterprise overview

## SAP offerings for Intelligent Enterprise

The SAP Intelligent Enterprise framework provides essential components and helps businesses to adopt capabilities and deliver business outcomes. In this section, we will first discuss the major components of Intelligent Enterprise. After that, we will discuss how they are integrated through business processes and suite qualities.

### Intelligent Suite and Industry Cloud

SAP offers the Intelligent Suite, an integrated suite of applications to support E2E business processes. This suite helps businesses to manage every part of their organization and processes, including customers, employees, supply chains, products, finance, and spend. This comprehensive solution suite brings together SAP S/4HANA, SAP SuccessFactors, customer experience, and intelligent spend solutions with out-of-the-box integrations, alongside critical business processes that every business will need, such as Lead to Cash, Design to Operate, Source to Pay, and Recruit to Retire. The Intelligent Suite is both well integrated and can be consumed in a modular way. It is also infrastructure-agnostic, which results in simplifying adoption and customer choices of running in SAP's cloud infrastructure or through partner cloud providers.

Intelligent Suite offers a great foundation with integrated E2E processes for all industries. Industry Cloud is an extension of Intelligent Suite with innovative industry cloud solutions built by SAP and its partners in SAP BTP. SAP's Industry Cloud is an open business process and technology platform to foster co-innovation between customers, partners, and SAP, to jointly create new business practices resulting in a set of solutions relevant to respective industries. Partners who are looking to extend Intelligent Enterprise can find open **application programming interfaces** (**APIs**), data models, commercialization models, and—of course—SAP BTP to innovate for different industries.

## BTP

SAP BTP is the technological foundation for the intelligent enterprise. It is a unified, business-centric, and open platform for SAP applications and the entire SAP ecosystem. In a nutshell, SAP BTP provides capabilities in the areas of application development, database and data management, analytics, **machine learning** (**ML**), **artificial intelligence** (**AI**), integration, and extension. It is the platform that integrates SAP's Intelligent Suite and the foundation of Industry Cloud. It provides businesses with what they need to transform their business, and the flexibility to run their business applications in multi-cloud environments. SAP BTP can be leveraged to integrate with your existing **information technology** (**IT**) landscape, extend SAP solutions including integration with third-party solutions, and enhance the ability to turn data into value.

## Business Network

Business Network helps organizations and their trading partners to become more agile and resilient and drive better business outcomes.

At its global *Sapphire Now* conference in June 2021, SAP announced a bold vision to create new business communities through SAP Business Network, which brings together SAP Ariba Network, SAP Logistics Business Network, and SAP Asset Intelligence Network. It brings together over 5 million organizations that will benefit from this connected community through the unified offering of SAP Business Network. The first major offering is a unified trading partner portal that provides new collaboration scenarios and enables greater responsiveness. It centralizes access to explore and collaborate with customers, supports intelligent trading partner onboarding and registration, and provides a highly configurable workbench enabling personalized experience based on roles.

In addition, buyers and trading partners can collaborate using shared data and workflows, applying network-wide intelligence to achieve informed business decisions.

## Sustainability management

Sustainability is one of the biggest challenges of our lifetime. Businesses must show accountability and operate in an intelligent way and embed sustainability management as part of core business processes. Sustainability must include raw material sourcing, manufacturing, logistics, or even recycling processes, so E2E supply chain transparency is critical.

SAP solutions have embedded analytical and transactional capabilities that integrate sustainability performance and insights into business processes, which provide a solid foundation to optimize business results and sustainability impacts together. This means businesses can manage product footprints holistically and understand carbon emission insights through the entire value chain. They can manage extended producer responsibility by keeping track of public commitments and new regulations, streamlining compliance processes, and leveraging business network intelligence to gain full **supply chain visibility (SCV)**.

## Experience Management

SAP introduced **Experience Management (XM)** with the capabilities of Qualtrics. To understand what XM is, let's start with what **O-data** and **X-data** are.

O-data is operational data; it's the insights from day-to-data operations, for all the business processes, in sales, service, **human resources (HR)**, finance, and procurement. O-data tells what is happening. X-data is experience data and is fundamentally different from O-data. It is the human factor—beliefs, emotions, intentions, and sentiments. X-data tells you why things are happening, as well as what matters most to your customers, employees, products, and brands.

SAP has the most comprehensive portfolio to help companies run their businesses, across all lines of business. This is where O-data comes from. Qualtrics is the XM platform to collect X-data from all kinds of channels. X-data adds insights into human factors, helping operational systems take action on every moment that matters, to optimize processes that lead to outcomes of better customer satisfaction and employee engagement, better product-market fit, and brand success.

When X-data connects with O-data, businesses can start to understand why things are happening and put in place necessary actions for improvements. This is the continuous feedback and improvement loop that we can summarize as a simple methodology of *listen, understand, and act*. This is what all businesses will need to win and grow in this experience economy.

## Business Process Intelligence

**Business Process Intelligence (BPI)** is the process layer within the SAP portfolio, combining process insights and improvement solutions from SAP and process mining and transformation technology through the acquisition of Signavio. It includes components such as process discovery, mining, design and simulate, improvement, rollout, and governance of workflows. BPI solutions help businesses to understand and transform their processes and lay the foundation to become the intelligent enterprise of the future.

## Multi-cloud infrastructure

SAP embraces a multi-cloud strategy and provides certain flexibilities for customers to run their applications on the infrastructure of their choice, either in SAP data centers or through a partnership with leading cloud providers such as **Amazon Web Services** (**AWS**), Microsoft Azure, **Google Cloud Platform** (**GCP**), and Alibaba Cloud in China. It helps customers to be more agile and works better with their own cloud strategies, providing necessary optimizations to increase cloud resiliency, **business continuity** (**BC**), security operations, and opportunities to reduce the **total cost of ownership** (**TCO**).

## Integration

A key part of SAP's Intelligent Enterprise strategy is integration, to provide out-of-the-box integration for E2E business processes in the cloud and in hybrid scenarios and provide a consistent **user experience** (**UX**) with a core set of suite-like qualities. The integration approach goes far beyond technical integration; instead, it offers a holistic integration of business processes, technology, and data. Together, it helps to lower efforts for customized integrations, shorten **time to value** (**TTV**), and reduce the complexity of operations. The integration also enables intelligence with connected data and insights.

### *Integrated business processes*

SAP is continuing to invest in integrated business processes across the portfolio, and has made significant progress with a cloud-first approach but also by enabling hybrid scenarios with SAP S/4HANA on-premises. Key processes include the following:

- Lead to Cash
- Recruit to Retire
- Source to Pay
- Design to Operate

**Lead to Cash**

Today, it is important for organizations to engage with their customers most effectively. The Lead to Cash process brings together **SAP Customer Experience** (**SAP CX**) solutions (including SAP Commerce Cloud, SAP Marketing Cloud, SAP Sales Cloud, SAP Service Cloud, SAP Customer Data Cloud, **SAP Configure Price Quote** (**SAP CPQ**), and more) and SAP S/4HANA to help organizations understand their customers' needs and meet their expectations.

The customer experience really starts from the initial interaction with prospects, all the way to order fulfillment, service delivery, or even the return process. A good experience requires seamless collaboration between marketing and sales teams, supported by capabilities through integration that allows customers to build qualified pipelines faster, automated opportunity updates to the quote creation process, and flexible pricing configurations.

The Lead to Cash process also enables new business models with the flexibility to sell physical products, service products, and subscription products in a unified way based on their own specific combinations.

## Recruit to Retire

The global pandemic has dramatically changed the way everyone works and how every organization engages its workforce, including both employees and external workers. This is where Recruit to Retire comes to play. The process brings together solutions of SAP SuccessFactors, SAP S/4HANA Cloud, SAP Concur, SAP Fieldglass, SAP Analytics Cloud, and Qualtrics. It provides an E2E HR process that enables businesses to understand and optimize all aspects through the entire lifecycle, from recruiting, onboarding, learning, performance, and even offboarding. It helps to manage the workforce in line with business objectives and take care of the employee experience.

Recruit to Retire is supported by three sub-processes, as outlined here:

- **Hire to Retire** covers employee experience through the employment lifecycle—for example, new hiring information shared across different modules of SAP SuccessFactors from recruiting to onboarding.

- **Travel to Reimburse** covers travel and expense management—for example, delta posting allows paid expense reports from SAP Concur to be adjusted for audit compliance and decreasing cost.

- **External Workforce** provides capabilities to engage with the contingent workforce—for example, settlement receipt prevents invoice variance and faster closure of transactions in SAP Fieldglass.

## Source to Pay

With economic volatility at an all-time high, customers have increased the need for procurement agility and integrated platforms more than ever before, including key priorities such as strengthening supply-chain resilience, transparency, and 360-degree visibility, centralized sourcing, persona-based guided buying, and contract management.

The Source to Pay process brings together best-of-breed SAP procurement applications (including SAP S/4HANA, SAP Ariba, SAP Concur, and SAP Fieldglass), along with SAP Business Network, on a common platform with integrated data models and UXs. The out-of-the-box real-time analytical insights and intelligence help to enhance decision-making. The process covers strategic, tactical, and operational procurement, as well as supplier management and collaboration, as outlined here:

- **Supplier Management and Collaboration** integrates supplier records with consistent qualification, segmentation, and supplier risk management.

- **Source and Contract** manages sourcing, contracting, and spend analysis processes for all types of spend—for example, direct and indirect materials and services.

- **Procure to Pay** provides an intuitive persona-based guided buying experience and invoice management capabilities on a single platform.

## Design to Operate

The Design to Operate process can help customers run resilient and sustainable supply chains. It provides capabilities to incorporate an E2E lifecycle of a product or asset from the design phase to its operation. The scenarios bring together SAP S/4HANA, **SAP Product Lifecycle Management (SAP PLM)**, SAP Integrated Business Planning, SAP Digital Manufacturing Cloud, **SAP Logistics Business Network (SAP LBN)**, SAP Asset Intelligence Network, **SAP Extended Warehouse Management (SAP EWM)**, and other solutions to address several sub-processes such as Idea to Market, Plan to Fulfill, and Acquire to Decommission, supporting both cloud-to-cloud and hybrid integrations. These sub-processes are outlined in more detail here:

- **Idea to Market** covers the inception of a product idea from its definition into product design and engineering requirements.

- **Plan to Fulfill** covers the journey of product-related information through the stages of supply and demand planning, manufacturing, and logistics.

- **Acquire to Decommission** captures the entire lifetime of an industrial asset from when it is received, onboarded, operated, and maintained, until decommissioning.

## *Suite qualities*

Essential suite qualities are required to provide a truly integrated Intelligent Suite, across the E2E processes, with a consistent and harmonized UX. For that, SAP defined a set of common qualities, as outlined here:

- **Seamless User Experience** supports a harmonized look and feel and navigation patterns based on Fiori experience and design principles.

- **Consistent Security and Identity Management** simplifies identity provisioning authentication and access management.

- **Aligned Domain Models** aligns business objects across applications, simplifies master data integration and reusability, and enables aligned APIs and business events.

- **Embedded and Cross-Product Analytics** integrates data across multiple products to provide a holistic view and gain new insights.

- **Coordinated Lifecycle Management** harmonizes tenant provisioning, configuration, and operations.

- **End-to-End Process Blueprints** provides reference architectures that can be implemented and extended based on customer requirements.

- **One Workflow Inbox** centralizes and simplifies workflow task management.

## RISE with SAP

We cannot talk about Intelligent Enterprise without talking about RISE with SAP, the latest **business transformation as a service (BTaaS)** offering from SAP. For many businesses, the transition will be a journey that is specific to their own experience. RISE with SAP includes one bundle of products and services that help businesses start their journey at their own pace and on their own terms. First, the offering includes the market-leading SAP S/4HANA Cloud **enterprise resource planning (ERP)**, SAP BTP as the technological foundation platform, and SAP Business Network with access to over 5 million connected businesses in the network.

Together with the ecosystem, RISE with SAP includes services and tools for business process design, cloud migrations, application lifecycle management, and learning content with SAP Enable Now.

RISE with SAP helps companies to accelerate their journey and transition to Intelligent Enterprise.

## Summary

We have now learned about Intelligent Enterprise and SAP's offerings for businesses to become intelligent enterprises through digital transformations. Through this chapter, we have learned about Intelligent Suite and Industry Cloud, Business Network, Sustainability Management, XM, and integration that comprise integrated business processes that span across multiple solutions and suite qualities to ensure consistent UXs.

In the next chapter, we will discuss the role of SAP BTP as the platform for Intelligent Enterprise and its core capabilities.

# 2

# SAP Business Technology Platform Overview

In the last chapter, we learned about the Intelligent Enterprise framework and how the components and capabilities are brought together to support businesses to become intelligent enterprises that are more resilient, profitable, and sustainable.

While SAP applications enable integrated business processes, companies will require additional flexibility to integrate with existing IT landscapes and extend SAP applications to industry-or company-specific needs. **SAP Business Technology Platform (SAP BTP)** is the platform for the intelligent enterprise to provide such flexibility, deliver business value through integration and extension, and transform data into value. It also enables different developer personnel to build innovations from a fully flexible programming model to a low-code/no-code model.

In this chapter, we will walk through the technologies behind SAP BTP and give you an overview of the capabilities of SAP BTP and what kind of use cases they support. As we will focus on the breadth of the platform first, there will be many products or terminologies being introduced. If something happens to be new to you, don't worry, we will explain it when we introduce it the first time or explain it in depth in later chapters. So, it is time for us to discuss the following topics:

- Why SAP BTP is different
- SAP BTP technology capabilities

## Why SAP BTP is different

In a nutshell, SAP BTP is the platform of Intelligent Enterprise that provides technology capabilities that help businesses to achieve agility, integration, extension, and creation of value from data. SAP BTP was first introduced in 2019, built on the legacy of SAP Cloud Platform, but it combined all other technology offerings from SAP to finally become a platform that is unified, business-centric, and open.

## Unified

SAP BTP is evolving to be a unified platform with a clear focus on business challenges. It brings together all the technology offerings from SAP on one platform. Based on the goal of unification, SAP decided to sunset the *SAP Cloud Platform* product name and merged the capabilities into SAP BTP, for example, **SAP Cloud Platform Integration Suite** is renamed **SAP Integration Suite**.

A unified platform offers a unified experience for customers. SAP is continuing to expand the value of SAP BTP by offering a simplified user experience and out-of-the-box integration and interoperability between SAP applications and technology. The unified platform also provides a consistent commercial model, a simplified platform cockpit, and a catalog of cloud services consumable for different runtimes.

## Business-centric

SAP BTP focuses on improving business outcomes and increases business-centricity by being tailored to applications and business processes. It is positioned for use cases along the key integration scenarios mentioned in the previous chapter and enables joint suite-like qualities across the applications, such as a harmonized look and feel, and consistent security and identity management.

The platform includes a semantic layer of business data. The SAP One Domain Model is the common data model that standardizes the key business objects across SAP applications. It is already used in the SAP Master Data Integration service for many master data objects, such as customers, workforce people, suppliers, products, and cost centers. The common data model is also serving as the foundation for APIs and business events, such as SAP Graph, as the simplified and unified API layer for Intelligent Enterprise scenarios. As SAP BTP evolves, the SAP One Domain Model will become more extensible and consumable.

Furthermore, SAP BTP can help companies to gain insights and generate value from data in a business context. It offers semantic data management capabilities through SAP HANA Cloud and SAP Data Warehouse Cloud, to connect enterprise data and break data silos. It automates the process of data integration and life cycle management and delivers cross-product analytics and dashboards to support data-driven decision-making.

SAP BTP also provides built-in security and compliance to ensure data security and privacy for business-critical information. It offers capabilities to help companies to manage enterprise-wide integrations across heterogeneous environments, including their existing IT and hybrid landscapes. SAP Integration Suite as part of SAP BTP can connect and contextualize processes and data, with more than 2,000 pre-configured integration packs.

## Open

SAP BTP is an open platform and builds on collaboration with partners and an open ecosystem.

Firstly, SAP BTP runs on top of multiple cloud **Infrastructure as a Service** (**IaaS**) layers, for both SAP data centers and through partner cloud infrastructures that give customers flexibility and choice. It offers a consumption-based commercial offering with different payment options and a free tier model to enable access to the broader SAP ecosystem at their pace of adoption.

Secondly, SAP BTP will enable direct access to a growing marketplace where partners and ecosystem participants can build, release, and monetize their solutions directly on the platform, and customers can easily consume them within one commercial model.

Lastly, SAP embraces and actively contributes to open source communities. Open projects Gardener and Kyma are such examples. Gardener is an open source project for multi-cloud infrastructure on top of Kubernetes. Kyma is a cloud-native extension platform. We will cover the details of Gardener and Kyma in a later chapter.

## SAP BTP technology capabilities

SAP BTP brings together a comprehensive set of technical capabilities and solutions, (which includes database and data management, analytics, application development and integration, and intelligent technologies) into one platform for both cloud and hybrid environments. *Figure 2.1* illustrates how SAP BTP fits into the Intelligent Enterprise framework described in the previous chapter:

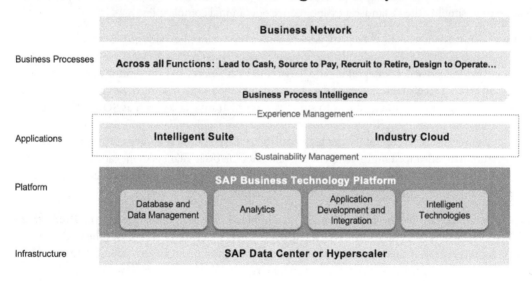

Figure 2.1: SAP BTP in Intelligent Enterprise

Now, let's get into the details of the technology offerings in each area, starting with database and data management.

## Database and data management

Organizations today are faced with the mandate of leveraging all the data assets to optimize business processes. The ability to collect, manage, and analyze data in real time is essential to compete in the digital economy. SAP's database and data management solutions help to manage enterprise data for their data-driven transformation and priorities. It includes offerings of SAP HANA, SAP HANA Cloud, SAP Data Intelligence Cloud, and more.

### SAP HANA

SAP HANA is one of the first in-memory data platforms to handle both **online analytics processing (OLAP)** and **online transactional processing (OLTP)** together in a single system simultaneously on the same dataset with unparallel performance. This is important as it enables running complex analytical operations in real time based on the latest information, without replicating data.

Even though SAP HANA is well known as an in-memory columnar **relational database management system (RDBMS)**, it has been taken a step further and provides built-in multi-mode support to store and process data types, such as geospatial, text, graphical, JSON, and time-series data. It also offers advanced search and analytics capabilities, as well as data integration capabilities for all types of data. By applying the built-in advanced capacities such as spatial analysis, text mining, predictive analytics, and machine learning, you can build new types of applications to meet your specific needs and achieve a faster time-to-value. The ability to process different types of data and workloads on a single system also helps to simplify the IT landscapes and reduce operational complexities.

Gaining a unified view of all enterprise data becomes more complex with growing data volumes. It is no longer feasible for a modern enterprise to physically aggregate data into one location. SAP HANA provides native data integration and federation with Smart Data Integration and Smart Data Access, to create a single logical view of data based on a unified security model. Besides, SAP HANA provides intelligent recommendations to simplify administrative tasks such as SQL optimization, data tiering, and monitoring. These capabilities enable a more agile and cost-efficient way to manage data. To support business continuity and high availability, SAP HANA supports a distributed scalable architecture with advanced multi-temperature and data life cycle management capabilities. Active and standby replicas can be deployed in geographically distributed locations for read access, load balancing, and failover through infrastructure automation.

In addition, SAP HANA provides embedded machine learning functions through the **Predictive Analysis Library (PAL)** and **Automated Predictive Library (APL)**. PAL provides the library with functions in the areas of clustering, classification, regression, time-series analysis, and statistics. APL provides automated predictive functions to generate regression and clustering models based on the dataset, which is simple to use for casual users.

Introduced in 2011, SAP HANA is now used by more than 54,000 customers to manage their critical enterprise data. SAP has also moved the majority of its Intelligent Suite applications off legacy databases onto SAP HANA, including SAP S/4HANA, SAP Ariba solutions, SAP SuccessFactors solutions, and SAP Customer Experience solutions. By doing so, applications can reunify the OLTP and OLAP with a simplified data model and leverage the speed of in-memory processing. For example, SAP Ariba solutions have improved UI response time by 40% on average, with 10 times improvement in search performance. SAP SuccessFactors HXM Suite runs on SAP HANA to enable unified reporting directly on source data with no latency. Query performance has been significantly improved. Besides, simplification of data models increases the speed of innovation.

To summarize, SAP HANA enables organizations to make better business decisions, innovate, deliver new services to their customers, simplify IT, and optimize operational costs. Most Intelligent Suite applications are running on HANA, which enables better integration with a simplified data model and makes cross-product analytics, machine learning, and **artificial intelligence** (**AI**) possible based on connected data. *Figure 2.2* summarizes the capabilities of SAP HANA:

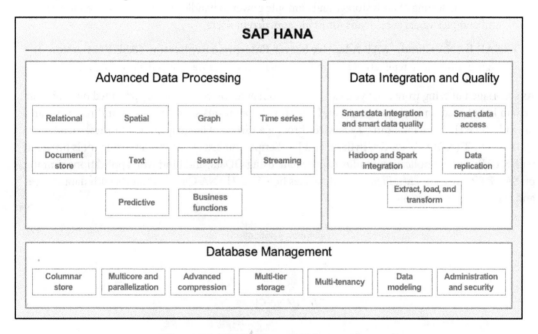

Figure 2.2: SAP HANA capabilities overview

## SAP HANA Cloud

SAP HANA Cloud is a data platform-as-a-service that offers SAP HANA natively in the cloud. SAP HANA Cloud inherits the capabilities of SAP HANA to store and process various types of data. In addition, it provides native data tiering with SAP HANA Cloud, Data Lake, and high-volume transaction processing with SAP Adaptive Server Enterprise. HANA Cloud also scales compute and storage resources separately and accesses data according to business needs for performance and provides more flexibility to manage costs.

SAP HANA Cloud includes the following components:

- **SAP HANA Cloud – SAP HANA Database** is the in-memory database for multi-model data processing that supports OLAP and OLTP in one system.

- **SAP HANA Cloud – Data Lake** is a fully managed cloud service for securely storing and analyzing large amounts of data that is infrequently updated. It leverages inexpensive storage options to lower costs while maintaining excellent performance and full SQL access to data.

- **SAP Adaptive Server Enterprise** (**ASE**) is a fully managed cloud service that enables extreme OLTP workloads in addition to real-time analytical capabilities. The ASE service is fully integrated with shared security and tenancy models, as well as development and monitoring tools. The cloud-native architecture of the ASE service efficiently accommodates independent and elastic scaling of both storage and compute power to handle extreme transaction processing and complex query workloads for many concurrent users.

- **SAP HANA Cloud – SAP Adaptive Server Enterprise Replication** (**ASE Replication**) is a high-performance replication system that synchronizes transactional data across ASE instances.

As a managed offering from SAP, you can benefit from guaranteed availability provided by SAP, scale system load based on business needs, and simplified operations such as backup and recovery, and upgrade. SAP HANA Cloud can be accessed through a variety of languages and libraries, such as Java (**JDBC**), .NET (**ADO.NET**), Go, Python, and JavaScript. You can create models using tools provided with SAP Business Application Studio, expose data using OData, and bind with applications running on SAP BTP environments. *Figure 2.3* illustrates how SAP HANA Cloud connects with data sources and consuming applications:

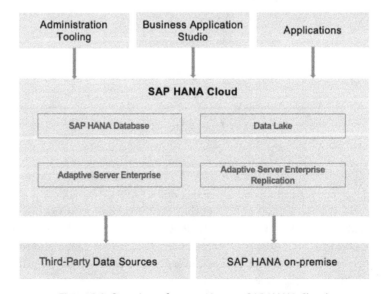

Figure 2.3: Overview of connections to SAP HANA Cloud

# Analytics

Analytics solutions as part of SAP BTP provide capabilities to connect and process all types of data. They enable companies to establish a single source of truth with cloud data warehousing, visualize insights with intuitive **business intelligence (BI)**, drive better business outcomes with collaborative enterprise planning, and turn insights into action with automated workflow and augmented analytics powered by **AI**. In this section, we will highlight SAP Analytics Cloud and SAP Data Warehouse Cloud.

## *SAP Analytics Cloud*

SAP Analytics Cloud is a **software-as-a-service (SaaS)** solution for analytics that includes BI, enterprise planning, and augmented analytics. This is important, as now businesses can have connected data to make confident decisions. In a nutshell, SAP Analytics Cloud includes the following core components:

- **Business intelligence**: A powerful combination of BI and analytics enables use cases to range from self-service data discovery and visualization, enterprise reporting at scale, embedded analytics for in-context insights, new analytical applications, and mobile consumption.

- **Enterprise planning**: To improve accuracy and efficiency for use cases such as budgeting, revenue forecasting, finance, workforce, and predictive planning. Users can simulate and run *what-if* scenarios to evaluate the pros and cons and determine the best way forward.

- **Augmented analytics**: Augmented with AI and predictive analytics to drive insights and improve decision-making, and achieved through a series of Smart features. The Smart features include Smart Predict to build actionable predictions, Search to Insights to enter questions in conversational language to get answers instantly, Smart Insights to focus on impact and contributor analysis for selected KPIs, and Smart Discovery to analyze patterns to identify outliers for anomaly detection.

SAP Analytics Cloud runs on top of SAP HANA databases, and users can perform real-time analytics on transactional data virtually through live connectivity. This helps users to view data instantly, and companies can rely on a single source of truth. Embedded analytics are available for SAP's Intelligent Suite cloud applications, which allows these applications to do reporting on live transactional data directly. For example, SAP SuccessFactors solutions have embedded SAP Analytics Cloud within existing workflows and enable HR professionals to better understand hiring, performance, attrition, and diversity, and to connect how people will impact business results.

Data can come from anywhere, and most businesses will have their own specific datasets. SAP Analytics Cloud, together with SAP Data Warehouse Cloud and SAP HANA Cloud, supports the ability to connect and combine data across enterprise landscapes. This enables organizations to incorporate analytics into existing business processes and accelerate time-to-value with out-of-the-box integration capabilities.

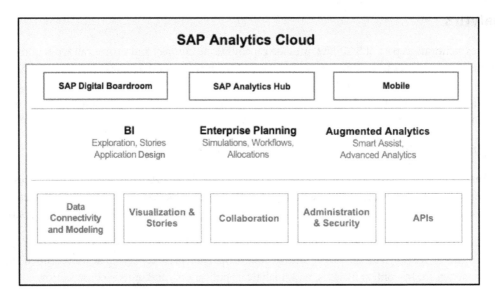

Figure 2.4: SAP Analytics Cloud overview

## SAP Data Warehouse Cloud

SAP Data Warehouse Cloud, meanwhile, is a new offering for data warehousing in the cloud that combines data management processes with advanced analytics. It is built on the powerful SAP HANA Cloud and works seamlessly with SAP Analytics Cloud.

SAP Data Warehouse Cloud provides a flexible, cloud-based option for the enterprise data warehouse, and is also designed to empower the line of business for self-service analytics through a business semantic layer. It supports a federate-first approach to reduce or completely avoid upfront data movement and a wide range of connectivity to SAP and non-SAP data sources. SAP Data Warehouse Cloud data objects are exposed as tables and views and can be integrated with external data pipelines and analytics tools. Typical scenarios for using SAP Data Warehouse Cloud include the following:

- Self-service data modeling and analytics by empowering line of business users via Spaces following the governance policies defined by administrators.

- Enable data democratization and lower the adoption barrier with a business semantic layer that abstracts from underneath physical data sources and accelerates time-to-insights.

- Enterprise data warehousing by leveraging SQL skills, built-in data transformation capabilities, as well as third-party and open source tooling for data integration and data processing. It also supports hybrid scenarios such as integration with **SAP BW/4HANA** (InfoCubes, Queries, and CompositeProviders) to ensure the reusability of BW data or other existing on-premises investments.

The Spaces concept in SAP Data Warehouse Cloud is the central element that provides the necessary isolation and enables collaboration between **lines of business (LoBs)** and IT to achieve the synthesis of data agility. Enterprise Spaces define and provide governed company-wide standards that can be extended in the departmental and individual Spaces using the same modeling mechanisms of the data and business layer. The individual data objects are only visible within their own Spaces. The data privacy and security rules are space-specific and support the fine granular definition of rules using row-level security. Auditing and activity logs are also supported at the object level.

SAP Data Warehouse Cloud's Data and Business Modeling services enable users to navigate data. First, the View Editor and Data Flow Editor are used for data modeling by defining connectivity to data sources and implementing complex data integration and transformation logic. Business Builder is the UI that allows data previews with filtering, sorting, profiling, data quality analysis, and basic data lineage. Some of the functionalities that come from SAP Data Intelligence are integrated as a cloud-based software service directly into SAP Data Warehouse Cloud.

As mentioned earlier, SAP Data Warehouse Cloud is closely integrated with SAP Analytics Cloud. Customers who already have a standalone instance of SAP Analytics Cloud can connect directly to SAP Data Warehouse Cloud's data objects. The two solutions provide a unified look and feel and share the same sets of common services, such as user management, and are delivered from the same data centers. *Figure 2.5* is a high-level overview of SAP Data Warehouse Cloud:

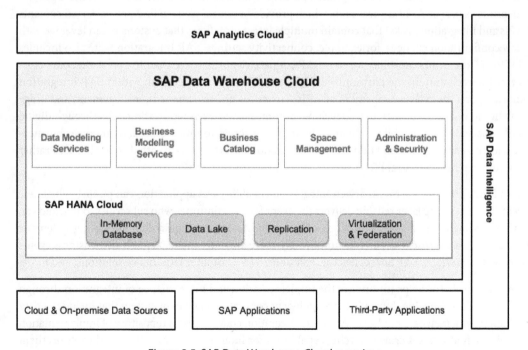

Figure 2.5: SAP Data Warehouse Cloud overview

## Application development and integration

The application development and integration capabilities of SAP BTP help companies to simplify application development, accelerate integration, automate business processes, and enable full flexibility to meet business needs on an extensible technology platform. As part of the solution package, SAP Integration Suite connects applications and data from SAP and third-party sources with prebuilt flows. SAP Extension Suite simplifies application development using flexible no-code, low-code, and pro-code capabilities to rapidly build and enhance SAP applications and increase development productivity and engagement through a harmonized digital experience.

### *SAP Integration Suite*

SAP Integration Suite combines integration capabilities such as Process Integration, API Management, Integration Advisor, and Open Connectors into a cohesive and simplified toolkit for enterprise integrations. It supports a variety of integration needs including business process optimization and automation, regulatory compliance, and creating new business models leveraging APIs. SAP Integration Suite is the integration layer of SAP BTP.

As you may experience in IT projects, you know a significant amount of time is spent building integrations; that is where the integration packs come to play and accelerate time to results. In SAP Integration Suite, there are more than 2,000 integration packs, 500 documented events, and 225 business process blueprints as part of API Business Hub, which provides a central place to find pre-packaged contents (APIs and integration packs) that contain multiple integration flows that customers can leverage with a few configuration changes, for example, connectivity settings. SAP Integration Suite also includes the Open Connectors capability for non-SAP connectivity, with more than 160 pre-built connectors to third-party solutions via harmonized RESTful APIs. API Management within SAP Integration Suite supports life cycle management of APIs – from design, development, management, and usage analytics to engagement with your developer community, or even monetizing APIs through digital marketplaces. These capabilities help to democratize access to integration and empower business users as citizen integrators to build or reuse integration flows for people with diverse skill sets, rather than fully relying on central IT.

Event Mesh provides the event-driven integration capability. An application can publish a business event. The messaging layer reliably delivers the event for any consumer who subscribes to that and can react accordingly. This enables a loosely coupled architecture that is required for integrating systems or services with a microservices architecture. Today, there are more than 500 published business events from SAP S/4HANA, SAP SuccessFactors solutions, SAP Customer Experience solutions, and more.

Integration Advisor helps to simplify the implementation and maintenance of integration through AI and machine learning. It provides an intelligent content management system that includes a data dictionary with metadata models of APIs and integration contents and a repository of implementation guidelines. It also offers crowdsourcing capabilities for interfaces and mappings and captures them in the knowledge base. By using machine learning and AI, Integration Advisor can automatically generate documentation, mapping guidelines, runtime artifacts, and validation rules for specific integration requirements.

Integration is the key to enabling Intelligent Enterprise, and SAP Integration Suite plays a significant role in integrating both technology and business processes to deliver value by accelerating innovation or reducing the complexity of operations. SAP Integration Suite includes the prebuilt integration packs to support the key business processes, such as lead to cash, source to pay, recruit to retire, and design to operate:

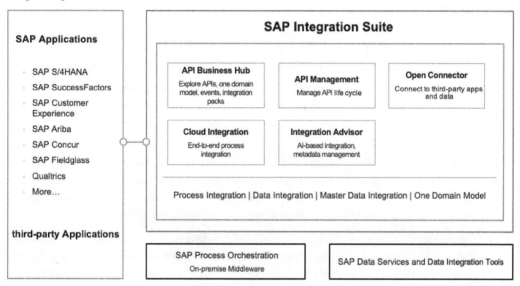

Figure 2.6: SAP Integration Suite overview

## *SAP Extension Suite*

As businesses are moving toward modern technologies and the cloud through digital transformation, maintaining existing applications while adopting emerging technologies becomes an increasingly complex task. SAP Extension Suite provides the necessary capabilities to improve development efficiency and productivity, and support different developer personas for citizens, LoB, or professional developers. With pre-built templates, enterprise-grade frameworks, ready-to-use technical and business services, and standard APIs, developers can build application extensions more quickly, from leveraging low-code/ no-code capabilities with fewer IT dependencies to having the flexibility to choose a development approach and runtimes that fit their needs.

There are mainly three types of extensibilities for SAP applications:

- **Classic extensibility** is the traditional method used to extend applications based on **SAP ERP Central Component** (**SAP ECC**) and SAP Business Suite applications. It is tightly coupled, and the customization code usually resides in the Z-namespace directly. Developers and consultants use customization and extension technologies such as ABAP, SAP GUI, and Web Dynpro.

- **In-app extensibility** was introduced with SAP S/4HANA. It provides the extension framework for building SAP Fiori-based customizations within the SAP S/4HANA system and works with SAP S/4HANA data and processes only.

- **Side-by-side extensibility** enables decoupled extensions. It helps to extend the business processes while keeping the core clean. It also allows developers to adopt the latest technologies and innovations, such as machine learning and AI, reusable business, and technical services.

Side-by-side extensibility is supported by SAP BTP through SAP Extension Suite, to enable businesses to address their business requirements in a modern way and innovate by adopting the latest technologies. The capabilities and use cases for SAP Extension Suite can be categorized into the following:

- **Digital experience**: This provides tools to help organizations to build and run applications that provide a consistent and engaging user experience through SAP Fiori-based web applications, mobile applications, and conversational bots. It also includes tools to enable end users to create business content and collaboration such as SAP Work Zone.

- **Development efficiency**: This offers capabilities to help developers rapidly build extensions and new applications. It includes low-code, graphical development tools, and programming frameworks such as SAP Business Application Studio and SAP Cloud Application Programming Model, which can help to increase development efficiency while ensuring consistent user experience. Multiple runtimes and frameworks are provided to meet different needs, such as Cloud Foundry, function-as-a-service through Extension Factory, and Enterprise Messaging to support event-driven service-oriented architecture. It also offers a low-code/no-code platform including the capabilities acquired through AppGyver.

- **Digital process automation**: This offers capabilities to automate, adapt, and improve business processes. With the intuitive and business user-friendly tools, users can leverage prebuilt templates to customize their processes or build new ones for their specific business needs. SAP Workflow Management and SAP **Intelligent Robotics Process Automation** (**iRPA**) are in this category.

*Figure 2.7* gives an overview of the use cases and capabilities that SAP Extension Suite supports:

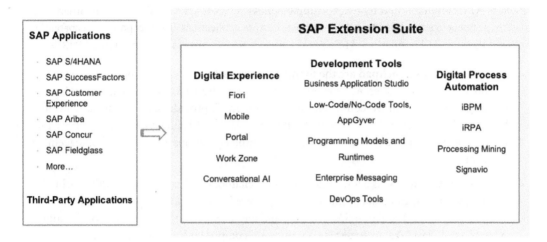

Figure 2.7: SAP Extension Suite overview

## Intelligent technologies

With the use of AI, organizations can get better insights to make better decisions, adopt business processes in real time by combining learnings from historic data, automate process steps, and free users from repetitive tasks.

AI is a cornerstone of the Intelligent Enterprise strategy. AI is infused into applications and business processes natively in SAP's Intelligent Suite applications. Through the embedded AI functionalities, customers can consume them directly as part of the standard applications. AI models are provided by SAP either as pre-trained models or trained on customers' own data. In this way, it simplifies the adoption and helps to bring AI to more users. Here are a few examples of SAP applications with AI embedded:

- **SAP S4/HANA**: This identifies slow-moving stock, reduces inventory carrying and warehouse management costs, and automates sales order creation from unstructured documents to speed up the process and improve quality.

- **SAP Concur**: This extracts information from documents such as user expense receipts and speeds up the entering and processing to provide a better user experience and reduce manual work.

- **SAP Service Cloud**: This automates ticket management by providing ticket classification and solution recommendations based on **natural language processing** (**NLP**).

SAP offers AI technology directly by exposing business services via SAP BTP for customers and ecosystem partners to extend SAP systems and create custom applications. These exposed AI capabilities are offered through AI Foundation, AI Business Services, SAP Conversational AI, and SAP iRPA:

- **AI Core and AI Launchpad** are the foundation for customers and partners to manage and extend SAP's AI capabilities. AI Core offers a robust and advanced environment for serving and training and allows unified consumption of AI content. It provides an upgraded architecture based on Kubernetes and serverless that is highly scalable. AI Launchpad is a new service that provides a central place to manage machine learning operations and life cycle management of the models.

- **SAP Conversational AI** is a low-code/low-touch chatbot building platform, with capabilities to build, train, test, and manage intelligent AI-powered chatbots to simplify business tasks and workflows across SAP and non-SAP products and improve user experience. SAP Conversational AI uses word-class **NLP** to analyze text inputs and compose responses to user queries.

- **iRPA** uses intelligent bots to automate repetitive manual processes and help people and organizations to redirect resources to high-value activities and processes. As a result, customers can save time and costs, and reduce human errors.

- **SAP AI Business Services** provide easy-to-use AI capabilities as reusable business services as part of SAP BTP that can help to solve specific business problems in various business processes. Such capacities include (but are not limited to) document information extraction, business entity recognition, data attribute recommendation, service ticket intelligence, and invoice object recommendation. AI Business Services are embedded in SAP applications already or can be integrated with other products such as SAP Conversational AI or used directly by any other applications.

*Figure 2.8* summarizes the AI capabilities of SAP:

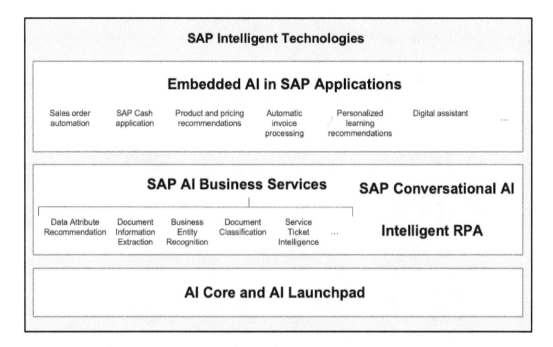

Figure 2.8: SAP AI capability overview

## Summary

In this chapter, we have discussed what BTP is and its key capabilities. BTP is the unified, business-centric, and open platform for Intelligent Enterprise, by offering differentiating capabilities around database and data management, analytics, application development and integration, and intelligent technologies such as AI and machine learning. By leveraging these capabilities, businesses can extend their business processes, create new innovations, accelerate time-to-value, and deliver a consistent and delightful user experience. Now that we have an overall picture of SAP BTP, let's get into the details in the next chapters.

# Part 2
# Foundations

On completing this part, you will get an understanding of the basic concepts that underpin SAP BTP and also familiarize yourself with how SAP BTP operates.

This part contains the following chapters:

- *Chapter 3, Establishing a Foundation for SAP Business Technology Platform*
- *Chapter 4, Security and Connectivity*
- *Chapter 5, Non-Functional Design for Operability*

# 3

# Establishing a Foundation for SAP Business Technology Platform

In previous chapters, you should have understood what **SAP Business Technology Platform (SAP BTP)** is and how SAP positions it in the Intelligent Enterprise ecosystem. You therefore shouldn't be surprised to see that this first practical chapter is dedicated to explaining the foundational elements of SAP BTP.

We know that you are eager to have a peek at what SAP BTP is, and we are at the point where things will slowly get practical. We say *slowly* because we need to establish the terminology and define the essential elements of SAP BTP first.

Don't forget that this book's audience is architects; therefore, we will not go into the nitty-gritty of every element—we would like to stay at a level of covering things that architects need to know to be able to design solutions and architectures.

Here, we also consider technical architects whose role may extend to creating a governance model for SAP BTP. But if you are a platform administrator, for example, don't expect to find all the details you need to operate SAP BTP in this book.

In this chapter, we're going to cover the following main topics:

- Environments and regions
- Commercial models
- Account model
- Services
- Account administration

# Technical requirements

As with many other cloud vendors, SAP provides trial options that make it possible to get your hands dirty at no expense. Currently, you have two options, as outlined here:

- Navigate to `https://developers.sap.com/tutorials/hcp-create-trial-account.html`, where you can find detailed instructions on how to create a trial account.

- Go to *SAP Store* at `https://store.sap.com` to subscribe to Pay-As-You-Go for SAP BTP by placing an order for free. After that, you can try SAP BTP services that offer free tier service plans.

# Environments and regions

In the SAP BTP context, *environment* is an overloaded term. So, when we say it, we may mean two similar but different things. Let's define the first one: at its foundation, SAP BTP provides frameworks, technologies, execution models, and tools for customers to develop and deploy applications that we refer to altogether as a **runtime environment** or, shortly, an environment.

SAP BTP has had an extensive evolution since it was first released. In this journey, SAP introduced different environments to provide platform services as well as runtimes for applications. As a result, there are four runtime environments in SAP BTP, as outlined here:

- **Neo environment**: This was the first and only environment when SAP BTP, then known as **SAP Cloud Platform** (**SCP**), was released originally. The technology underpinning this environment is SAP-proprietary and enables customers to develop and deploy HTML5, Java, and SAP HANA XS (JavaScript) applications. In addition, the Neo environment provides many platform services that fulfill an enterprise's cloud requirements—for example, integration, data, mobile, identity, connectivity, and so on.

- **Cloud Foundry (CF) environment**: SAP introduced this environment after embracing the open source **CF** technology. The CF environment makes it possible to develop applications in multiple programming languages and deploy them in supported runtimes, including Java and Node.js. In addition, SAP started to provide platform services on top of this environment while continuing to support the Neo environment. Today, the CF environment is at the center of the multi-environment foundation, where all innovations and new services are released. We will talk about multi-environment soon.

- **ABAP environment**: This environment is provisioned from within the CF environment and lets customers develop applications using the **Advanced Business Application Programming** (**ABAP**) language. If you have been working in the SAP ecosystem for a long time, you may think this is the good old ABAP, which is valid only to an extent, as this environment supports only the cloud release of ABAP, also known as **ABAP Steampunk**. As you may already know, SAP's newest **enterprise resource planning** (**ERP**) solution—that is, SAP S/4HANA—and some of their other products—for example, SAP Marketing Cloud, SAP Integrated Business Planning, and so on—are built on top of the ABAP platform (not necessarily ABAP Steampunk). Therefore, it may make sense to create extension applications for these products in the ABAP environment.

- **Kyma environment**: The newest to the game is the Kyma environment, a fully managed **Kubernetes** runtime enabling the creation of applications using serverless functions or microservices. If this is the first time you have heard of Kubernetes, you're missing a lot. We therefore highly recommend you learn about it and get yourself familiar with the concepts of containerization and microservices. We wouldn't be exaggerating when we say Kubernetes is becoming the *operating system* of the cloud. Kyma, being on top of Kubernetes, provides extensions to streamline the way applications are created and connected by easing some of the hardships of working with Kubernetes.

After releasing SAP BTP initially with the Neo environment, SAP changed its strategy from mainly two perspectives, as detailed here:

- Firstly, SAP embraced open source technologies—first, CF, and more recently, Kubernetes—for heavy lifting at the foundation level.

- Secondly, SAP decided to run SAP BTP on hyperscalers rather than its own data centers while giving customers the flexibility to choose a hyperscaler that best fit their requirements. With this shift in its strategy, SAP could focus more on providing differentiating platform services.

By the way, is this the first time you've heard the word *hyperscaler*? With this term, we mean the cloud vendors that provide the **infrastructure as a service** (**IaaS**) on which SAP BTP runs—for example, Amazon Web Services (AWS), Microsoft Azure, Google Cloud Platform (GCP), Alibaba, and so on; so, IaaS providers.

Now, we come to the second thing we may refer to when we say an *environment*, but before that, let's give a short definition of a term we will start using. A *subaccount* is an account-model element in which you use services and deploy your applications.

Historically, when there were only Neo and CF runtime environments, a subaccount was tightly coupled with one of them. Therefore, subaccounts were categorized with strict reference to the runtime environments—for example, a Neo subaccount or a CF subaccount.

With the strategy change, runtime environments became subordinate elements of the new types of subaccounts. Thus, a subaccount, whichever way it's managed under the hood, does not have a strict dependency on a runtime environment anymore. A subaccount can now exist with no runtime environment, or it can have one or many of the strategic runtime environments. This changed the basis for categorization because the new subaccounts could not be referred to with a specific runtime environment. So, a new twofold categorization emerged: *the Neo environment and the multi-environment*. SAP also refers to the multi-environment as the *multi-cloud foundation* and sometimes the *multi-cloud environment*.

The following screenshot shows the different SAP BTP environments available:

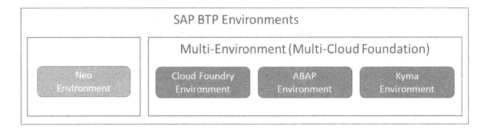

Figure 3.1: SAP BTP environments

Now that we know about environments, let's have a very brief introduction to services and then tackle the question of how to choose an environment.

## Services

It is better to define another concept at this point to gain a common understanding before we start using it very frequently going forward. So, what is a **service** in the SAP BTP context? When we use this term, we mostly use it at a generic level. A service is a managed capability provided through the platform to be used as a building block in our solutions—for example, it can facilitate building, deploying, and running applications, creating integration artifacts, storing data, managing workflows, and so on. We will only provide a definition here as we will discuss services extensively in a later section of this chapter.

## Which environment?

At this point, you should have already understood that we can consider the Neo environment to be no longer strategic. This shift of focus is not a secret as SAP releases all strategic innovations in the multi-cloud environment. In addition, SAP actively encourages its customers to transition to the strategic multi-environment.

If you are one of the first customers onboarded on SAP BTP, you may already have applications deployed and services enabled in the Neo environment. Don't worry; SAP continues supporting the Neo environment and will probably do so for a bit longer to protect the investments of its customers.

> **Important Note**
>
> If you have applications and services in the Neo environment, it's time to consider in your strategy how you will be migrating to the strategic multi-environment. You can get help from SAP on this. For more information, visit `https://help.sap.com/viewer/b017fc4f944e4eb5b31501b3d1b6a1f0/Cloud/en-US/aae4e0ae1cdf434b908c3c8cf3ea942a.html`.

Suppose you have a presence in the Neo environment and started a migration to the multi-environment. In that case, you will eventually face the challenging question of which environment to use. At this stage, the choice is between the Neo environment and the multi-environment. However, especially if you will be deploying applications on SAP BTP, you will come to a point where you need to select in which specific runtime environment you want to build your applications. We will discuss this in a later chapter.

The suggestions here depend on where you are with your transition and many other factors you need to consider with your strategy; however, we have some points that may help.

We would recommend using the Neo environment only in the following cases:

- If you are looking to onboard a service and if the service is only available in Neo—in this case, check the SAP roadmap to see whether they will soon release an alternative service in the multi-cloud environment. If that is the case, you need to decide whether you can delay your project until the new service is available. If your project cannot wait or if SAP doesn't have plans to release an alternative in the multi-cloud environment, the only option is to use the service available in the Neo environment.

- If you have heavily invested in the Neo environment and the following apply:

  - What you are looking to implement (an application or a service) is an integral part of an existing ecosystem in Neo.

  - Implementing the new requirement in the multi-cloud environment will introduce an unnecessary cost without a whole migration exercise.

It would be best to consider onboarding services or deploying applications in the multi-environment in all other cases. That said, migrating a single integration artifact or building a simple new application in the new environment without a plan for a complete migration may incur unnecessary costs. So, once you start the migration, it's also best to complete it as soon as possible to eliminate the administration overhead and reduce the overall cost, and bear in mind that the cost element depends on the commercial model with which you purchased SAP BTP. For example, you may need to align your migration completion date with the subscription contract expiration date to avoid sacrificing the remaining committed investment and eliminate the risk of an unnecessary contract extension.

Now that we know our environment options, let's discuss where we can run them.

> **Important Note**
> In this book, we will focus on the multi-environment as it's the strategic direction. This is in line with our suggestion for migrating away from Neo, and this way, we can reduce the complexity of the topics we discuss.

## Regions

Now that you know the different environment types in SAP BTP, we need to touch upon the concept of regions. If you are already familiar with cloud architectures, this wouldn't be a new topic, and a region is the same concept as you would see in other cloud contexts.

As should be clear by now, SAP provisions SAP BTP on top of cloud infrastructure. Yet, as a consumer of SAP BTP, you don't need to know the specifics about the infrastructure except when you are assessing the platform to make sure it fulfills specific requirements and when a service is provisioned directly with infrastructure-level configuration. At the lowest level, the platform is still running on machines in a data center, and for SAP BTP, this can be an SAP data center or one of the hyperscalers. So, the **region** corresponds to the geographical location of the data center where the infrastructure is running.

SAP BTP is provisioned with a multi-cloud strategy where customers have the flexibility of using it on a hyperscaler of their choice. In addition, customers can also choose to have SAP BTP on multiple hyperscalers—for example, for **business continuity** (**BC**) use cases or in line with their own multi-cloud strategy.

So, when specifying SAP BTP regions, we use two elements: a hyperscaler and the data center locality—for example, AWS Frankfurt, Microsoft Azure Netherlands, GCP US Central, and so on. Here, in the context of SAP BTP, your contract is with SAP, and you do not directly deal with hyperscalers.

You may wonder how to find in which regions SAP BTP is available; we will keep this a secret until later in this chapter. Okay—if you are so eager to know, make a detour to the *SAP Discovery Center* section and then come back to learn more about regions.

## Which region?

Now that we know there are multiple regions to choose from, it's time to discuss the factors you need to consider when selecting a region. You need to think about the following:

- **Service availability**: A service may be available only in some regions—for example, because SAP has newly released the service and is gradually making it available in regions.

- **Proximity**: Although the internet is much faster compared to the past, where you run SAP BTP (hence, how close it is to your **information technology** (**IT**) estate it communicates with and to your end users) is still a significant factor for performance. It would be best to run SAP BTP as close as possible to reduce network latency and response time.

- **Private Link Service availability**: We will discuss Private Link Service in a later chapter; however, at this stage, you can think of it as a private connection between SAP BTP and services in hyperscalers. If your IT estate has tight integration between SAP BTP and these services, this may be a factor when deciding on regions.

- **Legal requirements**: You may need to run SAP BTP only in certain geographies due to specific regulations that countries or industry regulators set. The regulations may necessitate you keeping the data, at rest and in transit, within the boundaries of a single country or multiple countries, such as in the **European Union (EU)** case. China is a good example here. Due to regulations, if you are operating in China, you most probably need to run SAP BTP in a China region—for example, Alibaba China.

- **Existing usage**: If you are already running SAP BTP in a region with several applications deployed and services enabled, you can choose to continue using the same region, although a different region may make sense when considering the other factors mentioned previously—for example, this may happen when SAP makes SAP BTP available in a new region. You can plan for migration if the benefits outweigh the cost of it.

Ideally, you may think you should choose a single region where you can have all your applications and services. However, after considering the aforementioned factors, you may end up with multiple regions, willingly or unwillingly. On the other hand, there are cases where having SAP BTP in multiple regions may make sense, such as in the following scenarios:

- You may need a higher level of BC for the application you deploy in SAP BTP. In that case, you may choose to deploy your application in multiple regions, which we will discuss in *Chapter 5, Non-Functional Design for Operability*.

- As a company, you may have your own multi-cloud strategy, which means you have a presence on multiple hyperscalers. For example, a large enterprise may choose to have the services for one of its **business units (BUs)** provisioned in Microsoft Azure and services for another BU in AWS or GCP. In line with this model, you can choose to have SAP BTP in multiple regions, coupling each to the same region of the hyperscaler of choice, as mentioned previously.

We have now laid the first tile in our SAP BTP foundation, and next, we will discuss our options for purchasing SAP BTP.

## Commercial models

SAP provides two main commercial models for enterprises to purchase SAP BTP, as outlined here:

- **Subscription-based model**: In this model, customers subscribe to one or multiple services. At the time of purchase, you negotiate with SAP to use a fixed set of services during a fixed term for a fixed price. When the term expires, you can extend your subscription.

- **Consumption-based model**: In this model, you do not need to fix the set of services you will be using, and you have two options, as follows:

  - If you establish a **Cloud Platform Enterprise Agreement** (**CPEA**) with SAP, you make an annual commitment to using SAP BTP over a fixed term with no restriction on which services you can use. SAP gives you a number of cloud credits you can consume by using SAP BTP services. During the agreement term, you can flexibly adjust what you are using by enabling, disabling, or ramping up/down the service utilization as long as you do not deplete your cloud credits. If you spend all your cloud credits, you will be charged with the list prices; you can also choose to top up.

  - If you are not ready to invest a committed amount, you can use the **Pay-As-You-Go** option. Here, you have all the flexibility with zero-commitment: no fixed set of services, no upfront spend commitment, and no fixed term.

## Which commercial model?

After SAP introduced CPEA, many customers went for it due to its flexibility, but if you purchased SAP BTP a long time ago, you might be on a subscription contract. SAP continues providing both subscription- and consumption-based commercial models to give customers options for the sake of flexibility.

SAP handles each commercial model differently, and you cannot combine them under the same agreement. However, there are transition paths from the subscription and pay-as-you-go models to the CPEA model because CPEA represents a well-established engagement with SAP.

Let's see a comparison chart for the commercial models to highlight what each offers in terms of critical commercial elements. You can view this here:

| | Subscription | Consumption | |
| | | CPEA | Pay-As-You-Go |
| --- | --- | --- | --- |
| **Set of services** | Specific services – single or bundled | Any | Any |
| **Usage amount** | Defined upfront; can be increased later | Flexible as long as cumulative consumption is within the committed amount; pay list prices if you exceed, and top-up possible | Flexible as long as you pay at the end of the month |
| **Commitment** | Upfront with a fixed price | Upfront for the entire consumption | None |
| **Minimum usage** | Required | Required | Not required |
| **Term** | Fixed | Fixed | None |
| **Billing term** | Pay in advance | Annually/Quarterly | Monthly |
| **Discounts** | Possible | Possible | Non-discountable |

Table 3.1: Comparison of SAP BTP commercial models

If your use of SAP solutions is not extensive—for example, you use cherrypicked solutions from SAP—it may make sense to use the subscription model. One way of buying SAP BTP subscriptions is through **SAP Store**. In SAP Store, you can browse SAP BTP services available for the subscription model. You can then make a purchase after you specify a configuration that consists of the quantity—for example, number of users, duration, and start date. If the product you want to purchase has prerequisites, SAP Store will provide you with a warning and let you know what they are. You can see an example of this in the following screenshot:

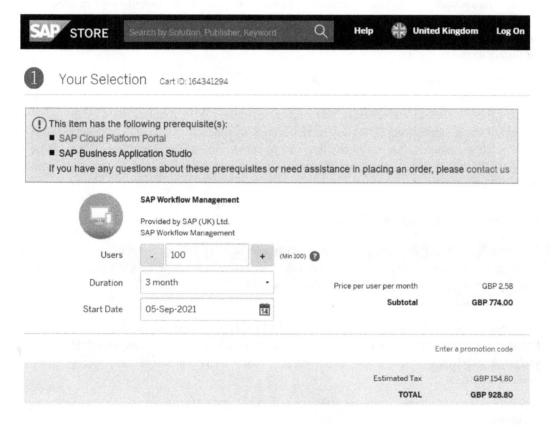

Figure 3.2: Making a purchase in SAP Store

As you can see in the preceding screenshot, if you want to subscribe to SAP Workflow Management, an SAP BTP service, you need to purchase a minimum quantity of 100 users for a minimum duration of 3 months. In addition, you are also required to subscribe to SAP BTP Portal and SAP Business Application Studio services, and they will have their own purchase configurations.

On the other hand, if you have extensive usage of several SAP products, you possibly have contracts with SAP, and you can get into another one for purchasing SAP BTP with a consumption-based model. Here, for well-established use cases for which you can easily decide the use of SAP BTP services, you can opt for a CPEA contract and benefit from possible volume-based or company-specific discounts. Of course, this requires proper planning to avoid over- or under-commitment. In addition, your CPEA contract can be part of your general cloud agreement with SAP. In that case, there may be another level of flexibility that allows you to exchange your cloud products and change quantities; hence, you can increase or reduce the cloud credits you have for SAP BTP.

Suppose you do not have a CPEA contract and want an enterprise-grade trial; or, maybe you have a CPEA contract but wish to isolate a specific use case from your CPEA consumption (for example, due to intra-company isolation). In that case, you can choose the Pay-As-You-Go model. But don't forget, with this model, you will not benefit from potential discounts, so you may pay extra in return for the additional flexibility.

It sounds as though Pay-As-You-Go is a better fit for companies new to SAP BTP that want to evaluate it where the confidence level in SAP BTP is somewhat high; for example, the trial is just a step for due diligence. Eventually, the contract can be transitioned to a CPEA contract retaining the global account. If you are an existing CPEA customer, having a separate Pay-As-You-Go contract wouldn't make much sense unless you can justify it. If you go above your CPEA commitment, you will be charged with the list prices anyway, and if your overconsumption becomes regular, you can top up your CPEA commitment.

## Trial accounts and the free tier

SAP provides SAP BTP in a trial environment where users can try to learn about its capabilities free of charge. It is a win-win situation for both the users—for example, developers—and SAP, where users gain experience by using SAP BTP, and this accelerates the adoption of SAP BTP, which in turn is a commercial gain for SAP.

As an individual, you can register to get a trial SAP BTP account that gives you access to many SAP BTP services free of charge for a limited time—that is, 30 days. You can extend this several times until you reach 365 days, after which SAP will delete your trial account. No worries, as you can create a new one after that.

> **Important Note**
> SAP BTP trial accounts are for personal use—for example, exploring SAP BTP capabilities—and you cannot use them for production.

Alternatively, you can use **free tier** service plans where available. This option is available for many services, and SAP plans to make it available for more services in the future. The free tier may eventually replace the trial account option as it provides an experience closer to enterprise accounts.

In the *Technical requirements* section at the beginning of this chapter, you can find a link to a tutorial explaining how you can get an SAP BTP trial account. In addition, you can also find information on how to subscribe to SAP BTP for using the free tier. The free tier can be used by enterprise customers as well. It may be a reasonable option for **proofs of concept** where it is possible to upgrade to a paid service plan without requiring a migration. As you would expect, free tier service plans have limited capacity, and support for the free tier is limited to SAP Community.

## Monitoring your consumption

Whichever commercial model you are on, you must keep an eye on your consumption. Otherwise, you may overspend your CPEA budget or subscribed amount, and in the case of Pay-As-You-Go, you may see a surprising amount on your monthly bill.

There are different ways to monitor your SAP BTP consumption. Firstly, SAP provides you with statistics and other consumption information on the **Usage Analytics** page when you log in to your account in SAP BTP Cockpit, as shown in the following screenshot. This page is available for different account-model levels we will discuss in a later section:

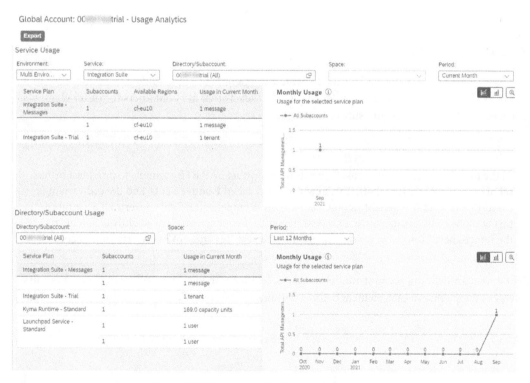

Figure 3.3: Usage analytics for a global account

In *Figure 3.3*, you can see the usage analytics for a global account. Have you figured out the **Export** button in the screenshot? You can click on this button to download detailed information on your consumption that you can use for further analysis. In the downloaded spreadsheet, you can find which services you consumed from the beginning of your contract period at the subaccount level with month-by-month metered actual usage and the cost. Based on your actual use, you can then make projections for your future consumption, which may signal any potential overspend; hence, top-up requirements. If you need to estimate costs for possible changes in consumption or new services you plan to enable, you can also use the *Estimator Tool* , which we will explain later in this chapter.

Suppose you need an automated way of retrieving usage data. In that case, you can use the **Usage Data Management** service and consume its **APIs** from, for example, an IT spend management or a reporting application. We will discuss how to do this in the section where we discuss services. With this API-based method, you can establish continuous monitoring and integrate your usage data for analytics use cases.

It would be best if you also use these analytics to optimize your consumption—for example, in the report, you can see whether there are services you have enabled but are not actually using. As mentioned before, some services incur costs even though you don't actually use them because SAP BTP reserves some capacity for them—for example, a Data Intelligence subscription, an Integration Suite subscription, a Kyma environment, and so on.

## Account model

SAP BTP's account model defines how its elements are organized in a structured way for administration purposes. For the primary hierarchy, there are three levels that are containers for other elements: global accounts, directories, and subaccounts.

> **Important Note**
>
> At the time of authoring this book, SAP was transforming SAP BTP accounts to provide a better set of cloud management tools. This new variant is called **Feature Set B**, and the old variant is called **Feature Set A**. This distinction will possibly disappear after SAP converts all accounts. In this book, we will assume you are on Feature Set B. If your screens look slightly different from the images here, don't worry; you will get the new features after SAP converts your account.

Before we start defining account-model elements, let's have an overview. Why not check it out first and try making sense of each element before reading its definition? Check out the following diagram:

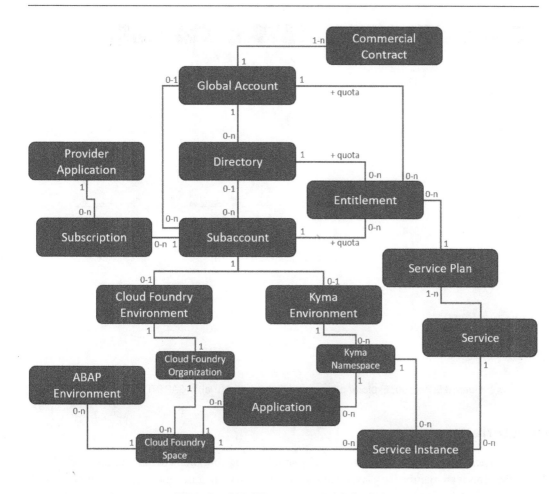

Figure 3.4: SAP BTP account-model elements

## Global accounts

A global account is the highest level in the hierarchy, and it corresponds to your contractual relationship with SAP. So, after you purchase SAP BTP, SAP will provide you with a global account and instructions to access it. Depending on your contracts with SAP, you may end up having multiple global accounts.

Global accounts are not associated with regions or environments, and they function as the topmost containers to include directories and subaccounts. In the following screenshot, you can see how SAP BTP Cockpit displays a global account having several directories and subaccounts:

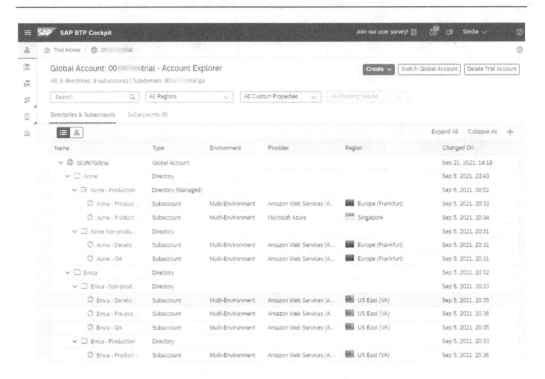

Figure 3.5: Account Explorer page of a global account (trial) in SAP BTP Cockpit

## Directories

Directories help organize the account model by simply being containers for subaccounts or other directories. This is an intermediary level where some properties—that is, entitlements and users—can be assigned at a higher level cumulatively for a set of subaccounts before distributing them to individual subaccounts. In addition, because you can set custom properties (tags) for directories, you can use them as an aggregation level for monitoring usage and cost.

Directories are optional and only available in accounts with Feature Set B. Directories can be nested to include other directories, as long as the entire account model has seven or fewer hierarchical levels. As with global accounts, you cannot associate directories with regions or environments.

## Subaccounts

We are now at the level where things get concrete, as subaccounts contain your operational SAP BTP elements. Therefore, subaccounts are associated with a region. This means the applications deployed and the services provisioned in a subaccount will be running in the subaccount's region. As you should remember from earlier chapters, when we refer to a region, it also contains the hyperscaler of choice.

After you create a subaccount, you can enable specific multi-cloud environments you want to use. As we discussed before, you can subscribe to some services with no attachment to a runtime environment, and for others, you need to create service instances attached to runtime environments. One thing to keep in mind about the Kyma environment is that you can choose to run your Kubernetes cluster in a region different from your subaccount's region.

As with directories, you can assign custom tags to your subaccounts so that you can identify them for particular reasons—for example, ownership, usage type, and so on.

## Elements specific to environments

In addition to the SAP BTP account model, the CF and Kyma environments have their own structural models.

The CF environment has two levels for structuring: an **organization** and **spaces** under it. In the SAP BTP context, when you enable a CF environment for a subaccount, the *organization* of the environment is 1-to-1 associated with the subaccount. Then, when you create organization spaces, they become subordinate elements of the subaccount.

Typically, you will deploy your applications and create service instances in spaces; therefore, you need at least one space in your subaccount. CF spaces provide a level of isolation; however, with the overarching account model of SAP BTP, isolation at this level is *generally* not used. This means you generally have only one space per subaccount.

Similarly, the Kyma environment has **namespaces** allowing a level of isolation, and you get a default namespace when you enable the environment.

## Entitlements

SAP starts metering the consumption of a service once it's provisioned, and it will cost you cloud credits if it's not an included service and you are not using the free tier. Therefore, after the structural elements are in place, you may want to set up a mechanism to control the number of services consumed in subaccounts. In order to make this possible, SAP BTP delivers the services with one or more pre-defined configuration variants that primarily define their costs. These variants are called **service plans**. For example, some services have service plans similar to T-shirt sizes (small, medium, and large).

SAP BTP facilitates the cost-controlling mechanism at two levels. First, with **entitlements**, you determine which services a subaccount or subaccounts of a directory can use in terms of service plans; for example, you entitle Subaccount A to use Service Plan x of Service 1. Then, attached to the entitlement, you assign a **quota** that specifies the upper limit of the quantity that service can be used in the subaccount.

As you can guess, at the top, there are entitlements and quotas SAP assigns to your global account that you are supposed to distribute to your subaccounts. If you have a CPEA or a Pay-As-You-Go contract, most of the entitlements for your global account will be unlimited because you can consume as much as you need, provided that it's within your consumption budget or you are happy to top up.

## Setting up your account model

It's now time for you to shape your own instance of an account model with the given elements. Indeed, you can use them in a way that fits your requirements, and there is always more than one correct way of doing this. When setting up your account model, the first primary challenge will be which subaccounts you need.

There are different factors here, and each of them may require you to add a set of subaccounts, which increases the landscape complexity; hence, administration overhead and the cost. Therefore, when planning, you need to set principles to optimize the number of subaccounts.

Most probably, the first dimension you would want to incorporate in your account model will be your change delivery strategy, which you likely already established for your on-premises systems. This means a separate subaccount for each landscape environment you have; for example, development, test (**quality assurance, or QA**), and production. This setup is generally the minimum many companies have. Additionally, you can have a separate pre-production environment to further safeguard delivery to the production environment and for activities such as performance testing. You can also have a sandbox environment to let teams explore options without contaminating the development environment. Finally, you can have a training environment that you specifically reserve for training purposes.

The change delivery in some companies may be quite complex, requiring more landscape environments; for example, some choose to have different sets of environments for the project stream and the business-as-usual (fixing live system incidents) stream.

Let's assume we have a landscape as depicted in the following diagram. This means we should start with six subaccounts:

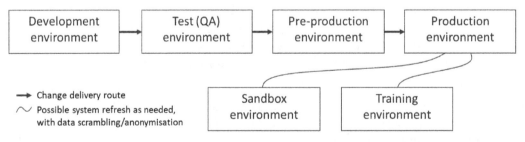

Figure 3.6: A typical set of landscape environments

Here, for your SAP BTP account model, you can consider choosing not to have a subaccount for some of the environment types. For example, in a setup where you don't foresee frequent and significant changes, you can plan training activities accordingly in the pre-production environment because the application version will stay stable and similar to production for a reasonably long time.

This is an opportunity for reducing the number of landscape environments. However, there are more factors that may require increasing the number, such as the following:

- **SAP BTP environment types**: You should remember our discussions about environment types from the earlier sections of this chapter. Suppose you are in the transitional period for migrating from Neo to multi-environment. In that case, you need to have subaccounts for both types until the migration is complete when you can decommission the Neo subaccounts. As we pointed out before, you need to target completing the migration as soon as possible to avoid the cost of running two sets of subaccounts.

- **SAP BTP service strategy changes**: Because SAP BTP has been in continuous development, there have been cases where SAP released a new service that offered a strategic alternative to an existing service; for example, SAP released the latest Integration Suite service as a strategic alternative to the existing independent integration services. Similarly, SAP released the newest HANA Cloud service as a strategic alternative to the existing HANA-as-a-service offerings. This type of strategy change means a migration within the multi-environment itself. Again, for technical or practical reasons, you may need to create a new set of environments for the migration.

- **Technical restrictions**: Let's give a direct example here. When SAP released the **Cloud Platform Integration (CPI)** service in the multi-environment, there was a restriction on the number of characters you could have for the subaccount's subdomain property. If you were planning to enable the service in an existing subaccount with a subdomain longer than the limit, SAP's advice was to create a new subaccount.

- **Project/product isolation**: There may be cases where you want to manage large or priority projects in a way that requires an isolated set of environments solely used for the project. This isolation can end before production, and the project can deliver to a shared production environment; but also, the isolation may go up to the production environment, which means you are segregating the product.

- **Business isolation**: Suppose your company has several **business units (BU)**. In that case, you may want to establish one set of subaccounts for each BU due to administrative or business requirements. If you consider doing this, bear in mind that the applications deployed for the BUs will most probably be independent of each other, and most platform services provide ways to isolate the artifacts of BUs. In that case, you may consider using the same set of environments for multiple BUs.

- **Regional requirements**: You should remember the section earlier in this chapter where we discussed regions and the cases in which you may require having SAP BTP on multiple regions. As subaccounts are attached to regions, a multi-region requirement means different sets of subaccounts.

So, let's solve an exercise to demonstrate what we have learned so far. How about creating an account and landscape model for a company with the following requirements? There is still some room for interpretations and assumptions; after working on yours, you can check *Figure 3.7* to see our solution:

1.  Company Alpha has two BUs and requires separation at the BU level.

2.  BU 1 has just completed a project and migrated from legacy software to SAP S/4HANA using a RISE with SAP offering. It now needs to set up its global account in SAP BTP.

3.  BU 1 plans to build some mission-critical applications; therefore, it needs to provide highly reliable business continuity measures for these applications.

4.  BU 1 has many end users and is happy to invest in providing training for these users. Also, BU 1 wants to allow power users and developers to innovate and trial new features without contaminating the change delivery environments.

5.  In addition, BU 1 needs a separate set of environments for its Product X because it wants to manage it independently; maybe it is considering commercializing the product. A small team will be developing and operating this product. They are okay with using the development environment for trial purposes and don't need a different training environment yet.

6.  BU 2 onboarded on SAP BTP a while back, and it has a presence in the Neo environment with a typical four-tier model.

7.  BU 2 has started migrating to the multi-environment and wants to keep its change delivery model the same, but it wants an additional environment for training end users.

You can see an example landscape for this exercise in the following screenshot:

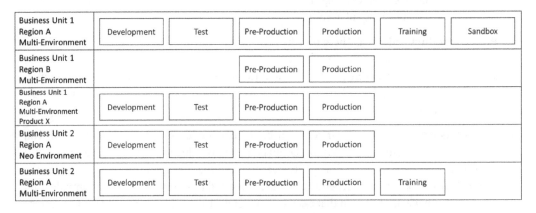

| | | | | | | |
| --- | --- | --- | --- | --- | --- | --- |
| Business Unit 1<br>Region A<br>Multi-Environment | Development | Test | Pre-Production | Production | Training | Sandbox |
| Business Unit 1<br>Region B<br>Multi-Environment | | | Pre-Production | Production | | |
| Business Unit 1<br>Region A<br>Multi-Environment<br>Product X | Development | Test | Pre-Production | Production | | |
| Business Unit 2<br>Region A<br>Neo Environment | Development | Test | Pre-Production | Production | | |
| Business Unit 2<br>Region A<br>Multi-Environment | Development | Test | Pre-Production | Production | Training | |

Figure 3.7: An example landscape fulfilling the requirements in the exercise

In our solution version, we should also note the following:

- In order to fulfill the business continuity requirement for BU 1, we propose two sets of subaccounts in two different regions, Region A and Region B. As the requirement is for BC, there is no need for development and test subaccounts in Region B. However, we have a pre-production subaccount in the second region where BC testing can be done.

- In response to *requirement 4*, we propose training and sandbox subaccounts in the primary region.

- There is a third set of subaccounts for BU 1 specifically set up for Product X development and operations as per its requirements.

- BU 2 already has a set of subaccounts in Neo. We propose a similar set of subaccounts for the new multi-environment setup, and we added a separate one for training.

With all the aforementioned factors adding new dimensions to your landscape, you may end up having tens of subaccounts, and their administration may become complicated. You may remember that SAP BTP has another element—that is, *directories*—for grouping subaccounts. Here, you have the freedom of how you want to group, and—most probably—pragmatic reasons will define your choice. For example, you can place the subaccounts in each row in our preceding example under a directory.

Furthermore, within these directories, you can add another level to separate production and non-production subaccounts. Here is a good piece of advice, though: don't exaggerate and end up with too many directory levels as this may eventually cause more pain than good. There is a limit on how many directory levels you can have anyways. For the entire account model, you can currently have a maximum of seven levels. One is for your global account, and another is for the subaccount level; hence, you are left with a maximum of five directory levels.

After making the landscape decision, you should consider which services you want to enable in each subaccount and with which configuration. We say *configuration* to take it at a more general level, but this primarily points to service plans and sizing considerations. It is not necessarily the same set of services you have to enable in every subaccount; for example, although you have a four-tier landscape, you can choose to enable the SAP Data Intelligence service in the production subaccount and only in one of the non-production subaccounts. With the two instances of SAP Data Intelligence, all non-production usage can co-exist safely with proper artifact isolation. This way, you can achieve cost savings.

When enabling services, you need to pay attention to which service plan you use because this will impact the cost. For this, you may need to do a sizing exercise where you need to define parameters. Here, you can use numbers from the business or get them from an existing system if, for example, you are moving functionality from on-premises to the cloud. With this input, you can use the *Estimator Tool* to calculate an estimated cost. We will explain the Estimator Tool later in this chapter.

# Services

At the beginning of this chapter, we already defined what a **service** is: it's a managed capability provided through the platform to be used as a building block in our solutions.

These can be *business services* that you can almost immediately incorporate into a business process providing industry-specific or **line of business** (**LOB**)-related capabilities, for example, Document and Reporting Compliance, Data Privacy Integration, Business Entity Recognition, and so on. Otherwise, they are *technical services* that do not directly relate to a business context; instead, you can use them to build technical elements and applications.

What we also need to clarify at this point is that in the SAP BTP context, a service can refer to different technical things, even though all of them are present together in a single service catalog/marketplace. Let's see them.

## Applications and subscriptions

An SAP BTP service can be an **application** that exists in a different provider environment to which you need to *subscribe* as a consumer before you can use it. These are like multi-tenant **software-as-a-service** (**SaaS**) applications; you have an isolated tenancy in the provider environment where the application runs on a managed and dedicated/shared infrastructure; hence, the boundary between **platform as a service** (**PaaS**) and SaaS gets blurry here. In any case, your data and processes are protected with appropriate isolation. Surely, for most SAP BTP services, the provider is SAP itself, and the application is built on top of SAP BTP.

Because you subscribe to a provider's application, SAP uses the term *subscription* to refer to your specific use of it. A subscription doesn't need a runtime environment in your subaccount. Your applications generally connect with these provider applications directly, without the platform's intervention—for example, a **HTTPS** communication managed by you and programming models can streamline this interaction.

Integration Suite, Workflow Management, Launchpad, Continuous Integration and Delivery, Event Mesh, and Business Application Studio are examples of this service type.

Your company may be on the other side of the subscription—that is, the provider of an application. In that case, you develop a multitenancy-aware application that, for example, uses proper routing mechanisms, Authorization and Trust Management Service for identity and access management (IAM), and so on. In addition, you can use the SaaS Provisioning service for managing subscriptions to your application.

# Runtime environments

Runtime environments are also considered services in the service marketplace. It's almost as though we are in a circular reference here, right? This is because of historical reasons we touched upon in an earlier section explaining environments.

You need a runtime environment in your subaccount if you want to deploy applications or use non-subscription services, which we will be explaining next. As we explained when discussing the SAP BTP account model, you can enable CF and Kyma runtime environments at the subaccount level. In contrast, the ABAP runtime environment needs a CF space.

When you create a CF runtime environment, SAP BTP assigns to the subaccount a memory quota that applications can use. Because SAP BTP's current service provisioning model is based on CF, some services become available only after CF is enabled in the subaccount.

When you create a Kyma runtime environment, SAP BTP reserves the infrastructure for running a managed Kubernetes cluster.

## Services and service instances

After handling the aforementioned special types, let's come to the kinds of services that are just reusable functionality reserved for consumption by your applications. To utilize these types of services, you need to create a **service instance** in an applicable SAP BTP runtime environment—that is, CF or Kyma. The service instances reserve resources in your subaccount, and they are primarily for your applications to communicate with them through APIs. Let's look at some examples here:

- **Backing services**: These are the services applications need to use in order to provide their full functionality, such as persisting data (database, object stores, and so on), storing and retrieving credentials, caching, and so on.

  For example, when you enable the SAP HANA Cloud service, SAP BTP provisions an instance of the database and the infrastructure it runs as reserved resources by the service instance. Similarly, when you create an Object Store service instance, SAP BTP arranges its infrastructure— for example, Microsoft Azure Blob storage, an AWS Simple Storage Service (S3) bucket, or a GCP Cloud Storage bucket—and through the created service instances, your applications can communicate with these backing services.

- **Other miscellaneous services**: For example, the Authorization and Trust Management service enables applications to fulfill IAM requirements through the foundational platform components—for example, authentication via the configured **identity provider (IdP)**.

Service instances can be attached to applications by creating **bindings** that deliver service credentials automatically to the bound applications. If you need to connect to a service instance directly—for example, from an external client—you can create a **service key** that generates access credentials. These include **Open Authorization 2 (OAuth 2)** elements, which you need to use for authorization before accessing service instance APIs. For example, the Kyma environment uses service keys to consume services in the CF environment; or, say, you have an IT spend management application that you want to connect to SAP BTP in order to retrieve consumption and cost information using the Usage Data Management service.

Here, after creating a service instance, you can create a service key that generates OAuth 2 credentials. Because the application is external, you cannot use bindings. Instead, the access information needs to be shared manually with the external application.

In *Figure 3.8*, you can see a diagram bringing the different types of services together. As you can see, there is one single service marketplace that includes all these services. If you are curious about the kernel services, we can say they are foundational components used internally within the platform and are not supposed to be directly consumed by customers.

One thing to note here: SAP's current strategic direction keeps CF and Kyma environments co-existing in SAP BTP. The current service provisioning model is more aligned with CF, and we don't yet know if this will be different in the future.

You can view the diagram here:

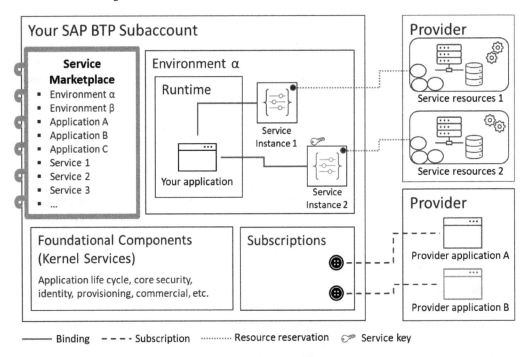

Figure 3.8: SAP BTP service types overview

## Connecting with external environments

You can define external services so that your applications can consume them similarly to SAP BTP's platform services. For example, after you configure your AWS or Azure account as a resource provider in SAP BTP, you can consume the supported services that are provisioned in the AWS or Azure platforms. Currently, SAP BTP supports PostgreSQL database services on AWS and Microsoft Azure. This way, you can create a PostgreSQL database in AWS or Azure and then build your application in SAP BTP to persist data in that database.

Another approach to achieving external service consumption is using user-provided services. First, you need to create a user-provided service instance that contains access details for the external service. This instance can now be attached to an application with a binding. As you remember, what a binding does is automatically deliver access information to the application to consume the external service. Compared to the first option, this is a less streamlined method.

In the opposite direction, you can also make external environments consume SAP BTP services as well. For this, you need to use the Service Manager service through SAP BTP Cockpit, the Service Manager **command-line interface (CLI)**, or Service Manager APIs. This connectivity option is valid for external Kubernetes clusters as well. Here, you would have an additional option—that is, SAP BTP Service Operator, which streamlines the interaction used by Kubernetes native tools.

## Taxonomy

Over time, SAP classified SAP BTP services under different categories. You've possibly had a peek through the contents of this book and have seen which categorization we adopted; that is, the high-level use cases for which SAP BTP provides services.

---

Important Note

There are some applications SAP built on top of SAP BTP, selling them as separate products. These are generally considered under the SAP BTP portfolio, although they are not directly available as SAP BTP services—for example, **SAP Analytics Cloud (SAC)** and **Identity Access Governance (IAG)**.

---

The following figure shows a basic categorization of SAP BTP services:

| Integration | Data-to-Value | Extensibility |
| --- | --- | --- |
| ▪ SAP Integration Suite | ▪ SAP HANA Cloud | ▪ SAP Workflow Management |
|   ▪ Cloud Integration |   ▪ HANA DB, ASE, Data Lake | ▪ SAP Intelligent RPA (iRPA) |
|   ▪ API Management | ▪ SAP Analytics Cloud | ▪ Cloud Foundry and Kyma |
|   ▪ API Business Hub | ▪ Data Warehouse Cloud |   Runtimes |
|   ▪ Open Connectors | ▪ PostgreSQL (Hyperscaler) | ▪ Authorization and Trust |
|   ▪ Integration Advisor | ▪ Redis (Hyperscaler) |   Management |
| ▪ Event Mesh | ▪ Object Store | ▪ Business Application Studio |
| ▪ ... | ▪ ... | ▪ Continuous Integration and |
|      ▪ SAP Data Intelligence | |   Delivery |
|      ▪ Master Data Integration | | ▪ ... |

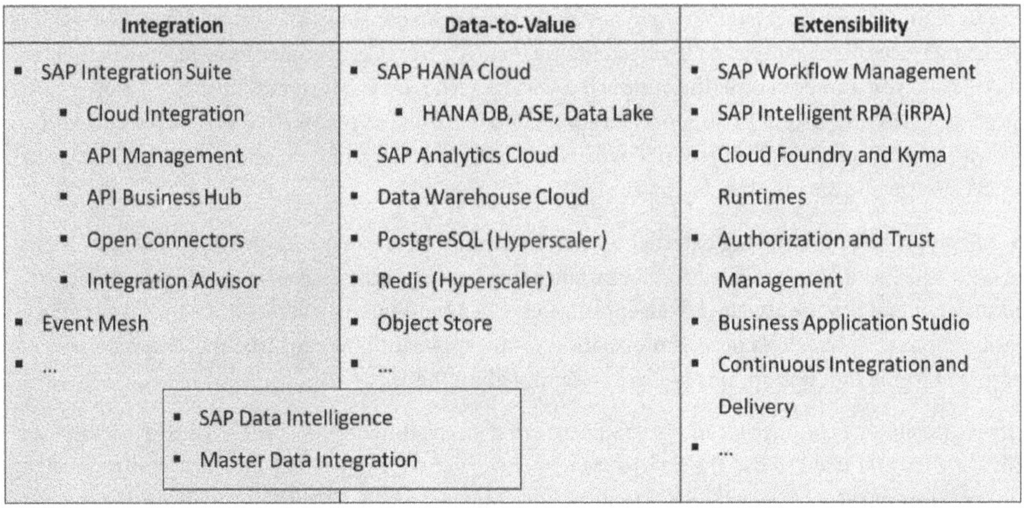

Figure 3.9: A basic categorization of SAP BTP services

Classification is not an easy task, and surely the functionalities of some services span multiple scenarios. In *Figure 3.9*, we wanted to give an overview and a sample of services for each category. Further listing all SAP BTP services and providing catalog information here would be a waste of space because we will explain most of them in later chapters with examples. Besides, there is a great online tool that fulfills service discovery requirements, and you do not need to wait long as we will discuss this in the next section.

## SAP Discovery Center

Who doesn't like a catalog that functions as a registry and has the following attributes:

- Is always up to date
- Includes a brief and effective summary of items
- Tags items for important attributes
- Provides detailed availability and pricing information
- Lists essential resources to get further information
- Includes guided training to learn more about how to use the items
- Shows a roadmap for the items' future direction
- Tells about success stories of others who used the items

We cannot see anyone raising their hands. Luckily, SAP provides such a superb catalog for SAP BTP—that is, **SAP Discovery Center**. So, don't take just our word for it; go and check yourself as it's at your fingertips at the following link: `https://discovery-center.cloud.sap/`.

While designing your solutions, SAP Discovery Center is your best companion to help you find your way among so many platform services. Let's see this with an example. Bear in mind that the following example is based on the content available at the time of authoring this book:

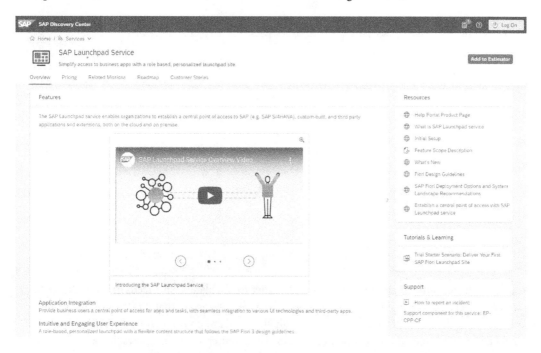

Figure 3.10: SAP Discovery Center overview page for SAP Launchpad service

As an architect working for Company A, Mary considers using the SAP Launchpad service in her design and needs to gather information. So, she navigates to SAP Discovery Center and searches for or browses the **SAP Launchpad Service** page. The screen looks like the one shown in *Figure 3.10*.

The **Overview** page tells her what the service is about and includes links to resources and tutorials. Next, she gets to the **Pricing** tab, which is shown in *Figure 3.11*. Company A has a CPEA contract. So, after ensuring the **CPEA** option is selected as the commercial model, she can see that two service plans are available: **Free** and **Standard**. The design is for a production solution end users will use. Thus, she thinks she should look into the **Standard** service plan.

Mary realizes there are two sets of pricing information, and it seems the region feature for EU access may impact the cost. Also, she needs to check whether the Launchpad service is available in the SAP BTP region in which her company already has subaccounts. She clicks on the globe button, which shows a map as in *Figure 3.12*, and it seems the service is available in the region she wants.

You can see the pricing page here:

Figure 3.11: SAP Discovery Center pricing page for SAP Launchpad service

So, how much will consuming this service cost? In order to calculate it, she needs to know the metric by which the service is charged. For the Launchpad service, she can see that it is the number of active users, and from the definition, it looks as though she needs to count anyone who would use the Launchpad service at any time during a month. From the requirements, she knows that approximately 6,000 users will be using this service, so she can base her calculation on this number. Checking the pricing table, it looks as though the quantity of 6,000 active users falls under the fifth pricing tier, which says **Up to 20,000**, and the price per unit for this tier is 0.79 **British pound sterling** (**GBP**)/month. So, for all users, that makes 6,000 x 0.79 = 4,740 GBP/month. Because Company A is on a CPEA contract, this will be the amount withdrawn monthly from the *cloud credits* balance for consuming the SAP Launchpad service.

> **Important Note**
>
> In contrast to many cloud vendors using cumulative pricing, SAP uses tiered pricing. In this model, you pay the entire quantity with the same price per unit of the tier to which your consumption corresponds. Therefore, once you identify the tier of your usage, other tiers have no place in your cost calculation.

The following figure shows the regions in which the SAP Launchpad service is available:

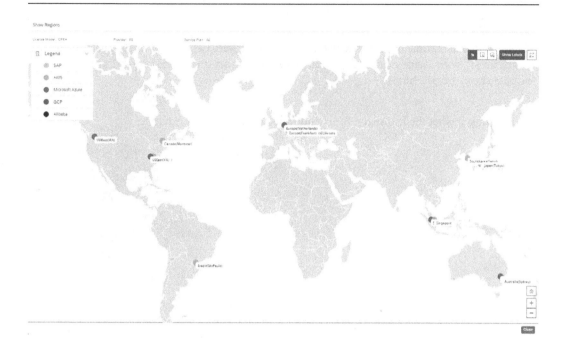

Figure 3.12: SAP Discovery Center regional map showing in which SAP
BTP regions the SAP Launchpad service is available

## Estimator Tool

In Mary's aforementioned scenario, there was only one service. The more services you need to consider, the more difficult it may become. Also, the metrics for some services require a deeper level of sizing exercises, such as SAP HANA Cloud, SAP Data Intelligence, and Kyma environments.

SAP provides a handy tool that helps customers neatly calculate prices. With the **Estimator Tool**, you can add multiple services and customize the factors that impact pricing. For example, check out the screenshot in *Figure 3.13*, where we added three services in the estimation. As you can see, besides providing the parameter values for service pricing metrics, we have also customized the estimator to do the following:

- Provide prices for the following:

  - Based on a specific region—that is, AWS Frankfurt

  - In our preferred currency—that is, GBP

  - For a particular commercial model—that is, CPEA

- Incorporate a discount of, say, 10%.

> **Important Note**
>
> You can access the Estimator Tool from within the SAP Discovery Center or by directly navigating to https://www.sap.com/uk/products/business-technology-platform/estimator-tool.html.

Let's take a look at what the Estimator Tool window looks like with our example:

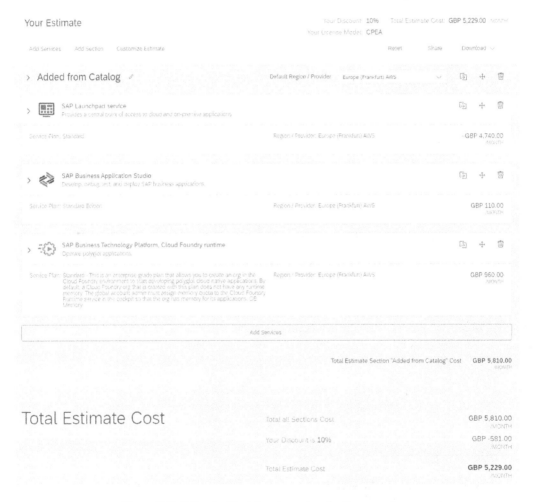

Figure 3.13: Estimator Tool showing prices for three services

As mentioned before, for some services, you need to have a more sophisticated sizing exercise to determine the cost. In such cases, SAP generally provides an abstract metric—that is, **capacity units**. By defining sizing-parameter values, a total number of capacity units is derived. In the tool, next to the metric input box label, a calculator icon appears for this type of service; upon clicking it, you will be taken to a sizing screen specifically tailored for the service. Let's take the SAP Data Intelligence service as an example. Multiple components may impact the cost, such as the number of pipelines, jobs, users, pre-trained machine learning (ML) services, and core ML services. For all related components, you can specify how many you need according to your requirements. In the following screenshot, you can see an example. It may not be a completed sizing exercise because our goal was to showcase different elements in the screenshot, but it should give you an idea:

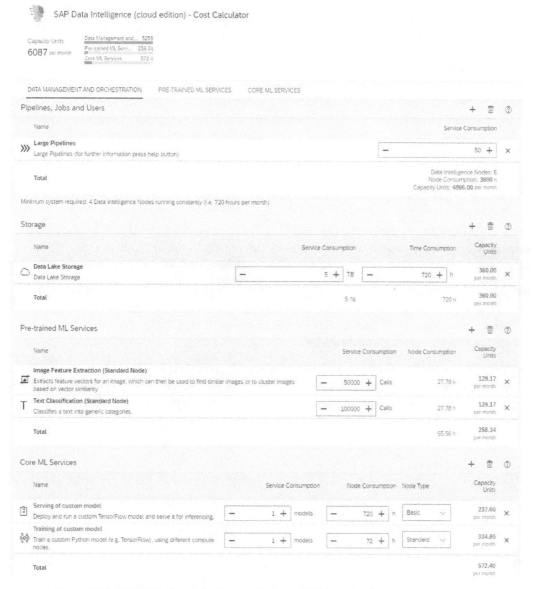

Figure 3.14: SAP BTP Estimator Tool – calculation of SAP Data Intelligence capacity units

As you can see, after our input, the number of capacity units is calculated as **6087 per month**. Now, you can close the sizing screen and go back to the Estimator Tool to enter this number as the metric value.

Next, let's learn more about account administration.

# Account administration

We have talked a lot about SAP BTP so far, and we understand there are lots of new concepts that need to sink in. Undoubtedly, the best way this can happen is when you try it yourself. So far, it has been all about foundational concepts, commercial models, and the SAP BTP account model. Now, let's look at the options around how you can manage all these. As an architect, you may not need to know the lowest-level details of account administration; however, having a high-level knowledge of it will help. So, we will keep it short and sweet. At the end of the day, you may want to know how to find your way around SAP BTP when designing architectures, and you may need to try things yourself.

You can manage your SAP BTP account mainly using three tools: SAP BTP Cockpit, the SAP BTP CLI, and SAP BTP APIs.

## SAP BTP Cockpit

SAP BTP Cockpit is a web-based **user interface (UI)** that lets users manage SAP BTP account-model elements using screen controls. The UI adheres to the account-model structure, and you can drill down from your global accounts to service instances where each has a dedicated administration screen.

Here, we should remind you of the note we provided at the beginning of the *Account model* section. Your Cockpit screens may look different from the screenshots in this book, depending on which feature set your global account is on. Also, SAP continues improving SAP BTP Cockpit; hence, changes in appearance over time wouldn't be surprising.

In *Figure 3.5* in a previous section, you already had a peek at the **Account Explorer** screen, which shows subordinate elements of the global account. As you can see, the screen displays information and contains buttons to make changes to your global account—for example, creating/updating/deleting a directory or a subaccount.

As another example, in the following screenshot, you can see the administration screen for a subaccount. It has a similar structure that displays essential information, and contains buttons for managing subordinate or linked elements:

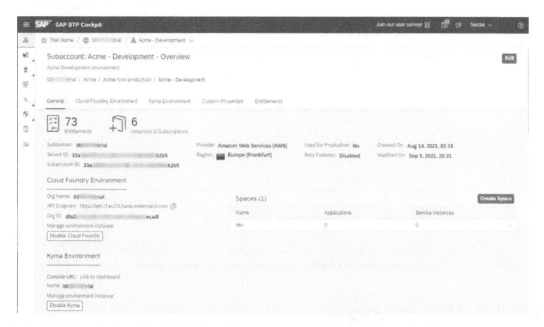

Figure 3.15: SAP BTP Cockpit – subaccount administration screen

> **Important Note**
> If you are stuck when using SAP BTP Cockpit, you can use the context-aware help by clicking the question-mark button. It's a great facility and provides rich content that will help with the page you are on, including essential information and links to the standard documentation. Try it, it's impressive.

Another interesting part of SAP BTP Cockpit is the **Service Marketplace**. Here, you can find all available services according to the entitlements assigned to the subaccount, as shown in Figure 3.16.

The following figure shows an overview of the **Service Marketplace**.

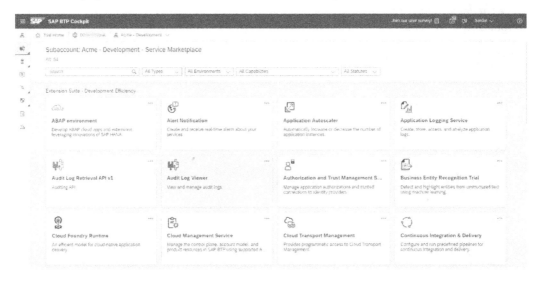

Figure 3.16: SAP BTP Cockpit – Service Marketplace

## SAP BTP CLI

It may look a bit abstract when you manage your account using SAP BTP Cockpit; however, under the hood, your account data is persisted somewhere, and there is an application processing that data.

As a convenience tool both internally for SAP and for customers, the BTP CLI provides a set of commands and other common CLI features for users who prefer working in a terminal.

This way, the BTP CLI enables scripting, which means you can create scripts to automate administrative tasks. Enabling automation is a crucial cost-optimization element in today's IT landscapes as operational requirements are much more dynamic.

You can use the BTP CLI to do everything you can do in SAP BTP Cockpit; for example, you can log in to your global account and manage all account-model elements.

> **Important Note**
> You can use the BTP CLI only for global accounts with Feature Set B.

If you have advanced use cases to manage CF elements of your subaccount, you can use the CF CLI. Similarly, with the **Service Manager Control** (**SMCTL**) command-line tool, you can run commands to manage service instances in your SAP BTP subaccount directly with Service Manager. Many SMCTL commands are available in the BTP CLI, though.

## SAP BTP administration APIs

SAP BTP provides a special set of APIs that you can use to manage your global account and its subordinate elements, as follows:

**Core Services for SAP BTP**: The APIs in this package use the Cloud Management, Usage Data Management, and Service Manager services; therefore, you need service instances in your subaccount accordingly. With these APIs, you can do the following:

- Manage your account-model elements—for example, global accounts, directories, subaccounts, and so on.
- Manage entitlements.
- Provision runtime environments.
- Get information about administrative events.
- Manage applications (as a provider) and subscriptions (as a consumer).
- Retrieve consumption information.
- Use SAP Service Manager for managing service instances, bindings, and so on.

**SAP Authorization and Trust Management Service**: These APIs can be used to manage IAM-related entities, as follows:

- Manage **role-based access control** (**RBAC**) elements—for example, roles, role collections, and so on.
- Manage IdPs of the subaccount.
- Manage security settings.
- Manage users and their authorizations.

We have just listed APIs that can be used for administrative purposes. There are many other APIs that you can use to consume the capabilities of SAP BTP platform services—for example, APIs for monitoring, connectivity, transport management, alert notification, and so on.

> **Important Note**
> For more information on SAP BTP APIs, you can visit SAP API Business Hub at `https://api.sap.com/` and search for SAP BTP.

As you would expect, these APIs are protected for security reasons, and you would need to get OAuth 2 authorization before you can use them. Any idea how you can achieve this? How about if we remind you that these APIs are exposing the functionality of SAP BTP services? If you don't have an answer, then maybe you should read (again) the part where we discuss service keys.

## Summary

We are now at the end of this chapter after going through so many foundational elements of SAP BTP. So, let's go back to the beginning and fast forward for a summary.

First, we learned which environments you could have in SAP BTP and in which regions SAP BTP was available. Next, we discussed different options to buy SAP BTP and how they compared. Then, it was time to see how SAP BTP components were structured in its account model, and we discussed how to set up your own account model based on an example. In the subsequent section, we had a good overview of what a service meant and also learned about SAP Discovery Center. Finally, in the last section, we briefly discussed the administration tools you could use to manage SAP BTP.

Now that we have laid out the essential foundational elements, we will go more technical in the next chapter and discuss two fundamental aspects you need to consider in your technical designs: security and connectivity.

# 4

# Security and Connectivity

After reading the previous chapters, SAP BTP should no longer be a stranger to you. Now, it is time to delve into the design aspects, and we will start with the one that is crucial to every organization: security.

After discussing security, we will touch upon the subject of connectivity, which is inherently related to security. Connectivity is all about paving the connection routes among several systems. And keeping these routes safe is of paramount importance.

In this chapter, we're going to cover the following main topics:

- Security in general

- **Identity and access management (IAM)** in SAP BTP

- Connectivity

After completing this chapter, you will be able to incorporate security aspects into your architecture design and include connectivity across several systems.

## Technical requirements

You might have already registered for an SAP BTP trial account, as suggested in the *Technical requirements* section of *Chapter 3, Establishing the Foundation for SAP Business Technology Platform*. If not, check it out and register for a trial account.

In this chapter, we will talk about an on-premise component called **SAP Cloud Connector**. If you want to get your hands dirty with it, you can download it from `https://tools.hana.ondemand.com/#cloud`. Also, for trial purposes, you can install on-premise SAP systems using SAP CAL at `https://cal.sap.com/`. Just be careful as these systems could incur very high costs.

## Security in general

The need for security is a reality in the IT world. If you haven't been to this side of it before, ask your company's security team, at what frequency does a cyberattack hit the company? Don't be surprised if the quantity is on a per-second scale.

Security implies there is something of high value that needs protection. At its core, it is the protected, confidential, or sensitive data that your company needs to keep safe. For example, data protection is related to regulatory compliance in the case of **personally identifiable information (PII)** such as in the EU's **General Data Protection Regulation (GDPR)**, the **California Consumer Privacy Act (CCPA)**, and China's **Personal Information Protection Law (PIPL)**. In the case of a data breach, a company could face severe penalties. More importantly, its prestige will be significantly damaged, which could have commercial consequences.

A cyberattack can paralyze a company's mission-critical systems and adversely impact its operational ability. Depending on its industry, the company could be impacted in different ways. For example, due to a cyberattack, a company might stop providing proper customer service, or its production line might come to a halt. If it's a government organization, this might cause political friction. And going a bit further, it could even become a matter of national security if the cyberattack is toward, for example, a state's defense system.

In the context of IT security, you might have already heard about the onion model or the Swiss cheese model. One uses the scales of an onion bulb, and the other has stacked slices of cheese. Both models suggest a layered approach to security; we will follow this approach. To begin, we will correlate the traditional onion model layers with the cloud service model components, as illustrated in *Figure 4.1*:

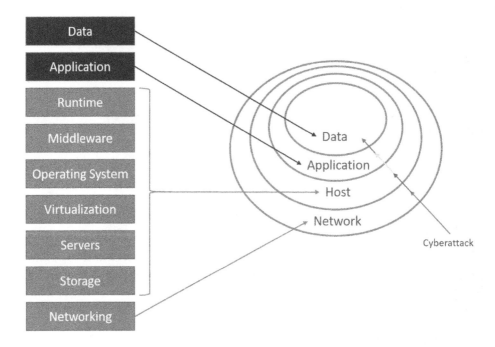

Figure 4.1: The cloud service model and onion model layers

The cloud service model is often used to explain the shared responsibility between the service provider and the customer. Because we are discussing security for SAP BTP, in *Figure 4.1*, according to the PaaS model, the customer is responsible for the application and data layers. In contrast, the rest of the components are under the provider's responsibility. As you would expect, the liability for each layer includes security as a crucial element. The more layers a cyberattack penetrates, the worse the implications are. Now, let's discuss these layers in more detail.

## Infrastructure security and the provider's security compliance

For SAP BTP, you have a contract with SAP; therefore, the responsibility of all cloud service model layers apart from application and data falls under SAP. Thus, regardless of which hyperscaler your SAP BTP subaccounts run on, your point of contact is SAP. That's why, from this point on, we will not always make an explicit distinction between SAP and the relevant hyperscaler.

You entrust your company's data to SAP as the cloud service provider. Surely, before doing that, you need to do due diligence and evaluate whether SAP meets the necessary security requirements. So, what kind of requirements can you think of?

To begin with, as you might remember from *Chapter 3*, SAP BTP runs on an infrastructure located in a data center that includes all the physical elements such as servers, disks, network devices, cables, and more. So, the first step should be to secure those elements. The cloud service provider ensures this by taking physical security measures such as using security cameras, employing staff after necessary background checks, only allowing authorized staff to administer the physical components, and preventing unauthorized access to the data center building.

The hosts in the provider's data center are not in a closed circuit and, surely, need to communicate with external elements. So, there are networking components that link your content to the outside world. This means there is a virtual attack surface susceptible to security intrusion; therefore, it needs protection. The data center provider should take necessary measures to prevent cyberattacks through this surface. These measures include firewalls, gateways, proxies, mechanisms to cope with **distributed denial-of-service (DDoS)** attacks, and advanced intrusion detection and prevention controls. To ensure these measures are properly in place, frequent penetration tests are performed.

So far, it was all about core security; however, to establish a good level of trust with the provider, you need to extend these controls further into other relevant areas such as privacy, confidentiality, availability, and processing integrity. All these aspects work hand in hand to determine the reliability of the cloud provider. Also, security is established not only against intrusion agents but also against different types of hazards, for example, equipment failures, disasters, power outages, fires, and more.

That said, as a customer, should you inspect the data centers on which SAP BTP is running? Of course, you have to ensure the provider meets all the trust standards, but continuously monitoring them would be an overburden for a typical company. Now, consider a large cloud provider with millions of customers. Each customer requesting an inspection for their own assurance purposes and the cloud provider dealing with such requests would be a huge inconvenience. So, there must be a better way.

We already gave away how the industry solved this challenge when we mentioned **standards**. Luckily, independent organizations create and maintain standards for the aforementioned aspects, such as the **International Organization for Standardization** (**ISO**) or a global network of national standards organizations in different countries, for example, the **British Standards Institution** (**BSI**). Other examples include the **American Institute of Certified Public Accountants** (**AICPA**) and the German Federal Office for Information Security (BSI in German). Cloud providers ensure they implement the necessary controls outlined by these organizations and get audited by independent parties, after which they can claim they comply with those standards.

For example, *Figure 4.2* illustrates the trust service categories defined by AICPA's **System and Organization Controls 2** (**SOC 2**) audit reports:

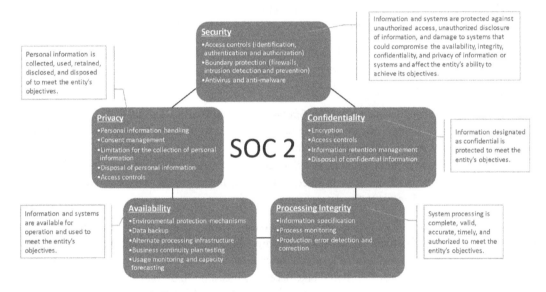

Figure 4.2: AICPA's SOC 2 trust service categories

We haven't explained all of this merely for general knowledge. If you are in the process of evaluating SAP BTP as a new platform to adopt or if your architecture design is ready for implementation, it is likely you would seek approval from your company's information security team. Firstly, let them know that SAP BTP complies with the following:

- ISO 27001 and ISO 22301
- AICPA's SOC 1, SOC 2, and SOC 3

- German BSI's C5

- FedRAMP (via SAP NS2)

- PCI DSS attestation (for SAP MultiCloud)

> **Important Note**
>
> If you need evidence of SAP BTP's compliance with the aforementioned standards, you can visit the *Compliance* section of the SAP Trust Center at `https://www.sap.com/uk/about/trust-center/certification-compliance.html`. Here, you can search for "*SAP Business Technology Platform*" to see a list of available audit reports and certificates. However, some reports such as SOC 2 are for a restricted audience, for example, customers with non-disclosure agreements, so you need to request them formally.

You might need to demonstrate that your design takes care of additional security requirements, including other infrastructure security elements such as data encryption. SAP BTP supports communication protocols with **Transport Layer Security** (**TLS**) for encrypting data in transit. In addition, there are options to establish additional communication security layers, which we will discuss later in this chapter. For the services that persist data, for example, SAP HANA Cloud, SAP supports data volume encryption and physical access control at the infrastructure level, which you can consider as a measure to secure data at rest.

So, we have discussed enough in terms of infrastructure-level security. Now, let's move on to the security topics at the application layer.

## Security at the application layer

In the previous section, we discussed how SAP ensures the security of cloud service layers below applications. There wasn't much you needed to handle as a customer. However, as you start using these services and building your applications on SAP BTP, they will process your data, and securing your data will be primarily your responsibility. SAP BTP doesn't leave you alone here; it provides capabilities that you can incorporate into your applications and service usage. In the following sections, you will see examples of this:

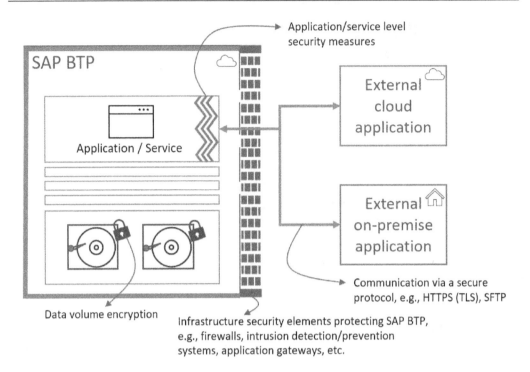

Figure 4.3: The core SAP BTP security elements

In *Figure 4.3*, you can see the core security elements illustrated together. Since we discussed the infrastructure aspects earlier, let's continue by taking our discussion to the application layer.

### Building secure applications

First, let's discuss what you need to do to build secure applications. This subject is quite broad and including all of its aspects here might not be the best idea as they need some prerequisite information, which you will learn later in this book when we discuss extensibility, integration, and data. So, this section will be a brief overview at this stage.

First of all, the responsibility of building secure applications is, as you might have guessed, with the application developers. They need to follow security practices to prevent attacks against the application, such as **cross-site scripting** (**XSS**), **SQL injection**, and more. To minimize the risk, it's best to implement automated security scans in the change delivery mechanism to detect the vulnerabilities before it's too late.

Next, the application needs to implement access controls by using SAP BTP's **Authentication and Trust Management service**, which enables the application to leverage the IAM entities, for example, trusted **identity providers** (**IdPs**), roles, and more. When used in relation to an application, this service is also referred to as **User Account and Authentication** (**UAA** or **XSUAA**). We will discuss IAM later in this chapter.

Let's suppose your application is accessing external services, including other applications or services in the same subaccount. In that case, it might be wiser to isolate the configuration that defines the parameters to access these external services. For this, you can use SAP BTP's **Destination service** to create and manage the destinations your applications can use. This service makes sure the connection details are safely kept and separated from your application code. Additionally, with the **Connectivity service**, you can access on-premise systems securely. We will discuss the destination and connectivity services later in this chapter:

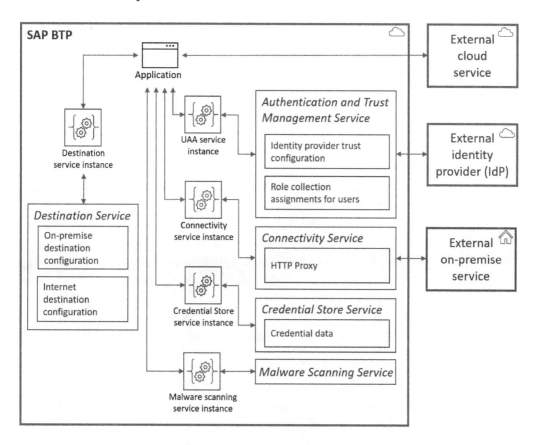

Figure 4.4: The SAP BTP helper services for building secure applications

Another SAP BTP service worth mentioning here is the **Credential Store service**. With this service, you can centrally store cryptographic entities such as passwords, keys, and keyrings. Then, applications can safely retrieve them at runtime through their service bindings and using the **JavaScript Object Signing and Encryption (JOSE)** framework.

Last but not least, we have the **Malware Scanning service** that you can use to scan the business documents processed in your applications. After binding this service, your application can make API calls to it and provide the business document in binary format. This call will then return the scanning result upon which your application can take further action, for example, deleting the file and creating a log record. Just to note, at the time of writing, this service is in beta version. So, check the SAP roadmap to find out more about it and whether it is available for production use.

Does this sound a bit overwhelming? In that case, programming frameworks and libraries such as SAPUI5, the application router, and CAP can give you peace of mind because they take care of the security concerns while streamlining certain aspects of programming such as database connections, authentication, **role-based access control (RBAC)**, API calls, and more. We will see some examples of these later in this book.

### Security features in SAP BTP services

The SAP BTP services are just applications similar to the ones you build, and as you might expect, the developers of these applications need to secure the applications properly. Therefore, these services might impose certain restrictions to make sure you use them securely. Besides, some come with security features specific to the service so that you, as a consumer, can use them. Let's list a subset of these features:

| The SAP BTP service | Security features |
|---|---|
| SAP HANA Cloud, SAP HANA Database | • Support for secure connections, for example, TLS for ODBC and JDBC<br><br>• External IdP for database platform users that can be used for SSO<br><br>• RBAC<br><br>• IP allowlists<br><br>• Data masking and anonymization<br><br>• Audit policies<br><br>• Secure internal credential store and SAP HANA secure user store |
| SAP HANA Cloud, SAP ASE Database | • Support for secure connections, for example, TLS for ODBC and JDBC<br><br>• Column-level encryption<br><br>• RBAC<br><br>• Audit logging |

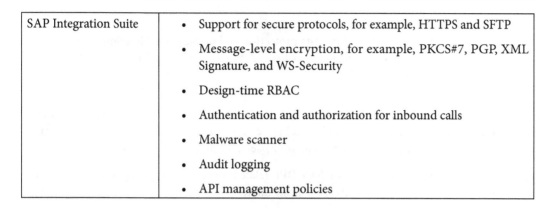

| SAP Integration Suite | • Support for secure protocols, for example, HTTPS and SFTP |
| | • Message-level encryption, for example, PKCS#7, PGP, XML Signature, and WS-Security |
| | • Design-time RBAC |
| | • Authentication and authorization for inbound calls |
| | • Malware scanner |
| | • Audit logging |
| | • API management policies |

Table 4.1: Examples of SAP BTP service-specific security features

Bear in mind that you are at the application layer, and the responsibility of using these features lies with you. So, you can choose whether to configure and control these features or not while considering the security implications.

## Data protection and privacy

When we talk about **Data Protection and Privacy (DPP)**, we are mainly referring to several legislations across the globe that regulate how organizations use certain types of data. Being one of the main motivations for establishing IT security, we already mentioned examples of such legislation at the beginning of this chapter.

All of the security measures we discussed in the previous sections can help organizations to be compliant with these legislations. However, DPP is not only about securing data against intruders or malicious users; it also requires the relevant data to be managed in a way that does not impact an individual's privacy. For example, a customer might wish to exercise their right to be forgotten. In that case, your organization needs to make sure that your systems do not store any PII of the customer. Another example of a compliance requirement is seeking your customers' consent to leverage their data for a given purpose.

Assuming all technical and organizational measures that protect the data are in place, SAP's specific concern for SAP BTP is then limited to only the personal data it stores for the platform operations. For this, SAP BTP persists limited user information and provides the necessary means for deleting this information if required.

After that, as the platform consumer, the responsibility of complying with DPP legislation mainly lies with you. You manage the data that is processed by the platform for your operations; hence, you need to take necessary precautions and establish compulsory mechanisms. Here, you can make use of some SAP BTP features for compliance. For example, you can use the RBAC feature to ensure only authorized users view the regulation-relevant data.

> **Important Note**
>
> For more information regarding SAP's data protection and privacy considerations, you can visit SAP Trust Center's *Privacy* section at `https://www.sap.com/about/trust-center/data-privacy.html`.

SAP BTP offers some business services that you can use to fulfill DPP requirements: Data Retention Management, Personal Data Manager, and Data Privacy Integration. With these services, you can manage the compliance aspects of personal data processed by your applications in SAP BTP.

Finally, here's a good piece of advice: if you have DPP-related concerns about using SAP BTP, do not hesitate to discuss them with SAP as this is a delicate matter.

So, we have now explained the core security concepts in detail. Next, let's go into more specific areas; next in line is IAM.

# IAM in SAP BTP

Securing applications does not mean you deploy them and let them run on their own in a box that no one can access. Someone will have access to the applications, but can it be just anyone? Maybe, but you might need to control this by only letting certain people have access to your application. But then, among those who are allowed to access the application, should everyone be able to use every capability and see every piece of data? Alternatively, should there be a further control level that only lets a subset of these people use a specific feature?

It looks like we are establishing a control mechanism that revolves around the people, that is, the users, and their access levels to the application. Defining this mechanism through a framework of policies and implementing technologies for operating this mechanism is called IAM.

In order to let some people have access or not have access to an application, the first step is to distinguish one from another. For this, we need to establish the person's **identity** based on their claim of who they are. They can do this by simply saying their name or maybe something that uniquely refers to them, such as an ID number or a username where uniqueness is guaranteed.

Before progressing further, let's spice things up. Earlier, for the sake of simplicity, we told the story using people as actors. However, in reality, the identity attempting to access an application can also be another application or something else, such as an IoT device.

## Authentication and authorization

Now that we have an answer to the question of "Who are you?", let's continue with the remaining procedures of IAM.

Let's suppose that you are a guard. Just because someone has claimed an identity, would you let them enter? Of course, you would not. Instead, you would try to establish the authenticity of their claim and verify they are who they claim to be. This is what **authentication** is all about. This can be done by simply challenging the identity claimant for a piece of information that is good enough to verify their claim. Yes, we know what you are thinking–maybe a password. Today, this is the simplest form of authentication. However, in response to evolving security challenges, the IT industry has come up with many sophisticated and more secure authentication methods using biometrics, such as fingerprints and retinal scans, and mobile devices, such as one-time SMS verification codes. Besides, additional factors are considered when authenticating users, such as their location, the devices they use, and more.

Let's continue with the metaphor we used earlier. The visitor is now authenticated and has just passed the gate. Can they do whatever they want? If not, there should be an additional level of questioning when they attempt to do an action. This is similar to the process of **authorization**, where a system checks whether the user has the privilege to perform a specific action and allows or denies the attempt accordingly.

For complex applications, assigning every user with all the actions they are authorized to perform and managing them will quickly become a hassle. To alleviate this inconvenience, multiple authorization items can be grouped together under a **role**, and users can be assigned to these roles. In general, these roles correlate with the job roles of the personas. Furthermore, SAP BTP introduces an additional aggregation level. The roles in SAP BTP are mostly attached to applications, and in order to group roles from multiple applications, **role collections** are used. Here, a role collection is not just a grouping container; instead, you can design it to correspond to the tasks a persona needs to perform. For example, a role collection for an *integration developer* can include all of the roles necessary for different capabilities of the Integration Suite service. Alternatively, a *data protection officer* can be assigned a role collection that contains the roles of the Personal Data Manager and Data Retention Management services. By using roles to determine whether a user is authorized to perform an action, you can implement RBAC.

What we have discussed so far should be enough to set the stage. However, before getting into the specifics of SAP BTP, let's discuss a crucial IAM component.

## What does an IdP do?

Let's suppose you only want to allow certain users to have access to your application. In that case, when developing your application, you can build a module to handle that side of things such as user registration and password setup. Additionally, when a user attempts to log in, your application can challenge them for their username and password. You can then check the username and password against the user records that your application stores and log the user in if successfully verified. This all sounds good. Now you need to develop several new applications and implement the same mechanism repeatedly for each application.

The user login stage is very significant for security. That's when you let the user through the gate to use your application and see the data. However, now, the security team says that you should only let users log in if they are accessing the application from certain locations. Here, location can be a geographical locality or an abstract location that is your company's IT security perimeter protected by firewalls.

They also suggest that your applications should challenge their users with **multi-factor authentication (MFA)**, where they need to provide multiple isolated pieces of information to be verified. If the number of required methods is set to two, this is called **two-factor authentication (2FA)**.

It looks like you should add these extra capabilities to your applications. Or is there a better way? Especially those of you with development experience should have already seen the opportunity here for reusability. You can create a separate application that uses these authentication features to serve as a central component. We call this type of application an **IdP**.

An IdP can handle most authentication aspects, and your other applications can integrate with it to delegate authentication tasks. This integration is based on a *trust relationship* that corresponds to the configuration at both ends of it. You can still choose to keep the essential authentication elements in your application in order to reduce dependency. However, you can delegate most of the complex authentication functionality to the IdP:

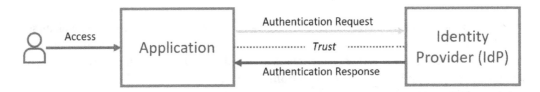

Figure 4.5: An application delegating authentication to the IdP

Having an IdP unlocks additional features. We can position it as a central component where many applications delegate authentication to the same IdP. Therefore, all integrated applications can uniformly benefit from the extra functionalities of the IdP. Let's suppose the IdP remembers it has already authenticated a user, for example, by using a session cookie it delivered to the user's browser when the user logged in to an application that trusts the IdP. In that case, it can choose not to challenge the user for a password again for subsequent authentication requests even though they are for different applications that also trust the same IdP. This convenience mechanism is called **single sign-on (SSO)**. Many companies also use SSO as a user experience enhancement as the users would not need to set and remember passwords for different systems.

There are standards that formalize the integration between an application and the IdP. This includes the security aspect since the trust relationship requires cryptographic functionality to be involved. The most prominent standards are **Security Assertion Markup Language (SAML)** and **OpenID Connect (OIDC)**. We will see a concrete example later when we discuss how SAP BTP uses SAML.

Following these standards, you can implement your own IdP. However, companies tend to go for commercial IdP solutions, such as Microsoft **Azure Active Directory (AAD)**. This is mainly due to the availability and scalability requirements. Also, these commercial products provide a good variety of additional features.

On top of authentication, you can delegate other IAM capabilities to the IdP at different levels. For example, you can base your RBAC implementation on the information managed by the IdP. For this, the IdP can send the information needed, for example, the groups the user belongs to, within the authentication response "and the application can use this information to check user's authorization".

Now that we have discussed all the essential elements, let's see how SAP BTP handles IAM.

## How does SAP BTP authenticate users?

Firstly, let's make a distinction between the two main types of users that access SAP BTP:

- **Platform users**: These users access the platform for technical and administrative purposes, such as using cloud management tools and services.
- **Business users**: These users access the business applications or services as end users.

SAP BTP does not manage identities directly; instead, it uses identity federation to delegate the management of identities to IdPs. However, for RBAC, the platform still needs to know minimal information about users so that roles can be assigned to users. The user records created for this purpose are called **shadow users**, and they are tightly coupled with the users managed by the IdP. You can create shadow users at both a global account level and a subaccount level and assign roles to them. Also, if users need to access Cloud Foundry organizations and spaces, they need to be added as organization or space members.

SAP BTP comes with a default IdP, *SAP ID Service* (except SAP BTP subaccounts in the China region). If you have been in the SAP world long enough, you probably have a **p-user** that you use to log in to SAP sites, including the SAP Community site. Also, you might have an **s-user** that is managed by your company and lets you log in to SAP sites, such as SAP Support, with your company identity. SAP ID Service provides and manages all these p-users and s-users. In addition, if you have multiple SAP ID Service users, you can link them to an **SAP Universal ID,** which conveniently groups multiple SAP IDs and provides one common user interface for logging in where you can select which specific user you want to log in with.

Besides the default IdP, SAP BTP also lets customers configure trust with multiple custom IdPs in a subaccount, given that they support the SAML 2.0 standard. So, for example, you can add your on-premise or cloud corporate IdP, such as Microsoft AAD, SAP Cloud Identity Services, Microsoft ADFS, Ping Identity, Okta, Forgerock, or OneLogin. If multiple IdPs are configured in a subaccount, it's possible to instruct an application on which IdP(s) to use.

With the trust configuration, you define which attributes the IdP includes in its authentication responses, and more importantly, which attribute it assigns as the *name identifier* that should match shadow user IDs in SAP BTP. You probably need to discuss these with your company's EUC team as they might suggest best practices.

> **Important Note**
> At the time of writing, you can only configure custom IdPs for business users, which means for platform users, SAP ID Service is the only option.

When a business user launches an application or a service, the SAP BTP Authentication and Trust Management service puts the IdP integration into action, and a SAML flow runs, as shown in *Figure 4.6*:

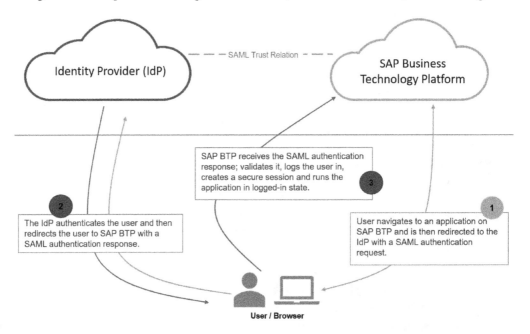

Figure 4.6: A SAML authentication flow for a user accessing an application or service in SAP BTP

As you can see in the preceding diagram, the SAML flow runs through the user's browser by using HTTP redirections where SAML artifacts are attached to the requests and responses. In SAML terms, SAP BTP acts as a *service provider* here. To be more precise, it is the UAA service instance that interacts with the SAML flow. If you are asking what UAA is, you should scroll back and read the *Building secure applications* section and maybe check out *Figure 4.4*.

With this setup, you can also achieve SSO, and the user can access an SAP BTP application with no authentication challenge if they were previously authenticated with the same IdP.

As an alternative to directly linking your corporate IdP to an SAP BTP subaccount, you can also configure **SAP Cloud Identity Services – Identity Authentication** as an IdP. If it fits your requirements, you can use it as the main IdP. Moreover, based on configured conditions, it can also act as a *proxy* between SAP BTP and another IdP, that is, your corporate IdP. Therefore, this alternative might give you an extra level of flexibility with identity federation. In *Figure 4.7*, you can see how a SAML flow happens with this setup:

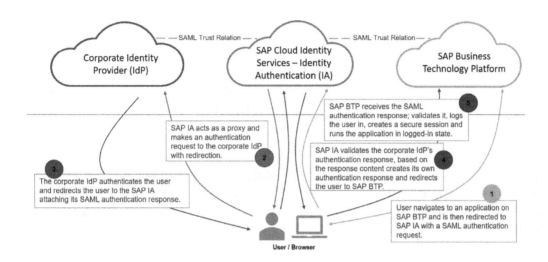

Figure 4.7: SAML authentication with SAP Cloud Identity Services – Identity Authentication

It might look complicated; however, all of these redirections and passings of SAML artifacts happen transparently once the trust relationships are set up.

Besides the capabilities mentioned previously, SAP Cloud Identity Services – Identity Authentication also supports advanced features. Some of them are listed here:

- Social login through popular providers such as LinkedIn, Twitter, Facebook, and Google

- 2FA, for example, FIDO2, the SAP Authenticator app, and SMS

- Risk-based authentication to allow, deny, or enforce 2FA for requests coming from a specific IP range

- Self-service processes for registration and password reset

- REST APIs for user management

- Custom privacy policies and terms of use

So, now you have learned how SAP BTP authenticates users. We will discuss integration-related authentication topics later. Next, let's look at how RBAC happens in SAP BTP.

## RBAC in SAP BTP

Previously, we defined the basic elements of RBAC from a general aspect. In this section, let's see how SAP BTP implements RBAC end to end.

Based on the requirements, developers can identify the basic authorization elements of an application to include them in the application's security descriptor:

- **Scopes**: These are the application functions that the user can only perform if they have the required authorization. For a simple application that maintains a data object, such as a sales order, typical examples would be *Display*, *Edit*, and *Delete*.

- **Attributes**: These are variables in the application's authorization context that are meant to be linked to the attributes of a user at a later stage.

After identifying the scopes and attributes, developers define **role templates** that bundle these elements together. **Roles** are instances of role templates. When an application is deployed, its role templates that don't contain an attribute are automatically instantiated to create roles. On the other hand, if the role template contains an attribute, then it requires human intervention to configure the attribute value that will be attached to the role.

Let's explain this with an example. A small university's registrar's office needs two new applications:

1.    Officers are divided into several teams that correspond to university departments.

2.    Officers will use the registry application to manage essential student information:

   - Although all officers can display and edit students' information, only the senior officers can delete records.

3.    Officers will use the course subscriptions application to manage students' course subscriptions:

   - Officers can only see the student records that belong to the department they look after.

   - Although all relevant officers, as per the preceding sub-point, can display course subscriptions, only the senior officers can edit and delete records.

4.    The university uses a central IdP and requires both applications to use identity federation and SSO. The trust relationship with the IdP is set so that the authentication response includes the authenticated user's team information:

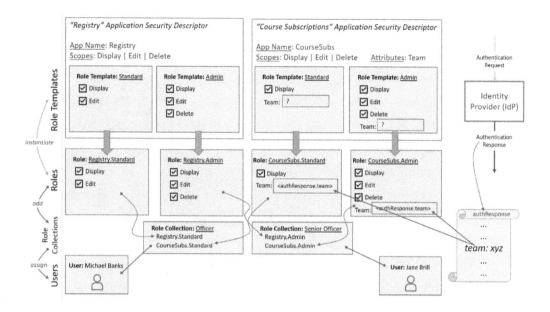

Figure 4.8: RBAC entities for the example scenario

In *Figure 4.8*, you can find an example solution that illustrates what entities you need to create and configure from development until role assignment. The developers created application security descriptors based on the requirements to include **scopes** such as Display, Edit, and Delete. Here, they followed a typical approach, although they could have also created two scopes for each application. For the second application, they also defined an *attribute* to fulfill the requirement (Refer to the first sub-point for step 3 in the preceding example). When these applications are deployed, for the first application, the *roles* are automatically generated. However, the roles for the second application need human intervention so that the `team` attribute can be configured. Here, administrators have the option of assigning static values and creating several roles for each value option. This would be fine if the variations were limited. However, in our example, they decided to make this flexible and link the attribute to the `team` information coming from the IdP. This way, they do not need to create a separate role for each team. Next, the administrators created two *role collections* for each persona: *Officer* and *Senior Officer*. Finally, they assigned the role collections to users as per their job titles.

For the services you onboard, the first part of the story is not in your control. After you subscribe to the service or create the service instance, the roles and role collections will appear in your subaccount. For example, in *Figure 4.9*, you can see the overview screen for the `Launchpad_Admin` role collection that SAP BTP delivers as part of the Launchpad service:

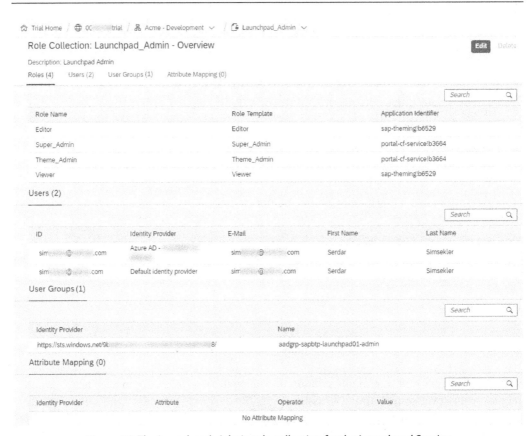

Figure 4.9: The Launchpad_Admin role collection for the Launchpad Service

Let's list what we can see in the preceding screenshot:

- The Launchpad service delivers four roles attached to the two applications that run the service.

- Under the **Users** section, you can see that there are two users to whom this role collection is assigned. You can also see that the users are controlled by different identity providers, one by Azure AD, and the other by the default identity provider, that is, the SAP ID service.

- When a user authenticates via an identity provider, it can send group information to which the user belongs. These groups and assignments are managed in the IdP. With the configuration under the **User Groups** section in the screenshot, it's made sure that if, for a user, the IdP response includes the information that the user belongs to the `aadgrp-sapbtp-launchpad01-admin` group, that user will be automatically assigned this role collection in SAP BTP.

- Similar to the user groups, other attributes sent by the IdP can also be used for automatic matching. However, in this example, this feature is not used.

Finally, let's touch upon the *administration roles*. These are the roles that are delivered with the platform and can be assigned to administrators who manage global accounts, directories, subaccounts, and other platform elements such as destinations and connectivity configuration. As you would expect, when SAP provisions your SAP BTP global account, they add at least one user you designated as a global administrator.

## Identity lifecycle management

In order to run the IAM processes, you need to persist identity information in a **user store** and manage the lifecycle of identities. The identity lifecycle is handled differently depending on the type of end users accessing an application:

- Applications used by the internal users of a company, such as employees and contractors

- Applications used by external users, for example, customers

Traditionally, IAM would cover the capabilities for the first application type. However, as the applications created for customers became more and more sophisticated, now IAM also covers the second application type. And in this latter case, the framework is also referred to as **Customer Identity and Access Management** (**CIAM**). In *Figure 4.10*, you can see the differences in identity lifecycle management for the two types of applications:

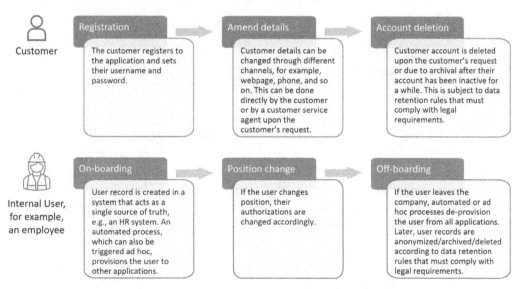

Figure 4.10: The identity life cycles for different types of users

As you can see in the preceding diagram, the main difference between the two lifecycle management approaches is who controls the identity events. In customer applications, customers themselves register to applications, whereas for internal users, the control is within an identity and access governance framework.

SAP has a SaaS offering, SAP Customer Data Cloud, that handles all CIAM aspects, including customer identity lifecycle management. As it's a different solution, we will not discuss it in this book.

To manage the identity lifecycle for a company's internal users, you can use the **SAP Cloud Identity Services – Identity Provisioning** service. This service reads identity data from a user store; generally, this is an HR system that acts as a single source of truth for employee data, such as SAP SuccessFactors. Identity Provisioning can then, optionally, send the identity data to a target system after transforming, filtering, and enriching it:

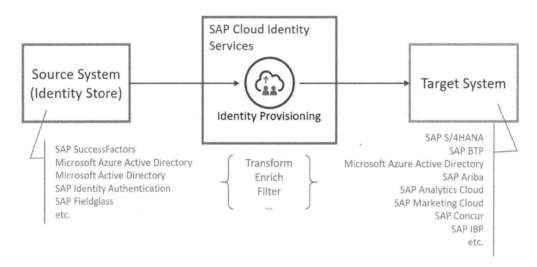

Figure 4.11: SAP Cloud Identity Services – Identity Provisioning

As you can see in *Figure 4.11*, you can use this service to provision user and role information to and from several types of on-premise and cloud systems. In addition, systems that are not explicitly supported with a specific connector can be integrated, given that the system implements the **System for Cross-Domain Identity Management (SCIM)** standard.

Suppose you have multiple source systems, for example, SAP SuccessFactors for employees and SAP Fieldglass for contingent workers. In that case, you can use the **Master Data Integration (MDI)** service to orchestrate the flow of identity data. Here, the identity data from source systems is replicated to MDI, and it acts as the source system for the Identity Provisioning service. For sophisticated orchestration requirements, you can also use SAP Integration Suite.

Identity provisioning is an area where you can easily harness the benefits of automation. For example, using the Identity Provisioning service, you can schedule jobs to synchronize identity data among systems with delta or full loads. This will ensure timely operations for joiners, movers, and leavers.

Let's discuss a specific risk scenario where we can make use of identity services to remove the risk. Suppose John has access to several SaaS applications within your company. One day, he finds a new job at a competitor company and leaves your company. After some time, he realizes he can still log in to the marketing cloud system where he can see your company's marketing plans. Surely, this is a big problem. So, what precautions would you take to remove this risk? Consider the following:

- You should establish a process, preferably automated, so that all the user accounts of a leaver are immediately deactivated after they leave.

- Identity federation and SSO function as a stopgap if the user account deactivation process is delayed. This is because processes for IdPs are deemed a priority and happen much faster. By deactivating John's user in the IdP, you ensure he cannot access any systems that rely on the IdP for authentication. In addition, with SSO, he would never need to have a password to access the systems. So, after leaving, he will not have the option to log in with a password.

We now know how to manage the identity lifecycle safely; however, there is more to this if you want to add extra governance features, and that is the next topic we will discuss.

## Governing identity access

With thousands of users and so many roles, enterprises have additional IAM requirements for introducing streamlined governance, efficiency, and additional guardrails. You can see some of these features in *Figure 4.12*.

SAP's solution for these requirements is **SAP Identity Access Governance (IAG)**. This solution is not part of SAP Cloud Identity Services, and SAP offers it as a separate product. However, it works well when integrated with SAP Cloud Identity Services.

If you had similar access governance requirements for your on-premise SAP systems, you might already have **SAP Access Control (AC)**, which is part of the **SAP Governance, Risk, and Compliance (GRC)** suite, in your landscape. Additionally, if you have well-established SAP AC processes, such as access request workflows, you might want to keep these and adopt SAP IAG for your cloud solutions. In that case, you can use **SAP IAG Bridge**, which allows you to run access request workflows for cloud applications in SAP AC, whereas SAP IAG handles mitigation controlling and provisioning:

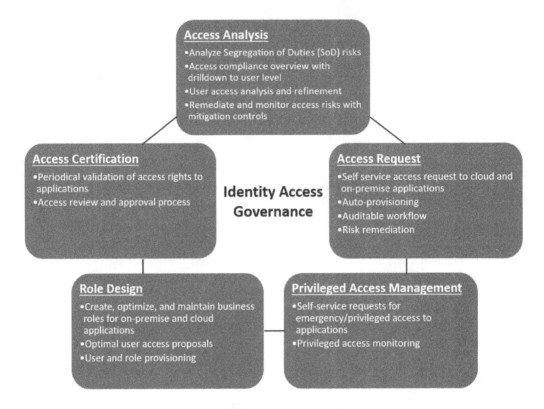

Figure 4.12: SAP IAG features

While facilitating the capabilities in the preceding diagram, SAP IAG lets you apply changes to a user's roles. In such cases, SAP IAG uses SAP Cloud Identity Services – Identity Provisioning to synchronize identity data.

## Audit logging

We can consider audit logging as a surveillance mechanism. It doesn't directly improve a system's security. However, it helps with the retrospective analysis of security events when they happen, and it might have a dissuasive effect on potential perpetrators. As a user of your company's IT applications, you agree with your company's terms of use, and you are accountable for how you use these applications.

For traceability of changes to important data entities, applications also record information regarding who created and changed database records and when. However, you cannot establish full accountability without storing data on other significant events generally linked to security or identity operations, such as logins, user information updates, role assignments, security setting changes, and more. Because audit logs can be used as evidence, for example, for legal purposes, they have to be persisted as immutable records. **SAP Audit Log service** stores all such information resulting from the consumption of SAP BTP services. At the time of writing, this service doesn't support logging functions for custom applications.

The SAP Audit Log service retains the logs for 90 days, after which they are deleted. To retrieve the audit logs, there are multiple options to choose from:

- You can view the audit logs using the Audit Log Viewer service that presents the log entries with a user interface.

- You can retrieve the audit logs using the Audit Log Retrieval API.

- You can request audit logs by creating a support ticket.

To better use audit logs, you can also replicate them in SAP Enterprise Threat Detection or a **Security Information and Event Management (SIEM)** system such as Azure Sentinel, IBM QRadar, Exabeam Fusion, and Splunk:

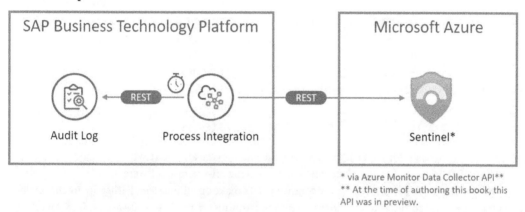

Figure 4.13: Integrating SAP BTP audit logs with Azure Sentinel

## IAM in hybrid environments

Although moving to the cloud has been the trend in the last decade, many companies still have on-premise SAP systems in their IT estate. This brings extra challenges when designing solutions. With this in mind, SAP's cloud identity solutions cater to hybrid environment requirements:

- SAP Cloud Identity Services – Identity Authentication supports identity federation with on-premise IdPs such as Microsoft ADFS. In addition, since it implements the SAML 2.0 standard, it can also provide authentication and SSO functionality to SAP NetWeaver systems where users access applications using the WebGUI (SAP GUI for HTML).

- SAP Cloud Identity Services – Identity Provisioning supports on-premise systems as source and target systems, such as SAP S/4HANA On-Premise, SAP NetWeaver ABAP (including SAP AC and SAP Identity Management), and Microsoft Active Directory.

- SAP IAG can coexist with the on-premise SAP AC and extend its use to the cloud using the SAP IAG Bridge.

We have covered a lot in terms of IAM, how it helps secure your SAP BTP applications, and how you can implement its processes using SAP solutions. Next, we will talk about connectivity, which inherently requires strict security.

# Connectivity

Infrastructure connectivity is a significant element in IT as operations can only continue with several technical components communicating with each other. Furthermore, with recent IT trends, the IT estates of companies have become far more modular in terms of the variety of solutions used. Also, almost all large companies have hybrid environments due to the hosting options that came with the cloud movement, that is, on-premise versus the cloud.

The connectivity aspect adds a new dimension to security considerations as you need to make sure the communication is kept secure. When architecting solutions with SAP BTP, the essential technical elements that underpin the connectivity are generally already in place, for instance, your networking infrastructure, network security standards, and more. You need to build on top of this foundation. Let's start with the challenge of establishing secure connectivity between SAP BTP and on-premise.

## Connecting SAP BTP and on-premise systems

Moving entirely to SaaS is not an easy target for large enterprises, and there will be a long transitional period until that becomes a reality. For some of them, having on-premise software might stay inevitable for an indefinite period. Before causing any confusion, let's make one thing clear. Earlier, we intentionally called it on-premise *software* to consider the case of running on-premise software on IaaS together with running the software in your own data center. In both cases, you need to set up the connectivity below the application layer. It would be a fair assumption that, in both cases, your systems are behind a network security layer, for example, firewalls, IaaS security elements, and more. So, from now on, when we say an on-premise, it can be either an on-premise software deployed in a hyperscaler IaaS or in any other data center, including a corporate's own data centers.

If these were just two on-premise systems to connect, you would make arrangements in the network components to allow communication between them. SAP BTP service endpoints are mostly open to the public internet. Some services, such as SAP HANA Cloud, provide you with security features such as IP allowlists. With them, you can define the IP ranges you allow to send traffic to the service endpoints of SAP HANA Cloud. You still have the option to allow all IPs, which makes the service publicly connectable. You do not have access to the layers below the application layer to make any network arrangements. And, for outbound traffic from SAP BTP, there is virtually no limitation.

### Connectivity service

On the SAP BTP side, the cloud applications can use the **Connectivity Service** to establish and manage the connectivity with the backend systems. The Connectivity service provides an HTTP proxy that receives requests from cloud applications and forwards them to the SAP Cloud Connector. As a reusable service, applications are required to be bound to a Connectivity service instance to obtain the necessary information to interact with the proxy, such as a hostname, a port number, or any internal authentication details.

## SAP Cloud Connector

When it comes to on-premise, things get a bit complicated. That is because you have complete control over how to expose your systems, and your approach will be selectively allowing access to ensure security. For example, you could open your firewalls to allow traffic from relevant SAP BTP IPs. However, your security team could raise concerns as this might be an extensive range of IPs, and it will be coming from a platform that is open to the internet.

SAP provides a solution that minimizes security risks when connecting SAP BTP and on-premise systems. **SAP Cloud Connector** functions as a link between SAP BTP and on-premise by creating a secure tunnel with the reverse proxy technique. In this approach, on-premise systems initiate the connection; hence, there is no need to add firewall rules for inbound connectivity from the internet to the on-premise systems. Here, the Cloud Connector must be able to access SAP BTP, which is allowed to make outbound connections through the proxy if you have one. Also, the Cloud Connector must have direct access to the on-premise systems.

The connectivity is not immediately in action just after you install the Cloud Connector. As you would expect, it gives you the control to configure which on-premise systems and which resources in those systems are accessible from SAP BTP. On the on-premise side, you can connect SAP BTP to any SAP or non-SAP backend system. However, for the cloud side, only SAP BTP and S/4HANA Cloud are supported. The connectivity is supported for the HTTP, LDAP, RFC, and TCP protocols, including their secure variants:

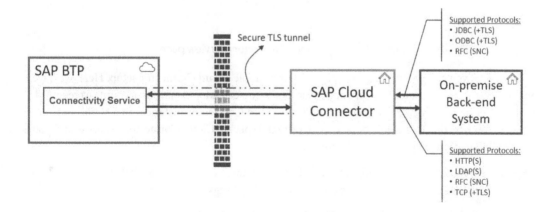

Figure 4.14: Connectivity between SAP BTP and on-premise systems with SAP Cloud Connector

As you can see in *Figure 4.14*, there are different constraints for the directions of the flows. The connectivity options are pretty flexible for communication from the cloud to the on-premise systems; this is primarily because TCP is supported. However, with great flexibility comes great responsibility. So, make sure the use case is justified and discuss it with your security and network teams if you are in doubt.

Only a limited number of connectivity options exist for communication from the on-premise systems to the cloud, and the arrangements for this direction are called **service channels**. Assuming you are using the newest SAP HANA Cloud and multi-environment, the only relevant option is to connect via RFC to ABAP systems in the cloud, including SAP S/4HANA Cloud:

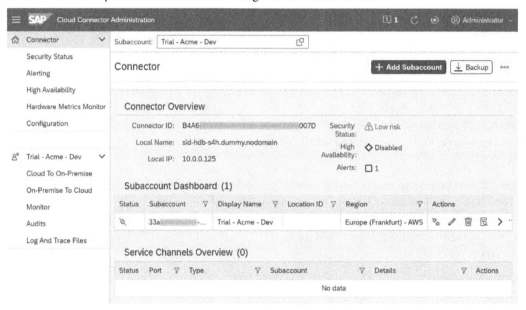

Figure 4.15: The SAP Cloud Connector overview page

In *Figure 4.15*, you can see the overview page of our example Cloud Connector setup. Here, we have configured one of the subaccounts in our trial account. You can add several subaccounts as required. On the other hand, you can also connect multiple Cloud Connector instances to a subaccount. In that case, you would need a stable handle to identify the specific Cloud Connector instance, and you can use the **Location ID** property of the instance for this.

In *Figure 4.16*, you can see our configuration defining a connection from the SAP BTP subaccount to an on-premise S/4HANA system. There are two important things to note here:

- You need to explicitly indicate which resources are accessible from SAP BTP by providing their URL paths for HTTP(S)-based connections and providing the function module names for RFC-based connections. It might be a good idea to be restrictive here, depending on your security needs. In our example, as shown in *Figure 4.16*, we configured SAP BTP to only have access to the resources served at the `/sap/opu/odata/` URL and all its sub-paths.

- You can assign a virtual hostname and port number that are different from the actual hostname and port number. This way, you can conceal this information for increased security. In our example, we defined the virtual hostname as `dev.s4h.acme` and the virtual port number as `1234`:

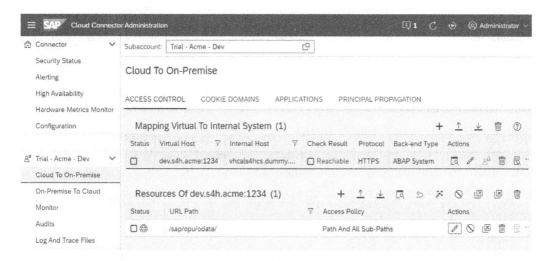

Figure 4.16: A SAP Cloud Connector cloud to on-premise connection example

Other administration-related features are listed as follows:

- You can establish high availability by installing a shadow instance to which the master instance automatically synchronizes the configuration.

- You can establish the monitoring of Cloud Connector with SAP Solution Manager.

- You can set the logging level, which also records audit logs.

- You can monitor the Cloud Connector instance using its UI or via its monitoring APIs. In addition, SAP BTP Cockpit has a Connectivity page that shows all Cloud Connector connections and their statuses.

### Other connectivity options

Typically, SAP Cloud Connector is the most reasonable way to establish backend connectivity for SAP BTP. However, you can also consider other options for specific cases, knowing that they might require extra administration and possibly have more security concerns to remediate. For example, the usual reverse proxy setup can be used where the connection from SAP BTP, hence, the internet, is received by the proxy and forwarded to your on-premise systems.

Connectivity options other than SAP Cloud Connector can be preferred in some other cases where broader connectivity is required. For instance, for the customers who onboarded SAP Data Intelligence at an early stage, the primary option was to set up a secure VPN connection between SAP Data Intelligence and the customer's on-premise boundary. This connectivity is still the option to connect SAP Data Intelligence to the private endpoints within your corporate's security perimeter.

For Kubernetes environments, you can use the **Connectivity Proxy** that works together with the Cloud Foundry Connectivity service and the UAA service to enable access to on-premise systems via the Cloud Connector.

## Destination service

To make an application communicate with another application, you need to provide information that specifies the connection destination. This information can be separated into three groups: the URL of the destination, the authentication details, and the other connection properties.

You can use the **Destination service** to store destination configurations safely, which also brings extra benefits:

1.  The Destination service formalizes how destinations are specified. By this, it encourages consistency in using destination configurations.
2.  By externalizing the destination configuration, you can use it in multiple places while managing it centrally. For instance, if you need to change a destination configuration, you will not need to change and deploy the applications using it.
3.  It introduces development efficiency by undertaking some authorization flow tasks where applicable. For example, it handles automatic OAuth2 token retrieval, building SAML assertion, caching tokens, and refreshing them. It also stores the artifacts, for example, certificates, for trust setups.
4.  It increases security so that sensitive information, such as passwords, is stored securely.

You can configure destinations at the subaccount level or the service instance level. For subscribed applications, you can also define destinations pointing to service instances so that the provider application can access service instances in your subaccount.

SAP BTP Cockpit provides a page where you can maintain destination configurations and other relevant elements. Alternatively, you can use the Destination service APIs, arrange your application's MTA descriptor that will deploy destinations via the Generic Application Content Deployment protocol, or provide the configuration in JSON format while creating a Destination service instance:

Figure 4.17: An example on-premise destination configuration

You can use the Destination service after binding an instance of it to your application. Using this instance, you can call the Destination service functions to retrieve static information about a destination's configuration along with information that the service generates, such as authentication tokens.

With the Destination service, it is also possible to configure on-premise destinations, as shown in *Figure 4.17*. For this, the configuration should include the proxy type as On-Premise and contain the URL with the virtual host and port details specified for the backend system in the Cloud Connector. Here, the protocol in the URL will be HTTP or RFC with no secure variants as the communication will be through the already established secure TLS tunnel.

For the cloud destinations, you need to set the destination proxy type to Internet. If your application is connecting to a cloud destination, you do not need to use the Connectivity service. With the information you obtain from the Destination service, you can call external cloud services, provided that you take care of other aspects, such as CORS for UI applications, by using the application router.

## Principal (user) propagation

In most cases, when setting connectivity between two applications, the called application will require you to authenticate the request before providing a successful response. In that case, you can configure the connectivity to include an arbitrary user, generally a technical user, and use basic authentication. Then, the called application will happily authenticate the user and respond accordingly. However, what happens if the called application requires the context of the same user?

For instance, Acme developers are building a new Customer Information Management application in SAP BTP. The application lets users maintain customer information by calling OData services from a backend SAP system. Irfan, as a senior customer service representative, can maintain any customer data. Ali, as an apprentice, can maintain all data apart from bank details.

The developers created an on-premise destination, as shown in *Figure 4.17*. It works fine; however, eventually, they realized that the authorization checks in the backend system were meaningless because the logged-in user was always the technical user, BPINST. Also, the change tracking was not really working because whenever a data record changes, the application had recorded the same technical user as the last changer.

What if they get the user context in the frontend application and hide the bank details fields in the UI? Well, this wouldn't work because a user can unhide the fields in the browser. So, checks at the frontend layer would never be sufficient.

You can solve this challenge using the **principal propagation** mechanism supported by the Connectivity service and the Cloud Connector. With principal propagation, the logged-in user of the cloud application is passed on to the Cloud Connector and then to the backend system. Principal propagation requires changes to be applied in the Cloud Connector and the target backend systems. After this setup, if you are using standard tools and libraries for developing cloud applications in BTP, enabling principal propagation is as easy as using a destination with the On-Premise proxy type. Other services such as the SAP Integration Suite service also make use of such destinations to access on-premise backend systems.

Our previous scenario deals with principal propagation for cloud-to-on-premise, which is a typical requirement in hybrid environments. However, principal propagation can also be achieved in cloud-to-cloud scenarios, and we will see the inner mechanics of both in the next section.

## The big connectivity picture

We are best situated to view the complete picture of how connectivity happens between an SAP BTP application and an on-premise system with the addition of principal propagation. Surely, we made some assumptions and simplifications when illustrating the following flows. Now, check out *Figure 4.18* and fasten your seat belts because this will be a roller-coaster journey:

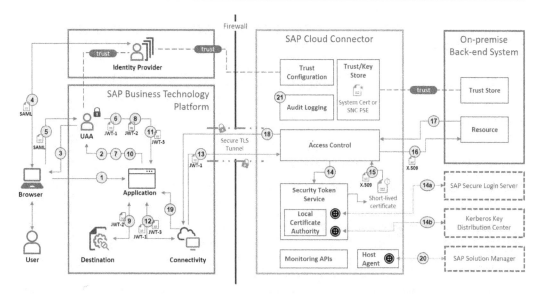

Figure 4.18: The connection flow from SAP BTP to on-premise with principal propagation

Let's decipher the diagram in *Figure 4.18*:

1.  The user launches the cloud application.

2.  Because there is no secure session, the cloud application forwards the user to the UAA service.

3.  Since there is no user context, UAA redirects the call to the IdP and initiates a SAML authentication flow.

4.  The IdP challenges the user for the username and password and, upon correct entry, generates a SAML token (authorization response) and responds to the browser with a redirection.

5.  The browser sends a request to the UAA service instance and attaches the SAML token.

6.  The UAA service extracts the identity information in the SAML token and creates a JWT token (JWT-1), which it returns to the application.

7.  Through the Destination service instance binding, the application retrieves the required parameters and calls the UAA service for authorization to access the Destination service instance.

8.  The UAA service creates a new JWT token (JWT-2) and returns it to the application.

9.  The application calls the Destination service instance after attaching JWT-2 to the request and retrieves the destination information for the on-premise system.

10. Through the Connectivity service instance binding, the application retrieves the required parameters and calls the UAA service for authorization to access the Connectivity service instance.

11. The UAA service creates a new JWT token (JWT-3) and returns it to the application.

12. The application retrieves the HTTP proxy details through the Connectivity service instance binding and creates an HTTP client. Then, it makes a request for the on-premise resource while attaching both JWT-1 and JWT-3 tokens.

13. The Connectivity service (HTTP proxy) forwards the request to the Cloud Connector through the secure TLS tunnel and attaches the JWT-1 token.

14. The Cloud Connector checks the request, that is, whether it's for a valid backend system and allowed resource, extracts identity information, and asks its security token service for a new token.

15. The Cloud Connector can, optionally, use SAP SSO Secure Login Service to retrieve the token.

16. The Cloud Connector can, optionally, use a Kerberos Key Distribution Center to retrieve the token.

17. The security token service creates a new token, such as a short-lived X.509 certificate, which includes identity information according to the Cloud Connector's principal propagation settings.

18. The Cloud Connector forwards the request to the backend system, attaching the X.509 certificate.

19. The backend system verifies the certificate, extracts identity information, and allows access to the resource with the propagated identity. Then, it responds to the Cloud Connector's request.

20. The Cloud Connector responds to the Connectivity service's (HTTP proxy) request through the secure TLS tunnel.

21. The application receives the response from the on-premise backend system resource.

22. Optionally, monitoring information flows to SAP Solution Manager.

23. During the flow, the Cloud Connector creates logs for troubleshooting and auditing purposes based on the logging level setting.

Now, let's do the same for a cloud-to-cloud principal propagation scenario where an SAP BTP application consumes another cloud resource, which can also be another SAP BTP application. For this type of flow, typically, you can use a destination whose authentication type is set to OAuth2SAMLBearerAssertion. Let's explain the flow depicted in *Figure 4.18*:

1. – 8. The same as the cloud-to-on-premise scenario above.

9. The application makes a call to the Destination service after attaching both JWT-1 and JWT-2 tokens.

10. The destination service extracts the identity information and generates a SAML assertion, which it signs with the subaccount's private key. Then, it sends a request to the OAuth2 token service as configured in the *destination* specification and attaches the SAML assertion to the request.

11. The OAuth2 token service verifies the SAML assertion and, upon successful verification, responds with an *access token*.

12. The Destination service returns to the application the destination specification and the access token.

13. The application makes a call to the resource URL and attaches the access token.

14. The external resource verifies the access token and responds to the request.

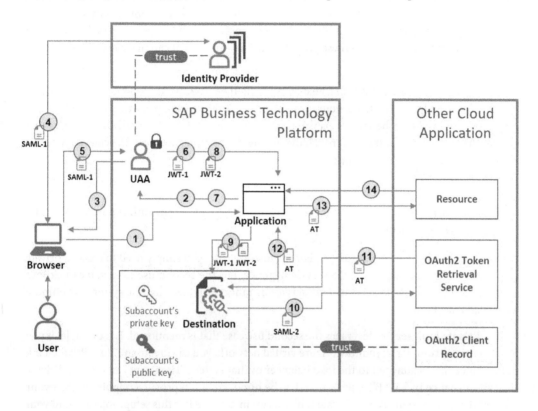

Figure 4.19: The connection flow from SAP BTP to another cloud application with principal propagation

For both flows, if you remove the principal propagation, the application won't need to pass on the JWT token identifying the user to the respective service. Instead, an authorization header as per the destination's authorization type will be sent with the request.

---

**Important Note**

Again, let's remind you that you can develop your application by focusing on what differentiates it and delegating most of the preceding tasks to standard frameworks and libraries that hide the complexity.

---

Well, by learning the two preceding scenarios, you are now familiar with how connectivity works in SAP BTP. Now, let's discuss the last topic of this chapter.

# Private Link service

Many enterprises work with at least one of the IaaS providers that lead the market, for example, Amazon, Microsoft, and Google. Therefore, providing secure and efficient connectivity within their platforms alongside customers' on-premise systems is important for these hyperscalers. Because SAP BTP runs on the infrastructure from these providers, under the hood, it can make use of the services hyperscalers offer.

Some IaaS providers offer a capability that enables access to the resources of certain services through a designated private endpoint created in your own virtual network; for example, *Azure Private Link* and *AWS PrivateLink*. Accessing the service via this private endpoint ensures the traffic from your virtual network to the target resource travels through the provider's backbone network. The connectivity can be established with two types of targets:

1.  To one of the provider's PaaS services
2.  To your own services, for instance, an SAP or non-SAP system running in VMs on the provider's infrastructure

Let's take *Azure Private Link* as an example. For the first use case, you simply need to create a private endpoint that targets the required PaaS service instance. For the second use case, you can expose your service through an *Azure Private Link service* instance, provided that the system is behind a standard load balancer.

SAP BTP's **Private Link service** leverages the second use case that is mentioned. For example, if you have such a system running in your own Azure virtual network, you can create an Azure Private Link service instance that is attached to the load balancer of that system. Then, you can create a Private Link service instance in SAP BTP, which, under the hood, creates a private endpoint within your subaccount that points to the Azure Private Link service instance. After this setup, you can bind your applications and use the private endpoint. This way, you ensure the traffic is isolated from the internet. Take a look at *Figure 4.19*, which illustrates this setup:

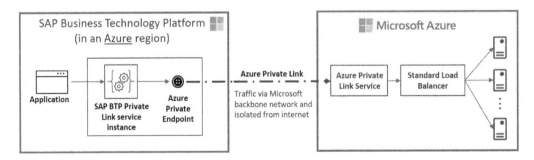

Figure 4.20: Accessing resources on Microsoft Azure via the Private Link service

Just to note, at the time of authoring this book, this service only supported a limited set of hyperscalers and regions. So, please check the SAP roadmap to find out more about it and whether it is available for production use.

## Summary

Well, this concludes our discussion on security and connectivity. Later in this book, we will continue touching upon security topics from different angles. However, what we have discussed so far should enable you to incorporate security in your SAP BTP architecture designs as a crucial ingredient.

In this chapter, you learned how SAP, as its provider, ensures the security of SAP BTP and how you can find out more about their compliance with the standards underpinning the security measures they apply. Because, as the consumer, you share the responsibility for securing the application and data layers, we discussed how you could achieve this when building your custom applications and when using SAP BTP services. As a closely related topic, we talked about data protection and privacy. Additionally, a large part of this chapter was about IAM. We briefly discussed IAM concepts at the generic level and then how SAP BTP implements its processes. Finally, we covered how SAP BTP securely connects to external systems and propagates user information.

In the next chapter, we will look at several design aspects that are grouped as non-functional design elements and constitute an integral part of your solution/technical designs.

# 5

# Non-Functional Design for Operability

In the previous chapters, we touched upon two crucial elements of architecture design: **security** and **connectivity**. However, there are several more aspects you need to consider in your designs. In the first part of this chapter, we will discuss these design elements and how you can address them when designing with **SAP Business Technology Platform** (**SAP BTP**).

Practically, your design is not merely for presentation purposes. Eventually, it needs to be realized as an implemented solution. As you know, the story never ends there, and the solution needs to be maintained until you don't need it anymore. As an architect, although your mindset is geared toward the design aspects, it will always help to know how SAP BTP operates.

You can design more robust architectures by also considering the second half of the story. So, the latter part of this chapter will cover topics around support elements.

Therefore, in this chapter, we are going to cover the following main topics:

- Non-functional design elements
- Understanding **service-level agreements** (**SLAs**)
- Getting support

## Technical requirements

This chapter does not have specific technical requirements. However, if you have already gone through the previous chapters, you should have a trial account that you can use to check some of the elements we will be discussing in this chapter.

# Non-functional design elements

Delivering a technology project is never for the sake of merely introducing technology. There must be a business case behind your design. The drivers of the business case may require an intensive design, especially if it is for executing strategic transformation. But sometimes, the design objective may be geared more toward ensuring stability. In such cases, as an architect, your role may be limited to ensuring no adverse deviations happen to the existing design, such as system upgrades aimed at keeping the lights on.

For business-driven demands, there are business requirements, while for technology-driven initiatives, there are technical requirements that eventually serve business purposes. For both types, you need to design with requirements that are not necessarily specified within the core motivation; however, they are essential if you wish to implement them successfully and ensure they operate properly. Furthermore, fulfilling these requirements contributes to the quality of the solution. These are categorized as **non-functional requirements** (**NFRs**), and as an architect, you produce **non-functional design** elements to address the related constraints. The naming here is a bit controversial; however, these are widely used terms.

Depending on the nature of the problem you are solving, some of these design elements may become more important than others, and some may even be irrelevant to your design. You can quantify some of these NFRs as they are based on measurable qualities. However, for others, you would need to specify the required quality, such as a feature. For example, you must specify what accessibility standards your solution design supports.

Now, let's discuss different types of NFRs.

> **Important Note**
> There are so many aspects that can be considered NFRs; some of the terms are used interchangeably, while some have overlapping scopes. Yet, each has its importance. We will discuss the NFRs that we believe need to be focused on more while briefly touching on others. So, let's get started.

## Security

**Security** is so vital that we had to discuss it by dedicating almost a whole chapter to it. After reading the previous chapter, you should already know about it and be able to design for NFRs such as the following:

- **Security**: In general, this involves encrypting the data that is in transit and the data that is at rest, which SAP BTP ensures at the infrastructure level.

- **Auditability**: For example, **SAP BTP Audit Recording** service that records important security events and changes.

- **Access and authorizations**: For example, allowing only certain users to act, for instance, via SAP BTP's role-based access control entities.

- **Regulatory**: For example, measures that are taken for data protection and privacy legislation or even for more specific levels, such as company policies and standards.

We have extensively discussed concrete examples of these in the previous chapter, so we'll leave it here for security. If you need to refresh your memory on these, just scroll back.

## Business continuity

This section will discuss several qualities that serve the eventual goal of ensuring steadiness for business operations. You may have already classified your solutions based on how crucial they are for your business; that is, their **business criticality**. Based on this classification, you need to think about the measures you want to take to keep your solutions running stably.

### Availability and resilience

There is always the possibility of the system components failing. Therefore, it would be best if you took precautions so that you're ready to remediate such incidents effectively and promptly. For cloud providers, it can be a problem with the data center's infrastructure elements, such as the power outlet or cooling system, as well as computer hardware problems, such as a hard disk or network device failure.

The first dimension for ensuring business continuity is maintaining the correct level of **availability** for your systems and applications. Ensuring availability typically transpires by introducing redundancy.

The cloud infrastructure providers arrange availability by introducing different isolation levels between fault domains and virtual separation for update domains. This gives the application's owner the choice to deploy their application in multiple separated infrastructure arrangements, as well as the option of automatic failover in case of failures.

#### General resilience concepts

In this book, we assume you have basic knowledge of these arrangements, such as **regions**, **availability zones**, and **availability sets**. Now, let's refresh our memory with a brief overview:

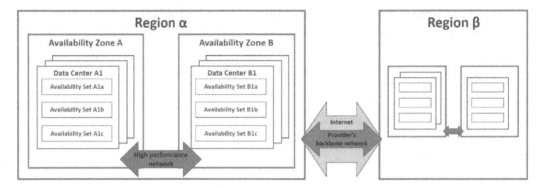

Figure 5.1: Availability level arrangements of a cloud infrastructure provider

Here, you can see different levels of arrangement that are typical to cloud infrastructure providers. By leveraging these, you can introduce availability at the following levels:

- **Local**: By deploying your application in multiple availability sets within the same zone, you can introduce a basic level of **high availability**, which protects your application against failures within a single location (for example, a hardware malfunction). With this level of redundancy, software updates for your application require less or even near-zero downtime because while you are updating one instance, another instance continues to serve the users.

- **Zonal**: By deploying your application in multiple availability zones, you extend the protection to cover the failures that affect an entire data center (for example, power outages, network infrastructure problems, or cooling system breakdowns).

- **Regional**: If your application is mission-critical and you cannot risk a prolonged downtime in the rare larger-scale cases of failures (such as disasters), then you can deploy your application in multiple regions.

The availability of a system is specified as a percentage of uptime during a unit of time; for example, 99.9% availability means approximately 44 minutes of downtime per month.

By introducing higher availability, you increase the **reliability** of your application. In addition, with regional redundancy, you enable maximum protection and have the option of **disaster recovery**.

Furthermore, for the highest level of availability, you need to ensure failures are detected early and fixed quickly. This requires proper monitoring, automated mechanisms, and a robust process for handling disruptions. The cost of your setup increases as you step up the protection and efficiency levels. Therefore, it's important to determine the level of availability for an application properly.

For solutions that include a persistence layer, redundancy needs to be accompanied  by a replication mechanism that synchronizes data between the storage instances  (for example, databases). This mechanism determines how quickly your application can recover (**recovery time objective (RTO)**) and the closest restore point for the data (**recovery point objective (RPO)**). Besides replication, data backups also contribute as a measure of **recoverability**.

In most cases, your solutions will contain several elements. Therefore, in such cases, you can initially think that your end-to-end solution is only as resilient as the resiliency of the weakest element in the design. To quantify this with a probabilistic approach, you can work out **composite availability** figures while considering the dependencies, fallback arrangements, individual component availabilities, and the technical flow for the critical scenarios.

Finally, like any technical deliverable, you should test your availability setup at project delivery and, later, continuously monitor to check whether its functionality is as expected. Furthermore, it is a good idea to test your disaster recovery arrangements with a certain frequency.

By incorporating all these aspects, your design will have a high level of **resilience** for your solution. Briefly, you need to introduce redundancy, eliminate single points of failure, and minimize the mean time to recovery so that you can make your solution resilient.

Now, let's discuss how you can achieve this in SAP BTP.

## Achieving resilient solutions with SAP BTP

As you may recall from our previous discussions on the cloud service models, the responsibility for ensuring resilience may be with the provider or you, as the consumer. Considering that SAP BTP is a **Platform as a Service (PaaS)**, the liability is with you when it's about your applications and your data. For other layers, the onus will be mainly on SAP. There are three types of arrangements that underpin your solution's resilience level:

- You can rely on the availability provided by SAP. We will discuss the level of availability that SAP promises in the *Understanding SLAs* section.

- For some services, SAP provides you with configuration options so that you can define the resilience level. In that case, it becomes a risk management question because the stricter measures you choose, the more you will pay for them. An example here is **SAP HANA Cloud, HANA database**. You have the option of creating HANA database **replicas** to increase availability and enable disaster recovery. We will discuss this later in this book.

- We can give another example here for the custom applications you deploy in SAP BTP. **SAP BTP Cloud Foundry** lets you use the availability zones of the region that your subaccount runs on, provided that the region has availability zones. When you create multiple instances for your application, the platform automatically distributes them across different availability zones, which means you achieve zonal redundancy, as shown in the following diagram:

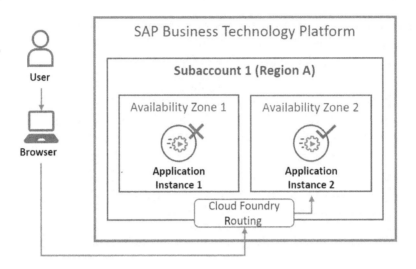

Figure 5.2: Built-in high availability setup for custom applications in the
SAP BTP Cloud Foundry runtime using availability zones

- You can design your solution with additional elements to increase the level of resilience. For example, you can create two instances of the same service in two different subaccounts that are located in different regions. Then, you can add a component such as Azure Traffic Manager, Azure Front Door, Amazon Route 53, or Akamai Ion. With these, you can monitor the primary service instance and automatically route the traffic to the secondary instance in case of failure:

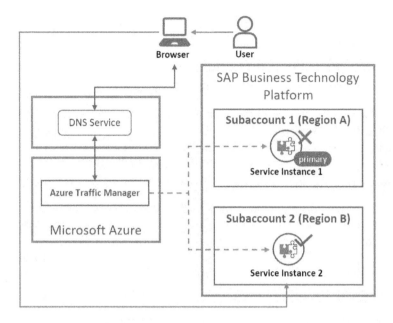

Figure 5.3: High availability setup with two service instances in different subaccounts

The preceding diagram illustrates a design that uses **Azure Traffic Manager**, which can route traffic to one of the multiple target endpoints. In this example, Azure Traffic Manager detects that the primary service instance is unavailable and makes sure that the request is routed to the secondary service instance. If applicable, you can also configure this routing so that it functions as a load balancer.

With this arrangement, you need to make sure the two instances have been configured in the same way unless it is explicitly required otherwise. Although you can do this manually, it's best to establish an automated change delivery pipeline that applies the same configuration to all instances.

## Backup and recovery

Traditional **backup and recovery** mechanisms can be a primary or secondary measure for the recoverability of your applications. Here, we can consider SAP BTP services under three groups:

- As the most primitive way, for some services, SAP BTP lets you export and import the data used by the service. The data, in this case, is generally the configuration data of a service, such as the **Destination** service, or **design-time artifacts** that are created in a service – for example, **SAP Integration Suite**. You can leverage the export/import functionality in different ways, provided that they are available for the service:

  - The UI application for the service may contain UI controls that can be used for backup and restore purposes (for example, buttons for export/import).

- You can use APIs to manage content for some services (for example, SAP Cloud Integration, the Destination service, and more).

- You can use the **Content Agent service**, which assembles content into archive files. You can then use these files in the **Cloud Transport Management** service to import content.

- SAP BTP automatically backs up the data stored by some services, such as **SAP HANA Cloud** and **PostgreSQL (hyperscaler option)**. For the SAP HANA database, besides the full daily backups, frequent log backups are taken so that backup-based RPO is no longer than 15 minutes. As an additional measure, the backups are replicated in other availability zones. The backups are not only safeguards for failures at the SAP side but also available for customers to initiate ad hoc recovery if needed.

- There are services for which none of the options we've discussed exist. For these, you need to establish a mechanism to take backups. For example, if you need a backup of the objects that have been stored with the **Object Store** service, you can implement your application to maintain objects in two different locations. For this specific service, bear in mind that the service plan you choose may already provide a level of redundancy at the infrastructure level.

All the resilience aspects we've discussed so far must be a part of your overall **business continuity plan**, which takes care of the process and event management aspects as well. By designing resilient solutions, you ensure operational stability. With this, you also ensure you don't lose data valuable to your business. Now, let's discuss some other non-functional requirements related to data management.

## Data management

Do you wish to read about how important data is again? We guess not since we have done that before. But remember, one essential motivation for securing your systems is protecting your data, and business continuity is meaningful if it helps you keep your data safe. So, let's continue learning about non-functional design elements in data management.

### Data lifecycle and retention

**Data** is valuable; however, it has a lifecycle and its operational value may depreciate. Besides, storing data is not free of cost, and considering data protection and privacy aspects, it may also become a liability. Therefore, if your design introduces new data entities, you need to define how long to retain this data based on legal or regulatory obligations and operational considerations.

Depending on how frequently a piece of data is accessed and how crucial it is for business operations, data can be classified into different **data temperature** categories such as hot, warm, and cold. In line with this categorization, you can store data in different technologies based on its temperature to optimize the storage cost.

For example, as we will discuss later in this book, SAP HANA Cloud supports **data tiering**, with which you can store the data in different integrated tiers. Here, only one copy of the data is stored, and you can optimize cost and performance by moving the data between these tiers. Typically, the data movement from hot to cold storage coincides with the age of the data. For example, financial data for older fiscal years can be moved to warm storage, whereas the data for the recent fiscal years stays in the hot tier.

The final step in the data lifecycle is **archiving**. Here, the data is archived with much cheaper storage technology because access is scarcely required. Once the data has been archived, it can be deleted from the operational storage. For some data types, you can also delete data without archiving it. By archiving or removing data, you slow down database growth and improve database query performance.

Your design needs to take care of the data protection and privacy perspectives as well. Thus, it would be best to define the rules for deleting privacy-related data as keeping it may be an unnecessary liability.

Furthermore, bear in mind that there may be overarching considerations that may override your data retention rules. For instance, when an inactive customer requests to exercise their right to be forgotten, you may need to erase their data, even though your retention rules advise a more extended retention period. Here, you may even need to erase their data from data archives. Or, if there is a legal hold for a customer, you may need to keep their data longer than the retention rules specified.

Let's consider this with an example: you are designing an application on SAP BTP that stores customer data in SAP HANA Cloud, HANA Database. For the application, you persist customers' names, email addresses, payment details, and orders. In your design, you can specify some data retention rules, as follows:

- If a customer has no active orders and their last order was fulfilled, do the following:

  - 1 year ago → Delete their payment details
  - 2 years ago → Delete their names and email addresses, and anonymize data for their orders (for example, change the customer IDs in the order records so that they cannot be linked to the particular customer)

- If an order belongs to a customer whose data has been deleted or anonymized, and the order fulfillment date is older than 5 years, archive the order data and delete it from the system.

> **Important Note**
> Don't confuse data archives with data backups. They are both copies of data; however, they serve different purposes. Archives are created for data retention, whereas backups are taken for recoverability.

Next, let's learn the importance of accuracy of data.

## Data quality

**Data** is valuable only if it serves a purpose. For this, you must capture data accurately so that your business operations are handled appropriately. For example, think of a customer service agent on the phone who cannot locate a customer's record because of a data problem. Or perhaps you're preparing an analytical report to present to senior stakeholders, and at the last minute, you realize that it doesn't consider a significant portion of the operational data because one of the data fields hasn't been populated correctly.

Lack of data quality is a chronic issue for many businesses as once it is widespread, it becomes very challenging to fix. For some companies, the problem even slows down the transformation they want to have.

Data quality generally becomes a problem for the master data that is entered manually by users. Therefore, you should consider data quality as a mandatory part of operational practice by incorporating necessary checks in the applications that are used and training the users. For this, you can use data management solutions such as **SAP Master Data Governance** (**MDG**), which can help improve data quality.

When designing solutions with custom applications in SAP BTP, you need to specify data rules to make sure users enter data accurately and without breaking integrity. These rules can specify mandatory fields, data validations, and dependencies. In addition, your design should indicate where the application can provide the user with input value suggestions. For some data types, it may be a good idea to leverage external services to validate data or obtain a list of accurate input value suggestions. A typical example of this is when your application needs to capture location data. SAP BTP provides the **Data Quality Management** (**DQM**) service, which offers cloud-based microservices for address cleansing, geocoding, and reverse geocoding. This service can be integrated with other SAP solutions such as SAP Data Intelligence. Furthermore, some solutions, such as SAP Cloud for Customer, come with prebuilt integration with the SAP DQM service.

Your application can call SAP DQM location microservices by providing an address as input and getting the cleansed address information that is also enriched with geolocation data. If the received response points to an error, your application can prevent users from saving the record unless they fix the problem. Don't forget that it should be the backend application, which ultimately checks the data's quality. Upon receiving the backend response, your frontend application can expose the error message and highlight the relevant data input components with error designation. Alternatively, your application can offer the user to input the cleansed address data automatically:

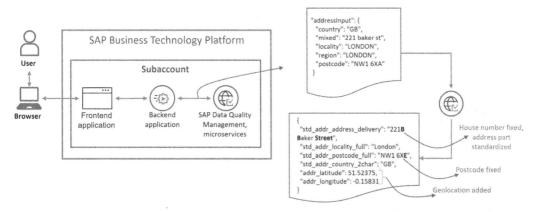

Figure 5.4: SAP BTP application using a SAP Data Quality Management location microservice

Here, you can see how **SAP DQM**, **microservices for location data** can be used to cleanse address data.

## Performance, capacity, and scalability

Do you remember that website that took so many seconds to load, and you haven't even waited to see what it exactly offers and navigated away to check another website? This example shows how important **performance** is for a software application. End users want responsive and performant applications. If your solution includes components that interact with users, its responsiveness is a crucial element of the user experience, promoting or hindering the adoption of your solution. Therefore, your solution design should also focus on the performance of each component and make sure the overall performance is acceptable.

Let's look at another example. Let's say you've designed a solution with an application that makes an expensive query at the database layer. Unfortunately, the query chokes the database processes and eventually brings the application to a halt. Are you looking for a quick resolution to the problem? How about doubling the sizes of the database server memory and CPU? You do that, and everything is back to normal. Or is it?

### Performance

There is often a correlation between performance and **capacity**. So, by increasing capacity, you can improve performance, which would saturate eventually. But we have bad news: capacity always comes with a cost. Do you still think the resolution in the preceding example was the best one? It may be. However, you can only decide this after making sure the technical resources have been utilized efficiently and by balancing performance and cost – that is, tuning the performance.

Let's take SAP HANA Cloud, HANA Database and list examples of the performance tuning options we have:

- You can work on the data model to check whether remodeling may help
- Use data partitioning to break large tables down into smaller parts
- Use hints to query data snapshots
- Proactively manage memory
- Manage workload with workload classes
- Tune settings for parallel execution of SQL statements

When it comes to the artifacts you create, you should take care of the performance aspect – for example, data model design with performance in mind, query optimization, avoiding unnecessary data retrieval, avoiding over-engineered modularization, and more. This is valid for the custom applications, integration flows, API management policies, SAP Data Intelligence graphs, and smaller code scripts you write inside these artifacts.

### Sizing/capacity

If it is about tuning performance, there must be a baseline. So, where does it start? As previously mentioned, performance and capacity are somewhat correlated, and this begins with your capacity allocation for a service instance. For this, you need to run a **sizing** exercise. In practice, we have seen some architects relying on their intuitions and others taking this as an exact science. In both cases, you need to consider the factors that will impact performance, quantify them, and allocate resources for the service instance accordingly. The specification for the sizing factors can start with requirements such as how many concurrent users need to use the application, or how many transactions the application needs to process in a minute.

Where sizing is important, you will see that SAP BTP gives you options so that you can optimize according to your requirements. While working on sizing, you can use the **Estimator Tool** to check how much your configuration will cost. You should remember this tool from *Chapter 3*. In the following screenshot, you can see the capacity unit estimator for SAP HANA Cloud, HANA Database, which can be accessed from the Estimator Tool:

| SAP HANA Database Configurations | | | | | ⓘ |
|---|---|---|---|---|---|
| Name | Amount | | Rate | Activity Hours | CU (per month) |
| **Memory**<br>Memory size of a SAP HANA database | − 128 + | GB | 0.025 CU / GB / Hour | 730 | 2336.00 CU |
| **Compute**<br>The number of vCPUs of a SAP HANA database | − 8 + | vCPUs | 0.184 CU / vCPU / Hour | 730 | 1074.56 CU |
| **Storage**<br>The disk storage space of a SAP HANA database | − 360 + | GB | 0.013 CU / 16 GB / Hour | 730<br>(fixed per month) | 213.52 CU |
| **Backup Storage**<br>The backup storage space of a SAP HANA database | − 2688 + | GB | 0.011 CU / 64 GB / Hour | 730<br>(fixed per month) | 337.26 CU |
| **Network Data Transfer**<br>The amount of network traffic | − 128 + | GB | 0.438 CU / GB | N/A | 56.06 CU |
| **SAP Cloud Connector**<br>Connect to an on-premise SAP HANA database | ◯⚪ | | 0.197 CU / Hour ⓘ | 730 | 0.00 CU |
| **Synchronous Replicas**<br>Number of synchronous replicas of a SAP HANA database | − 1 + | Replicas | ⓘ | 730 | 3624.09 CU |
| **Total Estimate** | | | | | 7641.49 CU |

Figure 5.5: Capacity unit estimator for SAP HANA Cloud, HANA Database

As we can see, SAP BTP allocates a technical resource capacity for your SAP HANA Database mainly in terms of memory, compute, storage, and network traffic. Similar estimators exist for other services such as SAP Data Intelligence and the Kyma environment. The details here explain how these elements impact the pricing; however, when configuring the service, a configuration element can be linked to another one for the sake of simplicity. For example, when creating a SAP HANA Cloud, HANA Database instance, you are given the option to select the memory size, which automatically determines the number of vCPUs.

Did you think sizing was a matter of the past as it was required for installing on-premise systems? Well, you see, the services you consume still run on some infrastructure. Therefore, from time to time, your input will be required, where your consumption will be correlated with reserved infrastructure capacity and the providers will reflect the cost to you accordingly.

The capacity you get will be linked to the pricing metric, and your entitlement for that metric may also impose constraints on performance elements, such as the bandwidth that's been allocated for your consumption. This will be more implicit as you get to models that abstract more layers above the infrastructure. For example, although you may have a level of flexibility to control performance in platform-as-a-service (PaaS), it is almost totally out of your control when it comes to software-as-a-service (SaaS) solutions.

Once you've established the initial capacity for a service, continuously monitor whether your requirements change so that you can take timely action for capacity adjustments when needed.

## *Scalability*

It is high time we talk about another cloud quality here, and that is **scalability**. Scalability is one of the primary motivations why companies move to the cloud – they want to use resources efficiently. Companies do not want to pay for infrastructure when they don't use it and enjoy the flexibility of using more resources when needed. With scalability, you can flexibly ramp up or ramp down the resources you use, depending on your requirements. Are you asking why we need sizing when creating a service instance, when we could use scaling? If so, you are missing the point that to scale, you need a baseline as a reference. And the sizing is required for establishing that baseline.

After onboarding to a service with the initial capacity configuration, you can leverage scaling options when your requirements change. Human intervention is more appropriate for services in which scaling has a significant impact and may not be that straightforward. For example, you can use SAP HANA Cloud Central to scale up or scale down your SAP HANA Cloud, HANA Database instance memory. At the time of writing this book, scale-out support for the SAP HANA database was still on the roadmap to be delivered later.

For your custom applications in the Cloud Foundry environment, SAP BTP provides both horizontal and vertical scalability options. You can define memory and disk quotas for your application when deploying it, and you can change these quotas for scaling up or scaling down without requiring a new deployment. The memory quota implicitly defines the CPU share of the application (for example, the Cloud Foundry environment guarantees a share of a quarter core per GB instance memory). Bear in mind that there are quota limits for the maximum instance memory per application and the maximum disk quota.

For horizontal scaling, you can add and remove application instances. As you may recall from the previous section on business continuity, SAP BTP automatically creates instances across multiple availability zones. That's why you can also achieve higher availability with horizontal scaling.

As horizontal scaling for applications can be achieved without human intervention, SAP BTP provides **Application Autoscaler**, which you can use to scale applications by adding or removing instances automatically. With Application Autoscaler, you can specify the following policies:

- **Dynamic policies**: Autoscaler acts based on changes in terms of CPU utilization, memory utilization, throughput, and response time metrics. Alternatively, you can define custom metrics for which you need to feed the quantity to the Autoscaler instance via its API.

- **Schedule-based policies**: Autoscaler scales the application based on a schedule. Therefore, you can use schedule-based policies when you know the periods during which your application will be accessed intensively.

So, you did the hard work and estimated the size for the service instance you use or the application you deploy. The natural next step is to verify your estimation based on actual data and calibrate it if needed. To do this, you need to monitor your service or application metrics, which is part of what we'll discuss in the next section.

## Observability

You must have seen movies where there is a group of people in a room with several huge monitors on the walls, and most of the people have computers in front of them as well. In the *Bourne* series, it's the CIA agents monitoring Jason Bourne's movements. In Apollo 13, it's the NASA workers in the Mission Control Center. And in many movies, it may be as simple as a building's concierge with a couple of screens.

All the people in these rooms are there for some common reasons:

- They want to respond to events swiftly when they happen.

- They want to proactively prevent events that may adversely impact their mission.

- They want to gather data that will help them retrospectively analyze past events so that they become lessons learned.

Besides, all the setups that are used in the rooms serve a common purpose. They support decision-making. For example, some monitors show real-time status data, while others display trend graphics. In some movie scenes, you may also hear an alarm going off to signal something significant has happened. With all these, people in the room can make decisions to direct the operation.

You need a similar setup to achieve your goal of running your applications and  systems smoothly. This setup should facilitate two things. First, with **observability**, you gain insights from the operational data produced in metrics, logs, and traces. With **monitoring**, you get to know about adverse events and why they happened. Here, the events can be performance or security-related, and monitoring depends on observability elements.

Where observability is crucial, SAP BTP provides necessary functionality so that you can observe and monitor the operations of the service. Let's look at some examples:

| SAP BTP Service | Monitoring Features |
| --- | --- |
| SAP HANA Cloud, SAP HANA Database | Using the SAP HANA Cockpit, Monitoring page (Figure 5.6), you can do the following:<br><br>• Observe memory usage, CPU usage, and disk usage<br>• Drill down to monitor CPU, memory, and disk performances with more detailed views<br>• Drill down to analyze workloads to see the top SQL statements, background jobs, and threads<br>• Check alerts, along with their details and proposed solutions<br>• Monitor table usage |
| SAP Data Intelligence | Using the SAP Data Intelligence Monitoring application, you can do the following:<br><br>• Observe memory and CPU usage with filtering options for graphs, statuses, users, and time ranges<br>• View recently executed graphs and drill down to their execution details, process logs, and metrics<br>• View and manage schedules |

| SAP Integration Suite | Using the Cloud Integration Monitoring dashboard, you can do the following:<br><br>• Monitor message processing and drill down to individual messages to see their statuses, properties, logs, and artifact details<br><br>• Manage the logging level<br><br>• Access audit logs and system log files<br><br>Using the Analytics view of the API Portal, you can do the following:<br><br>• View API traffic statistics in terms of the number of calls and response times<br><br>• View error statistics and error-prone APIs<br><br>SAP Integration Suite also supports out-of-the-box integration with Solution Manager and SAP Analytics Cloud. |
| --- | --- |

Table 5.1: Examples of SAP BTP service-specific monitoring features

The following screenshot shows the monitoring page of the SAP HANA Cockpit, which gives you an overview of the main monitoring categories. From this screen, you can click on the links to drill down to more detailed views for further analysis:

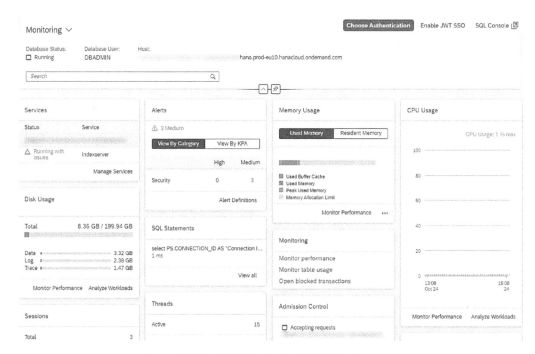

Figure 5.6: SAP HANA Cockpit – the Monitoring page

## Application logging for custom applications

As discussed previously, certain services provide the necessary information to monitor their operations. But how about custom applications?

This is where the **Application Logging service** enters the picture. By default, this service records logs from the Cloud Foundry router. In addition, if you want to log other information from your custom Cloud Foundry application explicitly, you can do so by creating an instance of this service and binding your application to it.

The SAP BTP Cloud Foundry environment uses *Elastic Stack*, a group of open source products, to record and visualize application logs. You can view the logs for your application by navigating to the application's page in the *Cloud Foundry space* and then selecting **Logs** from the menu. If you want more fun, you can click the **Open Kibana Dashboard** button to view dashboards and lots of information that's been logged for your applications. An example dashboard can be seen in the following screenshot.

In the Kyma environment, you have options in the console for viewing logs and metrics. These take you to **Grafana**, an open source observability platform, to query and visualize logs and metrics that have been collected from Kyma components:

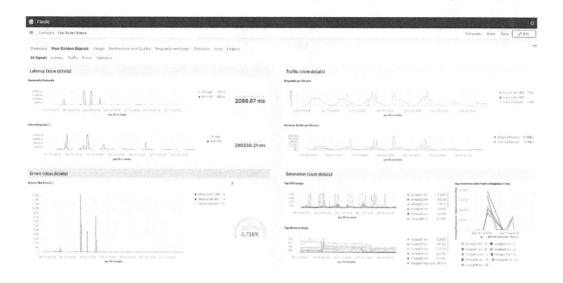

Figure 5.7 – The Kibana dashboard showing statistics for custom applications

> **Important Note**
> You should never let sensitive or confidential information, such as personal data, passwords, access tokens, and more, be collected in the logs.

## Alert notification

At the beginning of this section, the last element in our analogy was an alarm going off for significant events. It is analogous to **alert notification** in IT operations, which is an essential element of monitoring because you may need to race against time when remediating problems. Thus, you must be notified about the issues as soon as they happen.

The **SAP Alert Notification service for SAP BTP** comes to the rescue here. This service receives information about **events** in a predefined format and lets you configure three entities that help construct a notification pipeline, as follows:

- **Conditions**: Logical expressions that are based on event properties – for example, "[If] the `severity` of the event is equal to `Error`."

- **Actions**: A definition of how the service performs the notification. With an action, you configure technical details around predefined action types. With the full specification, actions correspond to **delivery channels**.

- **Subscriptions**: With subscriptions, you bring together conditions and actions to define the end-to-end notification process. You can add multiple conditions together to form a conjunct rule set and add multiple actions to push the events to multiple delivery channels:

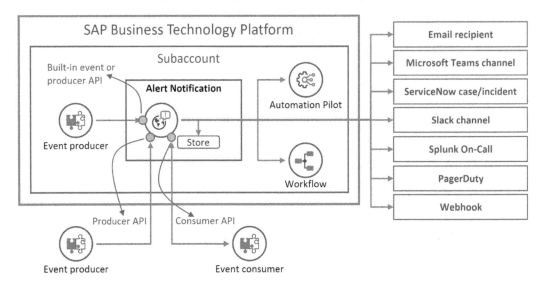

Figure 5.8: SAP Alert Notification service, sources, and delivery channels

The preceding diagram illustrates how you can use the SAP Notification Service. Let's discuss some of the details:

- There are built-in events for many SAP BTP services that become available as soon as you subscribe to the SAP Notification Service, such as SAP HANA Cloud, SAP Cloud Integration, SAP Cloud Transport Management, and more.

- An SAP BTP application or an external application can send event information to the SAP Alert Notification Service by using its Producer API.

- Applications can use the SAP Alert Notification Service Consumer API to pull events that are stored in the service's temporary storage or the events that have been undelivered for some reason.

- You can configure SAP Alert Notification Service actions to define delivery channels for many targets, such as email, ServiceNow, Microsoft Teams, and more.

An interesting action target here is the **SAP Automation Pilot**, which is another SAP BTP service. This service lets you create automation procedures using predefined platform commands or flexible commands to write scripts or make API calls. You can execute the commands, which can also be a set of other commands, in a scheduled manner, by using a URL trigger, via integration with the SAP Alert Notification Service, or through an API call.

Although not directly linked to observability, let's think of an interesting example for this service. Being a premium product, SAP HANA Cloud, HANA Database is not the cheapest on the market. As a result of having many environments for change delivery, sandbox, and training, you probably have several SAP HANA Cloud, HANA DB instances. But do you need all of them running all the time? Maybe one of your database administrators should stop the non-production instances every night and then start them again in the morning to save costs. You must be smelling the opportunity for automation here, and SAP Automation Pilot can help. For this example, let's also consider our hard-working developers who may need to work during the night from time to time. Let's build a solution step by step:

- Build an application that exposes a REST/OData API that, when queried, tells you whether a database can be stopped that night or not. The developers can use the UI of this application to mark a database as not to be stopped that night.

- Schedule an SAP Automation Pilot execution to run every night, which makes a call to the API and, according to the response, stops all applicable non-production databases.

- Schedule another SAP Automation Pilot execution to run every morning to start the databases.

### Traceability

Let's assume you are in a war room, troubleshooting a recent high-priority incident, or you are about to deliver a solution and must find the performance bottleneck. At that moment, if you had three wishes, one would be to have an end-to-end trace of how a request flows across multiple components. This trace is even more valuable when it correlates the requests of the same flow hitting each component. At the time of writing this book, unfortunately, no tools provide out-of-the-box traceability for SAP BTP. However, there are roadmap items that could deliver this.

### Tools

Let's briefly talk about the tools you can use for observability. If you have been using SAP on-premise solutions, most probably, you already have **SAP Solution Manager**, which provides monitoring capabilities. For customers who want a similar tool for cloud solutions, SAP provides **SAP Cloud Application Lifecycle Management (Cloud ALM)**, which comes included with SAP BTP and other cloud subscriptions. SAP Cloud ALM is still evolving, and capabilities for SAP BTP are on its roadmap. Finally, for system monitoring that extends from on-premise to the cloud with extra capabilities, **SAP Focused Run** can help as an observability solution. Contrary to the other two, SAP Focused Run is a paid product.

Apart from SAP solutions, you can leverage generic monitoring tools from the vendors, such as Dynatrace and AppDynamics. However, unlike on-premise monitoring, where you generally install agents on your systems, you may have restricted options for integrating your SAP cloud solutions to these tools. In most cases, this will be through the APIs to stream events, metrics, and statistics to the central monitoring tool.

Our suggestion for on-premise, cloud, or hybrid landscapes would be to use SAP-specific monitoring tools primarily because they are SAP-aware and have specifically crafted capabilities. After that, you can extend your monitoring to other generic tools for centralized operations.

With this, we conclude our discussion around observability and, in general, non-functional design elements. Surely, there are many other aspects that we can discuss under non-functional design. However, we will suffice here since we've discussed the major elements. Next, let's talk about how these become a part of an agreement between a supplier and a consumer.

## Understanding SLAs

As an architect, once you've gathered and understood the non-functional requirements for a solution, you must design an architecture that balances the quality of service and the cost to implement and operate it. With your solution becoming a service or a product, you need to convey a message to your stakeholders, customers, and users claiming at what levels you will fulfill the non-functional requirements. When quantified, these become **service-level objectives** (**SLOs**) – hence, quality of service targets. And by conveying these SLOs to your stakeholders, customers, and users, you get into **service-level agreements** (**SLAs**).

If you are delivering an in-house solution, the SLAs become the service quality that needs to satisfy your stakeholders. On the other hand, if you supply your solution to customers, the SLAs become part of the official and legal engagement between you and your customers. In the cloud, as everything is a service, the SLAs critically influence technology choices.

Depending on how much control you have over the operational elements, you may rely on service levels provided to you by other suppliers. If you have full control over all the components of a solution, you solely define its SLOs. For example, this is the case for hyperscalers. Their design choices primarily define the SLAs they can offer.

On the other hand, if you are building a solution on top of an as-a-service, you need to cascade the supplier's SLAs into your design's SLAs. Here, you can adjust an SLA if the supplier provides options; alternatively, you can add other components to your design to adjust your SLAs to the required level.

An SLA can be defined for any quality that can typically be quantified as an objective, such as web page load time, API response time, or database RTO/RPO. However, in the cloud, engagements are made prominently based on an availability SLA in terms of a percentage of uptime in a certain unit of time. For example, a supplier can offer a database-as-a-service with a 99.95% availability (uptime) SLA, which corresponds to a maximum of 22 minutes of downtime a month.

Generally, the availability SLA excludes the downtime that's required for planned maintenance activities that the customers are notified of in advance. This suggests that the suppliers may be correlating their SLAs to the risk probabilities they envisage.

At the end of the day, an SLA is a promise and can be unintentionally breached. In such cases, most suppliers offer a service credit. This can be considered a form of apology since it may not always compensate for the business impact of the disruption. In the end, the supplier's performance in consistently delivering the service within the SLAs determines its reliability. Customers want resilience, and suppliers strive to provide the maximum they can.

Finally, let's highlight something we have hinted at previously. Surely, you would want to provide the highest SLA possible. But, as with many things, this comes with additional costs. As an architect, you need to balance the SLA against the cost. So, anything you do to improve the SLA of your solution should justify its cost impact. For example, if the solution you are designing for is not mission-critical, 99.9% availability may be satisfactory. Yes, designing for 99.95% availability may introduce an extra uptime of 22 minutes per month, but you should think about whether this improvement is worth the additional implementation and operational costs.

## SAP BTP SLAs

Let's materialize what we have discussed so far by putting forward the SLA considerations for SAP BTP. As an architect designing solutions with SAP BTP, you rely on the SLAs that SAP BTP offers. These SLAs are part of the terms and conditions when you get into a formal engagement with SAP by purchasing SAP BTP. As part of the procurement, SAP provides the necessary documentation. Besides, in their generic forms, these documents are available in **SAP Trust Center** at `https://www.sap.com/uk/about/trust-center.html`. Here, you can navigate to the *Agreements* section and then to the *Cloud Services Agreements* section.

To understand the SAP BTP-related terms, you will need to check out several documents. Because these documents and their URLs are updated from time to time, we won't provide URLs here. Instead, you need to search for the latest version in SAP Trust Center. In addition, SAP provides documents that are specific to countries, so they will be in different languages. You can pick the one that suits your situation.

As mentioned previously, as with many software vendors, SAP refers to system availability as the primary SLA. So, let's go through the documents we can use to trace the SLA for SAP HANA Cloud as an example:

- **General Terms and Conditions for SAP Cloud Services**: As the name suggests, this document puts forward general terms and conditions with headings such as definitions, usage rights, responsibilities, warranties, and more. This document, then, refers to an applicable SLA or Supplement document.

- **Service Level Agreement for SAP Cloud Services**: This document considers SLAs that are generic for all SAP cloud solutions. Besides, it provides important definitions. With this document, we learn that system availability calculation excludes downtime due to planned maintenance. According to this document's version at the time of writing this book, SAP promises a system availability of 99.7% for its cloud solutions in general.

- **SAP Business Technology Platform Supplemental Terms and Conditions**: With this document, SAP provides terms and conditions specific to SAP BTP. Here, we learn that SAP increases its promise for the availability of SAP BTP to an SLA of 99.9%. However, the document says there may be deviations from this SLA and refers to another document – that is, the **Service Description Guide**.

- **SAP Business Technology Platform Service Description Guide**: This document contains details for all SAP BTP services in terms of their metric definitions, sizing considerations, and SLAs. For some sophisticated services, this document may refer to other supplement documents, and SAP HANA Cloud is one of them.

- **SAP HANA Cloud Supplement**: Finally, here, we will find specific information for SAP HANA Cloud. At the time of writing this book, the minimum SLA that SAP offers for SAP HANA Cloud is 99.9%. As discussed earlier, the document says it is up to the customer to improve an SLA of 99.95% by creating replicas. SAP does not refer to any SLAs for RTO and RPO.

It may not end there, and you may need to check your contract with SAP to see whether any specific agreement terms override these options.

## Working with SLAs

Now that you know how to check the SLAs for SAP BTP services, let's discuss how you can use this information. You must have already realized that we have been referring to availability SLA even though we use it generically as SLA. When discussing non-functional design for business continuity, we discussed how you could enhance resilience for your designs; however, we did that without specifying SLAs. The baseline SLA will be what you get from SAP BTP and, depending on your design, you may need to consider composite SLAs. As an example, let's take a custom application in the Cloud Foundry runtime:

- Suppose you deploy only one instance for the application. In that case, you should expect a SLA of 99.9% because the documentation provides a specific SLA only if you deploy multiple instances. Thus, with one instance, you are at the minimum SLA specified for SAP BTP.

- If you create multiple instances for your application, the SLA becomes 99.95% because SAP BTP, under the hood, deploys the application in different availability zones.

- If you want even more SLA and justify the cost of implementing and maintaining it, you can design a multi-region arrangement, as illustrated in *Figure 5.3*.

Checking the *Service Description Guide* when writing this book, we can see that most technical SAP BTP services are offered with 99.95% availability SLA, whereas business services generally have 99.7%. Although still on par with industry standards, the latter being lower is mainly because these services consist of several components, thus bringing the composite SLA down.

Now, let's see what you can do on the operations side. To begin with, you need to be aligned with SAP's maintenance and upgrade strategy for planned downtime. You are in the cloud now, and as you may already know, you cannot opt out of receiving a product update in most cases. To ensure this alignment, subscribe to cloud system notifications by going to `https://launchpad.support.sap.com/#/csns`.

To monitor the availability of SAP BTP services, you can use SAP's **Cloud Availability Center** (**CAC**) at `https://launchpad.support.sap.com/#/cacv2`. This tool provides detailed information on cloud service availability such as planned events, disruptions, timelines, disruption causes, and more. These two URLs are for SAP customers, so you will need an s-user to access these tools. For general information, you can visit `https://support.sap.com/en/my-support/systems-installations/cac.html`.

Finally, if, for a month, the availability you experience goes below the quantity set by the SLA, you can open an incident to request service credits, subject to the terms and conditions.

This concludes what we wanted to say about SLAs. Next, let's discuss how SAP supports SAP BTP and some peripheral considerations for you to make the most of SAP BTP.

# Getting support

With a fast-evolving cloud platform in hand, having vendor support becomes much more important to keep pace with it. On the other hand, the cloud vendors are keener to interact more intensely with customers for strategic alignment. Their success is measured not only by how much they sell but also by how much their solutions are adopted and consumed. The competition in the cloud market makes this mandatory. Therefore, it's advantageous for both the supplier and the customer to continuously monitor and maximize the consumption of cloud services. For the customer, this means they get what they pay for, while for the supplier, it increases the chance of the customer staying with them. Here, support quality is a key factor that accelerates adoption, eliminates roadblocks, and increases consumption.

## Support services

SAP has a support framework that provides various channels for a diverse set of requirements. For SAP cloud, which also includes SAP BTP, there are two primary support services:

- **Enterprise Support, cloud edition**: This is the standard support service level with no additional cost. Through this support channel, you can interact with the experts, get involved in Enterprise Support Academy training opportunities, and get access to tools such as SAP Solution Manager, SAP Cloud Application Lifecycle Management, and SAP Innovation and Optimization Pathfinder.

- **Preferred Success**: This is the improved support service that comes with a price. With this plan, you can get more proactive and tailored guidance that aims to increase the adoption and efficiency of SAP cloud technologies and solutions. In addition, you get faster issue resolution as the plan includes quicker target response times.

Apart from the support plans that apply to the SAP cloud, you can also benefit from premium engagement plans such as **SAP ActiveAttention** and **SAP MaxAttention**. SAP MaxAttention is the most exclusive level of premium engagement, and with it, you can enable the orchestration of all service and support engagements under one roof.

For reaching out to SAP support, you can report incidents in the **SAP Support Portal** at https://support.sap.com. When reporting incidents, it is important to provide the correct product function or component information so that your incident can be forwarded to the right team quickly. You can use the search functionality in the portal to find the right component. Alternatively, you can get this information at the **SAP Discovery Centre**. On the service information page, the support section will generally refer to the support component for the service:

Figure 5.9 – SAP Discovery Center – support information for the SAP Launchpad Service

The preceding screenshot shows the support section for the SAP Launchpad Service at the SAP Discovery Center. As you can see, it specifies the support component – that is, EP-CPP-CF – which you can use to raise an incident about the SAP Launchpad Service.

## People

When getting support for your SAP solutions, you may interact with people with different roles. Let's talk about some of them:

- **Account Executive**: This is the main point of contact for the business relationship between SAP and your company. In general, account executives deal with commercial matters, such as licenses and contracts. However, they can also step in for serious escalations. Apart from the industry account executive, who generally leads the customer account, you may also interact with other line-of-business account executives specialized in specific solutions.

- **Cloud Success Partner** (**CSP**): This role's main aim is to help customers successfully adopt, consume, and renew their investment in a specific SAP cloud solution. This role was previously known as **Cloud Engagement Executive** (**CEE**). For example, with your SAP BTP CSP, you can discuss any matter related to your consumption of SAP BTP, such as strategic alignment, technical issues, product information, and more.

- **Cloud Success Executive**: This role's aim is like CSP's; however, their responsibility is at a generic level and supports the account executive to coordinate cloud adoption across solutions and route cloud-related matters to specific CSPs where needed.

- **Technical Quality Manager** (**TQM**): This role manages the customer relationship for premium engagements and coordinates operational support activities. Their scope is not restricted to on-premise or cloud and can support customers with incidents, as well as general support matters, within the premium engagement terms.

Surely, there are people in other roles who support your relationship with SAP as a vendor. For example, when meeting with the aforementioned people, they can bring in experts from the product, solution advisory, RISE with SAP, or consulting teams where needed.

## Resources

There are a plethora of resources that you can leverage to maximize your use of SAP BTP, as well as help you find answers to your questions, including learning resources. Cloud technology is continuously changing, and you need to be proactive to upskill your teams to adopt new changes quickly. The following are the main resources you can go to:

- Read this book (it goes without saying, right?).

- Follow **SAP Community** at `https://community.sap.com`, where you can ask questions or answer others' questions to sharpen your skills. Besides, you can find thousands of blog posts that provide valuable information. SAP uses this channel to publicize information on new solutions or changes to existing solutions.

- Use **SAP Discovery Center** at `https://discovery-center.cloud.sap`.

- Explore **SAP Learning Journeys** for free at `https://learning.sap.com`.

- Watch courses and microlearning content in **openSAP** at `https://open.sap.com`. In ongoing courses, you can interact with the instructors, who are SAP experts. Besides, you can watch previously conducted courses at your own pace.

- Follow **SAP Developer Center**, where you can find hundreds of tutorials, trials, and other learning materials. Also, follow people such as **SAP Developer Advocates**, who create valuable content on various online channels.

- Use **SAP Help** at `https://help.sap.com/viewer/product/BTP`.

- Join SAP's **Customer Influence programs** such as **Customer Engagement Initiatives** (CEI) and **Early Adopter Care** (EAC). With these, you can get extra support for SAP solutions, get to know newly released features, and influence product development with your ideas.

- Attend significant events such as **SAP TechEd** and **SAPPHIRE NOW**, where SAP releases lots of new information and training content.

- Check out standard SAP training offerings, including **SAP Learning Hub** and in-class training.

- Leverage SAP initiatives such as **Intelligent Enterprise Institute**, **Co-Innovation Lab** (COIL), **Enterprise Support Advisory Council**, **Technical Academy**, and **SAP BTP Customer Value Network**.

- Finally, keep an eye on other books, virtual events, webinars, blogs, and articles – for example, webinars from SAP user groups such as **ASUG** and **UKISUG**.

## Summary

How did it go? We have gone through so many topics. First, we discussed non-functional design while concentrating on business continuity, data management, performance, capacity, scalability, and observability. For these, we set the stage first and then explained what SAP BTP provides for non-functional requirements and how you, as the consumer, can design solutions around the options you have.

In the second section, we touched upon SLAs that are primarily linked to the non-functional requirements around availability. After that, we showed you how you could find out the SLA's SAP promises for SAP BTP services so that you can cascade them in your design's resilience arrangements.

Finally, we talked about SAP support services, people you can interact with while getting support, and the primary resources you can use to get help.

This was the last chapter of the first part of this book. In the next chapter, we will start a new part, where we will delve into the topic of integration. Excited? Continue reading!

# Part 3
# Integration

This part will talk about Integration by providing integration architecture guidelines, considerations for producing an integration strategy, elaboration of two main integration styles, that is, process and data integration, and a brief look at other integration styles. You will also find details on SAP's cloud integration technologies and design examples that will make you better understand how to use these technologies.

This part contains the following chapters:

- *Chapter 6, Defining Integration Strategy*
- *Chapter 7, Cloud Integration*
- *Chapter 8, Data Integration*

6

# Defining Integration Strategy

*Intelligent enterprises are integrated enterprises* must be one of the most well-known mottos of SAP. With this, SAP underlines one of its strong suits in the on-premise world and declares its stance on having the same in the cloud.

For years, SAP products tackled complex integration scenarios well between a multitude of systems, including many line-of-business and industry solutions. Undoubtedly, the world has significantly changed since then. Today, things are much more interconnected, with many new paradigms resulting in many, more sophisticated integration requirements.

With the cloud, there are new types of challenges to solve. To begin with, SAP acquired several cloud companies in order to meet customer demands for cloud-based solutions. As such, the current SAP cloud product portfolio consists of many solutions built with different technology stacks and mindsets. Therefore, for many companies, it is not a trivial task to move all their applications to the cloud. There are many reasons why many companies still operate within hybrid landscapes. How about adding some innovative use cases to this mix, for example, the **internet of things** (**IoT**), distributed ledgers, and augmented reality? The heterogeneity of the landscape surely increases its complexity.

Your integration platform is the backbone of your IT application estate. Therefore, it requires a high level of attention so that it can facilitate all the different types of systems to work in harmony while running end-to-end business processes across them seamlessly.

In this chapter, we will talk about integration as part of digital transformation with a SAP-orientated approach and provide you with the necessary information so that you can create your own integration strategy. We will cover the following main topics:

- Integration methodology
- SAP's integration technologies
- Architectural considerations

# Technical requirements

In this chapter, we will mainly talk about methodology and strategy matters. However, it's better to have a trial SAP BTP account or an account with a free tier as described in the *Technical requirements* section of *Chapter 3*. This may help you explore some of the concepts that we will discuss in this chapter.

# Integration methodology

With so many different elements, integration is one of those areas where you need to be very systematic and well-organized. Otherwise, it will inevitably become a big mess, causing a significant administration overhead and inefficiency. Therefore, when shaping your integration strategy, your integration methodology is the first thing you should establish at its core.

## SAP Integration Solution Advisory Methodology

**SAP Integration Solution Advisory Methodology** (**SAP ISA-M**) is a set of guidelines and templates that formalizes an approach for SAP customers to shape their integration strategy methodically. Using SAP ISA-M can give you a head start in defining your integration strategy and help you align it with SAP's integration foundation. In this book, we use many integration concepts and approaches put forward by **SAP ISA-M** (**version 3.4**.) At the time of writing, SAP has newly released a capability under SAP Integration Suite, called **Integration Assessment**. This capability is the new way that SAP puts forward ISA-M for integration guidance with a tool-based approach. Now, let's establish a foundation by defining the integration concepts.

> **Important Note**
> To learn more about SAP ISA-M and get the latest updates, visit `https://www.sap.com/services/integration-solution-advisory-methodology.html`.

## Integration actors

Integration scenarios encompass a wide variety of interactions between different entities. First, let's talk about the main actors:

- **Applications**: No surprise here; applications are the main interaction surfaces. In an end-to-end integrated scenario, the flow can transpire through several types of applications. For example, this can start in a frontend application running in a browser, hit an authentication application for access control, then some business applications on different systems or platforms belonging to the same organization or different organizations. Between these, it's pretty possible that data mapping and other transformations will happen within the message content. Your integration platform can take care of some parts of this flow by formalizing them through reusable components and standards. This integration platform can consist of separate integration systems, as well as components embedded in the integrated applications to facilitate communication.

- **Users**: In many integration scenarios, an individual user interacts with applications that run within an integrated scenario. Here, users can be internal users, such as the employees of an organization, or external users, such as customers.

- **Things**: If we had talked about this several years ago, it would have sounded quite strange. However, today's world is more interconnected, and things have become smarter. Think of intelligent cities, smart home devices, sensors, smart vehicles, and smart wearables. These *things* run specialized applications that integrate with other elements.

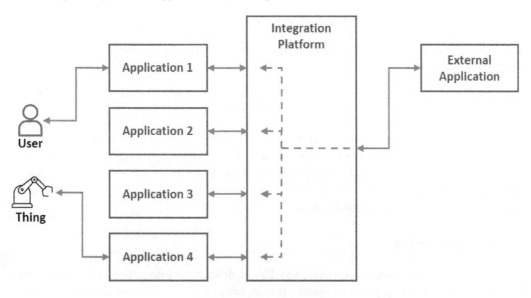

Figure 6.1: Integration actors

*Figure 6.1* is an illustration of how these actors interact. We already applied a best practice here – can you spot it? Yes, instead of using point-to-point integrations for applications, we created an integration platform to centralize, orchestrate, formalize, and govern integrations. Having said that, for certain scenarios, point-to-point integration may still be a reasonable option – for example, when integrating a decentralized SAP EWM based on SAP S/4HANA system with a core SAP S/4HANA system.

## Integration domains

As discussed at the beginning of this chapter, it's inevitable for many companies to have a hybrid landscape for several reasons. The cloud and on-premise require different mindsets regarding architecture design and operational aspects. Moreover, bringing them together in a hybrid landscape adds extra challenges. This is true of integration considerations as well. After defining integration actors, let's add the cloud versus on-premise dimension into the picture, which will extend it to define the **integration domains** that constitute the basis of integration patterns. *Figure 6.2* depicts all the integration domains that are formed by the combination of integration actors and software provisioning models:

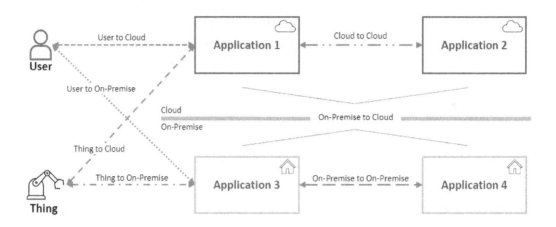

Figure 6.2: Integration domains

The cloud versus on-premise distinction arises from how the applications are hosted, secured, connected, and consumed. Although the way that applications are hosted is part of this distinction, when we say on-premise, we refer to the provisioning model of the software. Here, applications hosted in the **infrastructure-as-a-service (IaaS)** model can also be deemed on-premise, especially if you have a security boundary around them that is similar to an on-premise model.

## Integration styles

After establishing the integration domains, SAP ISA-M defines five **integration styles**, which are high-level integration categories. Furthermore, specific **integration use cases** are categorized under these integration styles.

### Process integration

When an overall business process spans multiple applications running on different systems and platforms, the parts of the process are chained by exchanging data in line with the business process logic. In this style, the generic use case can be defined as an **application-to-application (A2A)** integration. In addition, there are some specific use cases:

- **Business to business (B2B)**: This is when an overall process involves two separate business entities, and the process parts on each side are integrated based on standards such as **UN/EDIFACT** and **ANSI ASC X12**. These standards define syntax rules for messages, exchange protocols, and standard message types. For example, a company can use the UN/EDIFACT standard when sending advance shipping notifications to their customer business partners or when sending purchase orders to their suppliers. Here, the standards make the implementation and operation of the integration much easier at both ends:

Figure 6.3: A B2B integration use case

- **Business to government (B2G)**: This is when business entities integrate with government entities through predefined message formats that are put in place by the government authority. For example, a company submits its tax returns to the tax authority using the predefined message format dictated by that authority. The government authorities update these message formats in response to legal changes. Keeping up to date with these changes is one of the characteristics of B2G integration solutions:

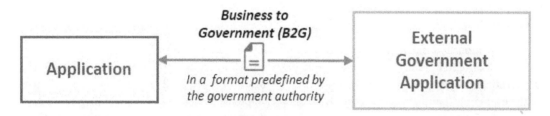

Figure 6.4: A B2G integration use case

- **Master Data Integration**: This use case being categorized under process integration may seem confusing when you read on about a specific integration style for data integration. There is surely a logic behind this. Master data is the core that underpins and makes all the data that your business uses meaningful. Therefore, master data generally gets replicated in multiple systems, and it's crucial to maintain its high quality. This use case refers to the continuous and process-led distribution of master data with robust integration at the *application layer*, rather than one-time or ad hoc data movements.

## Data integration

It's typical for an application to require data from other applications. If this happens through a business process at the application layer, then, as we previously discussed, it falls under process integration. However, there are cases where the nature of the integration requires intensive movement of data with no dependency on a process context. The application receiving the data can make use of it after it is moved in a data-orientated manner at the database layer. Since there is no attachment to a process, it's possible to transfer data quickly, in larger quantities, and through highly complex transformations.

A typical use case here is using **extract, transform, load** (**ETL**) mechanisms for replicating data, for example, from operational systems into warehousing or reporting systems. Another example use case would be orchestrating data from various sources through a pipeline to process **big data** for data science purposes.

This integration style also covers **data virtualization**, where data in remote data sources can be accessed without replicating data, as though it resides in the database running the query. Don't forget, when we talk about data integration, we are mostly at the *database layer* or the application layer, which uses data-orientated methods for integrating data.

### Analytics integration

The subject of this integration style is the interaction targeting users to expose data from various sources through an analytics platform that can also provide predictive and planning capabilities. The analytics platform can include one or many separate applications that orchestrate the data flow. It can also be an embedded application sitting close to the business application for specific analytics use cases. Typically, an analytical model is applied to the data to produce business insights for decision-making.

### User integration

This integration style caters to integration requirements for users accessing business applications through frontend applications. The existence of an interactive user introduces an additional dimension to an integration flow, as this mostly requires the integrated applications to be aware of the user context and act accordingly, for example, applying access controls or routing based on user context. You will remember our discussions in *Chapter 4, Security and Connectivity*, on the concept of **principal (user) propagation**, which solves the challenge of securely carrying user contexts between connected applications.

Another aspect related to user integration is providing users with a unified and integrated user experience for the applications that they use. This is relevant to the current status of SAP's cloud solutions portfolio, which includes several applications for a diverse set of technologies. For a seamless user experience, you can bring applications together in a common launchpad as the main entry point.

As another use case, we can mention the integration scenarios where users interact with mobile applications to consume backend business logic. Integration requirements specific to this use case, such as offline data synchronization, access management, and mobile device management, can be considered within the topic of user integration.

## Thing integration

With the technological advancements occurring around the **Internet of Things (IoT)** and similar innovations, sensors and smart devices are quickly becoming essential elements of our daily life. With these, the notion of **Industry 4.0** is created and we are at the verge of revolutionary impact on manufacturing with smart factories. These will eventually penetrate into more areas in our lives with smart cities, smart homes, smart hospitals, smart motorways, and so on. Similar to applications running business processes, these *things* integrate with other elements, and this integration style needs specific considerations, for example, device identities, storage limitations, and data streaming.

## Recap

Let's conclude this section with an overview of all the integration styles we have discussed, which are depicted here in *Figure 6.5*:

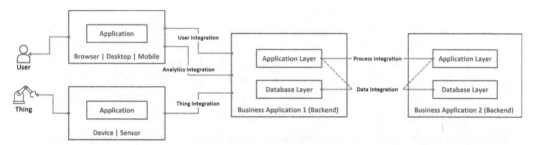

Figure 6.5: Integration styles

In the diagram, for the sake of simplicity, we haven't included a representation of the integration platform between integrated entities and a separate analytics platform that can be positioned between business applications and user applications.

Users interact with applications using a browser, desktop, or mobile clients. Then, the rest of the flow is an A2A integration. Similarly, things interact with the specialized applications that are deployed in devices or sensors.

Another fact that the diagram highlights is the distinction between process and data integration styles. The former happens between the application layers that run the business logic, whereas the latter primarily occurs at the database layer through data-orientated integration mechanisms.

Finally, there are integration patterns that can be categorized as **cross-use cases** since they can be applied through one or more integration styles. We will see examples of these later in the book, as in the following chapter, which will cover cloud integration.

## Approach

Now that we have discussed common integration concepts, let's put forward a typical integration methodology approach. We can consider establishing a common understanding of integration concepts to be a prerequisite for producing an integration strategy:

1.  To begin with, you need to be on top of your IT estate's integration map: gather the essential information for organizing it according to the foundational concepts. This can be in the form of a registry where you also note the information that will let you categorize integration scenarios for different purposes, such as business criticality, frequency, data volume, data sensitivity, and security. You should also include the in-progress and future use cases that you envisage implementing. With this comprehensive information discovery, you will know which integration domains and styles are relevant to your strategy and can carve out the integration use cases that you need to consider.

2.  As the next step for your integration use cases, you need to come up with the integration patterns that you find most feasible for your requirements. Then, complete these patterns with the technology and product choices that you make. Of course, SAP's integration technology offerings would satisfy all your integration requirements. However, every company has its own product and tool strategy depending on its vendor choices. In this book, we categorically presume that your integration strategy is SAP-orientated, and we will talk about SAP's integration technology offerings in the following section of this chapter.

    With your integration patterns defined, you can enrich them with integration best practices that you want to adopt when building integration artifacts. If relevant, high-level best practices can be a part of your strategy discussions, whereas you can put lower-level details into a separate document.

3.  The final part of your methodology should discuss how you govern integration in your company. With a complex hybrid landscape and numerous use cases, it's best to have a framework for continuous improvements and decision-making. This is also where you need to document the pillars of your change delivery process. For example, you can discuss how you will improve the change delivery mechanism so that cloud artifacts are maintained as evergreen while leveraging DevOps principles.

So far, it may look as though we have been discussing a static situation. But, surely, to produce a strategy document, you need to take these topics, provide an as-is snapshot, and discuss how you will arrive at the target state in line with your company's overall IT and business strategy. Beyond the core integration subjects that we have discussed thus far, there are other architectural matters for us to consider, which we will discuss in the last section of this chapter. Now, we will take a glimpse into SAP's integration technology offerings. This will give us a high-level understanding of the products and allow us to discuss product-specific strategic elements in the final section.

# SAP's integration technologies

With the proliferation and heterogeneity of products that serve our business requirements in tandem, SAP has to maintain a high standard for its integration platform offerings. On-premise offerings have been handling integration workloads for years. With cloud solutions now becoming more prominent, SAP's cloud integration technologies, which can be defined as an **enterprise integration platform as a service (EiPaaS)**, complement the on-premise integration products to form a complete suite of technologies for a hybrid integration platform.

*Figure 6.6* is an illustration of SAP's integration technology offerings. Now, let's briefly discuss them. In later chapters, we will delve deeper into specific topics and examples:

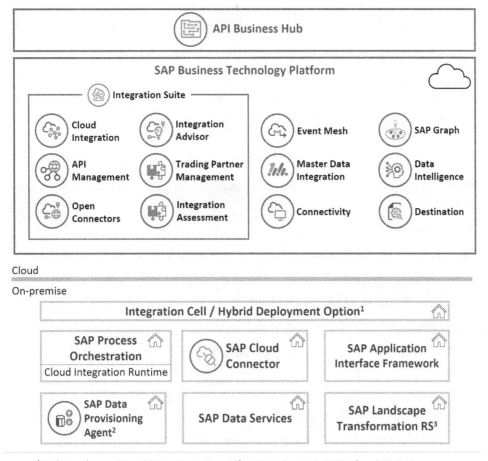

1) In the roadmap – Integration suite services and runtimes in a containerized environment.
2) SAP HANA Smart Data Integration (SDI) 3) SAP Landscape Transformation Replication Server (SLT)

Figure 6.6: SAP's hybrid integration platform

> **Important Note**
>
> Before getting any further into the details, let's explain a point that may confuse you. The term *Integration Suite* used to be a grouping term to refer to all integration-specific services. Then, SAP brought five of the integration services together as capabilities under one service and named the service *Integration Suite*. You will come across both uses frequently and need to derive from context which one is meant.

## SAP Integration Suite (service)

**SAP Integration Suite** is the collection of SAP's strategic core cloud-based integration services. At the time of writing, it contains six capabilities some of which used to be provisioned as individual services. SAP consolidated onboarding, some administrative tasks, and brought together these services under one umbrella. SAP may have further consolidation plans in its roadmap.

### Cloud Integration

The **Cloud Integration** capability, previously known as **Cloud Process Integration** (**CPI**), provides the tools for building flows that fulfill orchestration, mediation, transformation, and routing requirements within integration scenarios. Its web-based interface features the following:

- A discovery section that lists prepackaged out-of-the-box integration content that you can consume
- A development environment that lets you build and maintain integration flows using a graphical editor
- Monitoring for integration scenarios
- Operational administration tools

The Cloud Integration capability contains several adapters, which let you build A2A, B2B, and B2G integration flows between virtually any type of system.

### API Management

APIs are at the heart of digital transformation stories, as they provide a convenient way of exposing and consuming data. With **API Management**, you can do the following:

- Establish a layer for securing your APIs, as well as controlling how they are consumed, for example, by applying traffic management policies
- Leverage its data model to define and structure your APIs
- Use convenience features that are well integrated with other SAP BTP runtimes and services, for example, principal propagation
- Create a central catalog and publish APIs so that consumers can discover them
- Productize and monetize your APIs by creating rate plans and subscription billing

## Open Connectors

Typically, companies use several applications from different vendors, and it's almost unavoidable to build integration between these applications. Even though these applications are built with diverse technologies and serve different purposes, establishing integration between them generally has a set of similar tasks.

For non-SAP SaaS applications, such as Slack, Twitter, PayPal, ServiceNow, and Salesforce, **Open Connectors** takes care of these tasks and standardizes them by providing a layer that contains the following:

- RESTful APIs with harmonized **Uniform Resource Identifiers** (**URIs**) that are based on API provider categories and abstract the access to the actual API provider

- Normalized authentication, search, pagination, error handling, and bulk data processing based on common resources

- Common resource definitions to map data from multiple external applications into a canonical data model and a normalized form

By using Open Connectors, you do not need to deal with specific implementations of these non-SAP applications; instead, you use the standardized APIs. For example, with normalized authentication, you can connect to the API provider through a normalized authentication header without dealing with the specific authentication method required by the application. You just need to create an authenticated connector instance for the application once. Cloud Integration and API Management can also use this instance easily, as their integration building tools provide options specific to Open Connectors.

## Integration Advisor

Can you think of an enterprise that is ostracized with no connection to other organizations? The business world requires organizations to integrate their processes with other organizations and building integration between two different organizations is surely a difficult task. Luckily, industry standards such as UN/EDIFACT and ANSI ASC X12 come to the rescue to alleviate this challenge.

Standards provide a stable and consistent language between businesses. However, each business still needs to map the specific data model that they operate to the data models set forward by the standards. This can become a time-consuming activity with many interfaces to build and maintain. This is exactly where you can leverage **Integration Advisor**, which can provide proposals from a knowledge graph constructed using *machine learning* and crowdsourcing. Integration Advisor contains the following types of components:

- **Type systems**: This is a collection of well-documented information on standards and software vendor-specific formats. Type systems mainly include data types, code lists, and message structures.

- **Message implementation guidelines** (**MIGs**): A MIG is an interface specification based on a message defined in a type system. When you create a MIG, you add business context and can customize the message structure to your needs. For example, you can exclude certain data fields or change item cardinalities. With the click of a button, Integration Advisor can provide a proposal that mainly considers the business context that you set for the MIG. Then, you can go through the proposed changes and apply them to your specification.

- **Mapping guidelines** (**MAGs**): A MAG is a mapping specification between the data fields of two MIGs. Again, Integration Advisor can provide a proposal for the mappings based on the business context, and you can apply them to your MAG.

Once you complete your MAG, you can download the runtime artifacts that include files for syntax conversion and mapping scripts. Then, you can incorporate these files into your integration flow that you implement with, for example, SAP Integration Suite Cloud Integration or SAP PO.

### Trading Partner Management

The **Trading Partner Management** (**TPM**) capability extends what you build with Integration Advisor by creating, maintaining, executing, and monitoring B2B integration scenarios. Here, you can define your trading partners, systems, agreement templates, and agreements. As building blocks of agreements, you define the scenarios to which you also attach MIGs and MAGs. All this information is leveraged by integration flows to execute B2B integration scenarios. This capability also contains a monitoring section specific to B2B scenarios.

### Integration Assessment

The **Integration Assessment** capability provides a tool to create your integration methodology based on the SAP ISA-M that we discussed at the beginning of the chapter. You can configure elements of the ISA-M and create your version of the methodology, which can help you establish an integration governance framework. Besides providing the template for it, this service can guide integration architects and developers to comply with the methodology when implementing integration projects.

### Hybrid Integration Suite

At the time of writing, SAP have published their plans to release Integration Suite with hybrid deployment options. With this, SAP plans to introduce a component that can be deployed on-premise (including IaaS). This **hybrid integration cell** will complement SAP Integration Suite natively and provide similar runtime capabilities to running on-premise. However, the design and operations (for example, monitoring) will remain in the cloud. Using the hybrid deployment allows customers to run their on-premise-to-on-premise integration scenarios without going through the cloud, with the added benefit of designing the integration flows in the cloud.

# Other cloud-based integration services

Let's first highlight that although these are cloud-based services, like the SAP Integration Suite capabilities, they can also be used for integrating on-premise applications, for example, in a cloud to on-premise integration scenario.

## Connectivity and destination

We already touched upon these services in *Chapter 4, Security and Connectivity*, in which we discussed security and connectivity. Surely, connectivity between systems is a prerequisite for building integration between them. To refresh your memory, make sure to go back and read that chapter.

## Master Data Integration

As we mentioned before, master data is the core that underpins all the data that your business uses. In a heterogeneous landscape, this data typically needs to be replicated to several systems, and it is paramount to keep it consistent across all systems. This way, all these systems can work on the same data, which also helps processes be better aligned by reducing the exceptions caused by data problems.

The **Master Data Integration** service handles this integration with a *hub-and-spoke* architecture using the **SAP One Domain Model (ODM)** as the intermediary exchange format when distributing data changes to several systems. This makes the SAP ODM a common data model centrally defined for synchronizing business object data between multiple applications.

## SAP Graph

**SAP Graph** is the unified API for accessing the data managed in SAP solutions. The API retrieves the data mainly using a common data model. It provides a harmonious way of accessing data, assuming that it is integrated well between the applications. For example, suppose your application requires access to SAP-managed data and is indifferent to where the data is retrieved. In that case, you can use SAP Graph to reduce the complexity of implementing the data retrieval procedures.

## SAP Data Intelligence Cloud

As you will remember from the integration styles that we have previously discussed, specific tools are needed to handle data-orientated integration scenarios. These tools are supposed to tackle data in large volumes, in various forms, and with high-velocity ingestion.

**SAP Data Intelligence** caters to all these requirements providing ETL, pipelining, orchestration, and big data-relevant features. Besides this, it contains other capabilities that make it a one-stop shop for data management (cataloging, preparation, and quality), data integration, and data processing. SAP Data Intelligence can be provisioned as a service through SAP BTP or deployed on-premise.

### SAP Event Mesh

In a highly modular architecture, reducing the dependency between the components is reasonable. If the requirements do not dictate a synchronous request-response-based kind of communication, an event-driven approach can make the design more resilient, scalable, and agile. This approach is characteristically used in cloud-native applications that include several *microservices*. In this pattern, *events* published by a component are broadcasted to subscriber components to notify a state change in data. Typically, a **message broker** application handles the event broadcasting between the publisher and the subscribers.

**SAP Event Mesh** is a cloud service that acts as a message or event broker and provides messaging capabilities for an event-driven architecture. Considering SAP's intelligent enterprise vision, in which several applications are integrated, Event Mesh is a crucial component that robustly facilitates this integration, and also enables integration between the core SAP applications and sidecar extensions without disrupting the formalized business processes.

## On-premise components

Let's cover a brief overview of SAP's on-premise integration solutions to complete the picture:

- **SAP Process Orchestration** (**SAP PO**): SAP's on-premise middleware solution for building and running integration flows for orchestrating, operating, and governing integrations mainly for on-premise-orientated scenarios. Besides containing the integration core of its predecessor, that is, **SAP Process Integration** (**SAP PI**), SAP PO also includes **SAP Business Process Management** (**SAP BPM**) for modeling business processes and **SAP Business Rules Management** (**SAP BRM**) for rule handling.

  An essential feature to highlight about SAP PO is the embedded **Cloud Integration runtime** component. This means that you can deploy SAP Integration Suite Cloud Integration artifacts to your on-premise SAP PO system. The design work still needs to be done in Integration Suite, whereas the integration flow can be configured and run in SAP PO.

- **SAP Data Services**: SAP's on-premise data toolset that provides data integration, ETL, quality, profiling, and cleansing capabilities. SAP Data Services supports many SAP and non-SAP systems for building data integrations between them.

- **SAP Landscape Transformation Replication Server (SLT):** Another data tool mainly for data replication scenarios. Although SLT also supports non-ABAP systems, it is generally geared towards ABAP systems. It has powerful replication capabilities, which include real-time data replication. As such, it tends to be a key component in hybrid SAP landscapes, as it can facilitate data replication from on-premise systems to SAP HANA Cloud.

- **SAP Cloud Connector**: This connectivity solution functions as a reverse invoke proxy between SAP BTP and the on-premise landscape. It conveniently provides a secure tunnel for communication. We have already discussed SAP Cloud Connector in *Chapter 4, Security and Connectivity*.

- **SAP Data Provisioning Agent**: This is the on-premise part of the **SAP HANA Smart Data Integration** (**SDI**) technology, another real-time data replication tool. Compared to SLT, SDI is mainly used for replication scenarios where data moves from non-ABAP sources into SAP HANA and SAP HANA Cloud.

- **SAP Application Interface Framework** (**SAP AIF**): An application component that is embedded in SAP S/4HANA and SAP Business Suite systems. It complements SAP Integration Suite and SAP PO by providing capabilities at the application layer. At this layer, you can define additional data validations and value mappings. Moreover, SAP AIF's operational tools can be used to administer integrations without accessing the integration layer. Just to note, although it is embedded, SAP AIF is licensed separately and needs to be purchased before it can be used.

## SAP API Business Hub

**SAP API Business Hub** is a convenient directory where SAP presents prepackaged digital content for building integrations. In SAP API Business Hub, you can find prebuilt integration flows, APIs, events, CDS views, workflows, and domain models for the SAP ODM. It has an intuitive and well-structured user interface for exploring the available digital content. In addition, all the digital content elements are well-documented, and it is possible to do sandbox testing on APIs.

With the prebuilt integration flows, there are two options. Some of the integration flows are *configure-only* artifacts, for which you only configure the parameters and cannot change the flow design. Other integration flows are *editable*, and you have the option to edit them after copying them into your environment. As long as you don't edit an integration flow, which is always the case for configure-only flows, SAP will update it automatically.

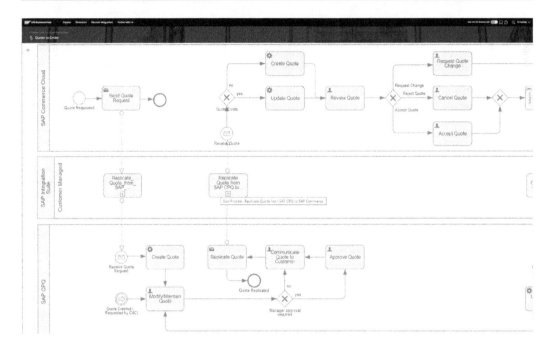

Figure 6.7: An example solution process flow diagram for SAP API Business Hub

In SAP API Business Hub, you can also explore **business processes**, in which SAP provides reference architecture models for solution variants. You can then view solution component diagrams, solution value flow diagrams, and solution data flow diagrams, which are excellent resources for understanding how SAP solutions work together to provide end-to-end business processes. In *Figure 6.7*, you can see an example solution process flow diagram. The figure contains part of the diagram for the **Quote-to-Order** (**Q2O**) process for the cloud deployment solution variant, which is a subprocess of the lead-to-cash business process.

> **Important Note**
> When architecting integration solutions, SAP API Business Hub will be one of your favorite resources. To access it, visit `https://api.sap.com`.

Besides SAP API Business Hub, for accelerating the implementation of standard integration scenarios, you can use the **Cloud Integration Automation Service** (**CIAS**), which helps automate the configuration of these integration scenarios.

# Architectural considerations

In the first section of this chapter, we followed a logical set of steps for building an integration methodology that can also form the foundation of your strategy. This methodology is meant to establish a systematic approach for building integrations in your IT estate.

Now, let's discuss some other aspects that you need to consider when defining your integration strategy.

## Technology

When producing integration patterns for your integration methodology, you should consider the integration technologies to be used. In the previous section, we briefly covered the integration technologies that SAP offers. If you are in the process of transitioning to the cloud, you are most likely leveraging several of the solutions in SAP's hybrid integration platform. However, if your aim is to eventually become a cloud-first or cloud-only company, you need to set your strategy to suggest how the transition of integration content to the cloud will happen.

For example, the strategic change may need to happen at different paces for different business units. Or, you can choose to have an overall strategy that suggests moving integrations to the cloud where at least one end of the integration is an application in the cloud.

As you can see, SAP PO may still have a place in your strategy for on-premise integrations, typically for performance and security reasons. Therefore, it is crucial to keep your SAP PO systems up to date. At the time of writing, your investments in SAP PO are secure until the end of 2027 (until the end of 2030 with the extended maintenance option), as long as you are on NetWeaver 7.5.

Here, SAP also provides (or plans to provide) some capabilities to alleviate the complexity of running a hybrid integration platform. In SAP PO, you have the Cloud Integration runtime component, which allows you to run SAP PO integration flows that are designed in the cloud. Again, as you will remember from what we have previously discussed, SAP plans to release a containerized integration runtime, as in a hybrid integration cell that can be deployed on-premise and run a broader set of integration artifacts designed in the cloud. As you may have already realized, these capabilities would also help your transition from on-premise to the cloud because then you would have all your artifacts designed in the cloud. However, let us remind ourselves that hybrid deployment model was an item on SAP's roadmap at the time of writing and SAP could change this roadmap at any time for any reason without notice. In addition, SAP's roadmap also includes an item that suggests provisioning a self-service migration assessment and a tool to migrate integration scenarios from SAP PO to SAP Integration Suite.

Over the years, SAP has released different integration services in SAP BTP. As you can guess, the first services were released in the **Neo environment**. Then, individual integration services were released in the **multi-environment**. Finally, and most recently, SAP bundled some of these integration services together under the common Integration Suite service. This means, at the time of writing, there were three different sets of integration services. If you have had SAP BTP for a while, you probably have cloud integrations implemented in the Neo environment and in the individual integration services in the multi-environment. Therefore, in your strategy, you need to consider moving your cloud integration implementations to the strategic Integration Suite service capabilities where applicable. SAP has plans for a migration utility. Besides this, there are automated migration and testing tools/services for this purpose available today from third-party vendors.

As we touched upon earlier in this chapter, SAP API Management enables you to monetize API consumption. So, if you have APIs for priceable consumption, then you can discuss the monetization elements in your strategy as well. We will discuss more on the relevant elements of SAP API Management in the next chapter, that is, *Chapter 7, Cloud Integration*.

Finally, it would be best to cover how SAP BTP integrates with other vendor platforms in your strategy. For example, you can discuss how to position SAP Cloud Connector in your hybrid landscape for connectivity or how to leverage SAP BTP's Private Link service to connect to Azure.

## Security

Security should have its own place in your integration strategy. It should explicitly suggest high-level security measures that need to be taken when implementing integrations. When implementing your integration in a PaaS offering, you need to make sure you fill in all the possible gaps according to its PaaS nature that would cause security breaches if left unattended. This includes very obvious precautions such as using TLS with applicable communication protocols, as well as specific security measures such as message-level encryption of messages that match certain sensitivity criteria.

With public integration endpoints, it will be much more crucial to implement robust authentication mechanisms. These may seem to be best practices; however, at a higher level, these also need to be part of your strategy to explain how you will secure your integration platform.

## Observability

It may be extra challenging to troubleshoot integration problems, as they may contain several different components, types of systems, and content types. Your integration platform, being a jam-packed hub, needs to be strictly monitored to avoid bottlenecks. You don't have much control over the resilience of cloud integration services, as they are managed by SAP; however, at a minimum, you need to monitor for performance and failure rates.

Your integration strategy should detail how monitoring, alerting, and traceability will be achieved for your integration platform. Here, you can refer to the out-of-the-box observability features that you can leverage in the built-in monitoring tools, as well as the observability-specific solutions such as **SAP Cloud ALM, SAP Solution Manager, SAP Focused Run**, and **SAP Alert Notification for SAP BTP**. In addition, from an analytics perspective, you can refer to the **SAP Cloud Integration Reporting Dashboard** that is delivered as standard content in **SAP Analytics Cloud**.

# Licensing

For on-premise systems, the licensing cost is based on the system infrastructure. For example, you would purchase perpetual licenses for SAP PO based on the number of CPU cores your SAP PO application runs on. After that, you typically pay a pre-agreed percentage of this license fee as the yearly maintenance fee for using SAP support where required. The crucial point here is to do the sizing properly, assuming the peak time workloads as well. As licenses cannot be reduced straightforwardly in on-premise licensing models, overestimating the required size may cause paying more than you need to. However, once established, you wouldn't have much room to optimize.

With SAP BTP, most enterprises choose the CPEA consumption model (check *Chapter 3, Establishing the Foundation for SAP Business Technology Platform,* if you need to refresh what this means). Therefore, using integration services will consume cloud credits based on their respective metrics.

For example, the Integration Suite service is priced based on the number of Integration Suite tenants that you have and the number of messages that are transmitted via the Integration Suite capabilities. As another example, SAP Data Intelligence Cloud is priced based on the infrastructure capacity that will be reserved for your usage. As you will remember, SAP's **Estimator Tool** and **sizing calculator** can help you understand the costs.

The cost of these services will be a significant factor when producing your strategy. Your strategy should also cover how you will be optimizing this cost, as a blank check may end up enabling rapid consumption of your cloud credits. This also requires you to establish continuous monitoring for the consumption of these services, so that you can detect anomalies and optimize if needed.

Let's ask a provocative question: if you have already paid for your on-premise SAP PO system license and must contractually continue paying the maintenance fee, how will you justify your business case for moving on-premise integrations to SAP Integration Suite?

Answering this question should be part of your integration strategy. The crucial justification point will be how the costs compare between the two options. As the deadline for the mainstream maintenance for SAP PO is currently in the future (at the time of writing), this gives you some time to take advantage of your investment in SAP PO. Assuming that you will be moving your integrations to the cloud over time, which means that your use of SAP PO will decline, one contractual facility that you can leverage is SAP's **cloud extension policy**. With this, you may partially terminate on-premise licenses and associated maintenance fees of unused capacity and instead subscribe to SAP cloud solutions. As this is a contractual matter and is subject to terms and conditions, you can discuss it with your account executive.

As the second type of facility, we will again refer to the capabilities that SAP provides (or plans to provide) for a hybrid integration platform. We have already discussed this previously in the *Technology* section of this chapter. With the on-premise deployment of integration artifacts designed in the cloud, running these integrations will be subject to on-premise licensing. This way, you can optimize when to move on-premise integrations to the cloud alongside your considerations around infrastructure reduction.

## Landscape

As you implement your integration content, you will deliver the changes for productive use within a defined process. In small landscapes where only *configure-only* integrations will be used, two tenants may suffice, for example, one for production and another for preview and testing. However, larger enterprises typically have more complex landscapes, which means multiple tenants for development, testing, and production. You need to define your tenant strategy primarily based on the following factors:

- **Cost**: As discussed in the *Licensing* section, each tenant incurs additional costs. So, you may want to limit the number of tenants, that is, the number of subaccounts in which you will provision the Integration Suite service.

- **Change delivery complexity**: Your established change delivery process may dictate how many Integration Suite tenants you need, for example, because you may need to map them to your on-premise landscape.

- **Subaccount strategy**: As discussed in *Chapter 3, Establishing the Foundation for SAP Business Technology Platform*, you should have already defined your subaccount strategy, for example, in line with your multi-cloud strategy. Following your subaccounts model, you need to decide whether an Integration Suite tenant should be provisioned as linked to that subaccount or not. This overlaps with the two previous factors for consideration as well.

In addition, for hybrid landscapes, your strategy should consider how Connectivity and Destination services are used, including SAP Cloud Connector as a component in the overall landscape architecture.

Finally, since we have touched upon it earlier, as part of your integration strategy, you can identify the change delivery mechanisms for your integration content. Here, you can elaborate on which tools to use when delivering a change. For example, SAP BTP **Continuous Integration and Delivery** (**CI/CD**), **Content Agent**, and **Cloud Transport Management** services can be part of your strategic change delivery process.

## Strategic alignment

Naturally, SAP's product strategy influences your integration strategy. TThe arguments we have discussed so far contain elements of this. Therefore, it's crucial to follow SAP's integration products strategy and re-align where required. SAP publicizes its strategy via different channels, including guides, blogs, SAP TechEd, **SAP Roadmap Explorer**, and ad hoc announcements.

> **Important Note**
> You can access SAP Roadmap Explorer via SAP Discovery Center or directly at the following link: `https://roadmaps.sap.com`.

While SAP acknowledges the prominence of on-premise integrations, it encourages its customers to move to the cloud. So, where your business case has room for discretion, it may be wise to weigh the decision in favor of the cloud-orientated options. While doing this, do not forget to re-evaluate your operating model to adapt it accordingly. In this way, integration will also become an essential element of innovation.

The heterogeneity of SAP's solutions portfolio makes master data integration and unified data access a priority for SAP. This means the Master Data Integration service, SAP ODM, and SAP Graph will play a key role in the future.

On top of the technology layer, one of the differentiating factors for SAP is the out-of-the-box content that it delivers for business needs. Considering the eventual cloud transition target moves toward SaaS solutions, standardizing your business processes and limiting modifications is a wise choice. Therefore, it is a good idea to encourage the use of out-of-the-box content where possible. SAP API Business Hub should be your default go-to resource when architecting solutions.

The use of standardized content and processes may become even more significant for B2B and B2G integrations. Formalizing these integration processes and leveraging the content provided by SAP will make implementing and maintaining integrations much more manageable. For example, for a company based in the UK, B2G integration can be considered an essential element of following the Making Tax Digital initiative.

We have discussed some examples that can be deduced from SAP's recent strategic moves and the direction of the IT industry. Following SAP's steps, together with what other vendors offer for integration, will give you the necessary hints for shaping your integration strategy.

# Summary

Integration platforms are at the heart of heterogeneous and hybrid IT landscapes. To manage the complex nature of integrations in these kinds of landscapes, it's very important to have a systematic methodology and produce a strategy that transforms and optimizes your integration platform.

In this chapter, we covered several topics that can help you build such a methodology and produce a complete strategy to achieve your transformation goals. We also established a common understanding before stepping into more practical examples for integration services.

We started by explaining SAP's recommended **Integration Solution Advisory Methodology** (**ISAM**), which also helps standardize integration concepts and terminology. Following the SAP ISAM, we discussed integration domains and styles. Then, we finalized the first section by putting forward an overview approach for building a concrete methodology for your integration requirements.

Next, we covered SAP's integration technologies and provided a helicopter view so that you could see SAP's integration portfolio. We will delve deeper into most of these technologies in the following chapters.

Finally, we discussed additional architectural considerations as examples that you can cover in your integration strategy.

The next chapter will dig deeper into cloud integration and elaborate the details of the relevant cloud integration solutions alongside design examples.

# 7

# Cloud Integration

We have covered a pretty broad range of high-level integration topics in the previous chapter. This chapter will delve into the cloud integration scenarios, design examples, and the tools you can use to build integration artifacts.

We have already discussed the philosophy behind integration, why it is crucial, and how to tackle the complexity of managing integration in a hybrid and heterogeneous landscape. Therefore, to avoid repetition, it will suffice to refer to the previous chapter to read such content.

It's now time to roll up our sleeves and move on to the practical side. We will adjust the detail level for architects in general so that they can grasp the essential information to incorporate integration services into their architecture designs. So, the content does not provide step-by-step details for building integration; instead, we will discuss topics from an architectural perspective.

As you may remember from the previous chapter, we have several integration styles and patterns. For the sake of maintaining focus, we will cover design discussions under cloud integration and data integration headings. The next chapter is specific to data integration, and in this chapter, we will cover several other integration styles. This includes cross-use cases that leverage different architecture styles to fulfill similar integration requirements, such as API-based integrations and event-driven integrations. This means that we will be talking about the capabilities under SAP Integration Suite, which will help you design architectures including A2A, B2B, and B2G integration use cases. In addition, we will also cover other integration-related SAP BTP services.

In this chapter, we're going to cover the following main topics:

- Designing application integration scenarios
- API-based integration
- Simplified connectivity with third-party applications
- Event-driven integration
- Master data integration

We will provide design examples in the last section to make things more tangible. So, bear with us until the end of the chapter.

# Technical requirements

The simplest way to try out the examples in this chapter is to get a trial SAP BTP account or an account with a free tier, as described in the *Technical requirements* section of *Chapter 3, Establishing the Foundation for SAP Business Technology Platform*.

# Designing application integration scenarios

Suppose you have already established an integration methodology. In this case, for a given scenario, you have done a big part of designing your integration simply because you will build on top of an integration pattern prescribed by your methodology.

We will start with designing typical process integration scenarios that can be implemented using the **Cloud Integration** capability of **SAP Integration Suite**.

As you may remember from our previous discussions, standards and protocols are crucial for integration, as they reduce complexity. There are several of them, and the more your integration platform supports, the better coverage you have for efficiently resolving integration challenges. Leveraging these together with the transformation, mediation, and orchestration capabilities, you can formulate and build integration flows.

## Anatomy of an integration flow

An **integration flow** is designed to process the message that traverses Cloud Integration. You can add operators called **steps** to your integration flow to define how it will process the message.

These steps can do the following:

- Transform the message content
- Convert between different formats
- Call external components to enrich message content
- Persist messages
- Apply security operations

An **integration process** consists of several of these steps. In an integration flow, there is one **main integration process**. In addition, you can create **local integration processes**, which can be used as subprocesses for modularization, and **exception subprocesses**, which can take control of the flow to handle exceptions.

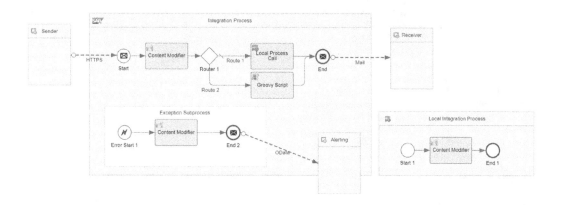

Figure 7.1: An integration flow designed in SAP Integration Suite's Cloud Integration

*Figure 7.1* shows an example of an integration flow. You can see the main integration process in the middle, which contains an **Exception Subprocess** and many integration steps. At the bottom right, there is a **Local Integration Process**.

Apart from integration processes and steps, there are two types of other elements in an integration flow:

- On the left, the integration flow has a **Sender**, representing the application that sends the message. Checking the arrow originating from the sender, we can see the incoming message is received using **HTTPS** protocol.

- Finally, there are two **Receiver** components. The upper one is the default destination, and by checking the arrow ending in that receiver, we can say the outgoing message is sent as an email. The receiver below (labeled as **Alerting**) seems to be placed for exception management where the exception subprocessor sends a message to another (alerting) application using **OData** protocol.

**Sender** and **Receiver** configuration is mainly based on the **adapter** type that is assigned to the connection and defines the communication format and parameters. Cloud Integration supports several out-of-the-box adapters that enable communication with virtually any system. These include technical adapters such as HTTPS, OData, SOAP, XI, IDoc, RFC, JDBC, JMS, SFTP, Kafka, AMQP, and Mail, as well as application adapters such as Ariba, SuccessFactors, AWS, Facebook, Twitter, Salesforce, and ServiceNow. You can also develop your custom adapters using the **Adapter Development Kit** (ADK).

## Message processing

In its simplest form, Cloud Integration functions as a message transformer and router between systems, enabling message exchange between them:

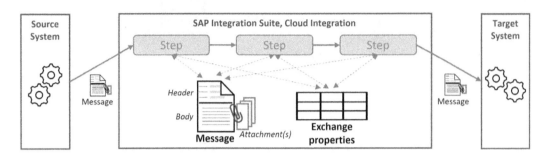

Figure 7.2: Basic message processing

As shown in *Figure 7.2*, the **Message** received from the sender system is handled through multiple integration process steps. Here, during the runtime of the message processing, the steps can modify data in the message **Header** and **Body**. With supporting adapters, it is also possible to handle attachments. In addition, the steps can create or delete transient data as **Exchange properties** in a key-value model. This provides a data container for the runtime session. The integration flow can maintain data in these properties without modifying the message. This is convenient when dealing with transient data that the target systems should not receive. As you can see in the figure, the only output of the integration flow is the message.

## Step types

Considering the scope of this book, let's have a brief look at the possible step types that can be used in integration flows. We will discuss persistence and message security step types under their specific sections. The other step types can be grouped as follows:

- **Events**: An integration flow has start and end events marking the beginning and termination of the integration processes or the entire flow. With different end events, you can set the final status of an integration flow. When the integration flow ends for certain adapter types, such as HTTPS, the processed message is also sent to the sender system as the response.

  In terms of start events, there are three main options. Typically, an integration flow is triggered by a message appropriately received by Cloud Integration. Secondly, for certain adapter types, such as SFTP and Mail, the connection needs to be configured with a **scheduler** so that Cloud Integration can poll the source system to retrieve integration content, such as files and emails. Finally, an integration can contain a **start timer** event that triggers the integration flow regarding the configured schedule.

- **Mappings**: Integration between two systems quite often requires a mapping to be defined between the data structures of source and destination systems. With this step type, you can define the rules for mapping by matching message structure fields, using predefined functions, and creating custom scripts. A mapping can be stored so that it can be reused in multiple flows.

- **Transformations**: Cloud Integration provides several options for transforming integration content. With **Content Modifier**, you can add or remove message headers and exchange properties. Besides this, you can modify the message body. With **Converters**, you can convert the message body into different formats, such as CSV, XML, JSON, and EDI. With **encoders** and **decoders**, you can encode or decode messages, compress them, or use MIME Multipart encoder/decoder to handle messages with attachments. There are more step types that you can use for transforming the message body content. Finally, you can write your **custom scripts** in Groovy or JavaScript to handle complex transformation requirements.

- **Calls**: You can use external call steps to make calls to external systems. You can then optionally use the response of the external system when processing the message of the integration flow. On the other hand, you can use local call steps to call local integration processes. As you may remember, these are modularization units to separate reusable process parts for reducing complexity. You can also make local calls in a loop.

- **Routing**: With these steps, you can create different processing branches, route the flow through one branch based on conditions, multicast the same message, split the message into smaller messages, and gather or join them together after branching.

- **Validators**: As a convenience of working with standard formats, an integration flow can include steps to validate messages, such as XML validation against an XML schema or an EDI message against an EDI schema.

## Persistence

As mentioned previously, Cloud Integration is primarily designed to process messages as it receives them and to complete the flow in a single runtime instance. However, some integration scenarios may require persisting messages or relevant information, and Cloud Integration provides capabilities to address these sophisticated use cases.

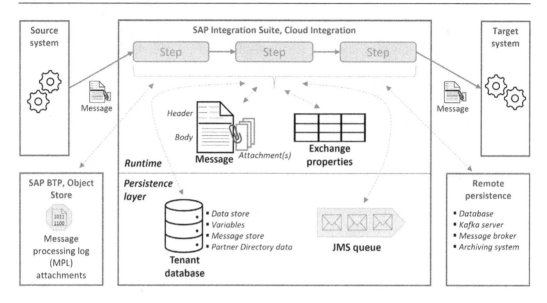

Figure 7.3: Message processing with persistence options

*Figure 7.3* extends the illustration of message processing by also showing the persistence options. For complex requirements, you can always store data in remote persistence options such as an external database, a Kafka server, or a message broker. For simpler use cases, you can use the internal storage options. Within the Cloud Integration tenant, there are two main containers: **Tenant database** and **Java Messaging Service (JMS) queues**.

## Tenant database

For typical data storage scenarios, you can persist data in the **tenant database**. You do not have direct access to the database. Here, you can store message parts in the **data store**, individual values as **variables**, and persist message bodies in the **message store**. Data stored in the **data store** or as **variables** can be set to have global or local visibility.

You may ask how **data store** and **message store** are different if they both store messages. Let us see how:

- In the **data store**, you can store messages and retrieve them to use in an integration flow when required. There is also a user interface for managing the **data store** content. This is a great convenience when data needs to be shared between two different flows or two executions of the same flow.

- On the other hand, a message in the **message store** can only be accessed after the integration flow that persisted the message is complete. The only way to access messages in the message store is by using Cloud Integration APIs. Perhaps you already understood the primary use of the **message store**. It's mainly for purposes such as auditing, where you need to store a snapshot of a message.

The **tenant database** also stores other data that is used by the Cloud Integration capability, including the **Partner Directory** entries managed for B2C integration artifacts. The **message processing log** (**MPL**) attachments are not stored in the **tenant database**; instead, they are persisted in an SAP BTP **Object Store** service instance.

### JMS queues

If the persistence requirement fits a *message queue* use case, such as asynchronous decoupling, you can use **JMS queues**, the second main form of data container in Cloud Integration. In fact, you can also use the **data store** for asynchronous decoupling. However, **JMS queues** are specifically built for this use case and provides extra features such as retrying message processing in case of failure. **JMS queues** support high-volume message processing; however, the data in the queue cannot be consumed multiple times due to the nature of queue processing. Although it is an internal component, **JMS queues** are incorporated into integration flows with specific sender and receiver adapters. This way, it's possible that data written to a queue can start the execution of listening flows.

## Message security

As expected from an enterprise-grade integration platform, Cloud Integration supports security at several levels.

For *data in transit*, you can use the supported adapters for secure protocols, such as HTTPS and SFTP. For *data at rest*, you have the encryption option to store data in data stores, message stores, and JMS queues.

Suppose your integration scenario requires processing encrypted messages. In that case, you can use the **encryptor** and **decryptor** steps that support PGP and PKCS7/CMS encryption. In addition, certain adapters, such as Mail and SOAP, support specific encryption capabilities.

You can enable *authentication* and *RBAC* measures for the execution of integration flows so that only authorized senders can trigger execution. Here, you have the options of basic authentication, OAuth 2.0, and client certificate authentication. As you would expect, basic authentication is not recommended for production use cases. The sender's authorization is checked through verification of whether the sender is using credentials of a runtime service instance that has the role defined by the integration flow. When forwarding the message to the receiver system with certain adapter types, such as SOAP, OData, HTTP, and XI, **principal propagation** is an option for authentication at the receiver side and lets the user context be sent to the receiver application. If you would like to refresh your memory about principal propagation, check out the relevant section in *Chapter 4, Security and Connectivity*.

For HTTP-based sender adapters, Cloud Integration supports **cross-site request forgery** (**CSRF**) protection to guard the communication against CSRF attacks. This is also valid for some HTTP-based receiver adapters, such as OData, and for others, the flow can be designed to include a CSRF protection mechanism.

For some integration scenarios, you may need to incorporate security materials, such as OAuth 2.0 credentials, passwords, **Pretty Good Privacy (PGP)** keyrings, and certificates in your flow design. Cloud Integration provides a secure store to keep these safely outside integration flows. After they are defined, integration flows can use these security materials by referring to this secure store.

Finally, let's remind ourselves of other security measures we discussed in *Chapter 4, Security and Connectivity*. You can enable the **malware scanner** at the tenant level for scanning the design-time artifacts. The tenant infrastructure complies with relevant standards, and finally, certain security events are logged for auditing purposes.

## Performance and capacity

Keep in mind that your Cloud Integration tenant has limited resources, for example, a 32 GB tenant database capacity in total. Therefore, it applies data retention rules, which means the data stored in the persistence layer gets deleted after a certain time period.

With limited resources, it's best to take necessary measures to use the available resources efficiently. For example, we can do the following:

- Restrict payload sizes
- Use pagination
- Schedule the flows reasonably

For instance, encrypting messages without a proper justification will adversely impact the overall performance of the flow execution.

If your persistence requirements exceed the capacity that Cloud Integration can offer or if it is for permanent storage, you can consider persisting data in remote storage.

**Custom scripts** can become blind spots, causing performance degradation. So, remember that you should use the flexibility offered by custom scripts wisely.

Finally, let's touch upon a special adapter, the **ProcessDirect adapter**, which you should use for flow-to-flow communication instead of calling flows through the internet. This eliminates unnecessary network latency and is useful when designing your integration scenario across multiple flows.

## Delivery procedure

Suppose you are given the business requirements for an integration scenario. What is the next thing to do to deliver the solution? You may remember some hints for answering this question from the previous chapter. Surely, we will refer to the *integration strategy and methodology* that sets the foundation of your integration delivery.

Similarly, you may remember **SAP API Business Hub** from this previous chapter. SAP API Business Hub contains prebuilt integration content that you can use to implement your integration scenarios in an accelerated way. This part of SAP API Business Hub is also embedded in the **Discover** section of the Cloud Integration tenants. Browsing this catalog of integration content, you can find prebuilt artifacts that you can copy to your tenant.

The available integration content is included in **integration packages**, which are containers for integration artifacts for a certain scenario. Cloud Integration also uses integration packages as an administrative unit to organize content. SAP API Business Hub integration packages come in two modes. A **configure-only** integration package does not allow you to change the package content; instead, it provides you with a set of parameters so that you can configure, deploy, and run the integration flow in a standard way. On the other hand, an **editable** integration package allows you to edit the content.

If you copy a configure-only or an editable integration package and use it as-is after configuration, you will get updates from SAP to apply automatically or manually. With editable integration packages, you no longer receive updates if you edit them. For some integration flows, SAP provides **customer exits**, at which point the standard flow can call a custom flow that extends its logic. This way, you do not touch the standard content while incorporating custom elements.

---

**Important Note**

When you use prebuilt integration content without modification to integrate two SAP solutions you own, the messages running through that integration flow are free of charge. As this is a commercial matter, we suggest you check terms and conditions with SAP.

---

As we mentioned configure-only packages, let's talk about **externalization**, a powerful feature you can use in your custom integration flows. With externalization, you abstract a set of integration configuration elements of a flow and link them to parameters that can be defined differently in different instances. This is mainly useful when you need to configure dissimilar configuration values for the same flow in different tenants, for example, in test and production.

When you copy standard integration content, you can configure or edit it in the **Design** section of Cloud Integration. Here, you can create custom integration artifacts, too.

After designing your integration flow, the simplest way to test it, or part of it, is using the simulation feature. By using simulation, you can debug your flow and fix problems.

An essential prerequisite for running your integration flow with actual sender and receiver systems is establishing the connectivity, especially when on-premise systems are involved. You may need to make firewall changes, outbound proxy allow listing, set up SAP Cloud Connector, and put in place security arrangements such as key exchanges. Furthermore, you may need to configure the participant systems to enable the integration mechanism at the application layer. For example, you need to maintain communication systems, users, and arrangements in SAP S/4HANA Cloud for running integration scenarios.

For transporting your integration content across tenants, for example, from a test tenant to a production tenant, you have several options. The simplest way is exporting the content as a file from the source tenant and then importing this file to the target tenant. However, this is error-prone and adds administration overhead; hence, it should only be used in exceptional cases.

On the other hand, you can link your tenant to an automated transport mechanism. This can be the **Enhanced Change and Transport System** (**CTS+**) on SAP NetWeaver ABAP if your mainstream change delivery mechanism is on-premise orientated. Alternatively, you can use the SAP BTP **Transport Management Service** (**TMS**) for cloud-based automated change delivery. In order to use these fully automated options, you also need to subscribe to the **Content Agent Service on SAP BTP.** This service helps manage transportable content. As the last option, you can download integration content as **Multi-Target Application Archive** (**MTAR**) files to manually feed them to CTS+ or TMS.

We recommend using one of the automated transport mechanisms. If you already have CTS+, you should use it. Based on your plans for transitioning to the cloud, you should establish the TMS option when you are ready. In order to decouple integration configuration elements from a specific tenant, you can use *externalization*, as we discussed previously. One last thing to keep in mind is that all the transport mechanisms will only transport the core integration content. You need to handle elements such as security materials and connectivity arrangements separately.

You can monitor your integration flows and access operational features in the **Monitor** section of Cloud Integration. For extensive observability options, you can go back to the *Observability* section in the previous chapter.

Finally, you can use the **B2B Scenarios** section of Cloud Integration, which constitutes the **Trading Partner Management** (**TPM**) capability of Integration Suite.

So, we have covered a lot about A2A cloud integration where SAP Integration Suite can function as the integration platform for transformation, orchestration, and mediation requirements. In the following section, we will discuss how the **API Management** (**APIM**) capability of SAP Integration Suite can cater to API-based cross-use case integration scenarios.

## API-based integration

**Application Programming Interfaces** (**APIs**) are at the heart of digital transformation, enabling the agility and openness required for rapidly interconnecting solutions. After all, they constitute a facet for data to be exposed and consumed between different layers of an enterprise's IT estate, or between applications of different entities. Therefore, a crucial design principle for APIs is to reduce complexity for the sake of convenience while acting as a contract between the provider and the consumer. This is similar to your mobile phone hiding the complexity of an entire telecommunications mechanism behind a simple call button. When using your mobile phone, you abide by the implicit contract and use this interface to make the call.

Considering the significant role of APIs, it is inevitable for a provider to have a control layer between the APIs and their consumers. This is why APIM solutions emerged in the IT world. This gatekeeping layer controls access to the APIs and then unlocks a further functionality tier for metering and monetization.

You can use SAP APIM to secure, manage, and govern your APIs through its governance structure, policy framework, and end-to-end API lifecycle management tools. Now, let's dig a little deeper into explaining how SAP APIM works.

## SAP APIM elements

The design-time elements of SAP APIM are managed in two parts. First, in the **API Portal**, you define the core runtime elements. The second part of SAP APIM is **API Business Hub Enterprise**, previously known as the *Developer Portal*. The resemblance of the name to *SAP API Business Hub* gives away the function of this part. API Business Hub Enterprise provides a platform to other developers where they can register themselves to discover the APIs you expose. After that, they can subscribe to API products with application subscriptions that allow them to consume your APIs.

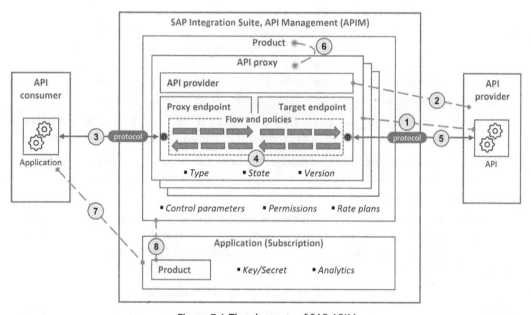

Figure 7.4: The elements of SAP APIM

*Figure 7.4* depicts most of the elements of SAP APIM, and now it's time to describe them. The dashed lines represent design-time relationships, and the continuous lines denote the runtime request-response pipeline. As you can remember, the primary function of SAP APIM is to be a control layer gatekeeping APIs. This implies that the API's business logic is typically implemented somewhere else. Therefore, you need to create an artifact that points to the API, the **API proxy**.

> **Important Note**
> Although an **API proxy** is a representation of the service exposed from a different system, SAP APIM sometimes refers to them together as the *API* when this distinction does not need to be explicit.

Let us look at the process:

1. First of all, an **API proxy** defines the connection endpoints. Since it is placed between the **consumer** and the **provider**, an **API proxy** contains the **proxy endpoint** exposed to the **consumer** and the **target endpoint** to route the request to the provider. For the **API proxy**, you can specify the state of the API, for example, active, alpha, or beta, and expose the API with different versions, too.

2. The **provider** is the system or application where the API business logic runs. Although you can directly specify the full URL for the **target endpoint**, a better way is to abstract the connection information of the target system by defining an **API provider**. This allows you to structure the APIs for easier maintenance as well.

3. The **API proxy** also defines the type of API that corresponds to the protocol used for the API-based integration; hence, it can be OData, REST, or SOAP. As you can manage the request content, it is possible to apply conversion between these protocols. When defining an **API provider**, you can specify which authentication method to use. This includes **principal propagation** for on-premise systems where the connectivity happens via SAP Cloud Connector.

4. At runtime, after receiving the request from the **consumer**, SAP APIM takes control. It then applies **policies** that are organized to be executed at certain parts of the request-response flow.

5. It then forwards the request to the **provider**; similarly, it conveys the response from the **provider** to the **consumer**. Some of the **policies** can be applied conditionally as well. We will talk about the types of **policies** shortly.

6. Now, let's briefly talk about how you can manage the consumption part of APIs. For this, you need to create **products** that contain one or many APIs. A **product** also specifies the **rate plans** for monetization, **permissions** to arrange who can discover and subscribe, and other access **control parameters**.

7. Via API Business Hub Enterprise, consumers can **subscribe** to these products.

8. We can also create applications in SAP APIM. Applications provide a **key-secret pair** for the **consumer** that is used for identification and authentication purposes.

Now, let us understand the APIM lifecycle.

## The APIM lifecycle

In general, the lifecycle stages correspond to the sections in APIM's API Portal user interface. You can see and navigate to these sections using the icons on the left-hand pane, the compass, pencil, and spanner icons, for instance. Similar to Cloud Integration, API Portal's **Discover** section has an embedded catalog from SAP API Business Hub and contains prebuilt integration content that you can copy and maintain in your tenant. Alternatively, you can create custom APIs. In the **Develop** section, you can maintain APIs, products, and policy templates. Here, when editing APIs, you can also maintain the API flow with policies, as shown in *Figure 7.5*:

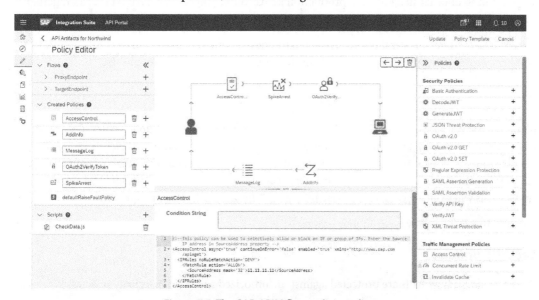

Figure 7.5: The SAP APIM flow policies editor

SAP APIM supports **OpenAPI Specification (OAS)** versions 2.0 and 3.0. This way, it also lets you maintain APIs using the **API Designer** editor.

When creating API proxies, you can retain the link between the API proxy and the provider backend service. This allows you to *synchronize* your API proxy when the backend service changes.

In the **Configure** section of the API Portal, you can manage API providers, certificates, and key-value maps. If you intend to monetize your APIs, you can define rate plans in the **Monetize** section of the API Portal, where you can also view the bills for the registered consumers. These rate plans can be assigned to API products.

After developing an API, you need to *deploy* it so that it becomes eligible to be included in an API product. Finally, when an API product is ready for consumption, you need to *publish* it so that it becomes available in API Business Hub Enterprise for developers to subscribe to before consuming the product's APIs.

During the development, you can test your APIs using the **Test** section of the API Portal. Alternatively, you can also use external HTTP clients, such as Postman. In addition, in the **Test** section, you can enable *debugging*, which records the API flow with additional information for inspection. As we pointed out previously, you can assign states to your API to mark their lifecycle stages, such as active, alpha, or beta. When you need to amend an API significantly while retaining the same base path, you can add *version* information to the full path, which helps with the administration of the APIs as well.

To transport your APIM artifacts between subaccounts, for example, from an instance in a test subaccount to another instance in a production subaccount, you can use SAP BTP TMS together with the Content Agent Service.

Finally, you can find statistical information in API Portal's **Analyze** section, such as call counts, the number of calls per response code, cache behavior, error counts, and response times.

## API policy types

It's time to talk about the policy types that SAP APIM can apply to an API flow, as they also solidify its controlling function. One important thing to keep in mind when adding policies to your APIs is the performance. Make sure every policy you add has a function that corresponds to a requirement. The performance of your API may be much more crucial, as the APIs can be consumed by user-facing applications where an acceptable response time is vital for an excellent user experience.

We can discuss the policy types in four groups.

### Security policies

You can manage how APIs are protected against unauthorized access with security policies:

- You can access security materials, such as *basic authorization* elements and access tokens. You can use these for authorization verification and convert the security content to send authorization artifacts to the provider.

- SAP APIM can also manage **OAuth 2.0 authorization flows**, generating and verifying access tokens and authorization codes.

- It can generate and verify **SAML assertions** and **JSON Web Tokens (JWTs)** as well.

- SAP APIM provides protection policies for *content-level attacks* by enforcing limits to JSON and XML structures or to any part of the message using *regular expressions* to detect threats.

### Traffic control policies

When you open your systems to external parties through SAP APIM, you may need to control the traffic for security or as part of commercial rate limiting:

- You can *limit access* to certain IPs.

- You can apply *quotas* to restrict the number of calls a consumer may make to an API.

- You can add a *Spike Arrest* policy to throttle the API access rate, mainly to protect backend systems against severe traffic spikes, such as **denial-of-service (DoS)** attacks.

- Traffic control also includes *caching* policies to improve performance. As you would expect, the cache has size limits; hence, you should use it reasonably.

### Mediation policies

As SAP APIM is an intermediary between the consumer and provider, it also lets you apply policies to manipulate the message content for mediation purposes:

- You can create or modify the request or response message using the **Assign Message** policy.

- If you need to access SAP APIM artifact data, such as products, applications, or developers, you can use the **Access Entity** policy.

- You can extract certain parts of the message.

- You can use a *key-value map* to temporarily store reusable data.

- You can *convert* between XML and JSON formats and also *transform* XML content using XSLT.

### Extension policies

For complex requirements, you may need to add more comprehensive policies:

- If you need to access external resources, you can use the **Service Callout** policy. With this policy, you can call resources via SAP APIM definitions, such as API proxies or API providers, or you can access them directly with their resource URL. There is a specific callout policy for *Open Connectors*, too.

- You can use the **Message Validation** policy to validate XML content against an XSD schema or SOAP content against a WSDL definition.

- You can send log messages to external log management services, such as Splunk and Loggly, using the **Message Logging** policy.

- Finally, you can add policies to add custom logic using *JavaScript* or *Python scripts*.

Well, you have learned a lot about SAP APIM and how you can use it as a layer to control access to your APIs. In the following section, we will discuss how you can use the Open Connectors capability of SAP Integration Suite as a convenience layer, formalizing integration with third-party applications.

## Simplified connectivity with third-party applications

Have we told you about how companies' IT landscapes are becoming more and more heterogeneous? Yes, we have, several times. And here we are again starting a section by pointing out this fact. This is because we will now be discussing an SAP Integration Suite capability, **Open Connectors**, that helps alleviate handling the integration challenges between applications from different vendors.

You can think of Open Connectors as a convenience layer that formalizes outgoing integration to third-party applications. So, what do we mean by that? First of all, you can build the required integration without using Open Connectors. However, it provides many features that accelerate the development of these integration scenarios.

## The elements of SAP Open Connectors

First, let's have a look at the structural elements of SAP Open Connectors that are depicted in *Figure 7.6*:

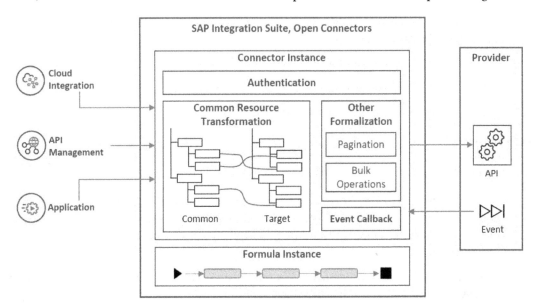

Figure 7.6: The elements of SAP Open Connectors

- **Connector**: A **connector** is a prebuilt integration component explicitly created for the target application such as ServiceNow, Salesforce, Twitter, and Google Drive. Therefore, a **connector** includes the information necessary to connect to the application and consume its APIs. So far, it sounds similar to an adapter, doesn't it? In addition, **connectors** support subscribing to events from the application providers. The best thing about **connectors** is that SAP manages them and keeps them up to date. **Connectors** are grouped under **hubs** by the primary function of their target applications. For example, the *Documents* hub includes Microsoft OneDrive, Google Drive, Evernote, Dropbox, Box, Azure Blob, and Amazon S3. SAP Open Connectors also allows the creation of custom connectors as well.

- **Connector instance**: To create integration with a supported third-party application, you create a **connector instance** by authenticating to an account on the **provider** side. Cloud Integration and APIM can leverage a **connector instance** that provides the third-party integration as part of a larger integration scenario.

- **Common resource**: You can expect applications that run similar functions to have similar data models; however, they are not always named or structured in the same way. With a **common resource**, you can create a canonical data model that can be mapped to many connectors with transformation definitions. This way, you can build with one data model when integrating with multiple third-party applications.

- **Formula**: You can create lightweight workflows to run simple integration scenarios with formulas. This is similar to a Cloud Integration flow. For example, an **event** from a third-party application can trigger a **formula** to send a message to another third-party application.

## Benefits

Now that we have a brief idea about how SAP Open Connectors works, let's check out its benefits:

- **Authentication**: SAP Open Connectors hides the complexity of authentication to the provider application. When calling an API via a connector instance, you need to authenticate with the Open Connectors credentials, and it handles the rest of the authentication with the application provider. So, for example, you can switch between different authentication methods, where available, without changing your Cloud Integration flow, which uses Open Connectors as the receiver.

- **Pagination**: An effective way to handle API calls that may return too many records is using **pagination**, which makes sure only a predefined number of records are received for one request. The response also includes a pointer to make a subsequent call to retrieve further records. Some APIs may support this natively; however, Open Connectors makes sure this is available for all connectors.

- **Bulk operations**: There are scenarios where you need to execute the function of an API for several records as input or output. Again, some APIs may support this natively, in which case Open Connectors wraps and leverages them. In other cases, Open Connectors makes this available so that the APIs can be called for bulk upload or download where applicable.

- **Stability**: Open Connectors can be considered as an abstraction layer for an outbound integration to a third-party application where its content is managed by SAP. Then, you can also further create common resources for canonical data models. With these, using Open Connectors enables stability where possible changes at the provider side don't necessarily require changes at your side.

This being said, let's also remind ourselves that depending on our requirements, we should also check the application-specific Cloud Integration adapters, for example, Salesforce, Workday, Microsoft, AWS, Twitter, and Facebook, as they may be more convenient options for building integration flows connecting to these applications.

Now, you have learned how SAP Open Connectors can help you build integrations with well-known third-party applications. Next, we will discuss a different approach, event-driven integration, which allows the development of integration scenarios for specific requirements.

# Event-driven integration

One of the many cloud qualities you are after when transitioning to the cloud is **scalability**. This is true for SaaS vendors since they need to scale significantly to serve numerous customers. Similarly, it is valid for end-user companies, especially when creating extensions while keeping the core clean. This is the ethos of the cloud, explicitly considering whether the future will be more geared towards SaaS and PaaS models.

Let's be a bit pedantic this time and define an **event** first. According to Cambridge Dictionary, an event is anything that happens, especially something important or unusual. This definition pretty much works when you apply it to the event concept in IT. For example, in business object-orientated models, the occurrence can be linked to a change in the state of an object, for example, a lifecycle status such as `BusinessPartner.changed`. This makes events more than mere messages, as they convey state-change information. This contrasts with the message-driven integration, where the message contains the established state of an object, as in **Representational State Transfer** (**REST**) or an action being triggered with a SOAP message.

If we are talking about integration, there must be participants: the **producer** or **source** application raises an event, and the **consumer** applications listen to it so that they can react to the event.

Just to avoid confusion, in essence, an event is an occurrence in the source system; however, when we talk about integration, we mean distributing the specification of the event. Going forward, we will use the term *event* for both of these concepts. Thinking along these lines, and as we alluded to before, what is distributed is still a message, but a special one that includes an event specification.

## Why do we need event-driven integration?

Earlier in this chapter, we discussed APIs and how vital they are to digital transformation. When reading a book section of this kind, you may think that the main concept discussed is the universal key to solving any challenge in that domain. So, upon reading, you may have believed you could use APIs to solve any integration challenge in the cloud efficiently. If you are an experienced architect, that thought should have faded out very quickly, as experience tells you that there is no key that opens every door. While APIs are essential elements of the cloud paradigm, there are cases where an **event-driven** approach would be the more reasonable way to implement integration scenarios. Wow, even when introducing event-driven integration, we based our argument on a comparison with API-based integration.

So, if it is all about an application sending information about a change that happened and another application receiving it, how is event-driven integration any different? At the beginning of this section, we already pointed out what underpins the rationale behind event-driven architectures: the requirement for a very high level of *scalability*. Scalability is essential within cloud-native applications and the integration between them. This is true for both design time, where you build solution components independently, and runtime, where these components need to run at scale.

An obstacle to scalability is the tight dependency between the components of a solution and **synchronous integration** is the leading producer of tight dependencies. So, if scalability is our primary concern, we need to break the tight dependency to introduce **loose coupling** of components with **asynchronous integration**. Lack of synchronicity may make it sound as though the integration cannot happen in near real-time; however, that's not the case. Yet, the receiver applications have the flexibility to consume messages at their own pace. Moreover, event-driven integration also unlocks other benefits, such as high availability, enhanced fault tolerance, high throughput, and low latency. For example, with loose coupling, Application A wouldn't necessarily depend on the integrated Application B and could continue running even though Application B is down.

All good, but why do we need *events*? At the end of the day, asynchronous integration can be achieved using message queues as well. For example, as you may remember, you can use JMS queues to build asynchronous integrations in Cloud Integration. In these kinds of scenarios, you are not necessarily fully decoupling the producer and the consumer; you are simply introducing asynchronicity with queues. In these integration scenarios, the producer still knows who the consumer is and creates the message accordingly.

When addressing higher scalability and throughput requirements, using events makes more sense mainly because the best way for the source application to initiate integration in isolation is by describing what happened and letting the consumer applications decide what to do. In this setup, the producer application can be agnostic toward consumer applications and doesn't care what technology they are built on, what format they expect the data in, or how they process the event. Furthermore, this kind of setup also makes positioning multiple consumers of the same event easier within an integration scenario.

Now that we have carved out the essentials, shall we establish event integration directly between producer and consumer applications? Surely not. It is not only because of the burden that this will offload to the applications but also mainly because it will not properly annihilate the tight dependency. There are many event-driven architecture patterns. One solution is to introduce a middleman application in between that is specially crafted for event-based integration. We call these **event brokers,** and they implement mechanisms to achieve event-driven integration. More theoretical discussion after this point would be beyond the scope of this book. So, as a concrete example, let's introduce SAP's offering and how it implements event-driven integration.

## SAP Event Mesh

**SAP Event Mesh** is an **event broker as a service** provisioned in SAP BTP. Actually, SAP Event Mesh can be leveraged as a message broker, providing patterns for asynchronous message-driven integration between a producer and a consumer application. This makes it a remote persistence option for integration flows built with SAP Integration Suite's Cloud Integration. However, we would like to promote its function in an event-driven integration here. This is because SAP adopts event-driven integration for applicable scenarios and enables events in its cloud and on-premise solutions.

The enablement of event-driven integration makes it easier to build side-by-side extensions. Considering the future direction for core business software is toward SaaS, this supports the relevant *keep the core clean* philosophy. SAP Event Mesh can play a central role here.

SAP Event Mesh implements an event-driven integration architecture using the **publish and subscribe (pub/sub) model**, with the following elements that are depicted in *Figure 7.7*:

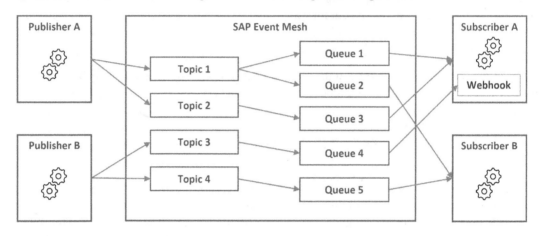

Figure 7.7: A typical pub-sub flow in SAP Event Mesh

- **Publisher**: The application that produces and sends the message.

- **Subscriber**: A receiver application that listens to published messages and reacts to them where needed.

- **Message client**: With message clients, you can organize integration contexts, as they contain the messaging elements. A message client corresponds to a *service instance* created in an SAP BTP subaccount. With this, they also provide isolation for runtime, as access to the messaging elements is made using the authentication credentials of the message client.

- **Queue**: Queues are the containers for the messages and define properties such as whether the broker should respect the time-to-live setting for the queue messages, which other queue to use as the **dead message queue**, and the maximum message size.

- **Topic**: Topics are the subject information against which the producer publishes the messages. In SAP Event Mesh, topics are defined implicitly through queue subscriptions.

- **Queue subscription**: A queue subscribes to one or many topics so that when a publisher sends a message to a topic, it can be written to the queue. Multiple queues can subscribe to the same topic as well.

- **Webhook subscription**: A webhook is an endpoint at the subscriber side, which is called by SAP Event Mesh to push the message. It is attached to a queue, with which connection details, such as URL and authentication, are defined.

SAP Event Mesh supports messaging-specific protocols **Advanced Message Queuing Protocol (AMQP)** and **Message Queuing Telemetry Transport (MQTT)**, as well as the HTTP-based REST APIs. In addition, it supports the following **Quality-of-Service (QoS)** levels:

- **At most once (0)**: This is when the published message is delivered with a best effort setup where no acknowledgment is expected from the receiver; therefore, from the publisher's perspective, it's a fire-and-forget scenario.

- **At least once (1)**: In this level, the message is kept in the queue until an acknowledgment is received from the subscriber. However, with this QoS level, the message can be delivered multiple times.

The publisher can send a message to a queue or a topic. At the receiving end, the subscribers can initiate the connection to SAP Event Mesh to consume the messages, which is a *pull* scenario. On the other hand, by defining webhook subscriptions, SAP Event Mesh can also send messages to the subscribers directly, which is a *push* scenario.

Have you noticed we have been using the term *message*? That's because we have been explaining messaging-level capabilities, which are also valid for event-driven integration. SAP standardizes event-driven integration between SAP solutions so that the required plumbing is in place for you. By configuring the publisher and subscriber systems, SAP Event Mesh can be located as the broker working in between.

When an event is published, it's possible to attach a large payload to send to the subscribers. This is called a **data event**; however, it has a significant problem. As you can remember, in an event-driven integration scenario, the publisher is agnostic toward subscribers. Therefore, when the publisher includes data in an event message, it cannot control which subscribers are allowed to see that data. This may expose a security risk. Furthermore, attaching large payloads to events is contrary to one of the motivations we had for event-driven integrations, that is, high throughput. That is why SAP Event Mesh limits the message size for any protocol to a maximum of 1 MB.

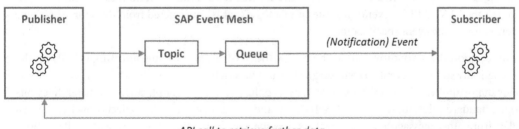

Figure 7.8: A notification event flow followed by an API call

From high throughput and security perspectives, a better option is using **notification events**, as depicted in *Figure 7.8*. Here, the publisher sends very lean information about the event, such as what happened, and the identifier of the business object impacted by the event. When the subscribers receive the event information, they can decide whether the event is relevant, and if needed, they can make a call to the publisher to retrieve further data. This way, the publisher can decide whether the subscriber can retrieve the data or not and which data it can retrieve. Notification events prevent the superfluous transmission of large event data to subscribers who do not need to know the details.

For event content, SAP adopts the **CloudEvents** specification for standardization. Here is an event specification with CloudEvents:

```
{
    "specversion": "1.0",
    "id": "e940019e-a96b-43d1-ae1c-585219493f50",
    "source": "/default/com.sstest.app01/1",
    "type": "com.sstest.app01.BusinessObject.Created/v1",
    "subject": "businessObjectId:1234567",
    "time": "2022-02-06T21:36:21Z",
    "comsstestapp01extension1" : "ssimsekler",
    "ccomsstestapp01othervalue" : 11,
    "datacontenttype" : "application/json",
    "data": {
        "businessObjectId": "1234567"
    }
}
```

Figure 7.9: An example CloudEvent

The CloudEvent in *Figure 7.9* contains some header data that includes metadata information and a *data* attribute for the event information. In simple terms, the example here says that a *Business Object* with the ID *1234567* was created. When SAP Event Mesh receives an event notification, for example, through the REST API for events, it routes it to a topic that is constructed from the source and type information in the event specification.

Another good thing to know is that the **SAP Cloud Application Programming** (**CAP**) model automatically supports event-driven integration and messaging with SAP Event Mesh. This unlocks many opportunities when developing extension applications, as the application can listen to events from a standard solution, such as SAP S/4HANA, and also emit events. This reflects how Event Mesh differs from other message and event brokers. It is specifically positioned to work with SAP solutions and understands SAP-specific context.

At the time of writing, SAP newly released a service called **Advanced Event Mesh** (also referred to as **SAP Integration Suite, Advanced Event Mesh**). As the name suggests, this service offers advanced features for adopting event-driven architecture including higher performance, support for larger messages, advanced event streaming, and analytics. Besides, this new service offers different deployment options with varying ownership models and connectivity models. For example, the service can be deployed with Kubernetes in an SAP-controlled or a customer-controlled region, and the connectivity can be via the public internet, private IP addresses, or a hybrid of both.

Before concluding this section, let's remember our condition of "if high scalability is required" for the scenarios where we are looking at event-driven integration as the solution. Event-driven integration doesn't necessarily compete to be the only pattern but complements other integration patterns. Yet, event-driven integration is prominent in the IT world because it is an inherent part of SaaS applications for scalability, works well with microservices, and is favorable in IoT communications for high throughput.

In the next section, we will discuss master data integration, which is closer to a process integration pattern, although it is used to integrate data.

# Master data integration

Previously, we touched upon the importance of master data and the challenges around it. Many enterprises struggle to keep their master data consistent and clean across multiple systems. Moreover, data silos start to emerge in various systems, which eventually cause inconsistencies. As these data silos become disconnected, they become obstacles to innovation. As you can guess, in heterogeneous and hybrid landscapes, the problem may become chronic and complicated to resolve after a certain point. Companies serious about their master data use master data management solutions such as **SAP Master Data Governance**.

One approach to tackling this challenge better is introducing a well-organized master data integration mechanism. By doing this, you can designate a *single source of truth* and distribute the master data to other relevant systems with consistency, keeping the data quality high.

With heterogeneous and hybrid landscapes in mind, SAP handles the master data integration mainly through two components:

- **SAP One-Domain Model (ODM)**
- **SAP Master Data Integration (MDI)**

From a different perspective, alongside the motivation of making life easier for customers dealing with a multitude of systems, with these solutions, SAP introduces a unified entry point and a master data access layer that spans the data of several solutions. Under the bonnet, modularization may make sense; however, most customers prefer a unified way of operating these solutions at the presentation layer.

## SAP ODM

SAP ODM is a coherent and harmonized enterprise data model that defines attributes and relationships for business objects that are used across several SAP solutions. The model can be viewed in SAP API Business Hub, as shown in *Figure 7.10*:

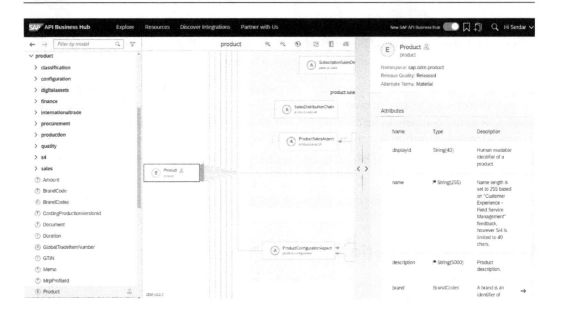

Figure 7.10: SAP ODM Product entity documentation in SAP API Business Hub

SAP ODM is the foundation for master data integration, and it's the centralized common model through which the data exchange happens. With this, SAP also uses it for the end-to-end business processes, such as lead-to-cash, retire-to-hire, and so forth, to run them seamlessly across multiple solutions.

SAP ODM is written in **Core Data Services (CDS) Design Language (CDL)**, and you easily embed it within applications implemented using the CAP model. In this way, you can write applications to extend core processes with a unified and coherent data model.

## SAP MDI

SAP MDI is an SAP BTP service that provides the foundation for distributing master data based on SAP ODM across several applications in a diverse landscape. SAP MDI aims to minimize the master-data-related challenges where business processes are spread across many different applications. It is also meant to support master data management solutions, for example, via SAP MDG, for ensuring the high quality of master data.

SAP MDI works in close relationship with the applications it supports. Therefore, enabling MDI requires a good amount of configuration to be done in the applications in which the master data will be distributed. At the time of writing, SAP MDI supported SAP S/4HANA, SAP Ariba, SAP SuccessFactors, SAP Sales/Service Cloud, SAP Customer Data Cloud, SAP Commerce Cloud, SAP Subscription Billing, SAP Concur, and SAP MDG:

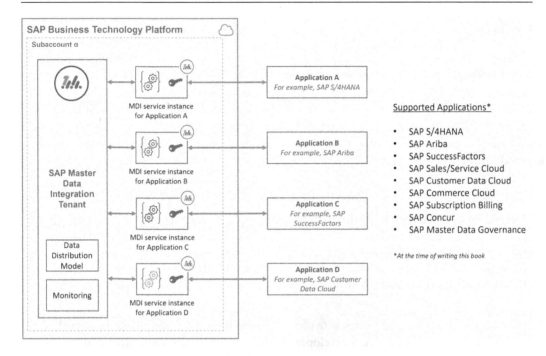

Figure 7.11: A SAP MDI setup with connected applications

*Figure 7.11* depicts a setup of SAP MDI together with connected applications. An SAP MDI tenant is provisioned through SAP BTP. You need to connect the applications to which the master data will be distributed to the tenant. To do this, you need to create an MDI **service instance** for each application. When creating the service instance, you provide the type of the application and other details as instance parameters. Each service instance works as a client for the connected application. For each service instance, you need to create at least one **service key**, which provides connection details. You may remember our service instance and service key discussions from *Chapter 3, Establishing the Foundation for SAP Business Technology Platform*. Then, you need to complete the configuration in the business application depending on its integration framework. Here, the main information you would require is the connection and access details that you obtain from the corresponding service key.

An SAP MDI tenant is provisioned when the first MDI service instance is created and is deleted when the last connected service instance is removed. Suppose you have requirements to establish separate master data distribution platforms, for example, for data isolation purposes. In that case, you need to use different subaccounts because there can be a maximum of one MDI tenant in a subaccount. Finally, you need to subscribe to an instance of the UI-based **SAP Master Data Integration (Orchestration)** application. This gives you a launchpad comprising applications that let you make MDI configurations, such as the distribution model, and monitor distribution status.

# SAP Graph

**SAP Graph** addresses the same challenge of data being spread across several solutions, which are diverse in terms of their data models and technology stacks. This is similar to SAP ODM. However, SAP ODM's approach looks at the subset of data and entities common across these solutions. SAP ODM provides the data model to be consumed by applications and mainly for master data exchange. In contrast, SAP Graph looks at the cumulative data model spanning all these applications to provide a unified API for accessing SAP data. With this, SAP Graph is technically middleware, and it actually uses SAP APIM under the bonnet.

> **Important Note**
>
> You may come across documents that say SAP Graph exposes data using SAP ODM. Although this was the intention during the incubation of SAP Graph, it looks as though the domain models for data exchange and unified API access had different requirements; hence, the implementation of the two drifted apart. Therefore, at the time of writing, the unified domain model that SAP Graph used was different from SAP ODM.

By unifying the API layer, SAP Graph provides a single endpoint to handle data. Besides this, it hides the landscape complexity from developers so that they can easily and conveniently develop applications accessing this data.

SAP Graph defines a common domain model that floats on top of the data models of the supported SAP solutions (at the time of writing, SAP S/4HANA, SAP SuccessFactors, and SAP Sales Cloud). It includes unified data entities and relationships between these entities in the form of associations or compositions. These entities also provide associations to the entities in the specific system in case the consumer needs to drill down to application-specific data.

Before consuming SAP Graph APIs, you need to complete certain configuration steps:

- Define SAP BTP destinations for the data sources. This includes connectivity setup and authentication arrangements as well.

- Create a configuration file for defining a **business data graph**. This file contains the following:

  - Your landscape information via the SAP BTP destinations as data sources.

  - Locating policies that specify rules on how to use data sources, for example, which system is the leading system to retrieve data.

  - Key mappings to enable navigation between data across different systems.

- Use **SAP Graph Toolkit** to activate the configuration file to create the business data graph in SAP BTP and obtain the URL to access APIs.

After creating the business data graph, you can consume it via **OData** APIs. This means you can access these REST APIs with additional OData features, such as $expand, $filter, and $top. After sending a request with the OData format, SAP Graph handles all the complexity based on business data graph configuration, navigates entities, applies key mappings, executes requested query rules, and retrieves data accordingly:

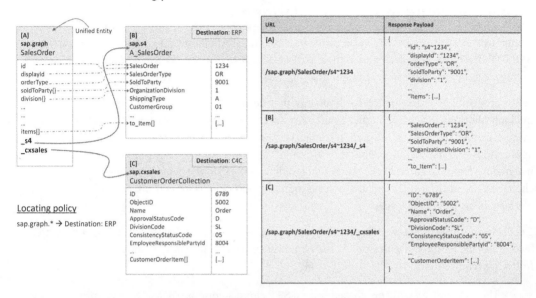

Figure 7.12: An example of entity relationships shown in SAP Graph

*Figure 7.12* shows an example unified entity, as in sap.graph/SalesOrder, whose data can be pulled from the SAP S/4HANA system defined by the **ERP** destination or from the SAP Sales Cloud system defined by the **C4C** destination. The locating policy of the business data graph has a rule that specifies the system at the **ERP** destination, hence the SAP S/4HANA system, as the leading system for sap.graph.* entities. Therefore, a request to /sap.graph/SalesOrder will retrieve data from the SAP S/4HANA system with the data model specified for the unified entity, [**A**].

If required, a request to /sap.graph/SalesOrder/<id>/_s4 can be made to read from the SAP S/4HANA system and return data with the data model defined for the SAP S/4HANA entity, [**B**]. Similarly, a request to /sap.graph/SalesOrder/<id>/_cxsales can be made to read from the SAP Sales Cloud system and return data with the data model defined for the SAP Sales Cloud entity, [**C**]. The data models for these entities are already defined in SAP Graph. You just need to create your business data graph, as explained previously. After that, you can make these requests to retrieve data, and use OData features for navigation, expands, and filters.

# Design examples

Now that we have covered quite a wide range of SAP Integration Suite capabilities, let's illustrate their use with example designs.

## A common cloud integration platform

**Company A** is investing heavily in executing its cloud transformation strategy and recently purchased SAP BTP. They have already migrated their SAP workloads to hyperscaler IaaS and there are hundreds of integration flows involving these systems.

When producing their integration methodology, they decided to build new cloud-relevant integrations in cloud offerings to achieve higher availability and better scalability. According to the company's integration methodology, an integration scenario is cloud-relevant if at least one of the main participant applications of the integration flow is in the cloud. They also adopted the practice to migrate these integrations from the current on-premises integration platform to the cloud when there is an extensive change to the integration. They are looking to migrate all cloud-relevant integrations to the cloud platform over the next few years.

Cecilia is a SAP architect working for Company A, and she is tasked with coming up with a high-level technical architecture design for the cloud integration platform that should also cater to the following requirements:

- The company recently purchased several SAP cloud solutions, such as SAP Commerce Cloud and SAP Marketing Cloud. In principle, they want to run the processes offered by these solutions as standardly as possible. Therefore, they would also like to leverage out-of-the-box integration content produced and managed by SAP for integration scenarios between these cloud solutions.

- The design should connect to the SAP systems in hyperscaler IaaS with minimum effort while providing maximum security.

- Some integration scenarios need the user context to be available in the backend service to apply authorizations for data retrieval and operations.

Surely, the requirements can be detailed further; however, Cecilia creates a design to be the core of the new cloud integration platform and cater to these generic requirements.

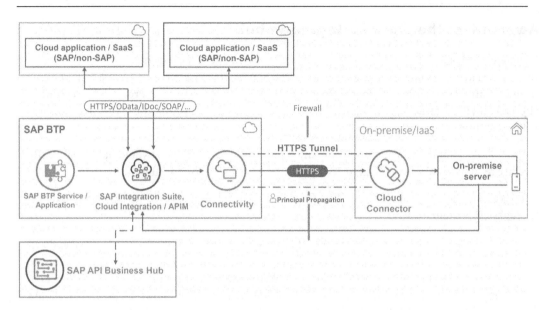

Figure 7.13: The design for a common cloud integration platform

As depicted in *Figure 7.13*, the design positions **SAP Integration Suite, Cloud Integration,** and **APIM** capabilities at the center. With these two (**Cloud Integration** and **APIM**), Company A can implement virtually any integration scenario.

The design includes **SAP API Business Hub** as the source for out-of-the-box prebuilt integration content that can be copied into the **Cloud Integration** tenant and operated for integration scenarios between SAP cloud solutions. As Company A wants to maximize the use of standard content and processes, they will not edit the integration content and keep receiving updates from SAP.

The design includes SAP **Cloud Connector** installed close to the SAP systems migrated to hyperscaler IaaS. Although IaaS is a cloud deployment model, the software is still on-premise, and therefore, the integration scenarios should be considered as cloud to on-premise. With SAP **Cloud Connector** and the SAP BTP **Connectivity** service, secure connectivity is established between SAP BTP and on-premise applications. This is the most convenient way, as it doesn't require low-level infrastructure changes, such as firewall changes, every time a new system needs to be connected to SAP BTP. In addition, SAP **Cloud Connector** provides secure connectivity.

Including SAP **Cloud Connector** in the design also unlocks the use of **principal propagation** by **Cloud Integration** and **APIM** to send the logged-in user context to the backend systems. This way, the backend system can check whether the user is authorized for the requested operation and record the actual username against the changelog.

## A version of the digital integration hub

**Company B** has a SAP Business Suite system that is hosted in one of the hyperscaler IaaS. Their digital channel includes a customer portal web application that needs to retrieve customer data from the SAP Business Suite system. Today, the main data retrieval happens through **SAP Process Orchestration** (**PO**) and **SAP Gateway** (**GW**), where these middleware systems eventually call the SAP Business Suite system to retrieve data.

As part of its cloud transformation, Company B purchased SAP BTP and would like to efficiently leverage its cloud qualities to integrate its digital channels and back-end enterprise systems.

Jacob is a senior technical architect working for Company B and needs to produce a design that fulfills the high-level requirements here:

- Today, Company B needs to make its customer portal unavailable when the IT team takes down the backend systems for maintenance. They want to improve the availability of their customer portal. At this initial stage, they are happy to restrict the customer portal to allow customers to only display their data when the backend systems are unavailable; however, the design should maximize the availability. They would also like to improve the response time for the services where possible, providing a performance boost for a better customer experience.

- Their middleware systems struggle to cope with peak loads. As they heavily invest in cloud transformation, they do not want to pay more for on-premise software licenses and maintenance fees. Instead, they prioritize migrating integrations to the cloud, which offers OpEx licensing models.

- They would like to control the access to the backend services and create a governance layer, as they have plans to introduce other internal and external applications to consume these services.

- Company B knows that they are beginning a transformation journey; therefore, at this initial stage, they want to keep the existing integrations and phase them out as they transition to the cloud.

While researching, Jacob comes across a pattern that may be applied for the solution, referred to as a **digital integration hub**, and tailors it as in *Figure 7.14* to fulfill the requirements.

Due to the monolith on-premise systems with heavy operational maintenance procedures and rigidness for scalability, it makes sense to replicate the most accessed business data to a cloud database. For this, Jacob includes the **SAP HANA Cloud, HANA DB** in the design. The business data in the SAP Business Suite system is replicated in near real time using the **SAP Landscape Transformation** (**SLT**) system. We will explore SAP SLT further in the next chapter.

Being an in-memory database, SAP HANA DB will provide faster data retrieval, too. To achieve higher availability, he proposes to create one **replica** for the SAP HANA Cloud, HANA DB, so that, in case of failure, the system can automatically switch over to this synchronously replicated database instance without disruption. Because this design is for a customer-facing application, the cost for the replica is justified. However, as a design principle, it is suggested that only the bare minimum data required for the customer portal is replicated and necessary governance is established.

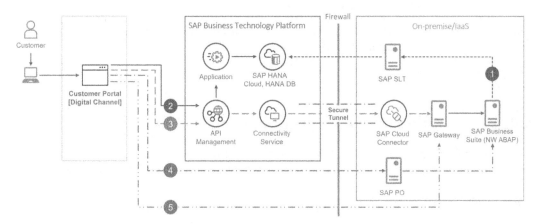

Figure 7.14: The design for a digital integration hub

We will cover application development in *Chapter 9* – just to briefly touch upon the relevant element in this design, a number of applications will be implemented and deployed in SAP BTP to read data from the HANA DB and expose them as OData services. These can be written in **Node.js** or **Java** using the CAP model, which makes the implementation and operation of these applications easy. Furthermore, to achieve higher availability for these applications, they will be deployed with a minimum of two instances, so that SAP BTP can automatically handle the workload routing in case of an application instance crash.

At the edge, the design includes the SAP APIM service as an access control layer through which the digital channels consume APIs. The APIs are exposed to the necessary security and traffic control policies provided by SAP APIM.

To cater to high-priority write scenarios, some APIs are implemented in SAP APIM that will consume the OData services exposed by the existing SAP GW hub system. These services access the backend SAP Business Suite system to execute business logic. SAP APIM calls these services safely through the secure tunnel created between the **SAP BTP Connectivity service** and **SAP Cloud Connector**.

To summarize, there are now five routes through which business data travels, as depicted in *Figure 7.14*:

1.  Shown with short, dashed lines, [- - -(1)- - -], the business data is replicated in near real time via SAP SLT to the SAP HANA Cloud, SAP HANA DB.

2.  Shown with solid lines, [--(2)--], the digital channel consumes a read API through SAP APIM, which retrieves data through applications, eventually reading data from the SAP HANA Cloud, HANA DB.

3.  Shown with long dashed lines, [– – (3) – –], the digital channel consumes a write API exposed by SAP APIM, which leverages the OData services in the on-premise SAP GW hub system to execute business logic at the back-end system.

4.  Shown with lines of dash and one dot, [ _._. (4) ._.], the digital channel consumes a web service via SAP PO, which then accesses the back-end system.

5.  Shown with lines of dash and two dots, [ _.._.. (5) .._...], the digital channel consumes a web service via SAP GW, which then accesses the back-end system.

## A B2G integration scenario for submitting tax returns

**Company C** is a company based in the United Kingdom. Through its Making Tax Digital initiative, the UK's tax authority (HMRC) requires companies to submit certain types of taxes electronically. Company C uses SAP S/4HANA on-premise as their finance system. All of their finance data resides in this SAP S/4HANA system, and they recently upgraded it to version 2021.

**Bilguun** is a solution architect working for Company C and needs to design a solution so that Company C can submit tax returns to the HMRC electronically. As the data source is an SAP system, he checks the options available in the SAP solution portfolio and designs the solution using the **Document and Reporting Compliance service**, a SaaS offering SAP built on SAP BTP:

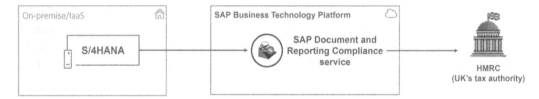

Figure 7.15: A solution design for electronic tax submission

As illustrated in *Figure 7.15*, in this solution, the business generates tax data using the standard functionality in the SAP S/4HANA system, which has been available since version 1610. After the data is generated, they can submit it to HMRC. With that, the SAP S/4HANA system forwards the tax data to the Document and Reporting Compliance service, which sends the tax data to HMRC. SAP manages this service; therefore, by using it, Company C offloads the responsibility of managing the electronic tax submission to this service. If HMRC requires a change to the electronic tax submission procedure, SAP applies it by updating this service.

# Using events to enhance business partner data

**Company D** needs to be prudent about the business partners they work with. Therefore, they would like to extend how they manage business partners in their SAP S/4HANA system.

After a business user creates a business partner record, the following is required:

- The new business partner needs to be categorized based on complex logic, which takes time.

- For certain types of business partners, a specific team needs to be informed to manage verifications that can only be done manually. The team uses Slack to keep track of such inbound verification notifications.

- For certain types of business partners, an email needs to be sent to a third-party supplier, so that they can run other checks for the business partner and notify Company D of the result via an API.

**Arina** is a technical architect working for Company D and produces a solution catering to the requirements above, as depicted in *Figure 7.16*:

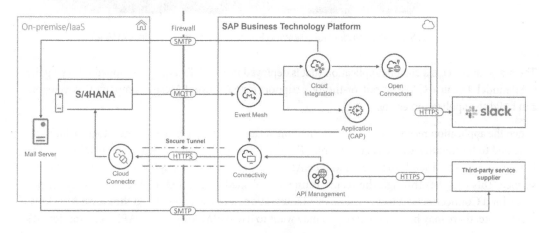

Figure 7.16: A solution design using events to enhance business partner data in S/4HANA

Let's check how the design components fulfill the requirements. The story starts with a change in SAP S/4HANA. Arina researched SAP API Business Hub and found that SAP S/4HANA publishes an event when a business partner is created, as you can see in *Figure 7.17*. This means she can use SAP Event Mesh so that subscriber applications can listen to this event and act accordingly. By the way, have you noticed that the example payload in the screenshot complies with the CloudEvents specification?

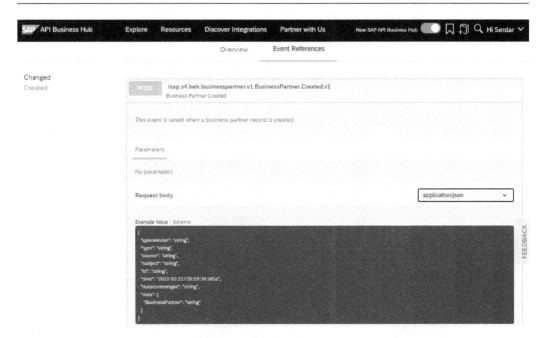

Figure 7.17: SAP API Business Hub showing Business Partner events in S/4HANA

The first subscriber is a custom application that is deployed in SAP BTP and is developed following the CAP model. Because CAP has out-of-the-box support for SAP Event Mesh, Company D developers can build the application easily.

When the application receives the event information, it can run the necessary business logic, which was specified to be complex in the requirements. The application calculates categorization values for the business partner and sends them back to the SAP S/4HANA system through a direct call to an OData service. This call goes through the secure tunnel established by the SAP BTP Connectivity service and Cloud Connector. Because it's an internal integration, it doesn't need to go through SAP APIM. Just to note, there may be cases where you may want to use APIM for internal API consumption. It's just not needed in this design.

The second subscriber is the Cloud Integration capability of the SAP Integration Suite service. When Cloud Integration receives the event, after any other transformation and mediation steps, it forwards the integration to two different receivers. The first receiver is an on-premise mail server, through which an email is sent to the third-party service provider. The second receiver is SAP Open Connectors, which can forward information to the Slack collaboration channel through the prebuilt connector.

We haven't included this in the diagram so as not to make it too crowded: both the custom application and the Cloud Integration flow can make calls to the SAP S/4HANA system to get further information and enrich message content.

Finally, the third-party service supplier calls an API exposed through SAP APIM, which forwards the request to the SAP S/4HANA system to update the business partner record accordingly. Again, this happens through the secure tunnel established by the SAP BTP Connectivity service and Cloud Connector.

## Summary

We must say there are lots of other topics that we could discuss under cloud integration. For example, we could delve into B2B integration implementation using Integration Advisor. Or talk about the industry, or LoB-specific standard integration platforms, such as **Ariba Cloud Integration Gateway** (**CIG**), Document and Reporting Compliance service, Peppol Exchange Service, multi-bank connectivity, market communication in **Cloud for Utilities** (**C4U**), or the Information Collaboration Hub for Life Sciences. However, covering all of these in this book would be beyond its scope. We believe this chapter's well-adjusted content is sufficient for architects to grasp most of the foundational concepts and design cloud integration architectures.

Integration is a vital domain for SAP; hence, it invests a lot to make its integration platform feature-rich so that it caters to almost all integration requirements, as expected from a complete **enterprise integration platform as a service** (**EiPaaS**). Besides, SAP invests in making this platform easy and convenient to use. This is where *low-code development* experience comes into the picture, as with the editor for building flows in Cloud Integration or the editor for managing API policies in APIM.

In the respective sections of this chapter, we have discussed the following:

- SAP Cloud Integration's transformation, mediation, and orchestration capabilities.

- How SAP APIM helps expose APIs securely and provides policies as a control layer.

- How SAP Open Connectors formalizes and accelerates building integrations with well-known third-party applications.

- Why we need event-driven integration and how SAP Event Mesh enables it.

- How SAP MDI and SAP ODM tackle master data integration.

- What SAP Graph offers and how it hides the complexity of large landscapes with several applications.

In the final section, we discussed many examples demonstrating these capabilities, which hopefully give you an idea of where you can leverage the SAP BTP integration services for addressing integration challenges.

In the next chapter, we will cover data integration. We will further discuss how data integration differs from the cloud integration topics we covered in this chapter. Then, we will delve into SAP solutions for data integration and work on some example designs.

# 8

# Data Integration

You may remember from the previous chapters that we separated data integration from other integration use cases covered under cloud integration. Since data integration differs from the process integration style, the patterns and tools used for these two categories are distinct.

With **data integration**, we bring together data from different sources so that the combined data has a meaning for a specific purpose. This may be for operational requirements; however, it is mostly for analytics and reporting purposes such as producing business insights or replicating data into a data warehouse. Data integration is also naturally relevant to big data and **artificial intelligence (AI)/ machine learning (ML)** use cases.

As you can remember, we covered master data integration in the previous chapter because its patterns and motivations are more akin to the process integration style.

We will cover the following topics in this chapter:

- Why do we need data integration?
- SAP Data Intelligence
- Other SAP solutions for data integration

## Technical requirements

The simplest way to try out the examples in this chapter is to get a trial **SAP Business Technology Platform (BTP)** account or an account with a free tier, as described in the *Technical requirements* section of *Chapter 3, Establishing a Foundation for SAP Business Technology Platform*.

## Why do we need data integration?

We have highlighted many times how today's world necessitates enterprises to be intelligent. This intelligence can only be established on the foundation of quality data that is managed systematically. **Hybrid** and **heterogeneous information technology (IT)** landscapes expose the usual challenge here because businesses need to bring together data from disparate sources in order to produce actionable insights.

Distributed data across several systems is one side of the story. With the recent advancements in the IT world, innovative businesses have a great appetite to exploit data that is sophisticated in many dimensions. In data science, these are formulated as the 5 V's of big data: **Volume**, **Variety**, **Velocity**, **Veracity**, and **Value**, as represented in the following diagram:

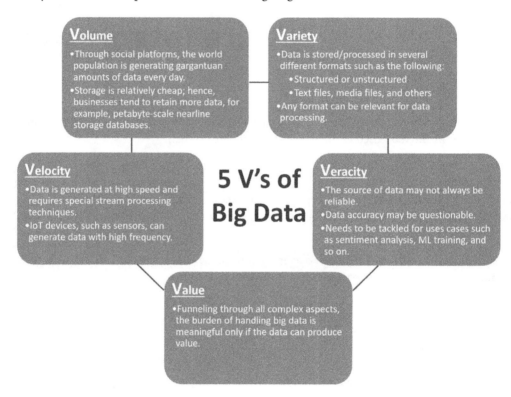

Figure 8.1: The 5 V's of big data

*Figure 8.1* illustrates the 5 V's of big data and provides brief examples. Although these dimensions define big data, they are still relevant when projected to smaller-scale data management. Leaving the other parts to you as a thought exercise, let's now focus on the *value* part and elaborate.

To harvest the fruits of your investment in establishing a data platform, you need to make sure the data can produce value. This is a prerequisite for an efficient digital transformation and an intelligent enterprise. When you remove this aspect from your motivation, you will face the trap of magpie culture, hoarding data for no beneficial purposes.

Let's understand some examples of how data can produce value, as follows:

- **Actionable insights**: The world is becoming extremely dynamic, where several intertwined factors influence a consequence. Businesses need to survive in this dynamism and efficiently deal with the chaos it creates. For that, the decision-makers heavily depend on data analytics, which provides them with actionable insights, such as the lights of a glide path for planes or a harbor lighthouse for ships. The decision-makers need access to concise data distilled into insights that help them see trends and set strategies.

- **Predictive analytics**: Predictive analytics can take insights to the next level, providing predictions. Although a human touch is inevitable for critical decisions, having the support of analytics done with an objective science would help. Predictive algorithms, AI, ML, and automation can unlock the next stage of digital transformation: **autonomous enterprises**.

- **Real-time stream processing**: With the **internet of things** (**IoT**) and mobile technologies, smart devices and sensors create a world that is more interconnected than ever. The technology can tackle high-velocity data by stream processing techniques to extract insight from streams of events and respond immediately to changing conditions. The streaming data can be fed into real-time monitoring dashboards for critical operations. For example, with **predictive maintenance**, sensor data can be used together with AI/ML and predictive analytics to predict anomalies in equipment. This is a foundational element of **Industry 4.0**.

Today, we have the technology to tackle data-related complexities and generate tremendous value. As a result, businesses implement data-to-value scenarios as a differentiator for gaining momentum in their competition.

For example, with the advanced technology in its foundation, **SAP HANA** brings **online transaction processing** (**OLTP**) and **online analytical processing** (**OLAP**) together in one database platform. Besides, with **Smart Data Access** (**SDA**), SAP HANA federates data access where a query can access data in a remote database without moving the persistent data. SDA lets you define a **data fabric** because the data is accessed as if it is all part of the same entity.

However, the aforementioned SAP HANA features have their use in certain circumstances and do not eliminate the need for data warehouses or moving persistent data from one database to another. Therefore, data integration and orchestration solutions are still relevant in modern architecture designs.

Now, let's return to the integration domain and see how data integration is different from process integration. At the end of the day, in both cases, data travels between systems, right?

## How is data integration different from process integration?

The main point separating data integration from other integration patterns is the integration scenario being **data oriented**. What does this mean?

In a process integration scenario, the amount of data that flows between applications is generally small because it deals with a particular business object. In some instances, such as searching, this may include multiple objects; however, the data volume is still relatively low. Besides, the integration needs to be at the process-aware application level because it runs explicitly for a business process and probably with the involvement of a user who is expecting to see results in a relatively short period of time.

As you can gather from our earlier discussions in this chapter, data integration is more about moving data where process integration techniques would not be efficient due to factors increasing complexity. Here, remember the 5 Vs we discussed earlier in this chapter. That's why we generally push down the operation to a lower level—that is, to the database level, where we can apply techniques that can deal with large amounts of data, tackle the processing of data generated with high frequency, or replicate data very fast. Alternatively, when the operation is at the application layer, it is specifically calibrated for the data perspective.

## Data integration techniques

For data integration, mainly depending on the complexity of the landscape, you can choose different techniques, as outlined here:

- You can consolidate data from several systems into a single platform, such as bringing data into a data warehouse system.

- You can move data between systems as required, such as synchronizing data between different systems—for example, by using **change data capture** (**CDC**) at the source.

- You can establish a layer that can retrieve data from different systems, concealing the complexity and presenting this layer as a unified data layer, such as SAP Graph.

- You can federate/virtualize data access, such as using SAP HANA SDA, as discussed earlier.

You can use **extract-transform-load** (**ETL**) procedures when you need to move data between systems. Most data integration solutions on the market provide ETL capabilities that include connectivity with different types of databases to retrieve or write data and functions for data transformation. For example, **SAP Data Services** is an on-premise solution that provides comprehensive data integration capabilities. Another example is **SAP Landscape Transformation Replication Server** (**SLT**), which offers powerful replication technology, especially for scenarios where the source is an **ABAP-based system**-based system.

If the integration target is an SAP HANA database, you can also use **SAP HANA Smart Data Integration** (**SDI**). With SDI, you can create flowgraphs that contain ETL procedures for reading data from a supported source database, transforming it, and writing it to the SAP HANA database.

On the other hand, if it is about processing event data that is generated with high frequency, you can leverage **complex event processing** (**CEP**) or **event stream processing** (**ESP**) technologies. Event brokers such as **SAP Event Mesh** can handle event processing to a certain degree. For more complex data, you can use technologies such as **SAP HANA Streaming Analytics**, **Apache Kafka**, and **Apache Flink,** which are specialized products for ESP scenarios. For example, these technologies can persist event streams in contrast to an event broker, which deletes an event after it's consumed. In addition, they can enrich, transform, filter, and combine data through the processing pipeline. Another feature these technologies can provide is **event sourcing**, where the system stores state change as a sequence of events by the time they happen. With event sourcing, you can reconstruct the state of an object that was valid at an arbitrary point in time.

SAP Data Intelligence is a strategic solution SAP offers; therefore, we will cover it in more detail in the next section. Afterward, we will also cover some of the technologies we mentioned previously.

# SAP Data Intelligence

Here, we discuss **SAP Data Intelligence** under the topic of data integration; however, calling it only a data integration tool would be a significant undervaluation. SAP positions it as an all-encompassing data management platform for governance, integration, orchestration, and processing of data. Besides, SAP Data Intelligence provides features to create, deploy and leverage ML models. For the sake of completeness, we will also briefly cover other SAP Data Intelligence features besides its data integration capabilities.

The following diagram depicts an overview of SAP Data Intelligence features and connection types it supports for implementing data management, integration, and ML use cases:

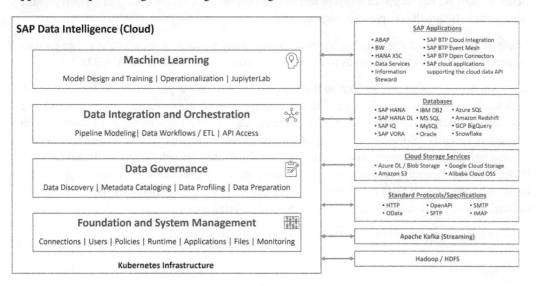

Figure 8.2: SAP Data Intelligence overview

## Foundations

Before getting into the capabilities, let's touch upon the architecture and foundation of SAP Data Intelligence. In fact, SAP Data Intelligence brings together the traditional data services SAP previously offered via SAP Data Hub and the ML features from the **SAP Leonardo Machine Learning Foundation (SAP Leonardo MLF)**. So, in a sense, SAP Data Intelligence is the successor for these two offerings.

> **Important note**
>
> At the time of writing this book, SAP announced two new SAP BTP services: **SAP AI Core** and **SAP AI Launchpad**. These services offer ML capabilities similar to SAP Data Intelligence; however, they are better suited for performance-intensive AI use cases. We are yet to see how SAP will position these offerings and the criteria to distinguish between use cases that better fit SAP Data Intelligence or SAP AI Core.

SAP Data Intelligence is built on top of a **Kubernetes** cluster. This makes the installation highly scalable and flexible to adjust under different performance requirements. The pipelines you build are deployed, executed, and managed as containerized applications.

You can install SAP Data Intelligence on-premise on an SAP-certified environment in your data center or an **infrastructure-as-a-service (IaaS)** provider's data center. On the other hand, you have the option of using SAP Data Intelligence Cloud, which is offered as a service via SAP BTP. The on-premise and cloud versions are equivalent in terms of features and capabilities, except the cloud version gets the latest features before the on-premise version.

After you have your SAP Data Intelligence environment ready, you can create users and assign **policies** to them. You can consider policies as roles that enable **role-based access control (RBAC)**.

Next, you need to define connections so that you can access data. As you can see in *Figure 8.2*, SAP Data Intelligence supports a plethora of connection types. With a connection, you basically define technical connectivity elements and authentication details. For SAP Data Intelligence Cloud, you can connect your tenant (Kubernetes cluster) to your on-premise systems via **SAP Cloud Connector**. Alternatively, you can connect via a **site-to-site virtual private network (VPN)** or **virtual network (VNet) peering**, depending on where your on-premise systems are hosted and the provider (hyperscaler) of the subaccount SAP Data Intelligence is provisioned. After the connectivity requirements are fulfilled, you can start using the capabilities of SAP Data Intelligence.

Here, you can see a screenshot of **SAP Data Intelligence Launchpad**:

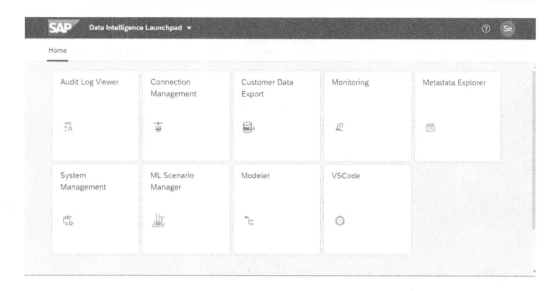

Figure 8.3: SAP Data Intelligence Launchpad

Launchpad is the single point of entry for all SAP Data Intelligence functionalities. Depending on the policies (roles) assigned to a user, the Launchpad can have a different number of tiles. Clicking on tiles navigates to applications, which we will discuss shortly. In addition, SAP Data Intelligence provides the flexibility to add other applications. For example, the **VSCode** application in *Figure 8.3* is a custom addition to the standard set of Launchpad tiles.

## Data governance

Let's make a start by thinking of a data scientist or a data engineer persona. You would be dealing with several data files with different structures, semantics, and formats so that you can produce value from an ocean of data. Before it becomes the task of finding a needle in a haystack, you need to adopt a systematic approach to handling the data. Without such an approach, as it goes with the popular saying among data scientists, your data lake may turn into a data swamp.

You can use SAP Data Intelligence's data governance capabilities to handle your data methodically. For example, after defining your connections, you can browse and *discover* data exposed from the corresponding systems. You can then produce metadata information and publish the data in the metadata catalog so that others can view or use the contents of the datasets. Next, you can *profile* the dataset so that more information about the dataset becomes available. After profiling, you can view the fact sheet for the dataset, which includes information such as column data types, unique keys, distinct values, percentage of null/blank values, and so on.

You can see an example of a fact sheet page here:

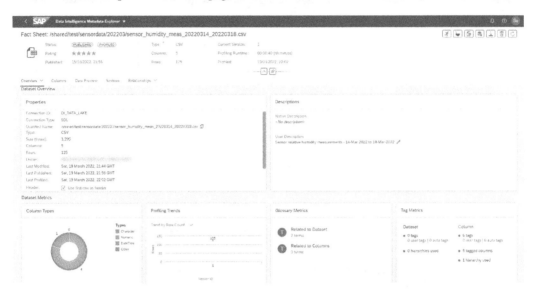

Figure 8.4: A fact sheet page for a dataset

The fact sheet page shown in *Figure 8.4* is for a dataset that comes from a comma-separated text file. Here, in addition to the information directly derived from the data, you can view and manage user descriptions, tags, relationships, reviews, and comments.

You can define **rules** for data validation and organize them under **rulebooks**. Then, you can run these rules for datasets to identify problems or anomalies. By using rules, you can realize the quality of your data and take necessary actions to improve its quality. If you are already using **SAP Information Steward** in your estate, SAP Data Intelligence can import rules from it via a connection or exported files. Lastly, you can create rules dashboards with scorecards to track trends in data quality.

You can create **glossaries** to add **terms** with their definitions to enrich semantics. You can then establish relationships between a term and another term, a dataset, a column of a dataset, a rulebook, or a rule.

After working on datasets by applying several operations to data from different sources, it may be important to remember the origins of the transformed data. By using **lineage** analysis, you can see where the data is coming from and the intermediary steps that transformed the data.

## Data integration and orchestration

Earlier, in the first section of this chapter, we already discussed the theoretical side of data integration and how it differs from process integration. As you may remember, data integration targets the challenges around cases where complexity increases in dimensions such as volume and frequency.

As a data platform, SAP Data Intelligence includes capabilities for processing data and moving data between several types of systems. You can create flow models for data integration and orchestration using these capabilities. In SAP Data Intelligence, these flow models are called **pipelines** or **graphs**. You will see these two terms used interchangeably. For consistency, we will use the term **pipeline** going forward. You can execute pipelines on an ad hoc basis or schedule them. If needed, you can schedule pipelines to run indefinitely.

## Modeler

The **SAP Data Intelligence Modeler** application is a graphical tool for creating and managing pipelines. As you can see in the following screenshot, it provides a canvas for adding a chain of operators to build pipelines. Behind the graphics, SAP Data Intelligence creates a **JavaScript Object Notation (JSON)** specification for the flow:

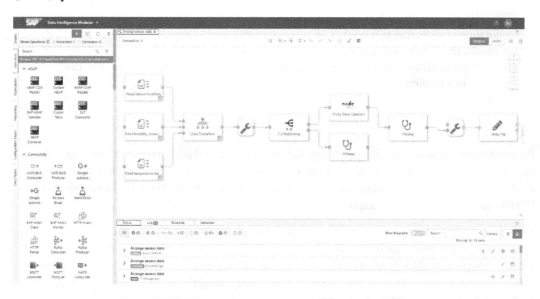

Figure 8.5: SAP Data Intelligence Modeler showing a pipeline

Using the Modeler, you can use one of the predefined graphs as a template for building your own pipeline. These can give you a head start when creating pipelines for typical scenarios. Besides, you can check them out as examples built by SAP.

Using the relevant section of the left pane, you can also access the repository to manage artifacts that are saved as files under several predefined folders. In addition, you can maintain operators, as well as configuration types and data types that are used in operators.

Finally, you can validate, run, schedule, and debug your pipelines using the Modeler. Relevant sections of the Modeler provide information on the execution of the graph, logs, failure reasons, metrics, and more.

### Operators

SAP Data Intelligence provides data functions in the form of **operators** that execute a single specific function. Operators include **input and output (I/O) ports** as required through which data flows. You create a pipeline by connecting a number of operators. There are more than 250 prebuilt operators. Let's briefly see what these operators do. But before we start, let's remind you that there are more examples than the ones we provide here. Also, it's always good to check the latest state of these operators as SAP adds new ones, and some may become deprecated.

> **Important note**
> At the time of authoring this book, SAP came up with a set of Generation 2 operators, which are practically new versions of operators that are not compatible with older operators and pipelines using older operators. Currently, you can use either Generation 1 or Generation 2 operators in a pipeline.

### ABAP operators

It's not surprising to see specific operators that access data in ABAP-based systems. The ABAP operators you include in a pipeline are actually just shells, and the processes of these operators are implemented in the ABAP system. Here, the ABAP system version and the **Data Migration Server (DMIS)** component version are important as they define the availability of operators and their versions.

For example, using **Core Data Services (CDS) / Operational Data Processing (ODP)** Reader operators, you can read data from **CDS views** and **ODP objects**. Alternatively, especially for **ERP Central Component (ECC)** systems and older **Suite for HANA (S/4HANA)** systems, you can establish a connection between SAP SLT (dedicated or embedded) using the SLT Connector operator and replicate tables from the source ABAP system.

The newer versions of these operators allow you to resume the execution of a pipeline in case it is stopped automatically or manually.

If needed, you can also create custom ABAP operators in your ABAP system by implementing a **business add-in (BAdI)**. By using custom operators, you can trigger the execution of custom logic in ABAP systems.

## Connectivity operators

This group of operators is for connecting to different SAP or non-SAP systems to read and write data. This includes generic protocol-level operators such as the following:

- **Hypertext Transfer Protocol (HTTP)** Client/Server operators

- **Message Queueing Telemetry Transport (MQTT)** Producer/Consumer operators

- **Web Application Messaging Protocol (WAMP)** Producer/Consumer operators

- Receive/Send Email operators (using **Internet Message Access Protocol (IMAP)** and **Simple Mail Transfer Protocol (SMTP)** protocols, respectively)

- OpenAPI Client operator, which can invoke **REpresentational State Transfer (REST)** services

- OpenAPI Servlow operator, which can serve **application programming interfaces (APIs)** by listening to calls made to a specific path

This group also includes product-specific operators, such as the following:

- **Amazon Web Services Simple Notification Service (AWS SNS)** Producer/Consumer operators

- **Google Pub/Sub** Producer/Consumer operators

- SAP HANA Client operator, which is a generic operator for executing **Structured Query Language (SQL)** statements and inserting data into an SAP HANA instance

- SAP HANA Monitor operator, which watches SAP HANA and outputs newly inserted rows

- **Kafka** Producer/Consumer operators

Finally, we can also consider in this group the operators that use the Flowagent subengine, such as the following:

- Table Replicator operator, which uses CDC technology and supports certain source and target connection types to replicate data between them

- Flowagent SQL Executor operator, which can execute arbitrary SQL statements in supported connection types

## Data workflow and external execution operators

Especially for orchestration purposes, you can invoke execution in external systems using data workflow and external execution operators. For example, you can start the execution of the following:

- SAP Business Warehouse (BW) process chains

- SAP HANA flowgraphs

- SAP Data Services jobs

- SAP Integration Suite, Cloud Integration iFlows

- Hadoop and Spark jobs

- Other SAP Data Intelligence pipelines

The data workflow operators return the execution status information, which means you can cascade them in data orchestration workflows with status feedback.

## SAP ML operators

We will briefly cover the ML capabilities of SAP Data Intelligence in the next section. To build your complete ML scenarios, you can create pipelines that include core ML operators. You can utilize these operators to train your models, submit model **key performance indicators (KPIs)**/metrics, deploy models, and send inference requests to your models or ML libraries in SAP HANA.

In addition to the core operators, you can use the functional services for typical ML scenarios such as image classification.

## File and structured data operators

It's typical to use files when dealing with data integration, especially for mass data processing. And as you can expect, SAP Data Intelligence provides operators to list, read, write, and delete files in supported connection types. Besides, you can use the Monitor Files operator, which polls the connected system for monitoring any file changes by comparing the list of files. The operator can highlight whether a file is added, changed, or removed.

If the data has a structure, the structured data operators can be used as they provide extra capabilities for structured data. For example, with the Data Transform operator, you can specify a set of transformation operations such as combining, aggregating, and joining datasets.

## Data quality operators

As part of a data integration scenario, you may want to improve the quality of data for which you can use the data quality operators. Here are some examples of operators you can use for different scenarios:

- Anonymization and Data Masking operators for protecting the privacy of individuals and other sensitive information

- Operators accessing **SAP Data Quality Management (DQM) microservices for location data** for address cleansing, and reverse geo lookups

- Person and Firm Cleanse operator for identifying people and firms data for cleansing purposes

- Validation Rule operator for building basic data validation rules to apply to data for filtering

### Custom processing operators

For complex data processing requirements, SAP Data Intelligence allows you to incorporate custom logic into your pipelines. For this, there are different alternatives. The easiest one is to use the processing operators that already exist in the list of prebuilt operators and provide you with a generic container to include your custom script. There are such operators for Python, R, Go, JavaScript and Node.js. You can also build scripts in **Continuous Computation Language** (**CCL**) for streaming analytics.

If you want to reuse the custom logic you build or encapsulate it in an operator structure, you can create custom operators in Modeler, as shown in the following diagram:

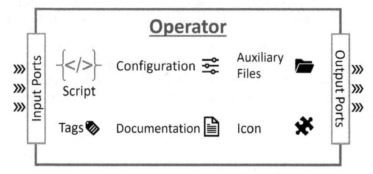

Figure 8.6 – Parts of an operator specification

As depicted in *Figure 8.6*, in order to create a custom operator, you need to specify the following:

- I/O ports so that the operator can interact with other operators in a pipeline. The input ports are used while listening to events that would trigger the execution of the operator. The output ports can provide input to the next operator in the pipeline. You can assign standard or custom data types to ports so that the pipeline engine can make sure the data flows consistently between operators.

- A script in one of the supported languages so that the operator runs the required logic to process data.

- Configuration parameters that can be used to configure the operator's function in a pipeline at design time.

- Tags that point to the type of container environment in which the operator will run its processing logic. When creating a custom operator, you select a built-in base operator. This base operator also determines the subengine, the foundational runtime environment that runs the operator and corresponds to a programming language. At the time of authoring this book, SAP Data Intelligence supported ABAP, Node.js, and Python subengines. Upon this foundation, you can also specify a specific container (Docker) environment to include extra elements such as libraries and frameworks for running the operator.

- Documentation that elaborates on the operator's function and provides specifications for its ports and configuration elements.

- Optional auxiliary files the script uses, such as binary executables.

- An icon that is displayed in the Modeler to represent the operator as a step.

**Utility operators**

Apart from the operators that are directly used for data processing, there are utility operators that can be used for convenience and design-time efficiency. For example, you can use the Wiretap operator by connecting it to the output of another operator whose output message you would like to inspect. Another example is the Application Logging operator, which you can use to write application messages as logs.

So far, we have covered a subset of operators, hoping they would be enough for you to grasp different types of operators and exemplify what they can do. You can get more information from the help documentation, which is also available within the Modeler. By concluding this section, we also complete the data integration section. Next, we will briefly touch upon the ML capabilities of SAP Data Intelligence.

# ML

SAP positions SAP Data Intelligence as a data management platform that allows data scientists to deal with all aspects of data processing using one single platform. This naturally includes ML tasks as well. SAP Data Intelligence is part of SAP's ML solutions, along with SAP HANA's ML capabilities and business AI services. As you may remember, this is practically a result of SAP Data Intelligence being the successor of the SAP Leonardo MLF. For example, in your pipelines, you can use the following SAP ML functional services, which can be added as operators in pipelines:

- Image classification

- Image feature extraction

- Optical character recognition (OCR)

- Similarity score

- Text classification

- Topic detection

SAP Data Intelligence provides more ML features than just using readily available services. Looking from a data scientist's perspective, it all starts with a dataset that is then profiled and prepared for further processing. We briefly covered the journey up to this point earlier in the *Data governance* section. At this point, the data scientist can begin developing an **ML scenario**.

You can register datasets to an ML scenario, which makes them consumable by the scenario via a unique technical **identifier (ID)**. Then, you can create **Jupyter notebooks** to run experiments on the dataset, including creating visualizations. As you can see in the following screenshot, in a Jupyter notebook, you can install Python libraries and run ML algorithms. For example, you can execute SAP HANA's **Predictive Analysis Library** (**PAL**) and **Automated Predictive Library** (**APL**) algorithms on data that resides in SAP HANA without moving it. Besides, you can leverage the **SAP Python software development kit** (**SDK**) **for Data Intelligence**, using which you can create and maintain SAP Data Intelligence elements, such as pipelines, configurations, and ML scenarios. Furthermore, you can use SAP Data Intelligence's scalable **Vora** database or use data from other connections, such as files from an Amazon **Simple Storage Service** (**S3**) bucket or the **Semantic Data Lake** (**SDL**):

Figure 8.7: An example Jupyter notebook in SAP Data Intelligence

When you are happy with your experiment, you can progress your work to create and execute pipelines to train your system. This way, you operationalize and productize your ML scenario. The metrics, KPIs, and models are saved as part of the ML scenario. Then, you can deploy your model upon which it becomes consumable by business applications via a REST API.

We will cover more about intelligent technologies in *Chapter 14, SAP Intelligent Technologies*. As we have stepped out of the main focus of this chapter, we needed to be very brief on this topic. Hoping that it provides essential information, let's get back to the topic of data integration by discussing other relevant SAP solutions.

## Other SAP solutions for data integration

SAP Data Intelligence is the future for data management; however, this doesn't mean it's the only tool you can use for data integration. As a strategic product, its focus is primarily on innovative use cases, and the support for older version software may have limitations. Nevertheless, you have other options, especially if you want to leverage your existing investment on on-premise tools or are just not ready to transition to a new tool. Let's briefly check out these other tools.

## SAP Data Services

**SAP Data Services**, previously known as **BusinessObjects Data Services (BODS)**, is a full-fledged on-premise data ETL tool. It supports powerful data transformation and quality features to move data between SAP and non-SAP systems.

If you have been an SAP customer for a while, you probably have SAP Data Services in your on-premise estate to handle data integration workloads as well as data migration requirements. Using jobs, you can build data flows that include transformation steps and move data in batch mode. In addition, SAP Data Services supports changed data capture for delta loads; however, its real-time replication capability is limited to responding to messages it receives—for example, from web applications.

As SAP Data Services has been the flagship data integration tool for on-premise, you may want to protect your investment in it. SAP acknowledges that the cloud transition is a long journey and there are valid reasons for on-premise usage. Therefore, SAP keeps supporting SAP Data Services. This includes the capability of SAP Data Intelligence to run SAP Data Services jobs in a remote system for data orchestration.

Let's think of an example. Levi is a solution architect and is working on designing a scenario that requires data from an SAP ECC system. The design includes SAP Data Intelligence to run pipelines for data processing. While designing, he realizes there is already an SAP Data Services job that reads the necessary data from the SAP ECC system. It looks as though the same data can be reused for the scenario he is working on, so he decides to leverage this existing investment to save time and cost. The flow in his design happens as depicted in the following diagram:

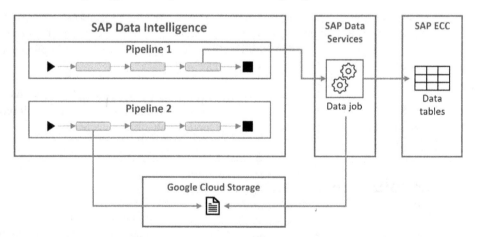

Figure 8.8: Data orchestration using SAP Data Services data jobs

Here's what happens:

1.  The first **SAP Data Intelligence** pipeline triggers the execution of the **SAP Data Services** job in one of its steps.

2.  Next, this job reads data from the **SAP ECC** system, applies transformation, and writes the transformed data to a file in **Google Cloud Storage**.

3.  Finally, another SAP Data Intelligence pipeline reads this file from **Google Cloud Storage** and uses it, for example, to enrich the data it's processing.

## SLT

One of the crucial elements of SAP's data management tools portfolio for on-premise is SLT. Before getting into what SLT is, we need to clarify a potential confusion point. There is another tool that is called **SAP Landscape Transformation**, and it is used for on-premise platform operations. What we are talking about here is the **SAP Landscape Transformation Replication Server**. It's a different product, and the widely used acronym for it is **SLT**. It's confusing because this acronym doesn't refer to the *Replication Server* part of the product's name.

The main use case where SLT shines is data replication from NetWeaver ABAP-based systems. SLT supports trigger-based *real-time* data replication, which is its most powerful feature, and can handle huge data volumes. You may remember how our example design for the digital integration hub pattern used SLT from the previous chapter.

As source systems, SLT supports all databases NetWeaver supports; hence, it supports non-SAP solutions based on these databases, too. In the source systems, changes are tracked by database triggers and are recorded in logging tables. SLT then reads the data from the application tables. Similarly, several SAP and non-SAP systems are supported as data replication targets. SLT writes changes to these systems using ABAP write modules, APIs, or database connections. Here, you have the flexibility to incorporate custom logic in read and write modules besides standard SLT capabilities such as filtering. After configuring SLT between source and target systems, you can initiate the initial load and then let SLT handle continuous delta replication.

SLT can be installed as a separate standalone system or used within the source or target systems (embedded or via the DMIS add-on) if they are ABAP-based systems. As the available features differ between S/4HANA and other systems and also between versions, you should check what is available for your system versions.

Although SAP Data Intelligence can access data in NetWeaver ABAP-based systems, its main focus is reading the data using CDS views, which is applicable for newer ABAP versions. For older systems, it can use SLT for table-based replication as well as the ODP interfaces.

Let's conclude our discussion on SLT with a basic example. Isidora is a solution architect tasked with producing a design for moving large volumes of data from three systems to a centralized data platform solution. These include an SAP S/4HANA version 2021 system, an SAP ECC 6.0 system, and an SAP BW on HANA system.

Her company uses SLT for replicating data from SAP systems to SAP HANA Cloud. Isidora finds out SAP Data Intelligence can access data in the **SAP S/4HANA** system using CDS views; however, she needs to include an SLT system in the design for the **SAP ECC** system.

The following diagram depicts the components included in Isidora's design:

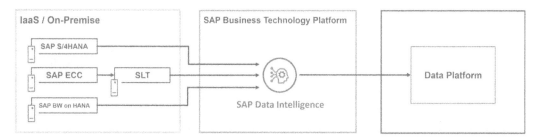

Figure 8.9: Using SAP Data Intelligence to read data from ABAP-based systems

As you can see in *Figure 8.9*, she positions **SLT** in between the **SAP ECC** system and **SAP Data Intelligence**. In this case, it's a standalone SLT system, as there is already one being used for other replication work, and provides flexibility for workload management.

### SDI

**Smart Data Integration** (**SDI**) is part of SAP HANA and provides ETL capabilities to load data into SAP HANA in batch and real time. It's coupled with **SAP HANA Smart Data Quality** (**SDQ**) for data-quality relevant features.

You may have already realized that SDI is built to load data only into SAP HANA as the target system. This can be an on-premise SAP HANA system or an SAP HANA Cloud instance. In order for SDI to work, you need to install the **Data Provisioning Agent** in the source system, which communicates with the **Data Provisioning Server** in SAP HANA for replicating data from the source system. For implementing the replication process, which can also include transformation steps, you need to develop flowgraphs or replication tasks, ideally using **SAP Business Application Studio** (**BAS**). SDI also provides REST APIs that you can use to execute and monitor flowgraphs. For example, SAP Data Intelligence uses these APIs to trigger flowgraphs. Using SDI, you can replicate data and data structures with an optional initial load. In addition, SDI provides partitioning if the data volume is very large.

The Data Provisioning Agent contains prebuilt adapters to communicate with the Data Provisioning Server from several types of source systems. Besides, you can create your own custom adapters if needed.

SDI is generally confused with SAP HANA SDA, another SAP HANA feature that allows the accessing of data in remote systems as if it is local to SAP HANA. Here, the idea is to access remote data via virtual objects without moving it, also referred to as data virtualization. SDI, on the other hand, is meant for moving data. We will also talk about SDI and SDA in the last part of this book.

For real-time data replication use cases where the target system is SAP HANA and the source system is—for example—an ABAP-based system, it seems we have two powerful options: SLT and SDI. Both have their advantages over the other. For example, you may already have SLT in your estate as it has been around for a while, which means you may want to protect your investment. SLT has better control and flexibility for ABAP-based source systems and supports several target systems. In addition, SLT is proven to handle huge volumes of data. On the other hand, SDI is native to SAP HANA, which means it runs within SAP HANA. The SDI development lifecycle can be aligned better with other SAP HANA artifacts, and if your team has SAP HANA skills, it may be easier to implement SDI, especially for leaner use cases. If SAP HANA Cloud is the target system, using SDI may mean that you do not need significant extra infrastructure resources. However, using SDI will put the load on SAP HANA, which may or may not be preferred.

As you can see, there is no clear-cut winner; hence, SAP keeps supporting both options. SDI may be a better choice if the main complexity of your use case is on the SAP HANA side or if you do not want to deal with an additional on-premise component. On the other hand, SLT may be the better alternative if you already use it, if the main complexity is at the source side (especially if it is an ABAP-based system), or if the data volume is really large. As usual, you need to assess these options, considering the specific requirements of your use case for a final decision.

### Other data integration solutions

So far, we have covered the flagship products from SAP's data integration solutions portfolio. However, some other offerings can be viable options in limited use cases.

**SAP Replication Server** (**SRS**) is another data replication tool SAP supports mainly to protect its customers' investments in solutions that got into the SAP products catalog with the Sybase acquisition. Although it can replicate data between different types of databases, it's mainly geared toward scenarios having **SAP Adaptive Server Enterprise** (**ASE**) or other Sybase products at the center.

**SAP Cloud Integration for Data Services** (**CI-DS**) is also a data integration tool with a specific scope. CI-DS is mainly used for bidirectional data transfer between **SAP Integrated Business Planning** (**IBP**) and on-premise SAP systems, such as SAP ECC, SAP S/4HANA, and SAP **Advanced Planner and Optimizer** (**APO**). It provides out-of-the-box content for such integration scenarios and relies on an on-premise agent for connectivity.

## Summary

This chapter focused on data integration, and we devoted most of it to SAP Data Intelligence since it is one of SAP's strategic tools for data management.

To set the stage, we discussed what data integration is and how it differs from process integration. While covering SAP Data Intelligence, we have been a bit cheeky and also briefly touched upon its capabilities not directly related to data integration. We believe this makes sense to provide a complete picture of SAP Data Intelligence capabilities.

Although it's strategic, SAP Data Intelligence may still need other components that complement its function, especially in hybrid landscapes and for protecting existing investments. Being one of the fastest-evolving SAP solutions, it may eventually become a one-stop shop for many data management requirements, from data governance to ML scenarios. However, there are other alternative solutions for data integration for now, and we concluded this chapter by briefly discussing them.

This chapter concludes the integration part, and with the next chapter, we will start discussing the extensibility capabilities of SAP BTP. First in line is the chapter for application development, where we will cover building applications using SAP BTP and the peripheral services that help application development.

# Part 4
# Extensibility

This part will help you understand how you can use SAP BTP to extend solutions at the innovation and agility layer by introducing the Extension Suite capabilities and use cases. We will also briefly cover what SAP BTP offers in the process automation area. Finally, if you are interested in learning more about containers and Kubernetes, the last chapter will give an overview as well as how SAP uses these technologies.

This part contains the following chapters:

- *Chapter 9, Application Development*
- *Chapter 10, Digital Process Automation*
- *Chapter 11, Containers and Kubernetes*

# 9
# Application Development

In this chapter, we are starting a whole new part of our book in which we will cover how SAP BTP facilitates application development. With the cloud transformation of business applications, especially with **Software-as-a-Service** (**SaaS**) solutions, businesses are encouraged to standardize their processes and leverage out-of-the-box functionality with the fit-to-standard mentality. However, the fast pace of change in IT and the impetus for innovation necessitate the development of extension applications to complement the core business solutions.

In the last decade, new application development paradigms emerged or gained traction. The open source movement has enabled large-scale collaboration, and together with connectivity and integration standards, it also improved the efficiency in interoperability between applications from different vendors. As a result, companies started using open source software in their commercial products, actively supporting their expansion and adoption. For example, SAP is a platinum member of Cloud Foundry, the **Platform-as-a-Service** (**PaaS**) foundation that underpins the SAP BTP multi-environment.

The application development capabilities of SAP BTP are primarily provided from the perspective of *extending* SAP's business solutions. Therefore, the relevant services are sometimes referred to as the **Extension Suite**. The naming here may be justified from certain aspects; however, using the application development services, you can also create independent and self-contained cloud applications on SAP BTP.

SAP BTP supports application development as a highly robust and flexible platform and includes best-of-breed development tools.

In this chapter, we will cover the following main topics:

- Implementing extensions
- Development platform types
- SAP BTP runtime environments
- Frontend applications
- Backend applications
- Mobile applications

- Application development tools

- Launchpad applications

- Non-functional design

- Other related services

- Deployment considerations

We will also apply what we learn to an example scenario for which we will produce an architecture design.

## Technical requirements

The simplest way to try out the examples in this chapter is to get a trial SAP BTP account or an account in which the free tier can be enabled, as described in the *Technical requirements* section of *Chapter 3*. For SAP AppGyver, you can sign up for free at `https://www.appgyver.com/` and check out how you can build applications with it. SAP may change this as they integrate SAP AppGyver into the SAP BTP ecosystem.

> **Note**
> Remember, this book is not meant to contain step-by-step instructions; instead, we provide higher-level design examples for architects, which should also work as pointers for those who want to dig deeper and learn the lower-level details.

## Implementing extensions

Do you need to implement an extension? We have started by asking this question on purpose. For business applications, there is a strong trend toward SaaS applications. With SaaS solutions, businesses expect to reduce the total cost of ownership by primarily staying away from the complexities of running the operations below the application layer. In such cases, companies are happy to give up on the flexibility of on-premise deployment models. As a result, we see the fit-to-standard approach is within the principles of most SAP S/4HANA transformation programs, where businesses intend to standardize their processes and align with the models put forward by the SaaS solutions. Some companies are much keener on standardization after the bad experience they've encountered due to the high level of modifications and customizations they've applied to their systems in the past.

On the other hand, as we learned in this chapter's introduction, creating extension applications is almost inevitable due to the fast-paced change in IT and the drive for innovation. These are motivations in addition to the traditional modification requirements where businesses change how an application runs processes so that they adapt them to their custom business needs. This, in a way, contradicts the trend that comes with SaaS solutions.

So, complete standardization is still too ambitious for many companies, and extensive customization is somewhat discouraged as it will bring many maintenance headaches. Acknowledging the reality of the dilemma between the two ends, SAP provides extensibility options at different levels, which helps its customers to adjust according to their requirements. While making these options available, SAP encourages keeping the core clean by using formalized extensibility methods.

SAP puts a massive effort into providing optimized business processes and delivers localization where needed. This is one of the primary strengths of SAP solutions. The main track for standard usage of these solutions is determined by the out-of-the-box models and processes provided in the solutions and the best practices suggested by SAP.

So, we agree that there will be custom-built extension applications. Before these applications get out of control, it would be wise to create a framework for extension governance and methodology. You may remember **SAP Integration Solution Advisory Methodology (ISA-M)** from *Chapter 6, Defining Integration Strategy*. Although not as established as ISA-M, there is a similar work for extensions called **SAP Application Extension Methodology**. You can check it out as a template for your extension governance framework. Another tool you can look at is the **SAP Extensibility Explorer**. Although the name is generic, its content is built specifically for SAP S/4HANA Cloud at the time of writing this book.

## Extensibility options

Before discussing the extensibility options, let's remind ourselves that we are looking at scenarios for implementing an extension in the cloud. Now, let's list the three layers where extensions can be relevant:

- **Data**: This is about extending the standard data model with extra data fields or even complete data entities peculiar to your processes. An extension at this layer generally cascades extensions in other layers.

- **Application**: In the application layer, an extension corresponds to a change in the business process flow or data processing. For example, you may change the business logic that determines a process milestone, amend the formula that calculates an aggregation, or manipulate data as per your custom requirements. For sophisticated extension requirements, this can even be an isolated application integrated into the standard business process and may have its own storage and user interface.

- **Presentation**: You may want to tailor the user interface according to your needs. This may be a user experience improvement, for example, by hiding unused fields or changing the layout. Another example would be adding new user interface components, such as showing static or dynamic text or displaying custom data with which you extended the standard data model.

Now, let's talk about extension options. Here, we will cover S/4HANA Cloud extensibility options. Be aware that we aim to provide a helicopter view so that you can observe how SAP BTP is positioned for implementing extensions.

If you come from a technical SAP background, you must know the concepts of **enhancements** and **modifications** in the on-premise ABAP-based SAP solutions. With modifications, you have the full power to change almost anything, whereas enhancements, such as **customer exits** and **business add-ins (BAdIs)**, provide a formalized and more controlled approach. Again, if you are a seasoned technical SAP professional, you must already know why to stay away from modifications and even complex enhancements unless they are really necessary since they complicate upgrades and transformations.

As you can expect, there is no modification option in SaaS applications since the vendor shares certain responsibilities and manages the underlying platform and the software, where modifications cannot be allowed. So, instead, formalized extension approaches are provided, which also guarantee stability as they are upgrade-proof. Let's look at them.

### In-app extensibility

Also called **key user extensibility**, this option includes low-code and no-code tools that enable users to implement extensions in a restricted scope. In addition, the tools are highly streamlined so that even key users, who do not necessarily have deep technical knowledge, can implement the extensions. Here, the extension points and the **extensible objects** are defined by SAP, which limits flexibility. Nevertheless, in-app extensibility caters to many business requirements.

For instance, with in-app extension tools in SAP S/4HANA Cloud, you can add a custom field at the data layer. Then, necessary extensions can be applied across all layers (for example, CDS views, business objects, and **Open Data (OData)** services to use the added field in business logic and the user interface.

### Developer extensibility

With this option, you have more flexibility to fulfill more complicated extension requirements. You can create fully custom development objects that interact with the core application components via released objects to maintain a stability contract between these and your custom development. For SAP S/4HANA Cloud, this means you can develop custom ABAP objects on the same stack of the SAP S/4HANA Cloud application. The interaction between these is based on lower-level ABAP components such as BAdIs, classes, interfaces, CDS views, behavior definitions, and authorization objects that are released for extension use cases.

### Side-by-side extensibility

With this extensibility option, you can detach your custom development fully from the main applications running the business process you would like to extend. This means you define the scope of extension and how much it relates to the standard business processes. Therefore, the extension relies on integration between the custom-developed objects and the standard applications, which happens mainly through APIs (OData or SOAP) and events. For SAP S/4HANA Cloud, you can also add BAPIs and IDocs to the list.

For side-by-side extensibility, the recommended environment is SAP BTP, which provides capabilities and facilities that work well with the SAP solutions. With SAP BTP, you can use ABAP or non-ABAP programming to create extension applications. We will discuss these shortly in a later section.

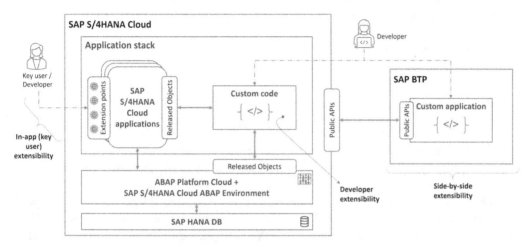

Figure 9.1 – Extensibility options for S/4HANA Cloud

The preceding diagram illustrates all extension options for SAP S/4HANA Cloud. As you can see, SAP BTP is mainly relevant for side-by-side extensibility, where you can create decoupled custom applications that integrate with SAP S/4HANA Cloud.

As mentioned previously, we deliberately started our discussion regarding application development by focusing on extensibility. This is because you should have an informed idea of what you aim to do with the application you are creating. While acknowledging the valid reasons for extension use cases, we want to highlight the importance of keeping the core clean and using the standard as much as possible.

That said, application development on SAP BTP cannot be confined to standard application scenarios only. As we mentioned previously, an extension can have a very loose relationship with standard applications and can be scoped as an extension to a business process in a broader aspect. Meanwhile, you can also create fully independent applications on SAP BTP. This includes, for example, creating SaaS applications that you can commercially offer to your customers, partnering with SAP to implement Industry Cloud solutions, or building cutting-edge innovative solutions to support your intelligent enterprise transformation.

# Development platform types

Over the last two decades, the way we develop software has changed dramatically. This is a result of several technological advancements, such as cloud, mobile, IoT, AI/ML, and more. In addition, agility in developing software gained importance due to increasing competition, and the IT industry came up with numerous programming languages, paradigms, frameworks, and patterns. With all these, the tools used by developers needed to support much more than coding. We will talk about tools in the *Application development tools* section later; here, we want to discuss the rise of a new development platform type, along with all these changes.

## Low-code/no-code development

One part of the story is about the tools and which convenience features they provide for developers. This includes hiding some of the complexity behind patterns, boilerplate codes, and reusability. For many scenarios, applications share similar components, and for the parts that differ from scenario to scenario, the development platform can let the developers provide them as configuration elements. If that is the case, why not bring a graphical editor to visualize the data model, application components, the flow, and the user interface structure while letting developers input specifics as configuration? This was the trend when **rapid application development (RAD)** approaches got traction in the IT world. RAD introduced elements that complemented traditional application development with tooling that made developers' lives easier.

Following the train of thought here, vendors took this to the next step, where all the aforementioned elements were abstracted at a separate layer hiding the generated code. So, the platform can take away control over the actual code running the application. What remains for the developer is almost a lean application description that can be converted into the lower-level design time and runtime elements as needed. Because these platforms require low code and even maybe no code at all for application development, they are called **low-code/no-code (LCNC)** development platforms.

If your requirements are straightforward to develop in this fashion, this sounds great, doesn't it? And there is one plus side to this as well. This convenience also means the entry barrier for learning to build such applications has become much lower. This is not only because of the capabilities provided by the LCNC platforms but also because the IT literacy of non-IT people has increased as a result of IT becoming an essential part of the business world and even our personal lives. Today, we call such people **citizen developers** as they are not necessarily dedicated developers; however, they have the skills to develop certain types of applications that would make their personal or work lives easier. Here, we can make a further distinction between no-code and low-code. However, the names are already quite intuitive, giving away what they mean.

The LCNC practices can be the main ethos of the platform if it is specifically for LCNC development. Besides, LCNC elements can also be embedded features of a development platform. You have already seen examples of this in previous chapters. For example, SAP Integration Suite and SAP Data Intelligence contain graphical editors that can be considered low-code components.

# Pro-code development

Are you a developer concerned that LCNC may threaten your job security? Feel no fear at all. The business world is very IT-orientated; we can almost say every sizable company is also a technology company, and lots of sophisticated IT work requires advanced programming techniques and flexibility. As this is the default mode for application development, it doesn't need a specific name; however, in contexts where development platforms are discussed, it is called **pro-code development**. As you can guess, this chapter is mostly about pro-code development. So, we will cut it short here and move on to the next section, where we will provide a comparison of the various development options.

# Comparison

There are use cases where LCNC development or pro-development is more appropriate, and this is mainly driven by the complexity of the application. The highly formalized development approach put forward by the LCNC platforms may become insufficient to implement sophisticated features, and the level of extensibility and performance optimization may be limited. On the other hand, the LCNC approach can save significant time and money for many use cases. LCNC platforms also allow citizen developers to develop creative solutions that help them do their job more efficiently, whereas getting the same functionality developed through pro-development delivery channels would be too bureaucratic, hence off-putting.

There is a gray area between the two ends where decision-making between the two approaches may be tricky. At the end of the day, these two approaches can co-exist. The fundamental requirement here is establishing an application development governance framework that identifies when to use which approach. It's best to keep LCNC platforms accessible to citizen developers as this will empower them while reducing the work funneled to the development teams, reducing their workload. For more complex cases that will be built by dedicated LCNC development teams, necessary controls and safeguards should be incorporated into the delivery mechanism of such applications. After these have been established, LCNC can provide remarkable opportunities for citizen developers and for developing certain application types.

# SAP AppGyver

So, as part of your IT estate, you should keep your options open and wish to invest in LCNC platforms. In terms of LCNC platform solutions, you have several options in the market. Concerning your SAP estate, you can use SAP's own offering, **SAP AppGyver**. If you plan to use another vendor's product, such as **Mendix** or **Microsoft Power Platform**, make sure you understand its capabilities around specific support for SAP solutions, such as native connectors or plugins.

> **Important Note**
>
> When deciding which LCNC product to use, consider the licensing impact of Digital Access (indirect use) as accessing SAP systems from third-party applications may require additional license entitlements. Check with your SAP Account Executive to see whether your use case is relevant to Digital Access licensing.

SAP AppGyver is mainly positioned as a no-code platform and, typical with LCNC platforms, it needs you to primarily define the following elements to build an application:

- **Data model**: You define the data model that will be used by the application. SAP AppGyver lets you use on-device storage, REST API integration, OData integration, and Google Firestore as data sources.

- **Pages**: You define several pages as required by your application. For each page, you set the layout, include page components, and apply data binding for the components that will be linked to the data sources. In pages, you can add logic so that your page can react to events. Here, SAP AppGyver allows you to add basic JavaScript code.

- **Navigation**: You can define the navigation flow between the application pages and configure the navigation menu and style navigation elements.

The following screenshot shows SAP AppGyver's page-building editor:

Figure 9.2 – Building a page for an SAP AppGyver application

On the left are screen components that you can drag and drop to the page. You can bind data to these elements and set other component properties using the right-hand pane. At the bottom, you can see the page-level logic elements where some flows are defined to respond to page events.

You can subscribe to SAP AppGyver through SAP BTP. When you start the subscribed application, it will launch the **Application Development Lobby**, a landing page for administrating your LCNC projects. Here, you can create and manage the following:

- Projects for developing no-code applications with SAP AppGyver

- Business applications that are implemented using the low-code features of **SAP Business Application Studio**, which we will discuss shortly in the *Application development tools* section of this chapter

Typically, LCNC platforms provide the convenience of building frontend applications. However, there are examples where similar LCNC approaches are applied to backend development as well. At the time of writing, SAP announced the upcoming release of **Visual Cloud Functions**, a cloud-powered backend development tool for SAP AppGyver. With Visual Cloud Functions, you will be able to create backend capabilities such as security, business logic, scheduling, and persistency with a no-code approach.

# SAP BTP runtime environments

There are several ways to build complex applications in SAP BTP. If, for example, you come from an ABAP development background, this may seem overwhelming. With ABAP, application development is quite formalized and many aspects such as authentication are taken care of by the underlying NetWeaver platform before the execution of the application becomes relevant. Before discussing the different types of applications that you can build on SAP BTP, let's have another look at SAP BTP runtime environments.

You may recall our discussion on SAP BTP environments from *Chapter 3, Establishing the Foundation for SAP Business Technology Platform*. SAP initially offered their proprietary Neo environment in the cloud, mainly supporting HTML5, Java, and HANA development. As you already know, although still supported for existing customers, the Neo environment is no longer strategic, and SAP is encouraging customers to transition to the strategic multi-environment. Under multi-environment, SAP offers three runtimes: Cloud Foundry, Kyma, and ABAP.

## Cloud Foundry runtime environment

**Cloud Foundry** (**CF**) is an open source application PaaS. Besides its foundational elements, it allows reusable services to be provisioned on the platform, which applications can leverage. It virtually supports any runtime using buildpacks, which provide framework and runtime support for applications. CF, as a platform, provides all the necessary tools for developing and deploying applications, as well as managing their lifecycles .

In *Chapter 3, Establishing the Foundation for SAP Business Technology Platform*, we discussed how services are structured and how SAP BTP encapsulates CF. So, if you need to refresh your memory, this is a good time to scroll back and have a quick read. Regardless of how they are built, most of the strategic SAP BTP services are provisioned through the service structure of the CF foundation underpinning an SAP BTP subaccount.

For application development, SAP BTP primarily supports Java, Node.js, and Python buildpacks; however, it's possible to bring your own language using community buildpacks, such as PHP, Ruby, and Go. Although the underlying CF platform is open to access, SAP is formalizing specific approaches to leverage the platform for deploying and running your applications. In principle, CF supports application development guided by **The Twelve-Factor App** methodology, which sets forth certain qualities that make applications cloud-native. You can visit `https://12factor.net` to learn more about this methodology.

## Kyma runtime environment

Virtualization and containers are the enablers of modern cloud technologies. Together with the microservice architecture, container technologies such as Docker and Kubernetes have recently become the norm for building cloud-native applications. In line with this trend, SAP started building **Kyma** on top of Kubernetes to enhance the way its functions are used and ease some of the hardships of working with Kubernetes. Later, SAP donated Kyma to the open source community.

With the Kyma environment, SAP BTP provides a fully managed Kubernetes cluster on which you can deploy high complexity cloud-native applications to leverage cloud qualities powered by Kubernetes, such as high scalability. Acknowledging that this is an interesting topic, we have a dedicated chapter, *Chapter 11, Containers and Kubernetes*, where you can find more information on the Kyma environment and how SAP uses Kubernetes.

## ABAP runtime environment

Good old **ABAP** has found its way to the cloud and is available as a runtime that is provisioned through the CF environment. As you would expect, teleported to the cloud, ABAP in SAP BTP is quite different from the traditional ABAP. Many of the traditional ABAP features that are linked to the underlying NetWeaver platform and user interface capabilities, such as Dynpros, are not supported in the cloud release of ABAP. Here, ABAP is positioned mainly for backend business logic. We'll leave it here for ABAP and cover it in a bit more detail later in the *Backend applications* section of this chapter.

## Choosing the right runtime environment

Again, with multiple options comes the question of which one to choose. Let's start from the easiest angle.

The ABAP environment can be your preferred option if the application you are building is an extension of an ABAP-based product, such as SAP S/4HANA. Another factor in favor of the ABAP environment would be your development workforce. You can consider the ABAP environment, especially if you have highly skilled ABAP developers who can develop an application more efficiently compared to other alternatives.

Then, it's between the CF and Kyma environments, where the boundary may be a bit blurry. So, here, we can say the following:

- If you want to implement a sophisticated application that you believe will evolve rapidly and extensively to respond to changing requirements, you can consider the Kyma environment.

- Otherwise, you do not need to deal with the complexities of the Kyma environment and can create Twelve-Factor cloud applications in the CF environment as it is streamlined for this.

- Some application runtimes are supported by the CF environment by default, whereas you still have the option of **Bring-Your-Own-Language** (**BYOL**) for other languages. However, doing so may amplify the complexity of deploying the application. If you are willing to deal with such complexity anyway, you can consider the Kyma environment instead of CF.

Finally, you need to take into account the cost of the runtimes as they are chargeable elements. Remember that the ABAP and Kyma environments may cost significant amounts as soon as you create them since they need reserved infrastructure elements. This, in a way, is linked to the complexity of the application, and you need to justify the cost if you want to use these environments. The ABAP environment comes with its SAP HANA database attached to it; this is one of the main reasons for its high price tag. On the other hand, typical with CAP applications, you will need a database, and if you use SAP HANA Cloud, that option may become costly altogether, comparable to the ABAP runtime option. You can see the pricing metrics in the following table:

| Runtime Environment | Pricing Metric | Description |
| --- | --- | --- |
| **Cloud Foundry** | Memory (GB) | Memory consumed by the deployed applications |
| **Kyma** | Capacity units are calculated based on the infrastructure elements. | VM size, number of additional nodes, storage capacity, and throughput |
| **ABAP** | Hours of persistent and runtime memory | Number of hours x memory (GB) |

Table 9.1 – Pricing metrics for runtime environments

> **Important Note**
>
> Kyma is the most recent addition to the environments and is a sign that SAP embraces the Kubernetes technology with a special focus. This may tempt you to pick Kyma as the environment of choice as you may think it's the newest, cutting-edge, and much shinier. However, a good piece of advice here would be to assess your options properly and first consider the CF environment, especially for low and medium-complexity applications.
>
> This chapter will mainly cover application development in the CF environment. This is mostly the case throughout this book unless we discuss other options explicitly.

Now, let's look at different types of applications and what SAP BTP offers for building them. With this, we will start designing an architecture in small steps and enhance it as we progress to further sections. Let's begin.

# Frontend applications

These are the applications presented to a solution's end users. The users interact with these applications to operate the overall functionality provided. Frontend applications can be specifically built for desktop, web, or mobile. Desktop applications are not relevant to our scope as web applications already provide more convenient ways for consuming cloud services within web browsers. In this section, we will cover web applications; we will touch upon mobile applications later.

Typically, a web application is supposed to present information and let the user interaction via the user interface elements (also called controls). A web application comprises three pillars that correspond to different web technologies:

- Page content, structure, and basic formatting → HTML
- Advanced formatting and theming → CSS
- The behavior of page elements and interaction → JavaScript and WebAssembly

As web applications became more widespread, the developer communities came up with efficiency solutions and introduced libraries and frameworks to streamline the development of web applications. Today, there are several frameworks, mostly open source, which make developing complex web applications much easier. Typically, these frameworks follow design patterns, such as **Model-View-Controller (MVC)**, which let developers provide what differentiates the application while concealing the complexity and repetitions. For example, Angular, React, and Vue are the most well-known JavaScript frameworks.

As web browsers are also used in mobile devices, web technologies support building **responsive applications** that can adjust the presentment of page content depending on the form factor of the device.

# The OData protocol

Before getting into the application development technologies, we need to talk about the OData protocol, which is a protocol that adds a layer on top of REST APIs to define best practices and streamline their use. For example, the OData specification includes resource identification documents such as the service document and the metadata document, making REST APIs more interoperable. OData services are specified with an entity data model using **Common Schema Definition Language (CSDL)**. Therefore, the metadata file is sometimes referred to with the generic term *CSDL document*. In addition, the OData protocol includes query options for complex filtering, pagination, expanding the data retrieval to related entities, free-text search, and so on.

The current version of the protocol is OData v4; however, at the time of writing this book, it was relatively new, and SAP was in the process of adopting this version, whereas OData v2 had strong support. In the SAP ecosystem, the backend technologies are architected to serve OData APIs, and frontend technologies are designed to work mainly with OData.

Taking this to the integration domain, OData is the preferred protocol for synchronous integration – for example, replacing the BAPI technology in SAP S/4HANA. Although the SOAP protocol is still mostly preferred (for instance, over IDocs in SAP S/4HANA) for asynchronous integration, there is ongoing work to make OData an option for such integration scenarios as well. Here, we will mainly talk about SAP S/4HANA; however, remember that SAP Netweaver has been supporting OData for a while, which means SAP Business Suite applications can expose OData services as well.

# SAPUI5/OpenUI5

The user experience qualities of a web application are essential for its adoption. With web browsers becoming the main canvas for applications, the competition was fast-paced and introduced lots of features that improved user experience. As more people had access to the web and mobile, the user experience became one of the top factors differentiating an application from its competitors.

Traditionally, SAP applications were shipped with proprietary user interface technologies such as **SAP GUI (Dynpros)**, **SAP Business Server Pages (BSP)**, **SAP WebDynpro**, and **SAP WebUI**. SAP still supports these technologies and even provides the **SAP Screen Personas** technology, which can be used to personalize and give an elegant touch to SAP GUI and WebDynpro applications.

As mentioned previously, with JavaScript frameworks becoming the industry standard for web frontend applications, SAP invested in developing a framework to be aligned with this trend. As a result, SAP introduced the **SAPUI5** technology, a JavaScript framework that includes several enterprise features. Leaving out some of the very specialized libraries, the framework is also available as open source with the name **OpenUI5**. SAP uses **UI5** when generically referring to these frameworks and relevant technologies and tools.

> **Important Note**
> For more information on UI5, you can visit `https://ui5.sap.com`.

As a web application framework, UI5 can be used to develop any web application. However, since it is the primary technology for SAP frontend applications, the most typical use case is where the application manages data from an SAP backend, such as SAP S/4HANA and Business Suite, or a backend application running on SAP BTP, where in both cases the **OData** protocol is used. This way, SAP efficiently formalizes how data is maintained through **Create, Read, Update, Delete, Query (CRUDQ)** data operations. For scenarios where OData APIs are not available, UI5 also natively supports REST APIs, and it is always possible to access any web resource and parse the response if needed.

As a best practice, UI5 applications follow the **MVC** pattern:

- **Model**: The data structure used by the application.
- **View**: How the model is presented in the user interface through screen controls – for example, input boxes, tables, date pickers, text areas, and more. The view also includes other elements such as the layout, margins, paddings, responsiveness, and so on.
- **Controller**: The engine that controls the interaction between the model and the view.

Besides the MVC components, UI5 allows developers to define **data bindings**, where a screen element is bound to a property or a more complex data structure in the data model. With data binding, any update in the model is immediately reflected in the view. If it's a two-way binding, a change in a screen control immediately changes the data model's content as well.

Since we need to keep things high-level, let's cover some UI5 features to give you an idea of what's available:

- As it's quite typical to have multiple views (for simplicity, let's consider them as pages), the UI5 framework also facilitates *routing* and *navigation* between them.
- UI5 applications run on smartphones, tablets, and desktops; they automatically adapt to the device and the operating system and can use functions specific to them, such as *device APIs*.
- UI5 supports *extensibility*, where it is possible to add, hide, and rearrange fields, as well as change their labels. The best part is that because UI5 uses a consistent layering structure, the changes made at the end user layer stay upgrade-safe and modification-free.
- Although UI5 applications support standard themes delivered by SAP, it is possible to customize and manage the *custom themes*, for example, for branding.
- UI5 supports multiple locales and lets developers define *multi-locale* properties, such as localized texts, in the application.
- As it's designed for enterprise applications, UI5 supports several *accessibility* features such as screen reader support based on ARIA and HTML standards, high contrast themes, and keyboard shortcuts.

Now that we've talked about SAPUI5, let's start designing our example architecture.

## Example architecture design

First, let's note that our example design is mainly for demonstration purposes. Here, we won't necessarily consider other aspects that may influence decisions, such as cost impacts, already existing solutions, and so on.

At this stage, we have an SAPUI5 application that connects to an on-premise SAP S/4HANA system to retrieve data for a specific group of customers and displays this information. The design would be similar if it were an SAP Business Suite system:

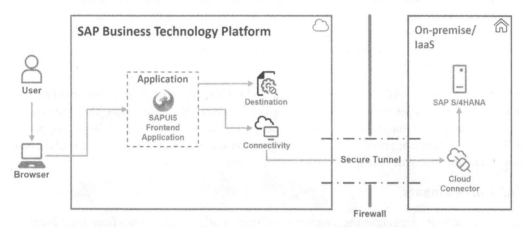

Figure 9.3 – Example architecture design – an SAPUI5 application and on-premise connectivity

Here, we have our SAPUI5 frontend application in the design, and it elegantly presents the customer information. Here, we will use what we learned from *Chapter 4, Security and Connectivity*: the application securely connects to the on-premise system via the **SAP BTP Connectivity service** and **SAP Cloud Connector**. The connection information is stored and retrieved via the **SAP BTP Destination service**. As we mentioned previously, we are at the very early stages of our design, and as you will see, this will evolve throughout this chapter. Here, we purposefully described the application as an elegant application. Let's see what we mean by that in the next section.

## SAP Fiori

SAPUI5 offers functionality across the complete set of frontend layers, including page structure, formatting, and behavior. It includes a broad set of prebuilt and configurable screen controls. For designing these controls and UX principles, SAP also introduced a common user experience for the frontend applications: **SAP Fiori**. SAP Fiori provides a modern, elegant, coherent, and cloud-ready design system that provides a consistent user experience across multiple platforms and device types.

> **Important Note**
> You can visit `https://www.sap.com/products/fiori.html` to learn more about SAP Fiori.

Today, SAP S/4HANA Cloud frontend applications are built with SAPUI5 and automatically use SAP Fiori as the user experience. This is valid for other SAP products that are based on ABAP in the cloud, such as SAP Marketing Cloud. SAP S/4HANA on-premise, on the other hand, includes SAP Fiori applications as well as older UI technologies, such as SAP GUI.

Because many of the other cloud products in SAP's portfolio are acquisitions, such as SAP Commerce Cloud, SAP Ariba, and so on, they use different UI technologies. However, SAP invests in unifying the user experience across these different solutions. As an extension to this investment, SAP released **UI5 Web Components** as a Fiori-compliant reusable UI elements library for web development frameworks other than UI5, such as React, Angular, and Vue, so that the Fiori experience can be extended to these frameworks.

Applications that use SAP Fiori design are called **SAP Fiori apps** and there are more than 2,000 of them. SAP designates some of the Fiori apps as **SAP Fiori Lighthouse apps**. These apps bring immediate business value mainly because they support tasks and processes that are not supported in SAP Business Suite or provide extensive simplification and efficiency compared to the traditional way of handling the same task in SAP Business Suite.

### SAP Fiori elements

The power of SAP's programming languages and frameworks mainly comes from their focus on developing enterprise-grade business applications. Looking closely, you can observe the prevalence of five typical floorplans used in business applications. By incorporating these floorplans into templates and creating patterns for the behavior models, SAP created **SAP Fiori elements**, a framework for accelerating the creation of SAPUI5 applications that use one of these floorplans.

Using SAP Fiori elements, developers can create an SAPUI5 application that uses **OData** and is underpinned by predefined views and controllers based on the selected floorplan. With this framework, the application automatically includes features for message handling, global edit flow, draft handling, keyboard shortcuts, and navigation. On top of this base, developers can add **annotations** to complete the application development. Annotations allow developers to tailor the application as per the requirements without needing to write JavaScript code. However, if needed, developers can still add JavaScript code for additional requirements. As you can see, SAP Fiori elements offer more than just layout templates.

With SAP Fiori elements, you can use one of the following floorplans:

- **List report**: Listing several items in a tabular format with a section at the top for defining and applying filters.
- **Worklist**: Listing several items in tabular form where no complex filtering is required.

- **Object page**: This page contains a header section for the highlighted properties of an object and then sections that contain other information about the object. This page can function as a form to create a new object or edit the properties of an existing object.

- **Overview page**: A page with several elements that contain high-level information for many areas in a well-organized way via cards. These cards can be list cards, table cards, stacks, or analytic cards, allowing the user to navigate to the specific application to drill down the details.

- **Analytical list page**: A page enriched with analytical elements that are generated from some transactional content. These elements may include filters and charts that interactively change the page's content.

The following screenshot shows a sample application built with SAP Fiori elements and the list report floorplan:

Figure 9.4 – An application built with SAP Fiori elements and a list report floorplan

Given that the backend services are in place, creating this frontend application takes much less time than creating it with freestyle SAPUI5 development. Next, let's take look at backend applications.

# Backend applications

Looking from a different point of view, there are some limitations to frontend applications:

- They are used via clients (for example, browsers), which run on end user devices; therefore, they have restricted resources to run applications.

- When they run within a browser, the data they use is exposed and easily accessible.

- They run specifically for the end user.

So, how can you leverage a database application that holds common business data managed by several users? Or, how about a resource-hungry application that needs to run complex business logic concurrently accessed by several users? How can you securely check whether the user is authorized to make the change they attempted?

To handle requirements such as these, we need applications that run at the backend - that is, a (virtual) machine that runs possibly somewhere else and can deal with these requirements. In a traditional SAP Business Suite world, backend applications are mainly the ABAP applications that run on servers where the SAP NetWeaver platform is installed. In the new world of the cloud, as we discussed previously, the cloud release of ABAP is still an option for backend application development. However, with SAP BTP, virtually, there is no restriction on which programming language and runtime you can use to implement your business logic as a backend application.

The flexibility of choosing any language makes SAP BTP a powerful application platform; however, SAP needs to consider efficiency; therefore, streamlines the way backend applications can be implemented by officially supporting a subset of possible runtimes. As discussed previously, these include Node. js, Java, and Python runtimes.

## Cloud Application Programming (CAP) model

Besides the supported runtimes, SAP also provides the **Cloud Application Programming** (**CAP**) model, a streamlined framework of languages, libraries, and tools offering an approach to building enterprise applications following best practices and efficient coding styles.

Without CAP, the developers are in a wild jungle with several ways of developing an application on SAP BTP. This level of flexibility is mostly unnecessary, and since SAP BTP is supposed to provide a platform for several complex business applications, non-standardization may hinder its adoption. At this point, CAP makes developers' lives much easier and tremendously accelerates application development by providing a formalized approach. CAP is mainly for backend application development in **Node.js** or **Java** runtimes, which are officially supported. In addition, CAP also supports serving SAP Fiori elements applications with little effort.

CAP provides an abstraction layer on top of application components. For example, at the heart of a CAP application is a data model specified with a *descriptive language*, **Core Data Services** (**CDS**), which is an abstraction layer on top of the actual database elements. When deployed, the CDS data model description creates, updates, or deletes the underlying database artifacts accordingly. With the data model in place, it is possible to call queries using the **CDS Query Language** (**CQL**). This is almost like in ABAP, where developers write the same Open SQL query to access the database, regardless of the specific database underlying the application platform. Another similarity is that the CAP framework takes care of all the hard work to manage the database connection.

From the data model description, it is quite straightforward to define services that manage data via **CRUDQ operations**, again using the CDS language. The services are, by default, exposed as OData services, and the CAP framework lets developers influence the standard operations by adding logic before or after their execution. Alternatively, it is possible to completely overwrite the logic for a data operation. Besides providing the CRUDQ data operations, services can also include **actions** and **events** to define other behaviors of data entities.

---

**Important Note**
You can visit `https://cap.cloud.sap` to learn more about CAP.

---

The CAP framework includes the usual application components, such as the following:

- **Access control and authorizations**: The CDS language provides annotations that can be used to control data entity exposure, which CRUDQ operations are allowed for the entity, and who can access the entity (even at a granular operation level) through role-based access controls. For this, the CAP framework leverages the **Authorization and Trust Management service (XSUAA)**. This means the user context can be made available to the application. Besides annotations, the user context can be used programmatically to check authorizations.

- **Messaging**: The CDS language allows you to define events for data entities, and CAP provides intrinsic support for emitting and receiving events. Although CAP's implementation for handling events is generic, it provides out-of-the-box support for **SAP Event Mesh** and the **CloudEvents** specification.

- **Databases**: With the data model specification, CAP handles the lifecycle of database artifacts as well as the runtime management of database access. The specifications can stay at a generic level, meaning the code can be deployed for any supported database, such as **SQLite** or **SAP HANA**. However, for complex use cases, it may be required to use database-specific elements to exploit native database features. SQLite is used for non-production purposes as it's a *lite* database. This means that at the time of writing, only SAP HANA is officially supported for productive use.

- **Localization**: Like UI5, the CAP framework supports localization and multiple locales. For example, application texts can be specified in multiple languages through text bundles.

- **Temporal data**: CAP provides intrinsic support for time-bound data entities, containing validity start and end dates. With this, it is possible to execute time-travel queries as well.

- **Media and binary data**: CAP supports serving media and any binary data. This means the data entities can contain media data that can be managed via the exposed services.

- **Data privacy**: The CDS language provides annotations to designate entities or entity fields for their relevance to data privacy. After defining a service interface, an application can be linked to **SAP Personal Data Manager** (a subscription in SAP BTP) so that personal data can be retrieved and changed for data privacy purposes. Furthermore, audit logging annotations can be added to log data operations to sensitive entities.

Next, we'll see an example architecture design.

## Example architecture design

Now that we know more about backend applications, let's extend our design so that it responds to a requirement where we need to implement business logic to enrich the customer data we receive from the backend system:

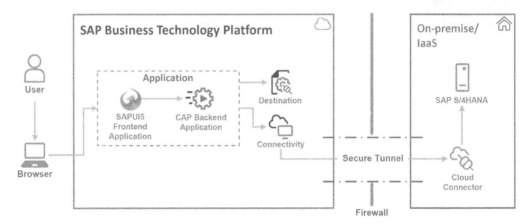

Figure 9.5 – Example architecture design – CAP application added

Here, we extended our design by adding the CAP application, which uses the same setup to connect to the on-premise backend system as an external service to consume its OData services.

## ABAP RESTful Application Programming (RAP) model

Besides embracing several open source technologies, SAP continues to position its proprietary programming language, ABAP, as a strategic element for cloud application development. ABAP supports modern application development paradigms with the new ABAP **RESTful Application Programming (RAP)** model. SAP came to this point through the evolution of different models for the interaction of frontend and backend applications in SAP S/4HANA. Like CAP, RAP also streamlines how the backend applications are developed and how they expose services for efficient consumption. Surely, RAP does this exclusively for the ABAP platform. And, when we say the ABAP platform, we mean both ABAP in SAP S/4HANA (on-premise and the cloud) and the SAP BTP ABAP runtime.

RAP has a similar approach to CAP, and the story begins with a data model specification. At the foundation, the database objects for persistency are controlled by the ABAP Dictionary. However, the RAP model includes other layers between this persistency layer and exposing services. On top of database tables, there are layers of views that mainly provide two benefits:

- They create a separate data model layer that is decoupled from the actual database tables. This provides flexibility as the database tables can be changed without impacting the applications relying on them.

- With a separate data modeling layer, application developers can restructure the underlying data, giving them the flexibility to tailor the data model that best fits the requirements.

For implementing these views, we have **ABAP Core Data Services** (**ABAP CDS**). Sounds familiar? Although they serve similar purposes, are built with similar principles, and have similar syntax, ABAP CDS and CAP CDS are different. And to make this even more confusing, there is another CDS flavor, HANA CDS, which again differs from the other two despite similarities in purpose and syntax:

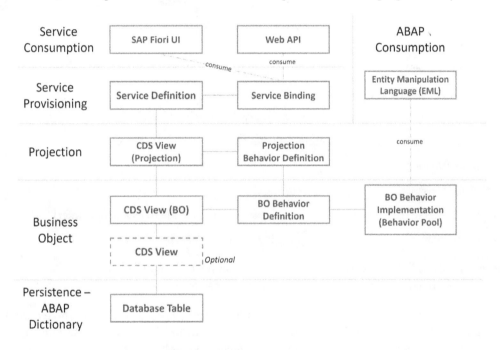

Figure 9.6 – ABAP RAP model elements

The preceding diagram illustrates the elements of the ABAP RAP model. Firstly, on top of database tables, you define a new data model for a **business object** (**BO**) using ABAP CDS. A business object corresponds to a real-world object we use in business processes, such as a purchase order or a product. The business object data model comprises a root (parent) node, such as a purchase order header, and optionally its child nodes, such as purchase order items. These are specified as **CDS views** that eventually use database tables as data sources. The parent and child entities are in a *composition* relationship, meaning the existence of the child entities depends on the existence of their parent entity. Depending on your requirements, you can implement an additional layer of CDS views before the BO CDS views to loosen the relationship between the BO data model and the ABAP Dictionary persistency model.

> **Important Note**
> A CDS view is a type of **CDS entity**, such as a CDS table function, CDS custom entity, and others. Therefore, sometimes, CDS views are referred to by using this generic term. To learn more about the ABAP CDS language, check out the ABAP CDS Development Guide in the SAP Help Portal.

After the data model for a business object has been specified, the next step is defining the **business object behavior**, including the following items:

- Draft enablement
- Numbering
- Feature control
- Authorizations
- Standard operations (create, update, delete, and lock)
- Actions (non-standard operations that modify the business object)
- Functions (non-standard read-only operations)
- Determinations
- Validations
- Prechecks (so that a request doesn't even reach and impact the transactional buffer)
- Augmentation (such as enriching incoming request content)

**Behavior pools** (ABAP classes) are created to implement the behavior elements, which is how the business object interacts. Here, behaviors can be defined mainly in two ways:

- **Managed**: With this option, the framework takes care of essential parts of the required implementation, such as the standard operations and the handling of the transaction buffer. This is generally recommended for new implementations as it gives a ready-to-run business object in a very short time, and you can focus on the business logic that differentiates the business object from others.

- **Unmanaged**: As you can guess, with this option, you need to implement all aspects of the business object. This is only recommended for use cases where it is reasonable to leverage existing business logic.

Implementing a business object is a tedious task; hence, it is preferable to have a generic one that implements a general data model and a wide variety of operations. On top of this foundational business object layer, another CDS view-based layer is implemented, which reuses the elements of the business object and defines a more specialized version of it. These views are called **projection views**. With a projection view, it is possible to refine the context specifically for the intended service and implement certain elements that help this specialization, such as UI annotations, default values, calculated virtual elements, and value helps. This can be considered a bottom-up approach where you first define a generic object and then define its version, which is meant to be used for the specific service you want to expose.

We are almost there. The business object is ready, and there is a projection that has been fine-tuned for the service we want to expose. At this point, a **service definition** is created to specify which CDS entities are in the scope of the provisioned service. A service definition mainly specifies this much and is not associated with a specific protocol (such as OData v2 or OData v4) or consumption type (that is, whether it is to be consumed by an SAP Fiori UI application or as a web API). To add this information and conclude the RAP model structure, a **service binding** is created. This is the last step to exposing the service for consumption.

After this point, the provisioned service needs to be attached to an access control structure so that it can be consumed:

- For **business users**, when accessing SAP Fiori UI applications, the service needs to be added to an **IAM app**, which needs to be included in a **business catalog**. Business users need to be assigned a **business role** that consists of the business catalog.

- For **system-to-system communication users**, the service needs to be added to a **communication scenario**, which is then included in a **communication arrangement** that contains the **communication user**.

RAP is primarily about exposing the business objects as OData services. However, in the ABAP platform, service bindings can also be created for direct SQL read access using the **Open Database Connectivity** (**ODBC**) driver. This way, tools that can leverage ODBC, such as Microsoft Excel, can use SQL queries directly to business objects. Similarly, a service binding can also use the SAP **Information Access** (**InA**) protocol for analytical queries, making it usable by SAP Analytics Cloud.

Now, let's consider some ABAP code that needs to access the business object within the same system. Should it use the services exposed by the RAP service provisioning layer? That would be overkill. Instead, the ABAP platform provides the **Entity Manipulation Language** (**EML**), which is contained in the ABAP language and allows business objects to be accessed internally.

You now have two options for developing a backend application on SAP BTP: CAP and RAP. Again, which one should you choose? The decision is not really about the programming models simply because they offer similar benefits for distinct runtimes. So, the competition is actually around the runtimes, which we briefly discussed in the *Choosing the right runtime environment* section.

## HANA applications

SAP HANA is more than a database; it's a platform that includes several other components tied to the core database element. SAP HANA can be used as a database in on-premise scenarios. In the past, SAP HANA was offered on SAP BTP via different services. The newest offering is **SAP HANA Cloud**, which includes an SAP HANA database and data lake in the cloud architecture. SAP encourages customers to migrate from the old offerings to SAP HANA Cloud.

We have a dedicated chapter, *Chapter 12*, *SAP HANA Cloud*, which covers SAP HANA Cloud in great detail, including an extensive *Development with SAP HANA* section.

You can create database artifacts and use SAP HANA as a database through its connectivity features, including ODBC, JDBC, **Smart Data Integration (SDI)**, **Smart Data Access (SDA)**, and so on. However, embedding HANA development in the CAP project structure is the most efficient option for most application development scenarios where CAP can be used. The data modeling part of CAP includes creating and managing the life cycle of some types of SAP HANA artifacts. You can also incorporate other HANA artifacts in your project and manage their lifecycles. This includes procedures written in **SQLScript**. SAP HANA procedures can also be managed through **ABAP Managed Database Procedures** (**AMDP**), which allows native consumption of these procedures and handling of their lifecycles.

## Example architecture design

For the sake of completeness of our example scenario, let's consider an additional requirement. So far, our CAP applications didn't have their own storage. Instead, we relied on them to run some sort of business logic for data enrichment, and they connected to the on-premise backend SAP S/4HANA system for the main data. Now, we have a new requirement to calculate ratings and other classification data for customers and store this information in the cloud.

For the calculations, we need data that can be replicated from the SAP S/4HANA system using existing CDS views that are replication enabled. We also need data from a second source, which is a non-SAP database that supports real-time change data capture. The calculation logic is quite data-intensive and should happen automatically whenever related data changes. Alternatively, it can be triggered manually so that you can see the calculation logs.

The rating and classification data should be available through OData APIs so that the existing SAPUI5 application can retrieve and display the information. This data should also be available to SAP Analytics Cloud to be used in dashboards efficiently. Finally, this data needs to be collated as a file and uploaded to an AWS S3 bucket for detached integration and data retention purposes:

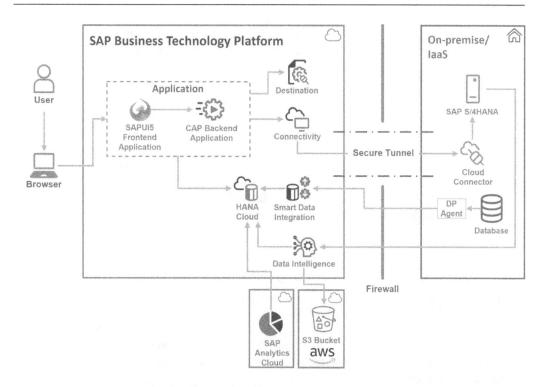

Figure 9.7 – Example architecture design – SAP HANA Cloud added

Let's update our architecture design with the necessary components, as shown in the preceding diagram. We now have an **SAP HANA Cloud, HANA Database** service instance that stores data for the solution. This includes the custom data model that is used for customer ratings and classification. The same instance also includes tables that contain data replicated from the SAP S/4HANA on-premise system CDS views via **SAP Data Intelligence**, as well as data replicated from the on-premise non-SAP database via **Smart Data Integration (SDI)**. The Data Provisioning (DP) agent at the source database side is part of SDI that allows you to transfer data to SAP HANA Cloud. Both data integration arrangements replicate delta changes in near-real time.

The CAP application contains services that manage data in SAP HANA Cloud and expose the data as OData services that are then consumed by the SAPUI5 application. The CAP application project also contains **HANA Deployment Infrastructure (HDI)** artifacts that are deployed in the database. This includes **SQLScript** procedures that do the calculations. Because these need data-intensive operations, we push down code to the database layer. The procedures can be executed by database triggers and can also be called on an ad hoc basis via CAP services.

SAP Data Intelligence is also used to run scheduled pipelines that read data from SAP HANA Cloud and write it as a file to an AWS S3 bucket. Finally, a *live connection* is established between SAP HANA Cloud and **SAP Analytics Cloud** so that the classification data can be used in analytics stories with near-real-time updates.

## SAP Cloud SDK

**SAP Cloud SDK** is a set of tools and libraries that aim to accelerate the development of cloud-native applications with mainly three elements:

- Providing an abstraction layer for SAP Business Technology Platform features such as connectivity, authentication, destinations, multi-tenancy, logging, and more.

- Facilitating easy integration with SAP cloud solutions such as SAP S/4HANA Cloud, SAP SuccessFactors, and others through type-safe client libraries, some of which are pre-generated and maintained by SAP. Others can be generated using the SDK tools.

- Providing other peripheral tools to make developing cloud-native applications easier.

The preceding definition may sound familiar to what we discussed regarding the **SAP Cloud Application Programming (CAP)** model. There is a bit of an overlap, and in fact, CAP leverages the SAP Cloud SDK under the hood. Let's continue our discussion by comparing the two as it may help you understand the SAP Cloud SDK.

CAP is an opinionated framework that encompasses all aspects of your development project and provides formalization for end-to-end application development. With CAP, some decisions are already made for you, including the principle of convention over configuration. This way, CAP guides your application development in a best-practices frame.

On the other hand, SAP Cloud SDK is more like an injectable tool for an arbitrary Java/JavaScript project. Yes, its tooling provides features such as generating an application; however, the SAP Cloud SDK doesn't enforce a structure for the entire application. Instead, it's more about making application development easier through abstractions and integrations.

CAP is more about implementing applications by building APIs; therefore, it defines what the application will be provisioning, whereas the SAP Cloud SDK focuses on consuming APIs.

```
1    import { BusinessPartner } from '@sap/cloud-sdk-vdm-business-partner-service';
2    ...
3    getBusinessPartners(): Promise<BusinessPartner[]> {
4        return BusinessPartner.requestBuilder()
5          .getAll()
6          .top(10)
7          .select(
8            BusinessPartner.BUSINESS_PARTNER,
9            BusinessPartner.FIRST_NAME,
10           BusinessPartner.LAST_NAME,
11           BusinessPartner.TO_BUSINESS_PARTNER_ADDRESS.select(
12             BusinessPartnerAddress.BUSINESS_PARTNER,
13             BusinessPartnerAddress.COUNTRY
14           )
15         )
16         .filter(
17           BusinessPartner.BUSINESS_PARTNER_CATEGORY.equals('1')
18         )
19         .execute({
20           destinationName: 's4hc01'
21         });
22   }
```

Figure 9.8 – A code snippet using SAP Cloud SDK

Let's look at the code in the preceding screenshot to solidify what we discussed earlier. This part of the code consumes the business partner service exposed by an SAP S/4HANA system:

- Line 1 imports a library, which is a pre-generated OData client for the SAP S/4HANA business partner service.

- You can see the OData query elements, such as restricting the number of returned records, selecting a subset of properties, filtering based on a condition, and expanding the query to a related entity.

- The property selection uses type-safe constants, as predefined by the library.

- Though not directly visible in this code snippet, the SAP Cloud SDK will handle authentication by interacting with the XSUAA service.

- The `execute` statement accepts a destination parameter and the SAP Cloud SDK knows how to use the **SAP BTP Destination service** before establishing connectivity.

As you can see, by having the SAP Cloud SDK, the developer can concentrate on what is required for the business logic and let the SAP Cloud SDK handle some of the lower-level details. Next, let's look at mobile applications.

# Mobile applications

For most of us, until we are awakened by a historical drama, we forget the fact that in the past, people used to live without mobile devices. They are such an integral part of our lives today; we learn, buy, pay, navigate, and entertain ourselves using these mobile devices. And indeed, we use them for business, too.

People, such as field engineers, depend on their mobile devices heavily to do their work. On the other hand, in the fast pace of business life, other roles also enjoy the flexibility that comes with mobility enabled by mobile applications. While rushing from one meeting to another, an executive can make use of mobile applications for most of the access they need to the business systems, such as approvals, worklists, analytics, and so on.

SAP BTP's mobile offerings are mainly grouped under **SAP Mobile Services**, which includes mobile development tools, and comprise management elements such as the application lifecycle, discovery service, push notifications, usage analytics, monitoring, identity, offline access, connectivity, and so on. Now, let's briefly discuss mobile development tools.

## SAP Mobile Development Kit

The **SAP Mobile Development Kit** (**MDK**) is an application development platform. The story of mobile application development with the SAP MDK starts with creating an application record in SAP Mobile Services Cockpit. Here, metadata information and desired mobile features are specified. After this step, a project can be generated, and in a supported editor, you can edit the pages, styling, and the application's behavior, mainly using a low-code development approach.

With the SAP MDK, you can build multi-channel applications, which means the same application can be deployed for mobile clients and also as web applications. For mobile devices, the mobile client translates the metadata, configuration, and scripts provided for the application into native code at runtime. This provides a native mobile experience to the user. For the web application, the web runtime takes care of the application running on the Cloud Foundry runtime.

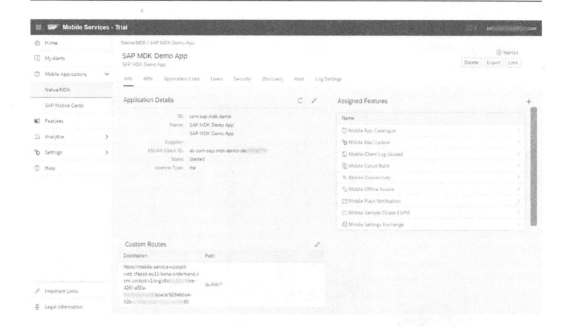

Figure 9.9 – SAP Mobile Services Cockpit showing the admin page of an MDK application

After an application has been deployed to SAP Mobile Services, you can use the client application, which you can install on your device, to launch the application either using its QR code (which you can obtain from SAP Mobile Services Cockpit) or via a URL with an application URI scheme For installing the client application, search *SAP Mobile Services Client* in the app store.

An example of the mobile features we alluded to previously is that you can configure push notifications in Cockpit using SAP Mobile Services. After slightly adjusting the application behavior in the editor, you can send push notifications to mobile devices. Another example of what SAP Mobile Services provides is that every time you deploy changes, SAP Mobile Services makes sure the mobile client is aware of the updates and asks the user to download the new version of the application. You can see a screenshot of SAP Mobile Services Cockpit in *Figure 9.9*, which also shows mobile features that are assigned to the application.

## SAP Mobile Cards

**SAP Mobile Cards** provides a low-code environment to design and publish stylish mobile cards that compactly contain business information. These cards allow user interaction, which means they can be used as entry points to business transactions or workflows.

Mobile cards can work as enriched notifications, quick worklist items, tickets, teasers, and wallet-style cards for various information-sharing purposes:

 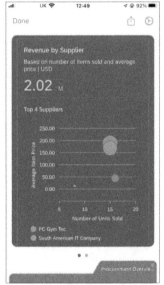 

Figure 9.10 – The SAP Mobile Cards app

*Figure 9.10* shows screenshots of some demo cards. With SAP Mobile Cards, you can auto-refresh cards so that they are always up to date, use integrated support for native apps (such as Mail, Maps, Messages, Phone, and SMS), and leverage offline support. If you want to have a peek, you can install the app on your mobile device to see the demo content.

## Mobile backend tools

Mobile applications can be deemed as frontend applications and typically need a backend for the heavy lifting, as discussed in the *Backend applications* section. **Mobile back-end tools** provide a toolset for modeling and generating OData services. After defining the core entity model, mobile-specific entities can be added to the OData CSDL document. The OData services can then be implemented using the generator tool, which creates a Java EE application. This application can be enhanced to have required elements such as routing and authentication so that it can be deployed on the SAP BTP Cloud Foundry runtime.

Customarily, mobile applications use existing OData services like those built using the previously discussed frameworks such as CAP and RAP, or the traditional services implemented in SAP Gateway. However, if your project is orientated around a mobile app, mobile back-end tools can be an option for implementing OData services conveniently. Generated OData services can be used by any application and are extensible through the hooks provided, which means you can tailor the business logic according to your requirements.

## Mobile Transaction Bridge

With **Mobile Transaction Bridge**, SAP Mobile Services takes a step into the ABAP world. You can create OData services from recorded **SAP GUI for HTML** transactions. First, you define the ABAP system to be connected, and Mobile Transaction Bridge gives you the tool to do the recording while running a transaction. The recording lets you specify elements that will be used for the OData specification. This includes annotations that are used to generate the mobile application UI. Using the recording, an OData metadata CSDL document is generated that puts forward actions and properties. This document is then published as an OData service, which can be natively attached to an SAP Mobile Services application or can be consumed directly by an external application.

From a recording, a mobile application can be designed using graphical tools that eventually generate the Mobile Transaction Bridge application project. Then, the project can be tailored and deployed like an SAP MDK application.

The target ABAP system needs to be provided as a destination for the runtime. You can use a destination defined in the SAP BTP Destination service or specify the destination explicitly. And, as you would expect, the ABAP system can be accessed via the SAP Cloud Connector if it's an on-premise system behind a firewall.

## SAP BTP SDK for iOS and SAP BTP SDK for Android

When it comes to building powerful native apps using the complete feature set of the native mobile application platforms, the story can start in a native application project on iOS or Android. This is where SAP provides the **SAP BTP SDK for iOS** and the **SAP BTP SDK for Android** to empower mobile application designers and developers with tools to accelerate the implementation process. This way, the applications can use platform features such as the fingerprint scanner, notifications, location services, and so on while nicely integrating with SAP BTP and providing a consistent enterprise-grade SAP Fiori user experience.

Although they are crafted for their specific platforms – that is, iOS and Android – the SDKs are built with the same mentality and work similarly. The SAP BTP SDK for iOS contains an **SDK Assistant** and the SAP BTP SDK for Android includes an **SDK Wizard**. These are used to generate mobile application projects into which the SDK libraries are incorporated. With this, the native applications are provided with a link to leverage SAP Mobile Services, and SAP Fiori controls are added.

Typically, app development happens as follows:

1. Install the SDK Assistant/Wizard.
2. Configure SAP Mobile Services in the SDK Assistant/Wizard.
3. Create an app record in SAP Mobile Services Cockpit and select the features you want your app to have, such as offline access, push notification, analytics, user feedback, and log upload. This is also where you configure SSO settings.

4. Generate the app development project in the SDK Assistant/Wizard by referring to the app record created in SAP Mobile Services.

5. Now, you can go wild and craft your native application with all the rich features that come with the mobile platform.

As mentioned previously, the SDKs also ensure the applications leverage the SAP Fiori design created specifically for the iOS and Android platforms. An essential part of the SAP BTP SDK for iOS is the **SAP Fiori for iOS Mentor**, which generates customized UI code snippets for SAP Fiori controls. Similarly, the SAP BTP SDK for Android includes the **SAP Fiori for Android Mentor**.

## Example architecture design

Let's enhance our example architecture design so that it includes a mobile application. This can be an SAP Mobile Cards application that sends important customer information as a card to subscribers or a native application that shows detailed customer information on mobile devices:

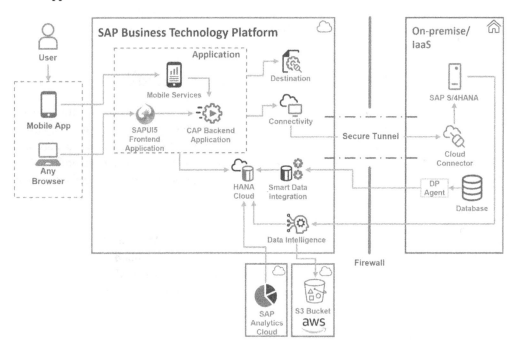

Figure 9.11 – Example architecture design – mobile app added

The preceding diagram shows the added mobile application elements. We have added mobile apps as a separate client that users can leverage to access mobile applications deployed in **SAP Mobile Services**. We have changed the label for the existing client type to reflect that it can be any browser, including browser apps running on mobile devices. So, the preceding diagram explicitly and expressly represents the mobile applications apart from browser access. SAP Mobile Services includes tools that can generate OData services that can be deployed in the CF runtime; however, for the sake of simplicity, we presume our mobile app consumes the services of the CAP backend application. Again, the **Application** box has connectors to the Destination and Connectivity services. This includes SAP Mobile Services consuming these services, too.

We have covered a lot about different types of applications and briefly discussed what they do, how they are developed, and how they are different. Now, let's take what we've covered so far as the core and delve into peripheral topics that complement core application development.

# Application development tools

When discussing low-code/no-code platforms, we talked about how application development has changed in recent years. Since the early years, it wasn't only the capabilities of programming languages and runtimes that advanced but also the ecosystem of application development peripherals that increased developer efficiency and made developers' lives easier. This was inevitable as application development scaled up tremendously; agility became a must with intense market competition and there was no room for low quality. Although it's not possible to cover everything that falls under this subject, let's briefly discuss some of these tools and how they can help.

## Integrated Development Environments (IDEs)

An **Integrated Development Environment** (IDE) is an application that facilitates software development by providing several capabilities for efficiency. At the core of an IDE is an editor where code is written. In addition, it can provide capabilities such as the following:

- Source code analysis, which checks for errors and quality issues
- Deployment automation for building, compiling, and deploying the code as applicable
- Debugging to find runtime issues and troubleshooting
- Organizing the development project's structure and searching source code
- Language support for syntax highlighting and code completion

Advanced IDEs can include visual programming features, wizards, and extensibility with plugins that provide several convenience features.

When it comes to SAP application development, we have several options; so, let's touch upon them.

### ABAP Development Tools (ADT) in Eclipse IDE

For traditional ABAP development, as some of you may remember, SAP ABAP Workbench was the development environment embedded in SAP NetWeaver. In terms of SAP BTP, this is not relevant. SAP has recently been encouraging developers to use the **Eclipse IDE** for traditional ABAP development, and some objects can only be developed there. On the other hand, developing ABAP in the cloud is only possible with the Eclipse IDE:

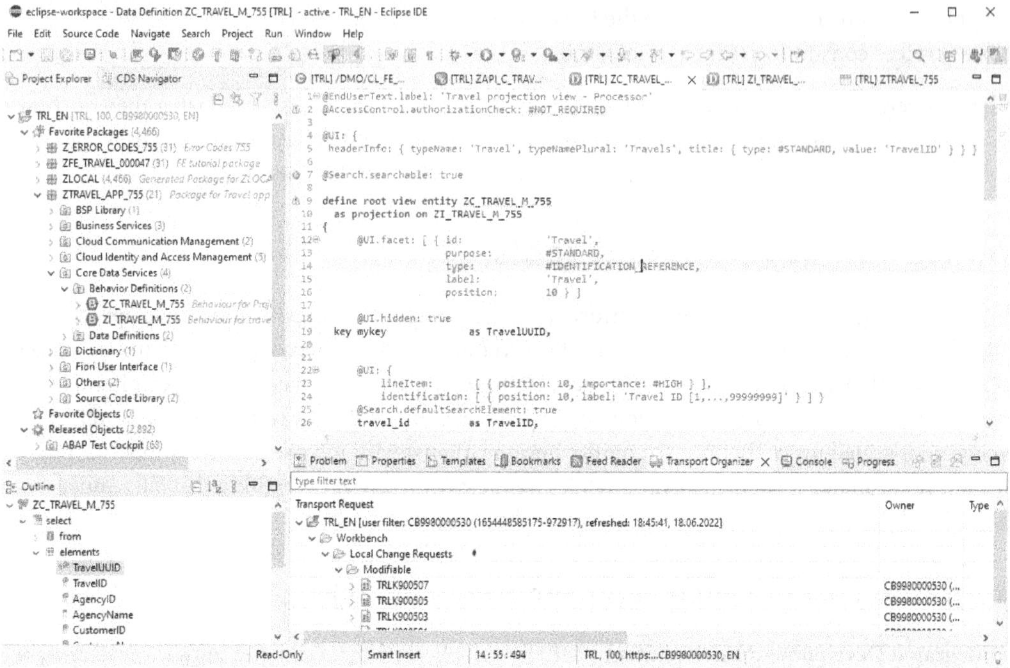

Figure 9.12 – ABAP development in the Eclipse IDE

As you can see, the Eclipse IDE provides a robust environment that includes advanced features for ABAP development.

## CAP and UI5 development

For developing CAP and UI5 applications, you are not limited and can develop these applications in almost any IDE you prefer. However, for the best development experience, there are two main options.

**SAP Business Application Studio** (**BAS**) is SAP's cloud-based IDE, which it offers specifically for SAP-relevant application development. Therefore, you can expect rich features that make SAP development much easier. Furthermore, as it is cloud-based and works on browsers, you can develop anywhere, so long as you have an internet connection. We will talk about SAP BAS in more detail shortly.

**Microsoft Visual Studio Code** is a desktop IDE (although its foundation allows cloud-based usage) that both SAP and the developer community support by providing plugins for convenience features. Note that it's different from Microsoft Visual Studio and can be considered a lightweight IDE mainly for web development:

Figure 9.13 – CAP and UI5 development in Visual Studio Code

*Figure 9.13* is a screenshot from Microsoft Visual Studio Code where a full-stack application is being developed. Microsoft Visual Studio Code is usually preferred, especially if you need to work offline. Many developers also like it because they are quite familiar with it as they use it extensively for other types of projects.

Also, note that you can also use the Eclipse IDE to develop CAP Java applications, and SAP provides tool support for this.

## HANA development

As you may recall, some SAP HANA artifacts can be created together with CAP and RAP development projects. However, if it's about creating native SAP HANA artifacts independently, you have two options: **SAP BAS** and the **Eclipse IDE**. Here, SAP BAS may provide a better developer experience, enriched with specific tools and convenient features. In old articles, you can see references to SAP HANA Studio, which is the Eclipse IDE with SAP HANA development tools.

Here, let's also mention **SAP HANA Database Explorer**, a web-based tool that comes as part of SAP HANA Cloud and allows you to work with SAP HANA artifacts. It offers IDE-like features such as managing artifacts, debugging, and executing SQL and SQLScript procedures.

## *Mobile development*

SAP BTP-related mobile application development starts by creating an application record in SAP Mobile Services. After this step, an SAP MDK application can be developed in SAP BAS, which provides specific tools for such applications:

Figure 9.14 – SAP BAS – editing an SAP MDK application page

The preceding screenshot is of SAP Business Application Studio while a page of an SAP MDK application is being edited.

Regarding native application development, SAP provides the SAP BTP SDKs for iOS and Android and assistant/wizard tools that generate the scaffold of an application project. Then, this project can be opened in a relevant development environment, such as Xcode for iOS or Android Studio for Android, to complete the development of the application.

## Other development types

Apart from the mainstream development paths mentioned previously, let's briefly note other development types:

- As you may recall, SAP BTP CF runtime supports virtually any programming runtime; this means you can build any application in any IDE and deploy the code in SAP BTP. Although this is not the mainstream route, it's possible so long as you can justify implementing applications this way.

- The Kyma environment lets you implement projects in any language and can be the preferred option, especially if your project has sophisticated requirements such as higher scalability. We covered the Kyma environment very briefly earlier in this chapter, and you can find more information in *Chapter 11, Containers and Kubernetes*.

- From our discussions in the previous chapters, you may remember that there were editors embedded in other SAP BTP services, such as the one for adding JavaScript or Groovy scripts in SAP Cloud Integration, and the pipeline operators that let you add scripts in SAP Data Intelligence.

- To highlight again, SAP AppGyver is a development platform where you can develop no-code applications. In addition, SAP BAS is also used for creating applications with a low-code approach.

- Some SAP cloud solutions have their own application development approaches, such as SAP Cloud for Customer's Cloud Application Studio, Java application development and SAP Spartacus for SAP Commerce Cloud, and so on. However, as they are not directly relevant to SAP BTP, they are outside the scope of this book.

We have talked about SAP BAS a lot, so now is the time for a proper introduction to it.

## Business Application Studio

As SAP's IDE offering, we thought we should cover **SAP BAS** in more detail.

As mentioned previously, SAP BAS is a cloud-based IDE and is accessible from anywhere with a browser, so long as there is an internet connection. It is based on the open source Eclipse Theia IDE framework, which is API-compatible with Microsoft Visual Studio Code. This means SAP BAS shares many Microsoft Visual Studio Code components, including the plugins written for it. On top of this base, SAP BAS contains many powerful features crafted for SAP application development.

After subscribing to the SAP BAS service on SAP BTP, you can create **dev spaces** with which you get an environment such as a Linux virtual machine where several tools relevant to SAP application programming are installed. You can even open a Terminal window and execute Linux commands in this environment:

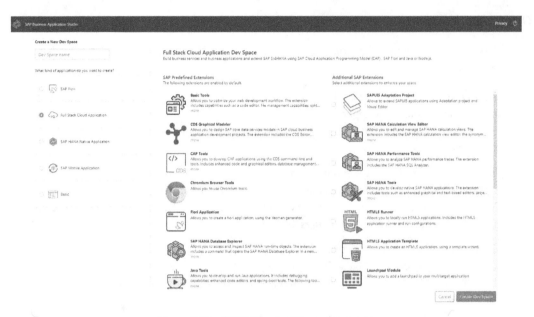

Figure 9.15 – SAP BAS – creating a dev space

As shown in the preceding screenshot, first, you specify an application type from a predefined list to create a **dev space**. This defines which extensions will be installed when creating the dev space. You can add other extensions when creating the dev space or later. These extensions provide additional capabilities you can use while developing an application.

In the previous sections, we mentioned you could use SAP BAS to develop CAP applications, SAP Fiori/UI5 applications, mobile applications, and SAP HANA native applications. With SAP BAS, developers get the following:

- Typical IDE editor features such as syntax highlighting and code completion

- Graphical editors for building UI screens, creating data models, and so on

- Visual editors that make maintaining important complex files easier

- Wizards with which applications and modules can be generated where necessary elements are automatically included

- Guided development to add specific features to applications

- Running applications in different run configurations, including local test runs

- Debugging applications for troubleshooting

- Git integration

- Terminal access

- Automation for deploying the SAP BTP CF runtime environment, SAP HANA, and SAP Mobile Services

Besides full-fledged application development, SAP BAS is also leveraged for application development while following a *low-code approach*. As you may recall from our previous discussions, when you launch the **Application Development Lobby**, in addition to the no-code SAP AppGyver option, you have the low-code business application development option, which loads a lite version of SAP BAS tailored for low-code development. It provides typical low-code application sections for data models, services, sample data, user interfaces, and workflows.

Another use case for SAP BAS is extending standard SAP Fiori (SAP Fiori elements and SAPUI5 freestyle) applications delivered in SAP S/4HANA. This provides additional flexibility compared to in-app extensibility. For this, you can create an **adaptation project** in SAP BAS and adapt UI elements, including the attached coding. Here, you only apply adaptation at places where the extensibility framework allows changes. And the project doesn't include the complete code for the application; instead, it includes references to the standard application and contains your adaptation code. Eventually, when you deploy, it creates an app variant that can also be included in SAP Fiori Launchpad.

## Other application development tools

Covering all application development tools in good detail is beyond the scope of this book. So, let's briefly touch upon some other types of application development tools:

- **Mock servers**: With mock servers, it is possible to test-run frontend applications without connection to an actual backend. This way, you can detach the timelines for frontend and backend application development, which means frontend developers can start development with no dependency on backend development, at least for some time. Based on an OData metadata document, a mock server can act as a pseudo server providing OData services with given mock data. The UI5 framework includes an OData mock server.

- **Test frameworks**: You can automate testing using several available testing frameworks and exploit the benefits of **test-driven development** (**TDD**) for a mature application delivery approach. UI5 framework has integrated testing tools such as **Qunit**, **Sinon**, **OPA**, and **Gherkin**. Similarly, CAP (Node.js) includes testing libraries with which you can write tests that run with **Mocha** and **Jest** frameworks. And, for ABAP, you can write **ABAP Unit** tests.

- **Command Line Interfaces (CLIs)**: The frameworks include tooling that can be leveraged by using operating system commands. For example, UI5 tooling includes the UI5 CLI, and CAP includes the CDS CLI to execute relevant framework features.

- **UI Theme Designer**: SAP invests in designing modern and elegant themes that are delivered as part of UI technologies, such as SAPUI5. In addition, you can create custom themes for your frontend applications. To create a custom theme, you start with one of the standard themes, customize it, and save it with a different name. Depending on your requirements, you can adjust the level of customization. For example, you can simply add your company logo and change the color palette for simple branding. Alternatively, you can make radical changes to the CSS and add custom CSS if you need a highly customized theme.

The content we've covered so far was mainly about implementing applications. However, the story doesn't end there; so, in the following sections, let's see what the next steps are.

# Launchpad applications

So, you have one application, you know its URL that you bookmarked, and you launch it using this bookmark. That's all good. How about when there are tens or maybe hundreds of applications that are relevant to your role at your company? Organizing them in your bookmarks wouldn't work after a point. Here, you must think about the administration side of controlling the visibility of these applications for several users.

To overcome the problems we mentioned earlier, an effective approach would be presenting these applications on a launchpad-style page to improve the digital experience.

## The SAP Launchpad service

With the **SAP Launchpad service**, you can establish a *central point of entry* for all users. You can configure how the applications are grouped and assign authorization elements to applications so that they are visible only to authorized users. As shown in the following screenshot, applications are represented by tiles that can show static and dynamic content. The size of these tiles can be configured, and you can also add links for the applications for which a smaller representation is sufficient. It's also possible to implement custom visualization for the tiles. The Launchpad's content can be organized with *spaces* (vertical tabs) and *groups* (horizontal panels):

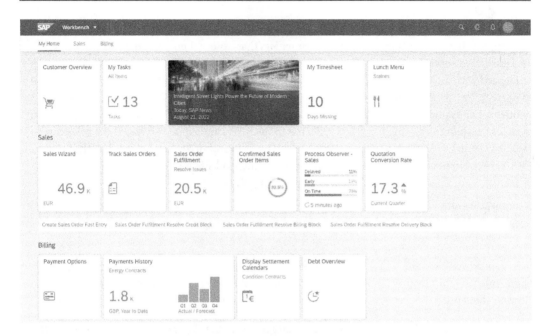

Figure 9.16 – An example SAP Launchpad site

While bringing several applications together in an organized way, the launchpad also provides a shell embracing all these applications. Technically, this enables a streamlined approach for application-to-application navigation, a common technical area where all applications can access, centralized user preferences, personalization, a common theme, an app finder, favorites, and so on.

> **Important Note**
>
> SAP Launchpad is like a spin-off of the SAP Cloud Portal service, which also includes freestyle portal capabilities. Although SAP continues to support the SAP Cloud Portal service, it announced it would not be enhancing its freestyle capabilities. SAP recommends that new projects adopt the SAP Launchpad service for essential launchpad capabilities and SAP Work Zone for enhanced content capabilities.

If you are familiar with SAP S/4HANA, you should know about the SAP Fiori Launchpad, which exposes its applications based on the SAP Netweaver (ABAP) platform. The SAP Launchpad service works with the same approach; however, it can be leveraged generically. You can integrate business content into the SAP Launchpad service by manually adding configuration on how an application can be launched. This is available for SAPUI5, WebDynpro ABAP, SAP GUI for HTML, and WebClient UI applications. You can also simply add URLs for straightforward navigation to applications.

As a more advanced option, you can integrate business content with *content integration/federation*. In this approach, there are supported content providers that expose their content in a format that the SAP Launchpad service can use. This way, a tighter integration is established where the content can be managed with less hassle. At the time of writing, this option is available for SAP S/4HANA (cloud and on-premise), SAP Business Suite, SAP BTP ABAP environment, SAP Enterprise Portal, SAP IBP, and others. For example, when you establish a content federation with an SAP S/4HANA system, you can expose certain roles, which are then reflected in the SAP Launchpad service. These roles can be attached to launchpad sites and assigned to SAP BTP users to authorize them. After that, the relevant SAP S/4HANA applications become available on the launchpad site for authorized users.

> **Important Note**
> By using content integration, you can establish central launchpads that span multiple solutions.

When you subscribe to the SAP Launchpad service, you get access to the **Site Manager**, which is a design-time tool for creating launchpad sites. The content of the launchpad is organized using the following elements:

- A **catalog** contains apps to technically classify them so that they are displayed together in the application finder.
- A **group** contains apps that will be displayed together on the launchpad as a group. This means that an app needs to be assigned to a group so that it can be visible on the launchpad.
- A **role** contains apps to define which users can access these apps. Roles are assigned to launchpad sites, and with this assignment, all the previous classification items and apps become relevant to the launchpad site.

You can extend the launchpad's functionality and its UI by developing **shell plugins**. Shell plugins are HTML5 applications that are deployed in the SAP BTP Cloud Foundry environment. You can also integrate **Enterprise Search** (SAP S/4HANA) to search for and access business data stored in SAP S/4HANA. There is a streamlined integration option that enables adding **SAP Task Center** tiles to a launchpad site. Finally, supported applications, such as SAP S/4HANA (cloud and on-premise), can provide *notifications* that can be shown on a launchpad site.

## SAP Work Zone

**SAP Work Zone** extends the capabilities of the SAP Launchpad service by adding premium user experience elements. Using SAP Work Zone, in addition to SAP Launchpad service capabilities, you can do the following:

- Design the page layouts with more flexibility
- Create a structure for different visibility levels using administrative areas, team workspaces, and sub-workspaces

- Add content with more variety by using widgets, such as images, slideshows, multimedia, rotating banners, polls, and so on

- Integrate external applications such as Microsoft Teams, Microsoft 365 Sharepoint Sites, SAP SuccessFactors Learning, SAP Cloud for Customer, and Google Drive

- Add chatbots

- Embed UI Integration Cards into pages

- Integrate OpenSocial gadgets

- Provide mobile experience with the SAP Work Zone mobile app

As you can see, SAP Work Zone is a platform for building digital workplace solutions that integrate content from various SAP and non-SAP solutions and function as an advanced central point of entry.

## SAP Mobile Start

The SAP Launchpad service provides great benefits for controlling how users access applications while improving the user experience. Following the same approach and tailoring it for mobile usage, **SAP Mobile Start** provides a launchpad experience using native mobile capabilities. With this, SAP Mobile Start is positioned as the native entry point to the SAP mobile experience, including native mobile apps delivered by SAP or customer apps:

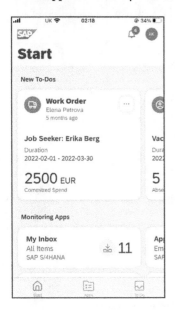

Figure 9.17 – SAP Mobile Start app

In essence, SAP Mobile Start leverages the SAP BTP Launchpad service, SAP Mobile Services, and other relevant SAP BTP services to provide a consolidated view across all mobile solutions.

In *Figure 9.17*, you can see screenshots from the SAP Mobile Start app, which has the following sections:

- The home area, which shows highlights and suggestions
- The application launch section, which lists available applications
- The **To Do** section for workflows, alerts, and notifications
- A dedicated Notification Center

## Example architecture design

Now that we know more about launchpad applications, let's incorporate them into our architecture design. Our example focuses on one application; however, let's add some launchpad components, assuming that the company will have more applications soon:

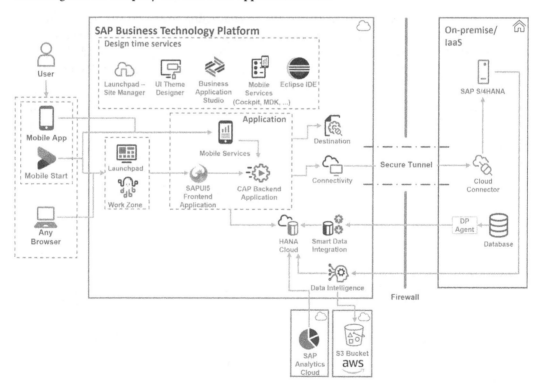

Figure 9.18 – Example architecture design – launchpad applications added

The preceding diagram shows that our design now includes the **SAP Launchpad service**, **SAP Work Zone**, **SAP Mobile Start**, and **Site Manager**. We preferred displaying SAP Mobile Start as a client application; however, as you may recall, at the backend, it uses SAP BTP. We have omitted showing the mobile app for SAP Work Zone for the sake of simplicity. As we discussed application development tools in the previous section, we have added design-time services to the diagram.

# Non-functional design

In *Chapter 4*, *Security and Connectivity*, and *Chapter 5*, *Non-Functional Design for Operability*, we extensively covered important non-functional design elements. If you need to refresh your memory, just scroll back and have a look. Here, let's briefly point out how SAP BTP application development services cater to some non-functional requirement categories:

- **Security**: You can bind applications to the XSUAA service so that they can utilize the authentication and RBAC capabilities. This binding can be done by running ad hoc commands or can be specified as a deployment element. Through XSUAA, applications can be made accessible only after the user authenticates, including the identity federation and **single sign-on (SSO)** capabilities provided by **SAP Identity Authentication Service** and/or the corporate identity provider. Similarly, by adding security specifications, such as role and role template definitions, the application can check a user's authorizations and reveal information or allow actions accordingly.

- **Availability**: SAP BTP CF uses the availability zones of the region on which your subaccount runs, provided that the region has availability zones. When you create multiple instances for your application, the platform automatically distributes them across different availability zones, achieving zonal redundancy. You don't need to add another service here as the runtime arranges this setup.

- **Scalability**: You can use the **Application Autoscaler service** to scale applications by automatically adding or removing instances based on specific policies.

- **Observability**: You can use the **Application Logging service** to record logs from your application, which helps troubleshoot problems. You can use the **Alert Notification service** to respond to certain events that happened in the application runtime, such as application crashes, deployment, and others. In addition, your applications can produce notification events and call the Alert Notification service to publish the event as an alert.

- **Accessibility**: We didn't cover this non-functional design element in the previous chapters; however, let's briefly talk about it here. With an inclusive mindset, one of your application design goals should be to enable access for people who need extra support for using the application. This is mainly relevant for frontend applications. For example, UI5 supports several accessibility features such as screen reader support based on ARIA and HTML standards, high contrast themes, keyboard shortcuts, and so on, following standards/guidelines such as the **Web Content Accessibility Guidelines (WCAG)** and the **Accessible Rich Internet Applications suite of web standards (WAI-ARIA) specification**.

Now, let's add some of the services we discussed in this section to our architecture design.

## Example architecture design

As a detail for the security requirements, let's assume we need to use **Microsoft Azure Active Directory (AAD)** as the corporate identity provider, while also providing an SSO capability. Besides, we also want the flexibility to manage third-party access to our application within the SAP team:

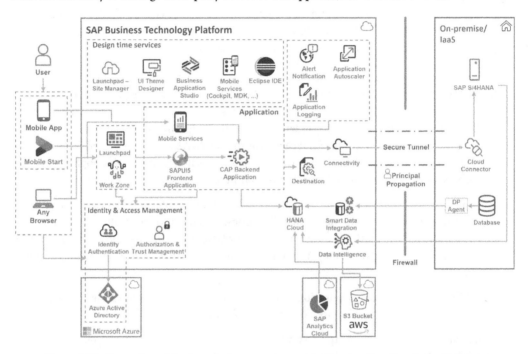

Figure 9.19 – Example architecture design – services added for non-functional requirements

In the preceding diagram, our example architecture design now shows the use of **Authorization and Trust Management**, which allows us to implement RBAC controls and provides integration with Microsoft AAD for single sign-on. We have **SAP Identity Authentication Service (IAS)** in between so that we have a layer where the internal SAP team can control user access, such as for emergency access of third-party support teams. Otherwise, SAP IAS is used in proxy mode, passing the authentication requests to the corporate identity provider for corporate users. With the addition of these IAM elements, the applications now have the logged-in user context. Besides, it's now possible to leverage *principal propagation* to use the actual user to authenticate to the backend system when consuming its services.

At the top right, we added the **Alert Notification service**, the **Application Logging service**, and the **Application Autoscaler service**, to exploit the observability and scalability features of SAP BTP, as discussed earlier in this section.

# Other related services

We have covered a lot so far, and as visible in the example architecture design, so many SAP BTP services can be involved in an application development scenario. But there is still room for extending our scenario with other services. The good side of all these services being available on SAP BTP is that it's easy to integrate them, the connectivity between them is efficient, and it's possible to manage their lifecycles together. Let's briefly cover other services that can be leveraged in an application development scenario:

- **SAP Integration Suite**: The best practice programming models suggest implementing services in an API-led approach. As you may recall, with both CAP and RAP, the end product is a set of OData APIs. So, in an inbound scenario, you can create a layer to control access and protect these APIs using the API Management capability of SAP Integration Suite. We discussed a digital integration hub design example in *Chapter 7, Cloud Integration*, which covered this scenario. For outbound integration, the applications can consume SAP Integration Suite endpoints. This can be a Cloud Integration flow, or an API proxy created in API Management to control outbound access and abstract the outbound service consumption.

- **SAP Process Automation**: Your application can make use of process automation elements, such as triggering workflows, using configured business rules, and so on. We will discuss this topic in more detail in the next chapter.

- **SAP Job Scheduling**: As the name suggests, you can schedule jobs to run once or with a recurring schedule. You provide an action endpoint, start times, and schedule as key inputs. The scheduled application needs to define and grant authorization scopes to the Job Scheduling service so that it can authenticate via OAuth 2.0 when calling the endpoint. Jobs can be created using the service dashboard or service APIs. For convenience, SAP provides a Node.js client library based on APIs. With these APIs, you can also manage the jobs and retrieve relevant information such as job details and run logs.

- **SAP Custom Domain**: The endpoints provided by the services and the deployed applications use a default subdomain. Although the customer defines the subdomain name, the main domain name comes from SAP's domain for SAP BTP – for example, *ondemand.com*. If you want to have a stable domain name with which you prefer to expose these endpoints, you can use the Custom Domain service to manage your custom domains, including route configurations and server certificates.

- **Other storage services**: Being SAP's strategic database offering, our examples included SAP HANA Cloud for persistent storage. This is also reflected in the programming models as they have the best out-of-the-box support for SAP HANA. However, you have the option to use **PostgreSQL** as a relational database, **Redis** for cache instances, and **Object Store** for object storage. SAP BTP manages these services through brokers that connect to hyperscalers where the storage service runs. There is no extra layer, such as functionality abstraction, provided by SAP for leveraging these services. So, for example, for the Object Store service, depending on the hyperscaler you chose, your application will be interacting with an Amazon S3 bucket, an Azure Blob Container, or a Google Cloud Storage bucket. Your application needs to read the credentials and access details from the environment variables and then use standard libraries provided by the hyperscalers to interact with these services.

- **SAP Document Management**: You can use this service to store and manage business documents. The difference from the Object Store is that here, the files are recognized as documents where additional metadata is specified for the files. Additionally, content management capabilities, such as versioning, are available. SAP BTP provides an *integration option* that allows applications to interact with the service via APIs. There is also an *application option* that comes with a web application to manage documents.

- **SAP Credential Store**: If your applications need to handle security elements such as passwords, keys, and keyrings, you can use the SAP Credential Store service to manage and use them securely.

- **SAP Forms Service by Adobe**: Using this service, you can generate print or interactive Adobe forms. The service acts like the **Adobe Document Services (ADS)** server. You can make REST API calls to the service endpoints by providing a form template and the form data. Accordingly, you will get the PDF file content. You can manage forms, templates, and schemas stored in the Template Store using APIs or the Template Store UI. You need to use the Adobe LiveCycle Designer application to design form templates.

Let's extend our example architecture design according to what we covered in this section.

## Example architecture design

Let's assume we want to expose the services implemented with the CAP applications so that they can be consumed by serverless functions implemented with Google Cloud Functions. In response to new requirements, we need to update customer data in SAP Marketing Cloud and also create a ServiceNow incident when certain conditions are met during the classification determination. Finally, let's assume one of the branches of our company has recently completed a greenfield implementation of SAP S/4HANA Cloud (public) and we would like to integrate customer data from this system using events:

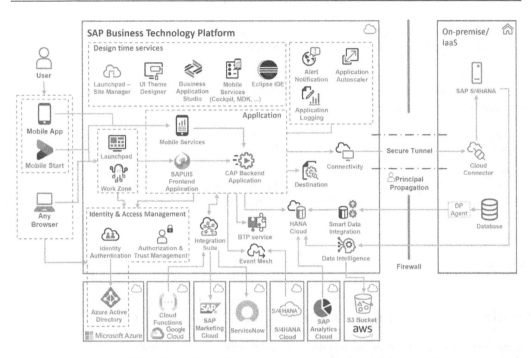

Figure 9.20 – Example architecture design – integration services added

The preceding diagram shows new additions to our example architecture design. The serverless function in Google Cloud can consume the APIs the CAP applications expose through API proxies created in **SAP API Management**. The CAP applications can trigger integration flows to call SAP Marketing Cloud OData services to update contact data for the customer. Similarly, it can trigger integration flows to create incidents in ServiceNow via the ServiceNow adapter or the ServiceNow connector in **SAP Open Connectors**. For all these integration scenarios, we added **SAP Integration Suite** in the design as the parent service to include the capabilities we mentioned previously.

There was a new SAP S/4HANA Cloud implementation and we wanted to use events to integrate customer data. For this, we can use **SAP Event Mesh** positioned as the event broker. As you may recall, CAP applications can consume events via the framework's out-of-the-box messaging capabilities with SAP Event Mesh.

# Deployment considerations

With the application development tools, you can develop locally and even test your application using mock data or by connecting the backing services. For commercial projects, you need to deliver your application by deploying it to a productive SAP BTP environment. The first target for deployment will be a development environment. Depending on your change delivery model, you should typically use a **source code management tool**, such as **Git**, which also helps with collaboration for developing code as a team. Your source code must be stored in a repository that supports your management tool. You have internet-facing options such as GitHub, GitLab, BitBucket, Azure Repos, and others. Alternatively, you can establish your own on-premise platform behind your firewall.

This is the starting point of your **continuous integration and continuous delivery (CI/CD)** approach. You can use the source code repository and establish a pipeline to automate your software delivery with necessary controls such as automated testing, code quality checks, security checks, and so on.

To establish a pipeline, you can leverage the **SAP Continuous Integration and Delivery service**, which comes with predefined pipelines for SAP BTP development scenarios, including CAP, Fiori/UI5 applications, Integration Suite artifacts, and container-based applications. You can connect your source code repository and establish Webhook connectivity for automation. Then, you can configure pipeline jobs using the service's job editor. Alternatively, you can add a configuration file to your project that includes job specifications. This allows you to specify pipelines as code, and this pipeline specification can be tracked for changes, together with the project code.

As an alternative to the SAP Continuous Integration and Delivery service, you can establish your own pipelines on other platforms such as **Jenkins**, **Azure DevOps**, and others.

## Continuous integration and the build pipeline

So, one part of the delivery pipeline is about continuous integration, where a state of the application code is built and deployed to the CF runtime. What does this mean?

Although there are other alternatives, the best practice deployment happens through **multi-target application archives (MTARs)**. A **multi-target application (MTA)** is an application package that contains code for different modules and can be deployed to different targets, such as an SAPUI5 module and a HANA DB module. When the application code is *built*, the builder application creates an archive (MTAR) file. The archive file contains the application code in a specific structure and compressed format. If you are familiar with JAVA development, this is similar to **web application archive (WAR)** files.

When the application is deployed, the application runtime makes sure the application is accessible via an endpoint and runs the application. In addition, other foundational tasks need to link multiple elements together for an application to run as expected:

- As you may recall from *Chapter 3, Establishing the Foundation for SAP Business Technology Platform*, applications use SAP BTP services via bindings. Although you can create service instances and bindings manually, the most convenient way is to automate their creation or make updates happen at the time of deployment.

- The CF runtime needs to know some properties to run the application, such as the amount of memory to be reserved for the application, the required input for the XSUAA service instance, and so on.

- Configurations are needed to build and deploy the application modules, such as what tool to use to build modules or their sequence.

To specify the configuration elements for these aspects, an **MTA descriptor** file (mta.yaml) is added to the project folder. Your MTA descriptor can include the specification for service instances and how the application will be bound to them.

For frontend applications, the static content is stored in the **HTML5 Application Repository service**, which provides features such as versioning, availability, caching, and so on. However, to access the static content, a dynamic runtime element is required mainly to serve the content via an endpoint, handle routing, and manage access features such as authentication and authorization. This can be accomplished by using an **application router** (**app router**). You can include an app router in your project by adding a standard package managed by SAP and a file for its configuration (xs-app.json).

As an economical option, SAP allows applications to use the app router of the SAP Launchpad service (or SAP Work Zone) if you are subscribed to it. In this case, you should specify a *managed application router* when creating your application.

## Continuous delivery and the release pipeline

After deploying an application to a development environment for continuous integration, you will need to take it up to the production environment to deliver it to the end users. This is where you can create a release pipeline that serves as a transport route for the deployment artifacts (for example, MTAR files). This pipeline typically deploys the application code to one or many test environments, optionally a pre-production environment, and finally to the production environment. You can set an approval process between the deployments so that they happen under control, for example, after the testing is signed off.

The **SAP Continuous Integration and Delivery service** can deploy the artifacts directly to the CF runtime. Alternatively, it can deliver them to the **SAP Cloud Transport Management service**, which allows you to manage the transportation of the content across different environments.

For content other than application code, such as the configuration of an SAP Launchpad service site, currently, the easiest option is to use the export/import capabilities. For a similar case for some of the SAP Integration Suite artifacts, the **SAP Content Agent service** could be used to assemble content as an MTAR file that the SAP Cloud Transport Management service can use:

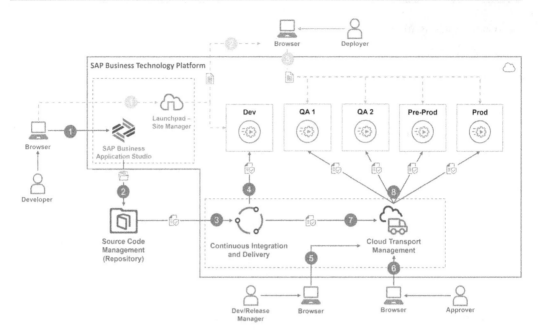

Figure 9.21 – CI and delivery setup with SAP BTP services

The preceding diagram illustrates a CI/CD setup using SAP BTP services. The route depicted with dashed lines is for the manual export/import mechanism for content such as launchpad site configuration. The route represented by solid lines is where SAP BTP services are used to deliver the change. The CI pipeline deals with deploying the committed code to the development environment and the delivery pipeline deals with deploying this code to subsequent environments until it is delivered to production. Here, approval mechanisms can be established so that the change delivery can happen in a controlled manner.

## Example scenario

Throughout this chapter, we talked about an example scenario with several requirements that revolved around use cases for application development. We enhanced the design as we covered new topics:

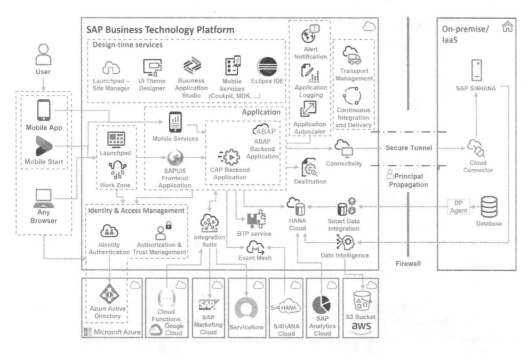

Figure 9.22 – Example architecture design including several application development-related services

In the preceding diagram, you can see the final version of our example architecture design with some adjustments to make it generic to show almost everything we covered in this chapter. Let's make it easier to spot the recent changes: We added ABAP as a backend application development option and the CI/CD relevant services.

## Summary

Well, this was a chapter with so much content, so you will need time for everything to sink in. With this chapter, we wanted to provide high-level content to architects so that they can consider application development options with SAP BTP.

We started by explaining the **extensibility** concept as SAP uses this aspect for application development. However, as we mentioned, it doesn't have to be an extension application that is tightly dependent on standard solutions. You can build independent applications using powerful features of SAP BTP application development features and services.

Then, we talked about LCNC application platforms and SAP's offerings in this area, including **SAP AppGyver**. For pro-code development, we continued by discussing three runtime environment options: **Cloud Foundry**, **ABAP**, and **Kyma**. After this, we came to the core of application development, where we covered different application types you can develop on SAP BTP, including frontend applications using **SAPUI5** and **SAP Fiori** and backend applications using the CAP and RAP models. We also briefly touched upon HANA database native development, while referring to a later chapter where it will be covered in more detail.

Next, we discussed **SAP Mobile Services** for mobile development, and then we covered application development tools, mainly IDE applications such as **SAP Business Application Studio**.

Then, we discussed launchpad applications for organizing how we present applications to end users. Here, we discussed the **SAP Launchpad service**, **SAP Work Zone**, and **SAP Mobile Start** as digital experience services.

We discussed non-functional design previously in dedicated chapters. Here, in this chapter, we wanted to correlate what we discussed previously with the application development aspects. Then, we briefly touched upon miscellaneous SAP BTP services that can be leveraged as peripheral capabilities next to the applications you develop. Finally, we discussed deployment considerations and highlighted essential topics and SAP BTP services in this area, such as the **SAP Continuous Integration and Delivery service** and the **SAP Cloud Transport Management service**.

You should now have an idea of how to develop applications in SAP BTP and understand the relevant concepts, processes, and services. In the next chapter, we will cover another exciting topic, digital process automation, and what SAP BTP offers in this area.

# 10

# Digital Process Automation

Businesses are always after automation opportunities to reduce time, effort, and cost. Automation also means fewer human errors, well-analyzed business processes, better-managed scalability, and more reliable business process insights. One use of automation is to offload labor-intensive but straightforward tasks, creating more bandwidth for tasks that generate more value and distinction with the human touch. Process automation can also become the glue for collaboration between business users by bringing together different ends of processes where human involvement is required. This significantly increases productivity and amplifies agility.

Being the enabler of the agility layer for businesses, SAP BTP includes **SAP Process Automation**, which brings together several aspects of digital process automation, offering a comprehensive toolset for the following:

- The direct consumption of business users by providing a low-code/no-code platform
- Building sophisticated solutions by developers via the advanced tools and features

In this chapter, we're going to cover the following main topics:

- Process automation in the intelligent enterprise
- SAP Process Automation

## Technical requirements

The simplest way to try out the examples in this chapter is to get a trial SAP BTP account or an account in which the free tier can be enabled, as described in the *Technical requirements* section of *Chapter 3, Establishing the Foundation for SAP Business Technology Platform*.

## Process automation in the intelligent enterprise

Like many of the concepts we have discussed so far, the use of process automation is linked to the broader intelligent enterprise domains. Putting what you learned in *Chapter 1, The Intelligent Enterprise,* and *Chapter 2*, *SAP Business Technology Platform Overview*, about how SAP BTP is positioned as the foundation layer, you can learn how SAP Process Automation interacts with **SAP Signavio**, which offers a platform for modeling and governing business processes, as well as producing intelligence and insights from them. This can be an important element of SAP S/4HANA transformations as many companies go for the greenfield implementation option and redesigning business processes is at the heart of it. SAP Signavio and SAP Process Automation form the process transformation suite, which helps customers with the tedious task of dichotomizing their current processes and building adoption routes so that their processes fit the standard and can keep the core clean.

SAP positions process automation as a core element of digitalization and a key platform for building solutions to respond to rapidly evolving customer requirements that will be dealt with by complex IT landscapes. As a result, SAP provides several prebuilt automation contents that support automation requirements in several lines of business. These can be found in the **SAP API Business Hub** or **SAP Process Automation Store**:

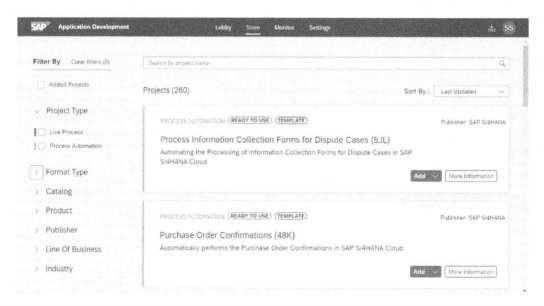

Figure 10.1 – SAP Process Automation Store

In *Figure 10.1*, you can see a screenshot from the SAP Process Automation Store. For example, you can find accelerators such as Capital Expenditure Approval Process, Purchase Requisition Approval and Release, Business Partner Payment Data Change Approval, Visibility on Order to Cash, Accrual Object Creation Approval, Vendor Onboarding, and so on. At the time of writing this book, there are more than 250 prebuilt automation projects in the store.

Another element of SAP's strategy for automation is seen in the tooling it offers. The immediate target audience for process automation is business users. As you may remember from our discussions on **low-code/no-code** (**LCNC**) platforms, we can call them *citizen developers*. This makes sense as business users can use their strong knowledge of business processes effectively when supported by a convenient platform, unlocking countless opportunities.

In general, we see process automation applied to the following use cases:

- Consolidating data from multiple sources

- Handling processes for high-volume transactions, such as entering data

- Digitizing business process journeys, especially across multiple applications and including human intervention points such as approvals

- Promoting process visibility, which is generally a pain point for many businesses for end-to-end processes where several steps happen by bouncing back and forth between different applications

To recap, with digital transformation, enterprises are looking at ways to simplify their processes and gain more visibility so that they can optimize them and recalibrate where needed. With SAP Signavio, companies can take care of the following:

- Process and journey modeling

- Process analysis and mining

- Process management and governance

When it is about building workflows and automation, SAP Process Automation enters the stage. SAP plans integration points between the two; for example, at the time of writing this book, there is a roadmap item that suggests content recommendations from SAP Signavio Process Insights can be incorporated into SAP Process Automation (SAP Signavio is beyond the scope of this book). Next, let's look at what SAP offers with SAP Process Automation.

# SAP Process Automation

Like many other SAP BTP services, **SAP Process Automation** resulted from the evolution of predecessor SAP BTP services. With SAP Process Automation, SAP brought together the **SAP Workflow Management** service and **SAP Robotics Process Automation** under the same umbrella. If you have been using SAP BTP for a while, this includes the **SAP Business Rules service**, which was previously merged with the Workflow Management service. At the time of writing, these services are not marked for removal from the catalog; the newer offering may lack some of the advanced features at this stage. However, we can say that SAP Process Automation is the strategic option. As usual, we expect SAP to continue to support the older service offerings for existing customers if they decide to remove these services from the catalog.

Besides bringing these services together, SAP also positions SAP Process Automation to provide mainly an LCNC experience so that citizen developers can also build process automation and workflow artifacts. This looks like part of SAP's strategy around LCNC offerings, and we may see further changes in this area as the offerings become more mature. At the time of writing this book, there are references to a unified design system that covers the LCNC offerings for process automation, application development, digital experience solutions, and chatbot tools.

With this brief introduction, let's explain how SAP Process Automation can be put into action. This should also give you an idea of the use cases where you can leverage it.

## Business processes

Launching the SAP Process Automation application takes you to a landing page that includes a lobby; this is where you can view and maintain your projects. This is quite similar to the Application Development Lobby for LCNC development that you launch for SAP AppGyver. At the time of writing this book, you can mainly create two types of projects: a **business process** or an **actions project**. An actions project is a wrapper that contains API definitions you upload using an OpenAPI specification document. This allows your business processes to call the included APIs as actions. Actions projects are quite lean projects; however, business processes can include several artifacts. Now, let's have a detailed look at them.

### Processes

After you create a business process project, you can create project artifacts under it. There are two main types of artifacts that can be triggered externally: processes and automations. So, in a business process project, you typically start by creating a process artifact or an automation artifact:

Figure 10.2 – SAP Process Automation – process builder

When you create a *process* artifact, the application takes you to the process builder to maintain the process steps, as shown in *Figure 10.2*. A process artifact brings together several steps that form a flow and can include other artifacts we will cover in the following sections.

Apart from project artifacts, which can be added to a process, other step types let you do the following:

- Add control elements such as conditions and branches

- Send an email where you can build the email body content using an editor that lets you use process content elements in the text

- Call an existing workflow in a process step

- Call an API that is wrapped in an actions project

At the time of writing this book, you can trigger a process either via a form by visiting the URL generated for it or from the **SAP Process Automation Monitoring** section by providing input manually.

### Automations

With an *automation* artifact, you can create process automation that can be executed by software robots that emulate human interaction with desktop and web applications. When deployed, an automation artifact uses the same runtime as the SAP Intelligent Robotic Process Automation service. Automation needs a **desktop agent** that can be installed on Microsoft Windows machines, including **virtual machines** (**VMs**). The desktop agent contains a set of connectors that define how the agent interacts with application technologies such as web applications, Microsoft Office applications, PDF files, and so on.

> **Important note**
> At the time of writing this book, automations are only supported on Microsoft Windows; support for other operating systems is on the roadmap.

The desktop agent can run in two modes:

- **Attended**: In this mode, the desktop agent is interactive, and a user needs to run automations manually.

- **Unattended**: In this mode, the desktop agent runs the automations in the background without interaction.

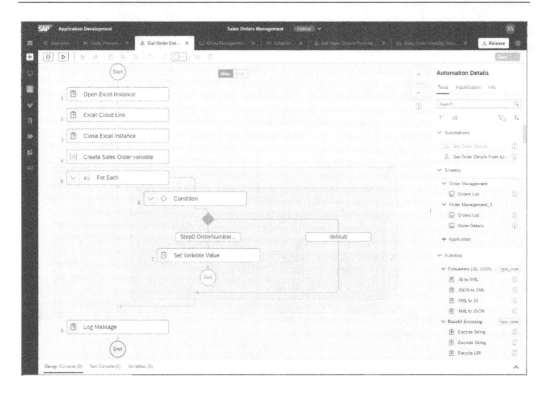

Figure 10.3 – SAP Process Automation – automation builder

As seen in *Figure 10.3*, automations are designed in a special automation editor that contains flow control elements, such as loops and conditions, as well as powerful features such as the following to interact with several applications:

- **File system**: File and folder operations such as renaming, moving, reading, and compressing files

- **Microsoft Excel file**: Operations on workbooks, worksheets, and cells such as getting/setting cell values, formatting cells, merging cells, and refreshing pivot tables

- **Microsoft Word**: Document and content operations such as replacing text and saving documents as PDF files

- **Microsoft PowerPoint**: Operations on slides such as deleting, duplicating, adding text, and formatting

- **Microsoft Outlook**: Email and calendar operations such as searching, sending emails, and creating meetings

- **PDF files**: Content operations such as searching text, splitting, merging, and extracting information from PDF invoices

- **HTTP**: For calling web services and downloading files

- **FTP**: Typical FTP operations such as uploading/downloading files and folder operations

- **Cryptography**: Cipher/decipher values and sign/encrypt/decrypt messages using keys or certificates

Most of the preceding operations require the relevant SDKs to be added to the project before they can be used in automation artifacts. SAP Process Automation lets you manage these SDK dependencies. It also notifies you when there is a new version and enables you to update the SDK version you've added to your project.

You can create **application** artifacts with which you capture an application running on your local machine, capture its screens, and identify the screen elements to use in your automation artifacts:

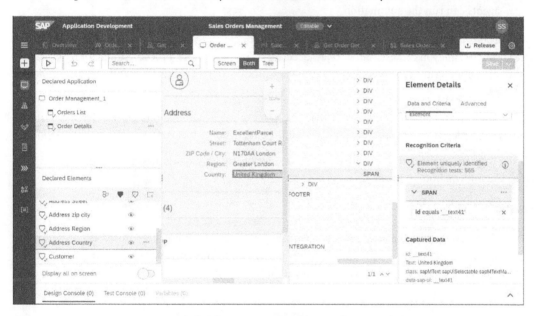

Figure 10.4 – SAP Process Automation – application editor

In *Figure 10.4*, you can see a screenshot of the application editor loaded with a web application. For the application, list and detail screens are captured, and several screen elements are declared through the HTML structure.

You can create **data type** artifacts to define simple and complex data types to be used in automation steps. Besides this, you can externalize variables by creating **environment variables**, which you can use in the automation artifacts of a project. The automation editor allows you to debug and test your automations. You can set watch variables and see the timeline of automation steps.

Automations can be triggered in three different ways:

- **API**: An API endpoint is generated, and the automation can be triggered by simply sending an HTTP request to this endpoint. The API uses OAuth2 authorization. Apart from this, an API key, which can be produced in the SAP Process Automation settings, needs to be provided with the request.

- **Attended**: With this option, the automation specification is distributed to agents, and users can manually execute the automation.

- **Schedule**: You can create a schedule that controls when automation jobs are created. SAP Process Automation supports complex schedule specifications and allows you to specify which agents can run the automation.

You can add *custom scripts* written in JavaScript for automation steps that require complex operations. In a custom script, you can use standard JavaScript and also access SAP Process Automation SDKs. In addition, custom scripts can accept input parameters, produce output parameters, and use environment variables.

In your project, you can create an *alert* artifact that you can use in automations to raise alerts. The alert artifact simply keeps an alert specification as an independent entity that can be reused by automations.

Finally, you can use *file* artifacts, which allow automations to directly access files, such as files containing reference information.

### Forms

We touched upon *form* artifacts earlier when we said you could trigger business processes using forms. In addition, you can use one or multiple forms as steps anywhere in your business process. As the name already suggests, forms are screens that gather user input:

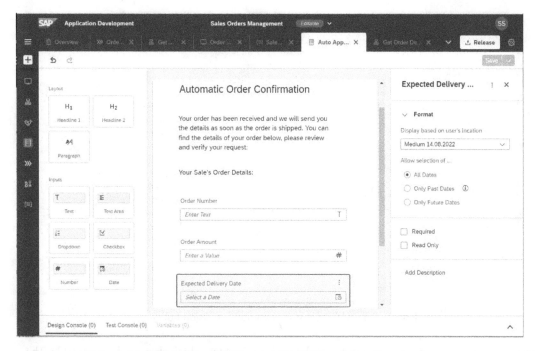

Figure 10.5 – SAP Process Automation – form editor

As you can see in *Figure 10.5*, when you create a form artifact, the application opens the form editor, where you can drag and drop form elements and maintain their attributes.

You can also create a standard form that lets users enter their input and click on a button to submit their entry. Secondly, you can create approval forms that show two buttons for approving and rejecting whatever is presented in the form. The process flow can then have separate branches for these two actions.

When a process flow executes a form step, a user task is created, which can be viewed in the **My Inbox** section of the SAP Process Automation application.

## Decisions

One of the essential elements of application development is implementing conditions such as the if-then-else blocks in application coding. The conditional structure can be set to influence the program flow, as well as to define business logic and data according to the conditions. This essential requirement is also part of business processes. With **decision** artifacts, you can build simple decision structures that can generate an output based on conditions and the provided input. In case you have experience in it, the mentality is similar to what **Business Rules Framework plus** (**BRFplus**) does as a form of on-premise decision service management:

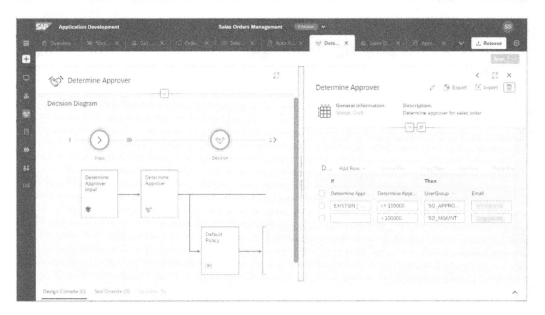

Figure 10.6 – SAP Process Automation – decision builder

In *Figure 10.6*, you can see a screenshot of the decision builder, which shows a decision table. The decision table can use the input parameters for the rule specification. When added as a step in a process, the inputs can be taken from process step elements or process metadata. For rule expressions and conditions, a set of predefined operators (such as mathematical or logical operators) and functions (such as time/duration functions, mathematical functions, and aggregate functions) can be used.

### Process visibility

After defining a business process, an important aspect is to gain visibility into how the process is performing. For this, SAP Process Automation lets you define several elements as process metadata, such as phases, events, states, attributes, and so on. You can then link these elements to define performance indicators.

The process visibility capability also works for processes that span multiple systems. For such visibility scenarios, you can add an external process definition as an **observed process** and add the required metadata for it so that its performance is incorporated into the indicators. Here, the external systems can send process data (events) via an API.

Finally, you can view process visibility content via the Process Workspace application, which can be configured as a standard application in the SAP Launchpad service. This gives you a dashboard that shows performance indicators and lets you apply filters to access process insights.

Now that we have an idea of the artifacts that can form business processes, let's look at what SAP Process Automation provides for monitoring business processes.

## Monitoring

SAP Process Automation provides a dedicated monitoring section that allows you to monitor process instances, automation jobs, and acquired events (events received from external systems for process visibility). In this section, you can also manage triggers, visibility scenarios, and processes; for example, you can trigger a new process instanc.

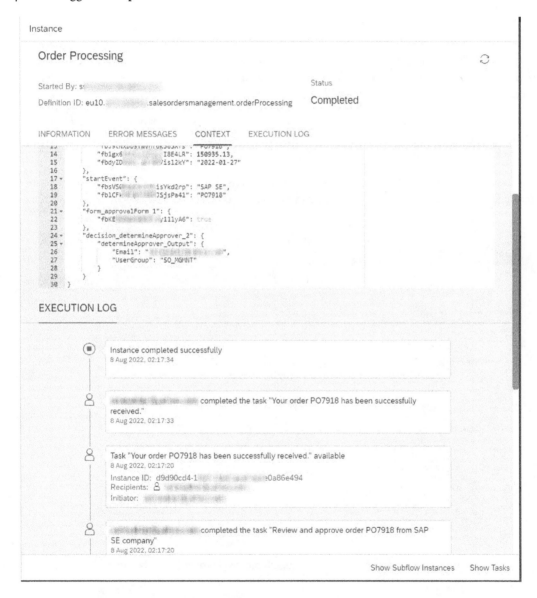

Figure 10.7 – SAP Process Automation – monitoring a process instance

*Figure 10.7* is a screenshot that shows monitoring a process instance. It provides information on the process instance's status, execution information, error messages, and instance context. It also provides an execution log in a timeline format.

At the time of writing this book, SAP has a roadmap item that can provide integration with **SAP Cloud ALM** for operations monitoring.

## Store

SAP Process Automation provides immediate benefits with prebuilt content, such as live process packages, bot templates, decisions, automations, and dashboards that can be imported from the **Store** section of the SAP Process Automation application or SAP API Business Hub.

The prebuilt content is an important differentiator of SAP Process Automation compared to other automation tools. The objects in the **Store** section are context-aware of SAP solutions, mainly SAP S/4HANA, and are mostly tied to SAP best practices.

The imported content can be tailored further by creating new process variants, configuring decisions, and configuring process visibility scenarios. This way, you can jump-start developing process automation:

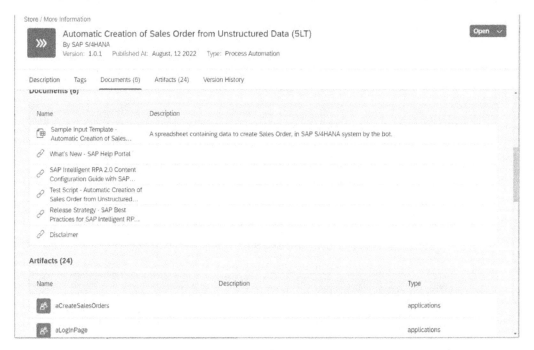

Figure 10.8 – SAP Process Automation – prebuilt process automation in the Store section

As shown in *Figure 10.8*, the prebuilt content comes with a good level of information and documentation. By browsing the content provided in the **Store** section, you can see several examples of how SAP implements business process artifacts. This can also give you hints on where you can apply process automation to address pain points in your business.

Many of the prebuilt automations implement typical use cases such as the following:

- Mass data input, for example, a bot reads several records from a spreadsheet file, and then uses each record to run a transaction such as creating purchase requisitions.

- A bot collects content from the user's email inbox, extracts information and runs transactions with it, for example, to upload journal entries.

- Approval processes for tracking and monitoring business transactions such as fixed asset transfers.

## Summary

In this chapter, we provided a very high-level look at process automation in the intelligent enterprise. Then, we covered SAP Process Automation, which is strategically positioned as an LCNC platform for creating processes, including workflow-type automations as well as robotic automations.

SAP Process Automation can provide remedies to many business pain points. It can be an enabler for reducing operational costs by automating tasks that are handled by people whose time can be channeled to activities that generate more business value. As such, SAP's current strategy to rebuild its automation offering as an LCNC platform is meaningful as it addresses IT resource shortages while letting business experts efficiently utilize their process knowledge. Besides SAP Process Automation, SAP BTP also offers services such as **SAP Task Center, Responsibility Management Service**, and **SAP AI Business Services** (covered in *Chapter 14, SAP Intelligent Technologies*), which can help implement automation use cases.

With the prebuilt content that includes SAP best practices, SAP Process Automation can be an integral part of SAP S/4HANA transformation programs. The same will continue to apply to further digital transformation programs as intelligent enterprises evolve into autonomous enterprises where hyperautomation technologies will surely be a powerful actor.

In the next chapter, we will go back to pro-code application development platforms with a trendy topic and cover containers and Kubernetes concerning how they are used in the SAP cloud ecosystem, especially in SAP BTP.

# 11

# Containers and Kubernetes

Cloud-native patterns and new cloud **operating systems** based on containers and Kubernetes have been growing rapidly over the past few years. Together with solutions through the viable ecosystem of the **Cloud Native Computing Foundation** (**CNCF** - `https://www.cncf.io/`), they have changed the development, delivery, and life cycle management of modern software.

**Containers and Kubernetes** have become the important cornerstones of building, running, and managing cloud services and applications. Like **virtual machines** (**VMs**), containers enable applications to share the OS kernel. Compared to VMs, a running container is less resource-intensive but retains isolation, thus improving resource utilization.

**Containers** are decoupled from the underlying infrastructure and portable across cloud and on-premises environments. Containers are created from images to produce identical environments across development, testing, and production deployments. Containers provide a good way to package all the necessary libraries, dependencies, and files for your applications; however, you need to manage the containers effectively and ensure that your applications are auto-scaling, and design for failures and recovery. This is where Kubernetes plays its part.

**Kubernetes** is a portable and extensible platform for managing containerized workloads and running distributed systems resiliently. It takes care of scaling and failover, facilitates declarative configuration and deployment patterns, and provides a self-healing ability, load balancing, and network traffic management. Kubernetes has evolved into the de facto industry standard for container orchestration.

Cloud-native technologies have enabled a new paradigm of software development and its capabilities. They have enabled agile development, **continuous integration and continuous deployment** (**CI/CD**), infrastructure automation, and a new way to structure teams, culture, and technology to manage complexity and unlock velocity.

SAP embraced cloud-native patterns and Kubernetes at an early stage, and has actively contributed to multiple CNCF projects, such as the open-source projects **Gardener** (`https://gardener.cloud/`) and **Kyma** (`https://kyma-project.io/`). Today, many SAP applications are already running on Kubernetes, while many others are in the process of migrating to Kubernetes. In SAP

**Business Technology Platform** (**BTP**), Kyma Runtime is the cloud-native extension platform and SAP BTP itself runs on top of Kubernetes, which is enabled by Gardener.

We will discuss Gardener and Kyma in more detail later. First, let's have a look at what we are going to cover in this chapter:

- What is Kubernetes and how does it enable a new type of architecture?

- Gardener as a managed Kubernetes service that is available in multi-cloud environment

- Kyma as the cloud-native extension platform of SAP BTP

- When should you use Cloud Foundry or Kubernetes?

## Understanding Kubernetes architecture

So, what is Kubernetes and how does it make cloud-native development much easier?

Initially developed by Google based on many years of running Linux containers both at a basic level and at scale, Kubernetes is a system for running and managing which containers run where, coordinating large numbers of containers, and facilitating communication between containers across hosts. In addition, Kubernetes provides a common infrastructure layer that abstracts underlying infrastructure environments, such as public, private, and hybrid clouds running in virtual or physical machines.

Kubernetes creates an abstraction layer that allows the developers and operators to work collectively and helps focus on control at the service level instead of the individual container level. If containers have empowered the productivity of individual developers, Kubernetes has allowed teams to compose services out of containers. This improved coordination has enhanced development velocity, service availability, and agility at scale.

To understand how Kubernetes provides the capacity to achieve those objectives, let's get a sense of how it is designed at a high level, as illustrated in *Figure 11.1*, and discuss each component in the following subsections.

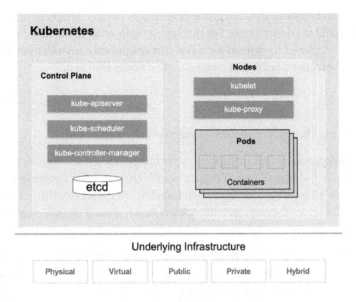

Figure 11.1: The Kubernetes architecture

Now let's take a look at the core components of Kubernetes.

## The control plane

In Kubernetes, users interact with the cluster by communicating with the API server, and the **control plane** is responsible for determining the best way to schedule the workload containers by examining the requirements and the current state of the system.

As part of the control plane, **etcd** is a lightweight distributed key-value store that Kubernetes uses to store configuration data, which can be accessed by each node in the clusters. It is used for service discovery and maintains the cluster state.

**kube-apiserver** is the API server that exposes the APIs and the main management point of the cluster, as it allows users to configure the workloads through REST API calls or the **kubectl** command-line interface.

**kube-scheduler** performs the actual task of assigning workloads to specific nodes in the cluster. It tracks the status and available capacity on each host, considers the resource needs of a Pod, and then schedules the Pods to the appropriate node.

**kube-controller-manager** contains serval controller functions in one and is responsible for implementing the procedures that fulfill the desired state. For example, a **replication controller** ensures the correct number of replicas is deployed as defined for a Pod. An **endpoints controller** populates endpoint objects and a **node controller** notices and responds when nodes go down.

## Nodes

The servers that perform the work of running containers are called **nodes**.

A **Pod** is the smallest deployment unit in the Kubernetes object model and represents a single instance of an application. Each Pod is made up of one or more tightly coupled containers that should be scheduled on the same node. Each node contains a **kubelet**, a small service that communicates with the control plane and assumes the responsibility of executing tasks and maintaining the state of work on the node server.

**kube-proxy** is a network proxy for facilitating network communications inside or outside of the Kubernetes cluster. It forwards requests to the correct containers, maintains network rules, and either replies on the OS's packet filtering layer or forwards the traffic itself.

## Blurring the layers of IaaS, PaaS, and SaaS

We often categorize our stacks into three layers – **infrastructure as a service (IaaS)**, **platform as a service (PaaS)**, and **software as a service (SaaS)**. Then, we classify all the components or services within these layers. For example, **VMware** falls into the IaaS layer, **Cloud Foundry** is a PaaS layer sitting on top of an IaaS, whereas cloud applications such as **SAP's Intelligent Suite** fall into the SaaS layer.

This classification helps with the **separation of concerns (SoC)** in terms of having the design patterns and tools focused on specific areas that add value. However, it still requires *glue* to connect the layers, which is typically the role of a **cloud platform**. So, when we think about this and the architecture of Kubernetes, what it essentially enables is a new style of architecture design that focuses on extensibility. This extensibility works across all layers, including hardware extensions.

By making use of containers and Kubernetes, we can move from machine-centric designs to application-centric and service-centric designs. We call this type of architecture cloud-native architecture, and Kubernetes is the key enabler that provides the flexibility of IaaS, the extensibility of PaaS, and the simplicity of SaaS. *Figure 11.2* illustrates how Kubernetes brings together the layers.

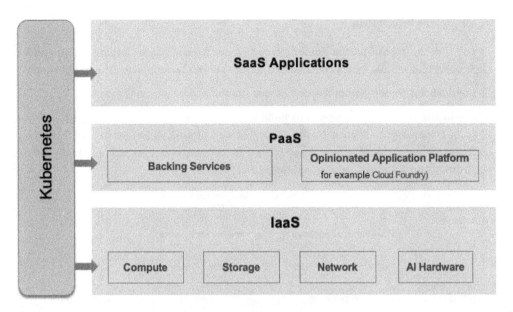

Figure 11.2: Kubernetes connects the layers

Now that we understand the Kubernetes architecture and how it enables application-centric and service-centric architecture design, let's next have a look at how we can interact with Kubernetes through its object model.

## Understanding Kubernetes objects

When we work with the Kubernetes API, we are ultimately dealing with Kubernetes objects, which are persistent entities that represent the states of different Kubernetes clusters and how the workloads are organized in Kubernetes. When creating an object in Kubernetes, we are basically telling the Kubernetes system our desired states, such as the following:

- Where an application needs to run

- The resources available to the application

- How the application will behave during restart policies, load balancing, or fault tolerance

More often than not, we create Kubernetes objects by providing information to the **kubectl** command-line terminal in a `.yaml` file. **kubectl** converts it into JSON and calls the Kubernetes API, and the control plane manages the object's actual state to match the desired state, as specified in the `.yaml` file. As such, it is important to understand the different types of objects that can be used to define the workloads in Kubernetes.

Here are some of the core objects:

- A **Pod** is the most basic unit in Kubernetes, which can contain one or multiple tightly coupled containers that should always be scheduled in the same node and share the same life cycle.

- A **ReplicaSet** defines the number of Pods that should be deployed in the cluster.

- A **Deployment** uses **ReplicaSets** as its building blocks and defines the life cycle of replicated Pods. A Deployment is likely to be the object that we will work with most frequently to create and manage workloads. Based on the Deployment, Kubernetes can adjust ReplicaSets, support applications for a rolling upgrade, and maintain event history.

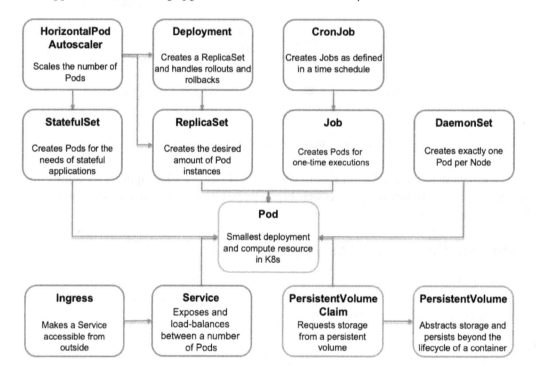

Figure 11.3: Kubernetes core objects

## Imperative and declarative

In Kubernetes, there are two ways to deploy objects, **imperatively** and **declaratively**.

The **imperative approach** outlines how a machine will do something and how it aligns with the operational model of a machine, such as kubectl commands, and is good for interactive experimentation.

In comparison, with a **declarative approach**, you declare the expected outcomes powered by the declarative Kubernetes API and the controllers. You can tell Kubernetes what you want to do, and it will deliver the outcome within some technical boundaries. This can be achieved by writing manifests in YAML/JSON using the `kubectl apply` command that refers to the manifest file. Here, the distinction is in *how* versus *what*. Declarative design is easier to understand and allows you to focus on problematic domains. Therefore, the declarative approach is used in most production deployments.

## Extensions and custom resources

Kubernetes is extensible through custom resources, which extend the Kubernetes API with resource types that are unavailable in the default Kubernetes installation. Custom resources are widely used by many projects, such as the **Istio service mesh**, **Kubeless Serverless Framework**, **TensorFlow machine learning framework**, and Kubernetes itself to make it more modular. There are two ways to create custom resources:

- **CustomResourceDefinitions (CRDs)** provide a simple way to create a custom object without any programming.

- **API aggregation** provides a programmable approach that allows for more control by writing your API server with custom business logic, validation, storage, and additional operations other than **create, read, update, and delete (CRUD)**.

Now, we have discussed the architecture patterns, core objects, and extension mechanisms of Kubernetes, demonstrating the benefits of enabling cloud-native development with its improved resiliency and velocity. For SAP BTP, Kubernetes is a key building block and the underlying layer for building new services and applications. Next, let's discuss what Kubernetes offers as a part of SAP BTP – **Gardener** and **Kyma**.

# Understanding Gardener

In many companies, it is the responsibility of a central infrastructure team to build and manage shared Kubernetes clusters, and teams are assigned namespaces to segregate the workloads. In a microservices architecture and DevOps model, teams are empowered to make decisions related to all aspects of any service, including the underlying infrastructure. A managed offering makes it much easier for teams to launch and operate their own Kubernetes clusters suited to their needs.

**Gardener** is a managed **Kubernetes as a Service (KaaS)** offering used as part of SAP BTP that works across on-premises and multiple cloud environments. In early 2017, SAP put together a small team to figure out how Kubernetes could work for SAP's workloads. Later in the same year, SAP joined the CNCF community as a Platinum member. This effort led to the creation of Gardener, with its first open-source commit on October 1, 2018: `https://github.com/gardener/gardener/commit/d9619d01845db8c7105d27596fdb7563158effe1`.

Gardener was created to run enterprise workloads in Kubernetes at scale, including day-2 operations. It is not only capable of provisioning thousands of Kubernetes clusters but also able to manage them 24/7 with scaling and observability capabilities. Some examples of these are rolling upgrades, a scaling control pane, and worker nodes. Gardener has a broad infrastructure coverage and runs on all SAP target infrastructures, on IaaS providers such as AWS, Azure, GCP, and Alibaba Cloud, as well as on OpenStack, VMware, and bare metal. Gardener supports multiple Linux OSs and provides the flexibility and portability of a managed and homogenous Kubernetes offering, together with multi-cloud support. Equally, minimizing the **total cost of ownership** (**TCO**) is one of the key design targets of Gardener. *Figure 11.4* summarizes and highlights the key features of Gardener.

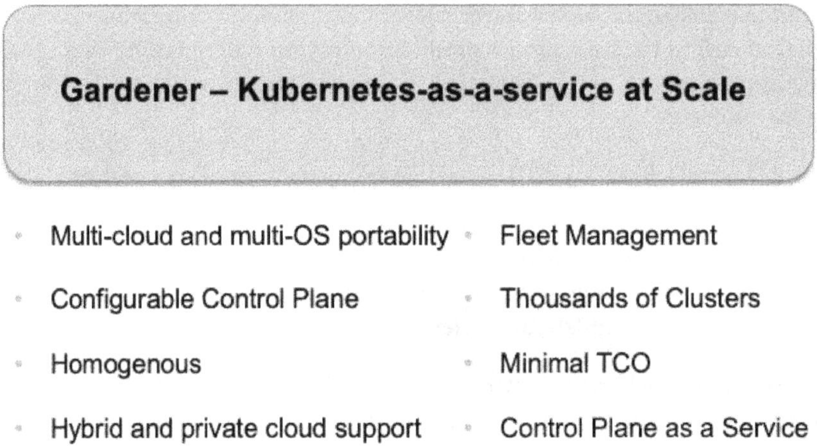

## Gardener – Kubernetes-as-a-service at Scale

- Multi-cloud and multi-OS portability
- Configurable Control Plane
- Homogenous
- Hybrid and private cloud support
- Fleet Management
- Thousands of Clusters
- Minimal TCO
- Control Plane as a Service

Figure 11.4: Overview of Gardener features

Next, let's discuss the unique architecture of Gardener, which uses Kubernetes to run Kubernetes itself to both improve resiliency and reduce TCO.

## Gardener architecture

So, what is unique about Gardener architecture?

The foundation of Gardener is Kubernetes itself. Gardener implements a special pattern to run Kubernetes inside Kubernetes in order to operate and manage a huge number of clusters with a minimal TCO.

When you explore the Gardener-managed end user clusters, you cannot find the control plane components that we discussed earlier in the *Understanding Kubernetes architecture* section, such as **kube-apiserver**, **kube-scheduler**, and **kube-control-manager**.

Instead, the control plane is deployed as a native Kubernetes workload and runs in Pods inside another Kubernetes cluster, which is called a **seed cluster**. In essence, what a seed cluster provides is a **control plane as a service** for the Kubernetes clusters running the actual workloads – the end user clusters. In

Gardener terms, these end user clusters are called **shoot clusters**. A seed cluster can potentially host and manage thousands of control planes of the many shoot clusters. This is its main difference from many other managed Kubernetes offerings. To provide necessary resiliency and business continuity requirements, it is recommended to have a seed cluster for each cloud provider and region.

So, how is this architecture achieved in reality?

Gardener implements a Kubernetes-Inception concept and is ultimately an aggregated API server that extends Kubernetes resources with custom resources, combined with a set of custom controllers. A shoot resource is the **CustomResourceDefinition (CRD)** used to declare the target status of an end user cluster. Gardener will pick up the definition and provision the actual shoot cluster. For every shoot, Gardener creates a namespace in the seed cluster with appropriate security policies.

There are controllers responsible for standard operations such as creating a cluster, performing regular health checks, or performing automated upgrades. Gardener implements the Kubernetes operator pattern to extend Kubernetes and follow its design principles. If you look into Gardener architecture, you will see its similarity to Kubernetes architecture. Shoot clusters are like Pods and seed clusters are like worker nodes. Gardener reuses the same concepts but creates another dimension of scalability in terms of distributed computing and resource management. *Table 11.1* compares the Gardener concepts with Kubernetes itself:

| Kubernetes | Gardener |
|---|---|
| Kubernetes API server | Gardener API server |
| Kubernetes controller manager | Gardener controller manager |
| Kubernetes scheduler | Gardener Scheduler |
| Kubelet | Gardenlet |
| Worker node | Seed cluster |
| Pod | Shoot cluster |

Table 11.1: Kubernetes versus Gardener

In Gardener, the controller manager manages the custom resources, while Gardener Scheduler is responsible for finding the appropriate seed cluster to host the control plane for a shoot cluster. Here is an example of the steps to create a shoot cluster in Gardener:

1. Gardener creates a namespace in the seed cluster that will host the control plane of a shoot cluster.

2. The control plane of a shoot cluster is deployed into the created namespace in the seed cluster, which contains the **Machine Controller Manager (MCM)** Pod.

3. The MCM creates machine CRDs in the seed cluster that specify the configuration and number of replicas for the shoot cluster.

4. Pods, PersistentVolumes, and load balancers are created by Kubernetes via the respective cloud and infrastructure provider, and the shoot cluster API server is up and running.

5. kube-system daemons and add-ons are deployed into the shoot cluster and the cluster becomes active.

*Figure 11.5* illustrates the Gardener architecture and how the aforementioned steps interact with different components.

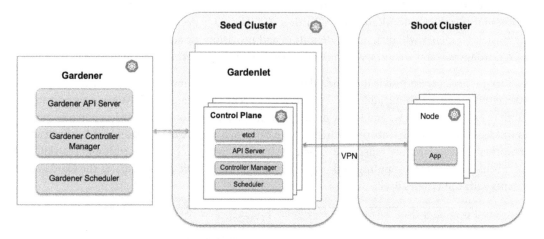

Figure 11.5: Overview of Gardener architecture

> **Important Note**
>
> Gardener is the underlying runtime of SAP BTP and many SAP applications. It is not necessarily visible to SAP customers who will build extensions or new applications on top of SAP BTP. However, it is helpful for you as an architect to understand this common infrastructure abstraction layer and its benefits. To learn more details about Gardener or even consider contributing to it, check out the open-source project at `https://gardener.cloud`.

## Understanding Kyma

If you have some applications that you'd like to extend in a cloud-native way, with the flexibility to use different technologies that can be scaled independently, or use event-based architecture and serverless functions, **Kyma** could be of interest to you.

So, what is Kyma?

Kyma is an open-source project designed natively on Kubernetes for extending applications using serverless computing and microservices architecture. Based on many years of experience in extending and customizing different SAP applications, Kyma was donated by SAP as an open-source project in 2018, with a mission statement to enable a flexible way of extending applications and with all the necessary tools to build cloud-native enterprise applications. Technically, Kyma picked the best projects from the growing CNCF community and glued them together to offer an integrated and simplified experience, equipped with the following out-of-the-box capabilities:

- Connecting any existing applications to a Kubernetes cluster and exposing its APIs and BusinessEvents securely. You can orchestrate heterogeneous landscapes to build common extensions. This is achieved by a component in Kyma called **Application Connector**.

- Implementing business logic in microservices or serverless functions using any programming language. Through its integration with connected applications, the extension logic can be triggered either by events or through API calls.

- Using built-in cloud services through the **Service Catalog**, which implements an **Open Service Broker** to consume business and technical backing services from GCP, Azure, and AWS in Kyma.

- Out-of-the-box observability for the functions and workloads running in Kyma, including logging, monitoring, metrics, and tracing.

- Using Knative features, such as Build, Serving, Eventing, and the Operator.

*Figure 11.6* illustrates the capabilities Kyma provides and the technical components it puts together.

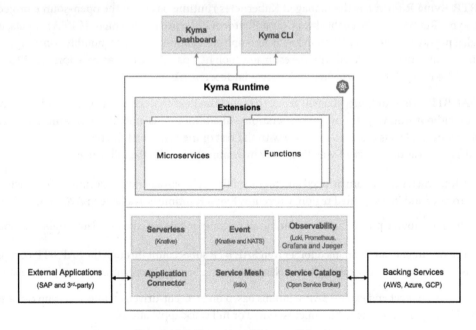

Figure 11.6: Overview of Kyma architecture

While most of the components in Kyma are based on CNCF open-source projects, **Application Connector** was created by the Kyma team at SAP to simplify connectivity and integration with enterprise applications, no matter whether they are within an on-premises or a cloud system. Application Connector helps to establish a secure connection with external applications and register the APIs and event catalogs of connected applications, delivers registered events, and maps an application to a Kyma namespace by using the registered APIs and events.

The registered applications are exposed in the Service Catalog and associated with the functions in Kyma through service binding. In this way, you can keep the extension code clean, and variables can be injected into functions automatically. Connectivity is secured using a client certificate verified by Istio and generated and stored as a **Kubernetes Secret**.

> **Important Note**
>
> **Knative** is an open-source project for building, deploying, and managing serverless and cloud-native applications in Kubernetes. It is an opinionated approach focusing on three areas: building containers and functions, serving and scaling workloads, and eventing. Kyma works and integrates well with Knative.

## SAP BTP, Kyma Runtime

**SAP BTP, Kyma Runtime** is the managed Kubernetes runtime based on the open-source project Kyma. Kyma Runtime can be enabled via **Cloud Platform Enterprise Agreement** (**CPEA**) credits, or through a **pay-as-you-go** (**PAYG**) model with zero upfront commitment. The monthly consumption of CPEA credits can be calculated with the estimator tool: `https://estimator-don4txf2p3.dispatcher.ap1.hana.ondemand.com/index.html`.

With SAP BTP, Kyma Runtime, you will get all the functionalities that the open-source project Kyma provides without worrying about cloud operations. In addition, it is embedded into the SAP BTP account model and so is easier to integrate with the rest of the SAP portfolio that uses SAP BTP as the underlying platform. Every Kyma Runtime environment includes the following:

- A Kubernetes cluster provisioned and managed through Gardener on a specified infrastructure provider and in a specified region. Currently, Kyma Runtime is available in AWS and Azure.

- The open-source project Kyma, including all its components based on the latest stable version.

A Kyma environment can be enabled for a given SAP BTP subaccount through the SAP BTP cockpit and runs in its dedicated Kubernetes cluster. Namespaces can be used to organize resources in a cluster.

In addition, to connect and extend SAP solutions based on an event-driven architecture, you can also use SAP BTP, Kyma Runtime to run microservices or full stack applications.

# When should you use Cloud Foundry or Kubernetes?

SAP BTP offers the Cloud Foundry application runtime, which is optimized for enterprise application developers to build stateless apps (that follows the 12-factor apps methodology) without worrying about the heavy lifting of deployment and scaling. Alongside Cloud Foundry, SAP BTP offers Kubernetes for both non-opinionated and opinionated workloads, supporting a broader range of technical capabilities and use cases. However, these additional capabilities come at the price of additional learning curves and effort in the day-to-day jobs of a developer. SAP's strategy is to make use of the benefits of to suit the different needs of its customers.

Equally, making the decision about which runtime to use requires sufficient information about the technology roadmap and means committing to a specific set of tools, technologies, support, and processes, as migrating from one to another can be very challenging. So, between Cloud Foundry's higher-level abstraction and higher development efficiency and Kubernetes' more flexible but lower level of technical capabilities, which do you choose for your use case? The short answer is "*it depends*." *Table 11.2* provides high-level guidelines on the decision criteria:

| Decision Criteria | Cloud Foundry | Kubernetes |
|---|---|---|
| Team skillset | Citizen developers and application developers need higher-level abstraction. | Cloud-native developers prefer to have low-level access and are comfortable with the level of complexity in exchange for the necessary flexibility. |
| Use case types | Stateless applications that follow the 12-factor apps methodology | Highly scalable microservices, stateful applications. |
| Infrastructure and regional coverage | Runs in hyper-scale public clouds only | Needs to support hybrid and private cloud environments as well |
| New technologies and services | Cloud Foundry-based business services and backing services | Wants to benefit from cloud-native capabilities, such as service mesh, the operator approach, the need for application-specific backing services (through Open Service Broker), or compatibility with special machine types (for example, for AI workloads). |

Table 11.2: Decision criteria between Cloud Foundry and Kubernetes

Please be aware that there is no one-size-fits-all and you will need to assess what will be more suitable for you.

## Summary

To recap, we have learned how containers and Kubernetes have helped to modernize software development and service delivery. We have also learned about the core components of Kubernetes, the object model on how we can interact with Kubernetes, and the support of custom resources and extension mechanisms.

Based on this, we have introduced how SAP embraces the cloud-native technology trend and contributes through its two major open-source projects: Gardener, focusing on multi-cloud Kubernetes provisioning and management, and Kyma, focusing on cloud-native application extension and development. Lastly, we have discussed the decision criteria for selecting the environment of choice for your use cases and how you can use this information to plan your projects to extend and build with SAP BTP.

Starting from the next chapter, we will focus on a new section of chapters on *data to value*. We will cover databases and data management capabilities, such as SAP HANA Cloud and SAP Data Warehouse Cloud, analytics, and intelligent technologies such as machine learning and artificial intelligence. Data is an exciting topic, and we have a lot to cover, so fasten your seatbelt; it will be a fun ride!

# Part 5
# Data to Value

This part dwells on how to use the data management capabilities in SAP BTP to address the challenges in integrating data, gaining insights, and delivering value in business contexts.

This part contains the following chapters:

- *Chapter 12, SAP HANA Cloud*
- *Chapter 13, SAP Data Warehouse Cloud and SAP Analytics Cloud*
- *Chapter 14, SAP Intelligent Technologies*

# 12

# SAP HANA Cloud

Applications are increasingly becoming data-driven, and data is generated by everything from enterprise applications and social media to smart devices. While companies are excited about the possibilities with all their data, how to manage data and extract value from it is becoming a common and urgent challenge. In the meantime, modern cloud design principles lead to an increasing number of distributed systems such as microservices architecture and cloud-native applications, resulting in increased complexity for integrating data.

In this chapter, we will introduce database and data management capabilities as part of **SAP BTP** and how they can help to address these challenges, such as accessing data, processing data, and how to get the maximum value from data. We will focus on the following topics:

- Data-driven use cases

- Data architecture concepts and patterns

- SAP HANA Cloud

- SAP HANA Cloud, HANA database

Before that, let's have a look at typical data-driven use cases, and data architecture concepts and patterns.

## Technical requirements

If you have already registered for an SAP BTP trial account, it is good enough to get hands-on experience with the products we are going to cover in this chapter.

## Data-driven use cases

Data is the core element for applications serving diverse use cases from traditional analytics and **machine learning (ML)/artificial intelligence (AI)** to data-intensive applications that combine both analytical and transactional workloads. All these applications generate data, and almost all enterprises today rely on multiple applications to support their business processes and fight with data accumulated in silos from different applications in their **information technology** (**IT**) landscapes. Furthermore, modern applications use a much larger number of data stores—such as objects, documents, and graphs—compared to legacy applications mainly leveraging a relational store. A modern data architecture supported by various data integration and processing technologies will need to address these challenges and hide the aforementioned underlying complexity.

Let's have a look at a concrete example based on an Intelligent Enterprise scenario to see how data and workflow can be integrated across SAP applications—for example, how to get an overview of and the ability to drill down into all workforce costs such as salary, bonus, travel, equipment, and the external workforce, all scattered among different systems such as SAP S/4HANA, SAP SuccessFactors, SAP Concur, and SAP Fieldglass.

S/4HANA is an **enterprise resource planning** (**ERP**) system that typically holds transactions such as salary, bonus, and payments; SAP SuccessFactors is a core **human resources** (**HR**) system that keeps all employee master data, including compensation details and bonus plans. SAP Ariba and SAP Fieldglass are procurement systems that employees use to order IT equipment and services, and SAP Concur provides information about business travel and expense reimbursement.

To get full visibility of workforce costs, data sitting in all these systems must be brought together in a harmonized way and be aggregated to calculate **key performance indicators** (**KPIs**). Besides employee salary, travel plans can be highly sensitive data and thus must be protected. Access control must be consistently enforced across all involved systems. In addition, insights derived from data can be fed back into systems to trigger new processes—for example, to apply a new travel policy based on budget situations and employee job families. The use case can be further extended with event-driven processing of data, to enable active notifications or other real-time interactions.

Derived from the aforementioned use case are typical data-driven scenarios in which data coming from multiple places must be combined, and should include both structured and unstructured data such as images and documents that are stored in various databases or storage systems.

The following list is not a complete list of all scenarios; rather, it provides a glimpse of common use cases that each company may have:

- **Data and process integration**: To enable business process and workflow integration based on data. In such integration scenarios, data is shared across multiple applications through aligned data models or **application programming interfaces** (**APIs**), or an integration middleware such as SAP Integration Suite. Data or events generated in one application can trigger actions in other applications. A loosely coupled event-driven pattern can be used to achieve integrations elegantly.

- **Cross-product analytics**: As with the workforce cost use case, it is essential to combine data from multiple sources to gain insights and realize the value of data. To be able to join data together, data harmonization is required, such as master data entities—for example, employee or cost center. Data can be connected both through federation that connects data virtually and replication into a central location for advanced processing. Data modeling and metadata management must be included, and analytical contents created must be extensible to meet different business needs—for example, adding a new data source.

- **ML/AI applications**: Apart from classical analytics applications, ML/AI applications usually need to process all types of data such as images, voices, videos, and sensor data from smart devices. Training of algorithms can be resource-intensive and requires underneath data platforms to support heavy computations. In this case, it would make more sense to extract data from source applications and consolidate this in a centralized data platform.

- **Data-intensive applications**: Require fast processing of huge amounts of data that often needs a distributed high-performance data platform with parallel execution. Such applications may involve ML/AI but with more focus on processing than training—for example, extracting information from invoices, monitoring sensor data, and performing searches over vast amounts of data. Besides, data pipelines with the necessary data lineage and **life-cycle management (LCM)** can provide transparency as data is usually processed in multiple steps.

# Data architecture concepts and patterns

To support the data-driven use cases, architecture concepts and patterns have evolved over the years to solve specific problems. Let's review them together, and later, we will discuss SAP data management capabilities in this context.

## OLTP, OLAP, HTAP

The terms **online transaction processing (OLTP)** and **online analytical processing (OLAP)** look similar but refer to two different kinds of data systems. An OLTP system captures and manages transactions in a database, in the form of insertion, updating, and deletion of data frequently. Tables in an OLTP database are usually normalized, and data integrity must be taken care of in case of any transaction failure. In comparison, OLAP's main operation is to extract multidimensional data for analytics, which has less frequent transactions but requires a longer time to process data as data needs to be denormalized and joined together by running complex queries to turn data into information.

The different requirements of OLTP and OLAP result in having different data systems optimized for their purposes. Data from one or more OLTP systems is ingested into OLAP systems through the process of **extract, transform, load (ETL)**. An ETL pipeline supported by various tools collects data from several sources, transforms it into the desired format, then loads it into a destination system such as an OLAP data warehouse to support analytics and **business intelligence (BI)** for insights. Depending on the use case, the ETL process can be very complex and requires extra storage, special care with data security, and privacy alongside data movement.

In some areas, using *after-the-fact* analysis is not acceptable. Organizations must respond quickly to business opportunities in real time. **Hybrid transactional/analytical processing (HTAP)** is a term that represents a data architecture that can handle both transactional and analytical workloads in one system, thus eliminating the need for multiple copies of the same data and the ETL process. HTAP has the potential to change existing business processes as well as create new ones by offering real-time decision-making based on live transactional data and the capability to run sophisticated analytics on large amounts of data. Most HTAP systems are enabled by in-memory and scalable transactional processing technologies. **SAP HANA** and its managed offering of SAP HANA Cloud are examples of such HTAP systems.

## NoSQL, big data, and cloud object stores

To extend the data architecture beyond **relational database management systems** (**RDBMS**), we cannot avoid talking about NoSQL and big data. NoSQL is not a product; rather, it's a collection of different data storage and processing systems to meet different kinds of needs.

NoSQL had a good run; it was created by Hadoop MapReduce in 2004 and was accelerated by Dynamo and BigTable in 2007. NoSQL has won in terms of popularity in the past decade by addressing one of the core limitations of traditional RDBMS—**scalability**, by starting with distributed system design and data management that provide **high availability** (**HA**) and scalability. In the **Consistency, Availability, and Partition Tolerance** (**CAP**) theorem, most NoSQL databases prioritize *A* and support eventual consistency for *C*. While it promises scalability and flexibility, NoSQL has fallen short in many areas, especially in its early days, such as no support for **Structured Query Language** (**SQL**), no support for transactions, and no schema management. It has also evolved from simple key-value stores to document stores, column family stores, and SQL on Files processing engines.

During its prime time, Hadoop and NoSQL technologies were often connected with big data, and this represents a whole ecosystem of technologies. In the past few years, we have seen consolidations in this space; however, it is still one of the key challenges many organizations face during data integration and building a future-proof data architecture. Besides, many NoSQL databases have added SQL-like capabilities such as the **Cassandra Query Language** (**CQL**) and **Spark SQL**, thus the term *NoSQL* itself is becoming obsolete.

In the meantime, cloud object stores such as **Amazon Web Services** (**AWS**) **Simple Storage Service** (**S3**) are becoming attractive and are the preferred storage solution for many companies. Object storage benefits from the mature infrastructure of cloud providers with low cost and built-in capabilities such as HA, scalability, and global and regional distribution, without worrying about the complexity of setting up and maintaining landscapes.

## Data federation and data replication

Given the complexity of the existing and ever-growing ecosystems of data technologies, how we can bring together data? Now, let's talk about data integration approaches such as data federation and data replication.

Data federation allows multiple databases to function as one. Data federation helps to remove data silos, resulting in more accurate, reliable, and consistent data. Data federation also avoids costs for redundant storage, software licenses, or extra data governance. Because it doesn't replicate or physically move data, it reduces the risk of data loss and makes it much easier to set up and manage authentication and authorization of data access.

However, data federation runs into limitations when data volumes and complexities are present—for example, HA and scalability, predictable low latency, and high performance. Data federation also falls short when sophisticated data cleaning and transformation are required. In such cases, data replication is the better approach. Creating multiple copies of data through data replication increases overall availability and reduces latency as data can be stored closer to its consumers. It also improves performance and provides more flexibility to run complex queries or advanced analytics with dedicated data stores optimized for workloads, instead of distributed fragile joins involving multiple databases and high network latency through data federation.

As there are advantages and disadvantages to both approaches, a modern data architecture will need to involve both and be able to switch between them seamlessly.

## SAP HANA Cloud

**SAP HANA Cloud** is a managed offering of the in-memory HTAP database SAP HANA. It inherits the capabilities of SAP HANA such as multi-model support (relational, hierarchies, graph, geo-spatial, semi-structured data), advanced analytical processing, and flexible data integration. As a cloud offering, all infrastructure layers such as compute, storage, and networking are automatically provisioned and monitored; backups and upgrades are taken care of automatically, so you can benefit from the reliability, scalability, integrated security, and productivity improvement of unified cloud-based tooling.

HANA Cloud supports a variety of use cases. It can act as a gateway to all enterprise data with virtual connections and data replications, be the backbone of advanced analytics and reporting with SAP Data Warehouse Cloud and SAP Analytics Cloud, and be the runtime database for your enterprise applications such as SAP Intelligent Suite applications.

In a nutshell, HANA Cloud is comprised of the following components to store and process various types of data:

- **SAP HANA Cloud, SAP HANA database**: This is an in-memory database for multi-model data processing, providing fast access and unmatchable performance.

- **SAP HANA Cloud, Data Lake**: Leverages inexpensive storage options to lower costs, while providing high performance for querying **petabytes** (**PB**) of relational data.

- **SAP Adaptive Server Enterprise (SAP ASE)**: Enables extreme OLTP scenarios for many concurrent users.

- **SAP HANA Cloud, SAP ASE Replication**: This is a log-based replication system that supports real-time data replication between ASE instances.

While multiple components have been introduced into SAP HANA Cloud to provide the necessary flexibility to scale data from an in-memory disk to an object store (SQL access to relational data in Parquet files), it allows picking the best option based on required qualities concerning performance, cost, or other **key performance indicators** (**KPIs**). The following diagram provides high-level guidance on data storage options in SAP HANA Cloud:

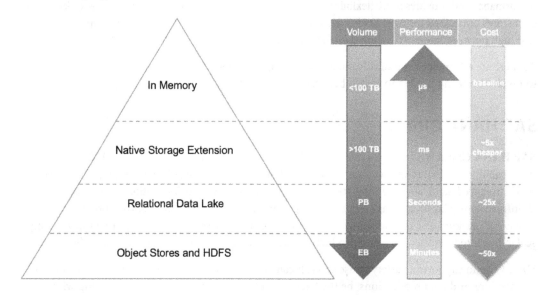

Figure 12.1: Data pyramid of SAP HANA Cloud

Besides this, HANA Cloud optimizes data access and query processing between different storage options—for example, sending child plan fragments to a remote source.

Rather than hold all data in memory, **Native Storage Extension** (**NSE**) is a built-in warm store to manage less frequently accessed data. NSE is enabled in SAP HANA Cloud by default. It uses techniques to only load pages related to your query into memory; you can use the `ALTER TABLE` and `CREATE TABLE` commands to specify which columns, tables, or table partitions are page-loadable through the `<load_unit> PAGE` value. NSE is transactionally consistent with in-memory hot data, included in backup and system replication operations, as a substantial increase of data capacity with overall good performance for SAP HANA to handle high-volume data.

SAP HANA Cloud, Data Lake, based on **Intelligent Query** (**IQ**) technology, is the **relational data lake** layer that scales independently and integrates with HANA Database through a highly optimized **Smart Data Access** (**SDA**) connection including query delegation. It also provides the capability to access cloud object storage such as AWS S3, and **Google Cloud Platform** (**GCP**) Cloud Storage.

SAP HANA Cloud runs on containers and Kubernetes managed through Gardener, mentioned in the previous chapter, to accommodate independent and elastic scaling of storage and computing, and provides HA, scalability, resiliency, and **total cost of ownership** (**TCO**) optimization.

> **Important Note**
> **SAP HANA Cloud** is the successor of **SAP HANA Service**, a managed HANA database offered through Neo and multi-cloud environments. SAP will continue to support the SAP HANA service for customers with existing contracts, but new customers are not eligible to buy the SAP HANA service anymore.

## Tools to access SAP HANA Cloud

One of the cloud benefits is to access SAP HANA Cloud through a centralized, unified **user experience** (**UX**) with powerful cloud-based tooling, all through web **user interfaces** (**UIs**). Depending on the role and task type, you can use one of the tools mentioned next to achieve your goals.

### SAP BTP Cockpit

SAP BTP Cockpit is an administration interface for managing almost all components and services in SAP BTP, such as global accounts, subaccounts, entitlements and quotas, subscriptions, and authentication and authorization. It is the starting point for creating and managing SAP HANA Cloud instances. To get an overview of your instances, navigate to the **Cloud Foundry** (**CF**) space and then choose **SAP HANA Cloud** in the navigation area. For each instance, you can check the status, memory, **central processing unit** (**CPU**), and storage consumption, or navigate to other cloud tools for more detailed administrative tasks.

### SAP HANA Cloud Central

SAP HANA Cloud Central is where you can create, edit, or delete your instances. The provisioning wizard allows users to configure options such as type of instance, **availability zones** (**AZs**) and replicas, network connectivity, and other settings.

Replica management is also supported; you can add a new replica to improve availability or initiate a takeover from an asynchronous replica for your HANA instance. In a recovery scenario, there are different options—you can either recover the backup into a new instance by using **Recreate Instance** or recover to a selected point in time of the same instance using **Start Recovery** if a backup is available, providing businesses options to meet their **business continuity** (**BC**) requirements.

### SAP HANA Cockpit

SAP HANA Cockpit is available for both HANA on-premises and HANA Cloud, providing a range of tools for database-level administrative and monitoring tasks. It is provisioned in the same CF space when the HANA Cloud instance is created, so you don't need to install it separately.

SAP HANA Cockpit aims to provide a single pane of glass for HANA database instances. It provides a SAP Fiori-based launchpad with real-time information in the form of tiles arranged in groups. Administrators can use it to manage multiple landscapes and instances with less effort, have more visibility of the overall system status with detailed metrics of each resource, and be alerted when attention is needed to prevent system downtime. SAP HANA Cockpit includes the following features:

- Managing database configurations and update parameters/values for different server types

- Managing database operations such as data volume encryption, automated backups, and data replications

- Monitoring and analyzing workloads, alerting, and diagnostics; monitoring service status, performance, and threads; and understanding resource utilization (CPU, memory, and disk) and SQL statement analysis

- Security administration (for example—manage users and roles, enable audit trails and policies, manage certificates, configure **identity providers (IdPs)**)

### SAP HANA Database Explorer

Integrated into SAP HANA Cockpit, SAP HANA Database Explorer is a tool for managing data and database objects of SAP HANA Cloud. You can browse the database catalog and check individual database schemes, tables, views, procedures, remote connections, or other objects. It includes the SQL console where you can execute SQL statements and analyze the query execution, or even debug an SQLScript procedure.

### SAP Business Application Studio

SAP Business Application Studio is the next generation of SAP Web IDE, offering a development environment for SAP BTP. You can launch SAP Business Application Studio from SAP BTP Cockpit. At the heart of SAP Business Application Studio are Dev Spaces, which are private environments such as isolated **virtual machines (VMs)** to develop, build, test, and run your code. Each Dev Space type includes tailored tools and preconfigured runtimes for the target development scenario—for example, SAP Fiori, mobile development, CAP-based (here, **CAP** refers to SAP **Cloud Application Programming Model**) applications, and certainly HANA native applications. The following screenshot shows the page to create a Dev Space for HANA development with default and additional predefined extensions:

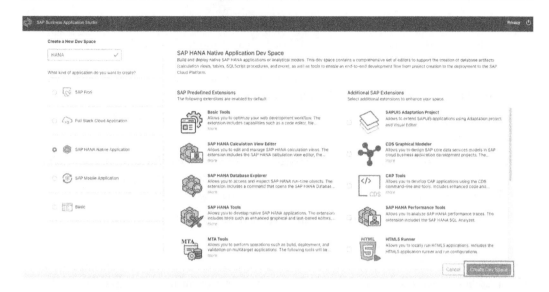

Figure 12.2: Creating a Dev Space for SAP HANA Native Development

> **Important Note**
>
> If you are using an SAP BTP trial account, SAP Business Application Studio may have already added it to your subaccount. Otherwise, enter the CF environment and find SAP Business Application Studio in the Service Marketplace and create a subscription. After that, it will appear in **Instances and Subscriptions** in SAP BTP Cockpit.

# SAP HANA Cloud, HANA Database

At the core of SAP HANA Cloud is the HANA database itself—the in-memory data platform. In this section, we will discuss topics you as an architect would like to know, from its system architecture, various development scenarios, data integration approaches, HA and BC, data encryption, feature compatibility, migration, and pricing, as well as its release strategy and data center availability. We have quite a lot to cover, so let's start!

## System architecture and server types

The HANA system is comprised of multiple server components running as different **operating system (OS)** processes and services in a host or a cluster of hosts. In SAP HANA Cloud, here are the core servers:

- **Name server**: Owns the information of the topology of the overall system. In a distributed system, it knows where the components are running and where data is located.

- **Index server**: Contains in-memory data stores. It segments all queries and contains several engines and processors for query executions, such as Planning Engine, Calculation Engine, and Store Procedure Processor. It also includes Transaction and Session Management for coordinating all database transactions and managing sessions and connections. An index server is not shared, and each tenant database must have its own index server.

- **Compile server**: Performs steps for compiling stored procedures written in SQLScript.

- **Data provisioning server (dpserver)**: Offered as part of **Smart Data Integration** (**SDI**), which provides data provisioning, data transformation, and data quality functions, adapters for remote sources, and a **software development kit** (**SDK**) for creating additional adapters.

- **SAP HANA Deployment Infrastructure Server (diserver)**: Simplifies the deployment of database objects using design-time artifacts.

You may notice that HANA Cloud has fewer servers in comparison to the HANA on-premises system, which has additional servers such as the preprocessor server used by the index server for text analysis and text search, or SAP HANA XS Advanced Services for HANA native application development. These server components are removed from HANA Cloud.

## Development with SAP HANA

There are multiple ways of developing applications with SAP HANA Cloud, from using HANA as the database runtime through **Java Database Connectivity** (**JDBC**)/**Open Database Connectivity** (**ODBC**) or **Object Relational Mapping** (**ORM**) frameworks, advanced data modeling, to native development with **HANA Deployment Infrastructure** (**HDI**) containers and using the CAP model to create full-stack applications. We will discuss these development scenarios next.

### Using SAP HANA Cloud as the database runtime

Just as with any other database, you can use HANA as the database runtime. In this case, you can use standard SQL statements to create, update, or delete database objects such as schemas, tables, and views, as well as run queries, join tables, filter data, and so on.

SAP HANA Client needs to be installed to provide a connection to the HANA Database using JDBC and ODBC, with the following connection strings respectively:

- **JDBC**: `"jdbc:sap://<endpoint>:<port>/?encrypt=true"`

- **ODBC**: `"driver=libodbcHDB.so; serverNode=<endpoint>:<port>;encrypt=Yes"`

The SAP HANA client also includes a command-line tool for executing database commands (for example, **Data Definition Language** (**DDL**); **Data Manipulation Language** (**DML**)) in a terminal window—**HDBSQL**. It can also execute commands from a script file for scheduled execution.

Drivers and libraries are supported for all major programming languages. For Node.js, `@sap/hana-client` can be used to connect and run SQL queries. It can be simply installed by running `npm install @sap/hana-client`. Find more details at `https://www.npmjs.com/package/@sap/hana-client`.

Similarly, Python, Go, Ruby, ADO.NET, and more programming languages and OSs are supported. You can check **SAP Note 2648274** for SAP HANA client interfaces at `https://launchpad.support.sap.com/#/notes/2648274`.

### Data modeling with SAP HANA Cloud

The modeling process involves the activities of slicing and dicing data in database tables by creating information views that can be used for reporting and decision-making. SAP HANA supports extended SQL views generated from design-time objects—modeled views. Historically, three types of modeled views were supported, which are attribute views, analytic views, and calculation views.

### Calculation View

The **Calculation View** combines the functionalities of all three types of views, and it is the only one supported in SAP HANA Cloud for modeling and analytical use cases.

Calculation Views allow data modelers to create advanced slices of data for analytics and multidimensional reports, by integrating various combinations of data (for example, entities and their relationships) to model a business use case. Data can be combined and processed with operations such as joins, unions, projections, and aggregations. If **CUBE** is selected as the data category, **Star Join** can be enabled to simplify the design process to join fact tables and dimensional tables. Advanced SQL logic can be applied, and in complex data models, multiple layers of Calculation Views can be combined. At the top of a Calculation View is the semantics node, where attributes (descriptive data such as customer **identifier** (**ID**) or sales order), measures (quantifiable data such as revenue or sales amount), and aggregation methods such as `AVG`, `SUM`, and `MAX` can be specified, which determines how the data will be exposed and consumed.

It is important to understand that Calculation Views are design-time artifacts and different from the corresponding database objects such as runtime objects. Actual database objects are created when the views are deployed (through HDI, which we will discuss in the *SAP HANA Native Development* section).

### SQLScript

**SQLScript** is the default programming language for writing database procedures in SAP HANA. SQLScript is a collection of SQL extensions—for example, data type extension with table types. A table type defines the name and attributes of an "internal table" that can be viewed as a temporary table without creating an actual database table. It can then be used to create table variables; the intermediate results of a SQL statement can be stored in the table variables and can be used as the data source for subsequent SQL queries.

An SQLScript procedure may contain SQL statements or call other procedures. Control flows such as `if/else` conditions and loops are supported, and a cursor can be opened to iterate through a result set. However, one of the key benefits of SQLScript is to embed data-intensive logic into the database layer to avoid massive data copies to the application layer and allow massive parallelization and execution of complex calculations inside HANA. Even though loops and cursors can process data in each row, it is always recommended to use read-only procedures with declarative table operators to allow mass data processing to achieve the best performance.

## SAP HANA Native Development

To understand how HANA Native Development has evolved, let's go back a little bit to the history of SAP HANA extended application services (XS Classics), XS Advanced, and the introduction of HDI. The following screenshot summarizes the major differences between them:

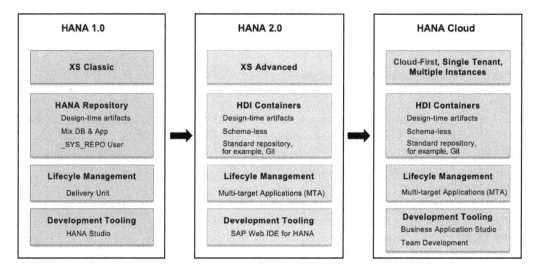

Figure 12.3: HANA Native Development evolution

HANA extended application services (XS Classic) were introduced in **HANA 1.0 Support Package Stack (SPS) 05** as an embedded lightweight application server that includes web-based **HyperText Transfer Protocol** (HTTP) and **Open Data Protocol** (OData) services. It is tightly coupled with database objects and uses database permissions and database user `_SYS_REPO` for content management in HANA Repository. All roles are global roles in the database and owned, built, and granted with privileges of `_SYS_REPO`. Content isolation is only possible using schemas and packages. **SAP HANA XS Javascript** (XSJS)—server-side JavaScript—and oData are the only programming interfaces supported in XS Classic, using HANA Studio and Web Development Workbench as development environments.

Introduced in HANA 1.0 SPS 11 and widely adopted in HANA 2.0, SAP HANA XS Advanced is an enhanced application server, based on the learning of the limitations of XS Classic such as scalability and the demands of more programming language support such as Java and Node.js. In XS Advanced, contents are deployed into organizations and spaces as with a CF environment; content isolation is achieved by the introduction of HDI containers. Roles are owned by schema-level technical users created by HDI that are separated from application development roles. Instead of using HANA Repository, it uses standard repositories such as Git.

SAP HANA Cloud implements a cloud-first approach for native development. Multi-tenancy is achieved by creating multiple HANA instances, and each instance itself is a single-tenant database. HDI continues to be the core of HANA Native Development in HANA Cloud and has been nicely integrated with development tooling such as Business Application Studio; for example, you can bind your application to an HDI container deployed in a BTP CF environment. Even though HDI was introduced together with XS Advanced, they are not dependent upon each other; XS Advanced is not even included in HANA Cloud.

## Understanding HDI

To understand HANA native development, the first thing is to understand what HDI is and the key benefits of using HDI. You may have heard about HDI containers and wondered how they relate to **multi-tenant database containers** (**MDC**) or Docker containers. The fact is it has nothing to do with either of them. So, what is HDI?

In a nutshell, HDI is a component and mechanism in SAP HANA to simplify the deployment of database objects using declarative design-time artifacts. It ensures a consistent deployment and implements transactional all-or-nothing deployment by checking dependencies and grants that multiple objects are deployed in the right sequences.

HDI offers a declarative approach to creating database objects; otherwise, these would be created through SQL DDL in imperative statements such as CREATE TABLE. The declarative way allows you to describe the desired target state in a design-time file and let HDI take care of the creation when the design-time file is deployed. This approach offers a higher level of abstraction that is easier to understand and more flexible and powerful to write logic than plain SQL. Design-time files can be versioned in a source code management system such as Git and can be used to ship database contents, just as with other application code. HDI only covers the deployment of database objects such as tables, views, and procedures, not non-database contents such as web and application code.

Isolation is one of the key features of HDI, achieved through HDI containers. In a HANA database, an arbitrary number of HDI containers can be created, and each container is implemented by a set of database schemas technically and isolated from other containers through schema-level access controls. Application developers don't need to explicitly specify the schema name in SQL statements, and this enables schema-independent code. Instead, the following schemas are created by HDI under the hood:

- **Container runtime schema**: <schema>, which contains application database objects that are accessible by the application at runtime.

- **Container metadata schema**: <schema>#DI contains design-time files, dependencies between objects, and additional metadata required for the deployment process.

- **Object owner schema**: `<schema>#OO` represents the technical user created as the HDI container's object owner (also known as #OO user). The object owner is a restricted database user who has a `CREATE ANY` privilege on the schema but no external privilege by default. The schema itself is empty.

- **Design-time user schema**: `<schema>_<user>_DT` represents technical users used for creating database objects from design-time artifacts.

- **Runtime application user schema**: `<schema>_<user>_RT` represents technical users to access runtime database objects by the applications.

Deployment into HDI containers includes two steps: first, upload design-time artifacts into the container metadata schema, then deploy the contents in the metadata schema into the database. The uploaded design-time artifacts are organized in virtual filesystems in HDI. For each HDI container, there are two virtual filesystems. Newly uploaded design-time files are stored in the `work` filesystem first, and then promoted to the "deployed" file time during the deployment, and corresponding database objects are created or updated in the container schema. The deployment operation, as well as uploading design-time files, is invoked by calling the HDI APIs (based on SQL procedures) generated in the container metadata schema when a container is created. The following screenshot shows an example of generated HDI schemas and the HDI API procedures of a HANA database project created in Business Application Studio named MYHANA:

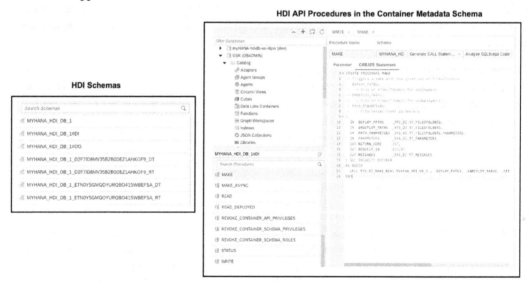

Figure 12.4: HDI schemas and HDI API procedures

HDI uses container-specific technical users; there are different technical users for different tasks—for example, the technical user that is used to create application database objects should have no access to the metadata schema and HDI API procedures and ensure runtime users only have access privileges on the container schema. These technical users are created in the object owner, design-time, and runtime user schemas. Cross-container access is prevented by default but can be enabled by granting necessary privileges explicitly and creating synonym binding configurations in the .hdbsynonym file. To be able to access objects in another container, the container's object owner user will require corresponding access privileges on objects in the target schema—for example, grant a SELECT privilege of the target schema to the #OO user with the GRANT/ADMIN option. Synonym binding is also applicable when you need access to a non-HDI-managed schema.

The following diagram illustrates how deployment to an HDI container works in steps:

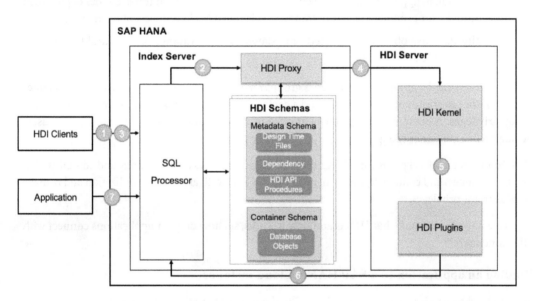

Figure 12.5: HDI deployment steps

The steps go like this:

1. HDC clients (for example, through Business Application Studio in the CF environment) upload the design-time files by calling a container-specific WRITE API procedure to SQL Processor.

2. SQL Processor delegates to the HDI proxy library to write the files to the "work" virtual filesystem in the container metadata schema.

3. Once uploaded, the HDI clients call the MAKE API procedure to trigger the deployment of involved contents in the virtual filesystem, which is dispatched to the HDI proxy again.

4. The HDI proxy calls the HDI server. The HDI server reads the files from the container metadata schema.

5.  The HDI kernel in the HDI server calls the HDI plugins for the different types of design-time files—for example, .hdbtable for table definition, .hdbprocedure for stored procedures definition, as well as **Core Data Services** (**CDS**) files. The mapping between plugins and file types can be configured in a configuration file (.hdiconfig, a join file that contains a list of bindings between design-time artifact file types and plugins and their versions). The plugins interpret the files and extract dependencies to determine the deployment order and translate them into SQL statements to be executed.

6.  The HDI kernel evaluates the extracted dependency information and calls the plugins to execute SQL to apply changes in the container schema, after which transactional deployment is ensured—for example, the entire transaction is rolled back in the event of an error.

7.  Finally, database objects are created or updated in the container schema and then can be accessed by the applications.

HDI containers can be grouped via container groups for administrative purposes. An HDI container administrator can create container groups, add a container to a container group, and manage container group privileges. A container group role is granted to the container object owners (the #OO user) belonging to a container group.

HDI Administration Cockpit, as part of SAP HANA Cockpit, provides the monitoring and administration of HDI containers and container groups that you can use to investigate resource utilization and manage administrator privileges.

You have now understood what HDI is and how it works; so, how do your applications connect with HDI containers?

**Binding an application to a SAP HANA Cloud instance**

You can bind an application to a SAP HANA Cloud instance through a schema or an HDI container, through a SAP HANA service broker instance (**SAP HANA Schemas & HDI Containers**) that provides schema and hdi-shared service plans, as shown in the following screenshot:

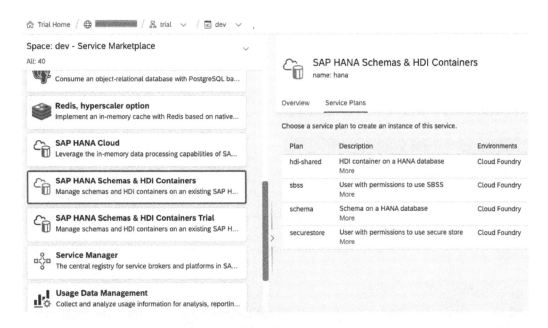

Figure 12.6: SAP HANA Schemas & HDI Containers' service plans

The schema service plan can be used to create a plain schema that you can manage manually. Consider using it if you want to use an ORM framework or use HANA as the database runtime only.

The hdi-shared service plan is used to create a broker instance to bind an application deployed in SAP BTP to an HDI container via the HDI Deployer. The HDI Deployer is essentially a Node.js (@ sap/hdi-deploy) based deployment module for HDI-based persistence models. Usually, the HDI Deployer is already packaged into the db module as part of a **multi-target application (MTA)**. The HDI Deployer can also be used without MTAs; to install it manually, simply run the following command:

```
npm i @sap/hdi-deploy
```

The following screenshot shows the configuration in an MTA.yaml file and credentials applications received once bound to an HDI container. The binding enables applications to access the HDI container without worrying about database access and connections. You will also see that the technical users mentioned previously (such as <schema>_<user>_DT and <schema>_<user>_RT) are used to access the corresponding design-time and runtime objects:

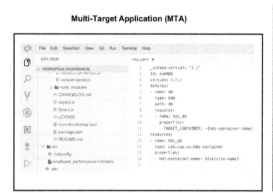

Figure 12.7: Application binding to an HDI container

## CAP, CDS, and HANA Cloud

SAP CAP is a development framework for enterprise applications that provides the necessary libraries and out-of-box capabilities to speed up development. CAP is an opinionated framework based on a core set of open source and SAP technologies.

CDS is the universal modeling language and backbone of CAP that allows you to define domain models, services, queries, and expressions in a declarative way. CDS models are plain JavaScript objects based on **Core Schema Notation (CSN)**, an open specification based on **JavaScript Object Notation (JSON)** Schema, which is used to generate target models such as OData/**Entity Data Model (EDM)** or OpenAPI, and database persistence models.

CDS, in combination with HDI previously discussed, is basically how CAP-based applications work with HANA Cloud. An entity created by CDS that serves as a façade of the objects is called a façade entity. The façade entity handles CDS-to-database-type mapping—for example, map an entity name to a database object name; map elements of an entity to database table columns; map the data types. You can create entities, associations, and compositions to capture the relationships between entities. It is possible to create either new database objects or use existing ones in a CDS model. To tell CDS that an object is already in the database, just add the `@cds.persistence.exists` annotation so that it will not be generated again. To understand more about CAP, please visit `https://cap.cloud.sap/docs/`.

**HANA ML libraries**

SAP HANA includes **Automated Predictive Library (APL)** and **Predictive Analysis Library (PAL)** to support ML and data mining capabilities covering a variety of algorithms and predictive models such as clustering, classification, regression, time-series forecasting, and more. The regression models and classification models implement a "gradient boosting" approach that applies learnings from each iteration step to provide a more accurate modeling result.

Both APL and PAL are installed in SAP HANA Cloud by default. However, they require Script Server to execute functions. Script Server is not enabled by default and can be enabled or disabled in SAP HANA Cloud Central.

> **Important Note**
>
> APL can also be called in Python via the Python ML client for SAP HANA (`hana-ml`). More details on `hana-ml` can be found at `https://help.sap.com/doc/1d0ebfe5e8dd44d09606814d83308d4b/2.0.05/en-US/html/hana_ml.html`.

## Data integration through federation and replication

In SAP HANA Cloud, you can create virtual tables through federation to access remote data as it was stored as a local table or use data replication.

A virtual table creates a link to a physical table in another HANA instance or other database, and data is read from the remote table and translated to HANA data types, in batches or in real time. While this gives the advantage that data doesn't need to be copied (thus reducing time), accessing data remotely might not be the ideal approach if you need to run complex queries by joining multiple tables spanning across different databases or have a specific need for query performance. In that case, data replication is recommended, and you can also set up replications automatically, such as by using **remote table replication**.

Next, we will have a look at the different technologies available in HANA Cloud to support the different scenarios of federating or replicating data into SAP HANA Cloud from various sources—SDA and SDI. The following screenshot shows different methods for remote access when SAP HANA Cloud is the target system:

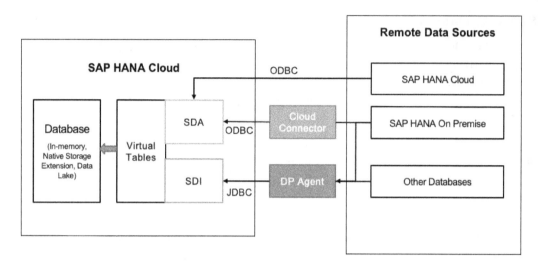

Figure 12.8: SAP HANA Cloud Data integration options

Here, the following applies:

- If the source system is also SAP HANA Cloud, SDA is the simplest way to use the ODBC adapter.

- If the source system is a non-HANA database, SDI with the **Data Provisioning Agent** (**DP Agent**) should be used.

- If the source system is a SAP HANA on-premises database, either SDA (ODBC) or SDI with DB Agent (JDBC) can be used. Cloud Connector is needed if the one-premise HANA is protected by a firewall.

> **Important Note**
>
> SDA and SDI support a different set of connections. The list of supported remote sources is also different between SAP HANA Cloud and SAP HANA On-Premise. New sources can be added or removed from a new release; see *SAP Note 2600176 – SAP HANA Smart Data Access Supported Remote Sources* for the latest information at https://launchpad.support.sap.com/#/notes/2600176 and SDI **Product Availability Matrix** (**PAM**) at https://support.sap.com/content/dam/launchpad/en_us/pam/pam-essentials/TIP/PAM_HANA_SDI_2_0.pdf.

## Data encryption

Data encryption at rest and in transit has become a mandatory requirement in modern system architecture. Encryption in transit protects data if communications are intercepted during data movement; for instance, **Transport Layer Security** (**TLS**) is often used for encrypting information—encrypted before transmission and decrypted on arrival.

Encryption at rest protects data while stored and can be applied at different layers such as database, application, or the underneath storage layer at the disk volume level. However, storing encryption keys on the same server as data no longer meets security standards for many companies. Several standards exist, depending on the industry—for example, **Payment Card Industry Data Security Standard** (**PCI DSS**) defines the duration of the period until keys must be rotated. **Federal Information Processing Standard Publication 140-2** (**FIPS 140-2**) defines security levels and where to store encryption keys.

There are two types of encryption keys: symmetric and asymmetric. The symmetric approach uses the same key for encryption and decryption, while the asymmetric approach uses a pair of public and private keys that are mathematically related, to encrypt data with a public key and decrypt data with the corresponding private key. As the asymmetric approach is computationally intensive, it is often used for encrypting keys named **key encryption keys** (**KEKs**), while the actual data is encrypted by a **data encryption key** (**DEK**) using the symmetric approach. DEKs encrypted with KEKs are typically stored separately outside of a **key management system** (**KMS**) or a **hardware security module** (**HSM**). KEKs used to encrypt DEKs never leave the KMS or HSM. This hybrid approach is often referred to as envelop encryption, as illustrated in the following diagram:

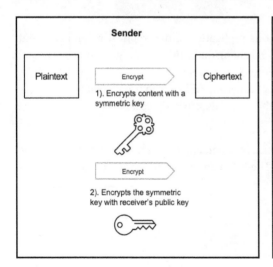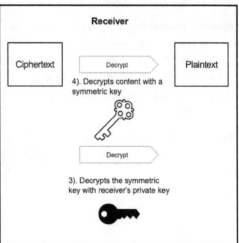

Figure 12.9: Envelop encryption with symmetric and asymmetric keys

In SAP BTP, **SAP Data Custodian** is the KMS fulfilling the compliance requirement for encryption keys, which provides a consistent way to manage the life cycle, including key rotations, secure storage of encryption keys, and audit logs for transparency. It integrates with the hyperscaler provider's KMS and HSM services that meet *FIPS 140-2 Level 2* and *FIPS 140-2 Level 3* compliance respectively. SAP HANA Cloud uses SAP Data Custodian to provide advanced encryption capabilities to enable customers to supply and manage their keys.

## HA and BC

HA and BC are important, especially for mission-critical systems. SAP HANA Cloud provides multiple available options based on different business needs, leveraging the multiple AZs provided by the underneath cloud infrastructures.

When creating a new instance through SAP HANA Cloud Central, you can define an AZ of interest to place the instance, which allows placing the database instance as close as possible to the applications to ensure low latency between the systems. For instances running on top of Microsoft Azure, it is possible to derive the AZs based on your Azure subscription ID automatically.

If you have your HANA Cloud instance running and want to extend it with a HA setup— with redundant instances called replicas—you can enable synchronous replication between multiple instances within the same AZ; redo log shipping and replay are enabled continuously. Consistency between the instances is the top priority here, and the replication mechanism guarantees that a transaction is committed only when applied in both instances. SAP HANA comes with built-in failure detection with autonomous takeover if one instance is unavailable.

For **disaster recovery** (**DR**) purposes, multiple zone replication allows replicating all persistent data across zones via an asynchronous replication mechanism. In this case, it guarantees eventual consistency; the database doesn't wait for replication to be completed, so you may lose data in the event of a disruption. Failover doesn't happen automatically; you will need to trigger failover manually following your DR procedures and after accepting the risk of data loss. Once failover is triggered, the DR failover is fully automated.

The HA and DR setup can be combined if your applications demand the highest level of BC. Besides, a near-zero downtime upgrade can be achieved. The following diagram summarizes the various options to consider:

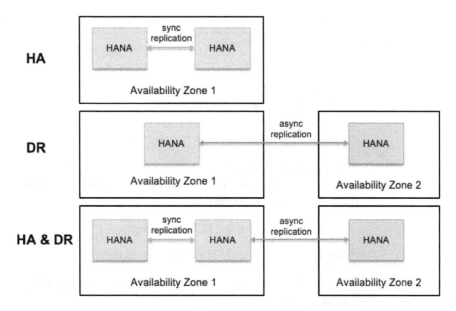

Figure 12.10: SAP HANA Cloud HA/DR options

No surprise that additional replicas incur additional costs. The cost of each replica is the same as the cost of the primary instance. So, it is your business decision to strike a balance between availability and cost, and it is recommended by SAP to plan BC for mission-critical systems.

Finally, there is an option to recreate an existing database instance in another AZ. Recreation will take longer than replication and should only be considered if no other alternative options are available. It is recommended to only take this option once you have filed a support ticket with SAP and have been advised to proceed with the recreation option.

## Compatibility and migration

In early 2019, SAP made a decision to split code and prioritize a cloud-first approach and move HANA architecture towards cloud-native qualities such as elasticity and scalability. All the new features and most of the development will be available for cloud-first. To protect the existing investment of customers and safeguard the transition, SAP also keeps the on-premises code line without radical changes but still delivers improvements. Selective features developed for the cloud can potentially be introduced back to an on-premise edition as well. As a result of the code split and the decision to innovate in cloud-first, there are some features originally developed for on-premises that are not supported in HANA Cloud. The following table lists features not available in HANA Cloud. It is not an exhaustive list but provides an initial checklist if you are considering migrating to SAP HANA Cloud and want to compare it with your existing HANA systems:

| Areas | Features |
|---|---|
| System management and operation | Direct access to OS level |
| | SAP HANA MDC |
| | SAP host agent |
| | Various system privileges (USER ADMIN, DATA ADMIN, EXTENDED STORAGE ADMIN, and more) |
| | Various built-in procedures and functions—graph nodes; anonymization nodes; history table option; column store cache option; import/export options |
| | Ability to disable logging, LCM, Delta log |
| | Volume input/output (I/O) statistics; result caching |
| | Scale-out and SQL plan stability (planned but not available initially) |
| Data definition | Data-type creation |
| | Full-text indexing, geocode indexes, non-unique inverted hash indexes |
| | Time-series tables, flexible tables, history tables, temporary row tables |
| | BusinessObjects Explorer (BO Explorer) including SQL extensions |
| Data processing | Text analysis and text mining |
| | SAP HANA dynamic tiering (DT) |
| | SAP HANA External Machine Learning (EML) library; TensorFlow integration) |
| | SAP HANA Smart Data Quality (SDQ) |
| | Hive integration; R integration |
| | Capture and replay |
| | Live cache |

| Application development | SAP HANA XS Advanced (XCA) and SAP HANA XS Classic; includes native OData services and a built-in job scheduler |
| | SAP HANA Repository |
| | SAP HANA CDS |
| | Multidimensional Expressions (MDX) |
| | Attribute and analytic views |
| Tooling | SAP HANA Studio |
| | Enterprise Architect Designer (EAD) |
| Security | Client-side encryption |
| | SYSTEM user access (replaced by DBADMIN) |

Table 12.1: Feature compatibility of HANA Cloud with HANA On-Premise

> **Important Note**
>
> For the latest information on feature compatibility, please check the help document at `https://help.sap.com/viewer/3c53bc7b58934a9795b6dd8c7e28cf05/hanacloud/en-US/11cc86c44d0b4dd3bf70e16870d9d4df.html`.

SAP HANA Cloud offers many advantages in comparison with previous versions, such as HA, a built-in data lake, and more. After thorough assessments and if you are planning to migrate to HANA Cloud, here are typical steps to check:

1.  During the pre-migration assessment and planning phase, it is important to get familiar with the feature capabilities and the differences in SAP HANA Cloud, review your requirements and understand the incompatibilities, and decide how you want to address them. You should also review the data center regions you plan to use and make sure SAP BTP and SAP HANA Cloud are offered in the target regions. Most importantly, have a clear objective for the migration and plan the necessary resources for the migration project.

2.  During the preparation phase, necessary **proofs-of-concept (PoCs)** should be performed for validating architecture assumptions, changes, and alternatives. Development and testing environments should be provisioned, and all tools and support services should be prepared. Besides this, the target production environment should be provisioned and configured.

3. During the development and validation phases, incompatible database objects and contents should be either removed or converted (for example, legacy database artifacts such as attribute views and flowgraphs should be converted to HDI contents), and dependencies identified and resolved. Multiple testing and validation efforts need to be executed, such as functional testing, load and performance testing, full regression testing, data integrity testing, and migration testing itself.

4. Finally, there is the deployment or migration phase, to deploy the actual application and database content and migrate production data from the source system(s). Security, observability, and operational monitoring should be enabled at the target, migrated data, and application functionality is validated and ready for use. The migration is usually done during a maintenance window.

5. If you are migrating from the SAP HANA service to SAP HANA Cloud, there is a Self-Service Migration tool provided to check compatibility and identify and migrate database objects, schemas, and data.

Please keep in mind that each database migration is unique and needs to be very well planned to minimize downtime and avoid disruptions. Depending on the complexity of your HANA landscape and your use case, the self-service tool might not be sufficient, or your migration process could be very different from what was described previously, so please consult your SAP support before planning the migration.

## Pricing

SAP HANA Cloud instances are sized based on the memory size, in 16 **gigabytes** (**GB**) blocks with a minimum of two blocks (32 GB). Compute and storage are allocated automatically—one **virtual CPU** (**vCPU**) per block of memory and 120 GB for the first 32 GB of memory, plus 40 GB for each additional 16 GB of memory. Backup storage is added separately, and all provisioned storage is a fixed cost per month, while compute is not charged when an instance is not running. Network data transfer is charged for all data leaving the database, such as reading data from the database to the applications.

The pricing of SAP HANA Cloud is based on the concept of *capacity units*, which are calculated based on compute, storage, and network needed. Each component within SAP HANA Cloud has a different unit of measure and capacity-unit value.

To calculate the number of capacity units, you can use the *SAP HANA Cloud Capacity Unit Estimator* at `https://hcsizingestimator.cfapps.eu10.hana.ondemand.com/`.

## Release strategy and data center availability

Unlike other services in SAP BTP, SAP HANA Cloud has a release strategy that includes service level and component level. The service level includes administration tools such as SAP HANA Cloud Central and SAP HANA Cockpit, which are updated frequently, all managed by SAP, and you are always working with the latest version. The component levels, such as SAP HANA Cloud, SAP HANA

Database, and SAP HANA Cloud, and Data Lake, have different release strategies. As you are planning the upgrade or adopting a new feature, it is important to understand the differences, as outlined here:

- SAP HANA Cloud, SAP HANA Database follows a **quarterly release cycle (QRC)**; for example, QRC 1/2022 means a release in the first quarter of the year 2022. A release can be used for up to 7 months and will be upgraded to the next release automatically in a maintenance window. Customers will be notified before the upgrade. You can also perform a manual upgrade if necessary.

- SAP HANA Cloud, Data Lake also follows a QRC. The latest version is immediately available for new instances; however, existing instances will not be upgraded automatically until 40 days after the release date. Otherwise, you can request a manual upgrade before that.

- SAP HANA Cloud, SAP Adaptive Server Enterprise, and SAP HANA Cloud, SAP Adaptive Server Enterprise Replication don't have a release every quarter and don't perform automatic upgrades at the time of writing this book.

SAP HANA Cloud is offered as part of the SAP BTP CF environment and is available in multiple regions. SAP will continue to expand the services to new regions; check `https://discovery-center.cloud.sap/serviceCatalog/sap-hana-cloud` for the latest information.

## SAP HANA Cloud, Data Lake

SAP HANA Cloud is built as a central point to access data from multiple sources and multiple formats (for example, **comma-separated values (CSV)**; Parquet) while providing options to keep performance and cost balanced via flexible data storage options through data virtualization.

**SAP HANA Cloud, Data Lake** is an optional extension to SAP HANA Cloud, HANA Database, based on SAP IQ, an efficient disk-based relational store. It is optimized for OLAP workloads and large volumes of data, supporting storage capacity from hundreds of **terabytes (TB)** to multiple petabytes, with the full support of SQL. The data lake storage is much cheaper and stores all data on disk. To use the data lake, tables and schemas are created in the data lake and linked to the HANA database through virtual tables through an optimized high-speed SDA capability to match data types and query data.

SAP HANA Cloud, Data Lake further allows a native integration and high-speed data ingest from cloud object stores such as AWS S3. It provides an SQL on Files capability to efficiently process data files stored in the data lake through SQL queries, without loading data into the database.

From an operational perspective, it is a natively integrated part of HANA Cloud and shares a common security mechanism, tenancy model, and tooling with HANA Cloud. However, it scales independently to accommodate data volume and workload complexity increases and separate provisioning of computing and storage. You can also create a standalone data lake in SAP BTP Cockpit directly or integrate a data lake as part of the SAP HANA Cloud data pyramid.

Technically, the Data Lake is comprised of two components: the Data Lake IQ and Data Lake Files. Data Lake IQ is managed by the HANA database and provides SQL analysis for large volumes of structured data. Data Lake Files uses data lake file containers to store unstructured, semi-structured, and structured data. A Data Lake Files container is a managed object store that integrates with cloud object stores. Here is a high-level architecture diagram that shows how Data Lake works with HANA Database:

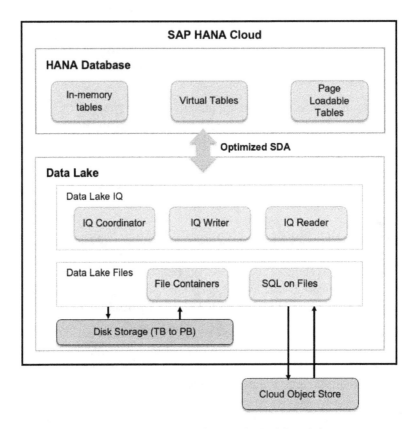

Figure 12.11: HANA Database and HANA Data Lake

## SQL execution and SQL reference for Data Lake

When Data Lake is configured with maximum HANA database compatibility, all SQL statements, procedures, and views are embedded in the REMOTE_EXECUTE procedure. Here is an example of creating a Data Lake IQ view:

```
CALL SYSHDL_CONTAINER1.REMOTE_EXECUTE('
    CREATE VIEW VIEW_T AS SELECT * FROM T
');
```

HANA Database connects with the Data Lake IQ via container groups that isolate data and access control to each relationship container. Each relational container has a dedicated connection with HANA database. A single query can include both HANA in-memory tables and virtual tables pointing to Data Lake IQ tables in relational containers. Joins are possible between tables in relational containers or between relational containers' tables and HANA database tables. The following diagram illustrates the execution of SQL statements involving the HANA database and Data Lake IQ tables:

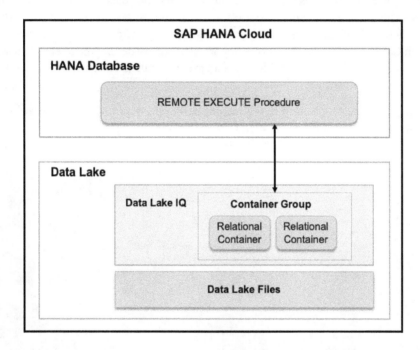

Figure 12.12: SQL execution from HANA Database to Data Lake

As Data Lake IQ also provides a standalone setup with a full feature set, two SQL references are available for the different setups. The standalone setup uses SQL syntax derived from on-premises IQ; however, the HANA-managed Data Lake IQ uses HANA syntax customized for data lake IQ users. The SQL reference for HANA managed Data Lake IQ can be found at https://help.sap.com/viewer/a898e08b84f21015969fa437e89860c8/QRC_3_2021/en-US/74814c5dca454066804e5670fa2fe4f5.html.

SQL on Files is included in Data Lake IQ and enabled automatically, allowing you to query data directly without loading data into Data Lake IQ. SQL on Files is useful in a scenario where you need to access a large volume of structured data stored as files in The Data Lake. It supports running SQL analysis on top of three file types: CSV, Parquet, and Apache **Optimized Row Columnar (ORC)**.

## Summary

Well, we covered quite a lot in this chapter. As this is the first chapter of "data to value," we started this chapter by discussing typical data-driven use cases and data architecture patterns to support various use cases.

The key element of this chapter was SAP HANA Cloud. We first introduced the different components of SAP HANA Cloud, its server types, and tools to access and work with HANA Cloud. Then, we focused on different development scenarios, from using HANA Cloud as the database runtime, modeling with Calculation Views, and—more importantly—native development, especially with the HDI. We briefly discussed SAP HANA Cloud Data Lake as a built-in extension of HANA database for large- volume data processing.

In the next chapter, we will look at other products as part of the *data-to-value* offerings, especially SAP Data Warehouse Cloud and SAP Analytics Cloud.

# 13
# SAP Data Warehouse Cloud and SAP Analytics Cloud

In the previous chapter, we discussed SAP HANA Cloud as the managed offering of HANA that can be used as the database runtime for data modeling and HANA native development.

We will continue our *data-to-value* journey and learn about the data management solutions built on top of SAP HANA and how they can help translate enterprise data into business insights.

In this chapter, we will focus on the following topics:

- SAP **Data Warehouse Cloud (DWC)**
- **SAP Analytics Cloud (SAC)**

Through this chapter, you will learn about the advanced modeling capabilities and collaboration that are provided through a virtualized workspace called Space in SAP DWC, as well as data visualization, **Business Intelligence (BI)**, and augmented analytics in SAC.

Let's get started!

## Technical requirements

To experiment with SAP DWC, you will require an SAP BTP trial account. An SAP DWC trial tenant can be requested at https://www.sap.com/products/data-warehouse-cloud/trial. html, while an SAC trial tenant can be requested at https://www.sap.com/products/ cloud-analytics/trial.html.

## SAP Data Warehouse Cloud (DWC)

Before we introduce what SAP DWC is, first, let's understand the differences between a **data lake** and a **data warehouse**.

A **data lake** is a data repository that holds a large amount of raw data in its natural format, often coming from disparate sources, including a mix of structured, semi-structured (CSV, XML, and JSON), and unstructured data formats. It offers an effective solution for collecting and storing large amounts of data but doesn't necessarily need to process it until it is required for use.

In contrast, **data warehousing** has a more focused use case that is optimized to store and transform large amounts of data for advanced queries and analytics in a more structured relational database. It has two key functions: it acts as a federated repository of business data, and then as the query execution and processing engine of the data. The goal of a modern data warehouse is to gain insights from data. To support that, it usually includes building blocks such as the following:

- Data preparation
- A global semantic layer
- Governance and policy
- Data integration with various data sources, including data lakes

SAP DWC is an offering in the cloud that's designed for both technical and business users to provide modern and unified data modeling and warehousing as a service that enables users to integrate, transform, model, and gain insights from data.

Collaborations in DWC are enabled through a virtual workspace called **Space** so that the different departments can work on the same datasets, with necessary isolation and security policies defined at each Space level. DWC separates the data layer and business layer. With the data layer, data engineers can create their models with a technical approach; the business layer empowers business users to easily drag and drop to model and explore data.

As it is built on top of SAP HANA Cloud, the broad data management capabilities discussed in the previous chapter are supported in DWC as well. Besides this, you can benefit from its cloud qualities as a fully managed offering, such as high frequency of releases, ease of use, high availability and reliability, and low maintenance effort.

## Use cases

SAP DWC allows you to converge data from SAP and non-SAP applications into a fully managed cloud environment that helps simplify the data warehousing landscape. It supports a variety of use cases, such as the following scenarios:

- As the enterprise data warehouse consolidates data across cloud and on-premise environments, it reuses data models from on-premise SAP **Business Warehouse** (**BW**) with built-in SQL and data transformation capabilities and acts as the acceleration layer for BI use cases.
- It enables self-service data modeling for business users with an intuitive drag-and-drop UI fully governed by the IT department. Business semantic modeling is separated from data modeling and physical data storage.

- It democratizes enterprise data by utilizing pre-built business content from SAP and partners to support end-to-end business scenarios and speed up time to insights.

- It enables a true collaboration model around the data through cross-space collaboration and data sharing and extends the reach to more data for various industries and **lines of business** (**LoB**), such as through Data Marketplace.

- It provides seamless integration with SAC for advanced analytics and visualizations.

Next, let's explore another concept of SAP DWC, space.

## Understanding Space

**Space** is one of the key concepts in SAP DWC. Spaces are essentially isolated virtual environments, but collaboration can be achieved through sharing across spaces, which allows the different departments to have their own spaces, such as between LoBs and IT.

Working with data in DWC means creating a Space or accessing an existing Space. Each Space is allocated a certain amount of disk and memory storage that can be specified when it is created. DWC follows the same data tiering concept as SAP HANA Cloud.

The status of all Space storage utilization is shown on the **Space Management** page, with a color-coding system of *red*, *green*, or *blue* to indicate the resource usage. It is important to keep an eye on Space usage. When a Space exceeds its quota, it can be locked and operations such as creating new models are not allowed. In that case, you can delete unwanted data or increase the Space's quota to unlock the Space. You can also configure the workload classes by specifying the priority of a Space range from 0 (lowest) to 8 (highest). From a job scheduling perspective, statements in a higher-priority Space will be executed first. The default priority is five; priority nine is reserved for system operations.

DWC also provides a **command-line interface** (**CLI**) (`@sap/dwc-cli`) to automate the management of Spaces. You can use the CLI to create, read, update, or delete a Space, assign members, update Space properties, and more. Here is an example of creating a space: `$ dwc spaces create -H <Server_URL> -p <Passcode> -f </path/to/definition/file.json>`.

More information about `@sap/dwc-cli` can be found at `https://www.npmjs.com/package/@sap/dwc-cli`.

DWC maintains access rights by assigning roles to users. Within DWC, only one user can be assigned as the System Owner, who has full access to all application areas. A user with the Administrator role has full privilege for the entire DWC tenant, such as creating users and spaces, creating custom roles, and assigning them to other users. A Space Administrator has full access to a Space and can create the data access controls of a Space, as well as leverage the Content Network to import pre-delivered contents into a Space. There are other roles with fewer permissions, such as the Integrator role, which can manage the data connections, create database users, and connect HDI containers with Spaces. A Modeler can manage objects through the Data Builder and Business Builder areas of a Space, while Viewers only have read access to objects in a Space.

## Connectivity and data integration

SAP DWC provides various options for integrating and ingesting data from a wide variety of sources, for both SAP and non-SAP data sources. DWC runs on top of the HANA Cloud database, so it can benefit from the data integration options of HANA Cloud such as **Smart Data Access** (**SDA**) and **Smart Data Integration** (**SDI**). You can also write data to the Space through its Open SQL schema and associate it with data artifacts in an HDI container. SDI also provides additional integration options to non-SAP data sources through its Data Provisioning Agent and adaptors. Besides this, you can leverage the SAP BW metadata and data through SAP BW Bridge. Now, let's have a look at these data integration options.

### Access to the HANA database

Sometimes, you may want to work directly with the underlying HANA Cloud database of DWC to leverage its advanced capabilities; for example, using HANA machine learning libraries. In that case, you will need to create a database user as an Administrator, which is a technical user that can be used to connect with the underlying HANA database.

For each database user, an Open SQL schema is created. An Open SQL shema used to connect with your SQL clients, which can be granted write access to perform DDL and DML operations, such as ingesting data into a DWC.

You can also run the DWC-specific stored procedure known as `"DWC_GLOBAL"."GRANT_ PRIVILEGE_TO_SPACE"` to grant write privilege to the individual tables. DWC users can always read data in the Open SQL schema for modeling in Data Builder. For read access, the database user can also read the data from a Space through the Space Schema if the data has been exposed.

If you already have data in an HDI Container or want to consume the data and models in your Space from your existing HDI container, you can create an SAP support ticket to map the HDI container with the DWC Space. Once mapped, objects in the HDI container are available in Data Builder; this scenario is referred to as HDI Ingestion. Instead, you can access Space objects in the HDI container, which is referred to as the HDI Consumption scenario.

To use HANA machine learning libraries (APL and PAL) in DWC, the HANA Script Server must be enabled for the underlying HANA database. At the time of writing, you will need to create an SAP support ticket to create the database user with the required authorizations.

### Connecting with SAP HANA Cloud, data lake

To access a large amount of data, you can connect a DWC Space to SAP HANA Cloud, data lake. You will also need to create an SAP support ticket to associate the data lake with a DWC tenant. At the time of writing, only one Space of a DWC tenant can be assigned to access the data lake.

Once connected, the tables in the data lake can be accessed in DWC via the virtual tables in the Open SQL schema. DWC provides two stored procedures to create and access the tables in the data lake:

- Uses the `"DWC_GLOBAL"."DATA_LAKE_EXECUTE"` stored procedure to create tables in the data lake

- Uses the `"DWC_GLOBAL"."DATA_LAKE_CREATE_VIRTUAL_TABLE"` stored procedure to create virtual tables in the Open SQL schema that refer to the tables in the data lake

Once the virtual tables have been created, they can be consumed in Data Builder for modeling.

### Connecting with SAP Data Intelligence Cloud

**SAP Data Intelligence Cloud** is a data integration platform that provides capabilities for data pipeline, data discovery, and automated data processing. Depending on the use cases, you may need to integrate with Data Intelligence Cloud from DWC, such as via Kafka integration, or apply advanced data transformations with ML/AI models.

Accessing DWC data is done through the underlying HANA database tables. Here, a database user with the necessary privilege to read and write data in your DWC Space is required. In the connection management area of the DWC tenant, a connection needs to be created to read data from DWC in the data pipelines of SAP Data Intelligence Cloud.

Processed data can be written back to the DWC Space and become available in Data Builder to explore and model the data.

### Connectivity to other data sources

SAP DWC supports connections with a wide variety of sources for data integration and ingestion. This can be achieved by leveraging **SAP HANA Smart Data Integration** (**SDI**) and the **Data Provisioning Agent**. You can also create a custom adapter and register it with DWC to extend the integration with additional data sources. Depending on the connection types and their configurations, different features can be used.

The following features are supported in DWC:

- Remote tables are supported in the graphical and SQL views, as well as the entity-relationship models of Data Builder, to access data remotely.

- Data flows are supported in Data Builder Data Flow to connect with SAP's cloud applications, such as SAP SuccessFactors, using the Cloud Data Integration APIs or generic OData APIs.

- Model import is supported in Business Builder so that existing metadata and data from SAP BW4/HANA can be reused. This is done by generating DWC objects translated from BW objects (InfoObject, CompositeProvider, and Query) and accessing data directly from the BW system via remote tables.

If you wish to view the full list of supported connection types, please check out `https://help.sap.com/viewer/9f804b8efa8043539289f42f372c4862/cloud/en-US/eb85e157ab654152bd68a8714036e463.html`.

### SAP BW Bridge for SAP DWC

In TechEd 2021, SAP introduced SAP BW Bridge for SAP DWC, which allows customers to leverage DWC to support existing investments in their on-premise SAP BW systems and skills in ABAP. The target scenarios for SAP BW Bridge include, but are not limited to, the following:

- Converting SAP BW (BW7.3 and upward) to the cloud while retaining existing data and data flows and leveraging SAC as the consumption layer
- Hybrid scenarios for combining SAP BW4/HANA data and DWC data first, before gradually transitioning the SAP BW4/HANA data flow to DWC

Technically, SAP BW Bridge provides the capabilities for ABAP-based data extraction up to the **CompositeProvider** level and offers SAP BW4/HANA-like environments in the cloud. However, SAP BW Bridge doesn't include the OLAP engine and query execution, and add-ons such as the planning engine. Instead, it's recommended that customers use SAC for planning. Strategically, SAP will continue to invest and evolve SAP DWC so that it becomes the foundation for planning use cases in the future.

In terms of the data sources, it is primarily intended for **Operational Data Provisioning** (**ODP**)-based source systems such as ODP-BW, ODP-HANA, ODP-SAP (for SAP S/4HANA), ODP-CDS, and ODP-SLT.

In SAP BW Bridge, customers can use the web-based SAP BW Bridge Cockpit, Eclipse-based BW modeling tools, and ABAP development tools for administration, modeling, and development tasks; the overall experience is very similar to SAP BW4/HANA. At the time of writing, users are still required to work on both BW and DWC environments with these different tools. These tools will be merged to provide a consistent user experience in the cloud in the future.

To enable SAP BW Bridge, a dedicated Space for SAP BW Bridge must be provisioned in the DWC tenant. This Space has a specific type that is different from any other Space. This generated DWC Space contains the connection to an SAP HANA Cloud **Smart Data Access** (**SDA**) endpoint and an HTTP-based ABAP endpoint, which can be used to connect the SAP BW Bridge environment with the DWC tenant and the external scheme of the HANA Cloud database underneath SAP BW Bridge, for moving data between the systems. This connection is generated by the provisioning process automatically and cannot be changed by a user. No additional connection can be created in this dedicated Space as it is restricted to SAP BW Bridge only.

Once connected, the tables of SAP BW Bridge can be exposed in the SAP BW Bridge Space in DWC as remote tables. The main purpose of this Space is to import the objects from SAP BW Bridge as remote tables and share them with other Spaces using the cross-space sharing mechanism, which can be used for data modeling. Users cannot create new tables, views, or data flows in this generated space.

During the import, objects in SAP BW Bridge are organized by InfoAreas and underneath data tables of InfoObjects; here, DataStore Objects can be imported into the SAP BW Bridge Space. Within standard DWC Spaces, the shared remote tables can be accessed, combined, and enriched using standard DWC functionalities. Remote table monitoring and remote query monitoring are supported via the Data Integration Monitor.

Finally, SAP BW customers can choose to convert on-premise BW contents using conversion tools, starting from SAP BW7.4, and will support SAP BW7.5 and SAP BW4/HANA in the future. Please check the SAP Roadmap Explorer for the future roadmap of DWC at `https://roadmaps.sap.com/board?PRODUCT=73555000100800002141&range=CURRENT-LAST#Q4%202021`:

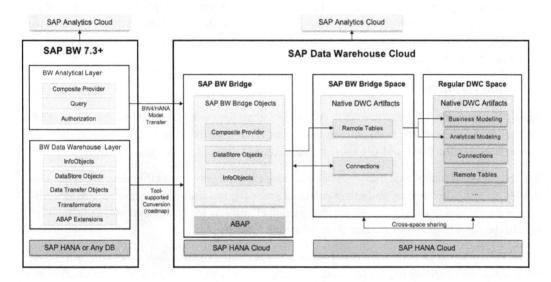

Figure 13.1 – SAP BW Bridge to SAP DWC

Well, we have covered quite a lot, and it might seem quite complicated, but *Figure 13.1* gives a good visual recap of what we just discussed.

## Data Integration Monitor

While there are multiple ways to integrate data with DWC, how do you monitor and manage the connections and data replications from the source systems? This is what the **Data Integration Monitor** can help with.

It works like a dashboard and allows you to drill down into the details of a Space. The following capabilities are supported in the Data Integration Monitor:

- **Remote Table Monitor** to monitor remote tables deployed in the Space, configure data replication options, and refresh the frequency

- **View Persistency Monitor** to set up persisted views for graphical or SQL views to improve performance as data is replicated and stored locally

- **Data Flow Monitor** to view and monitor the execution of the flow of the data from source to target and the data transformations in between

- **Remote Query Monitor** to monitor and analyze the remote query statements and how the communications between the underlying HANA database of the DWC tenant and the remote source systems work

Depending on the use cases, you can decide to access remote data directly or replicate the data to local storage. Both snapshot-based replication (can be scheduled) and real-time replication based on change data capturing are supported. Instead of remote tables, you can also pre-compute the modeled views and configure the data replication for them. Not all the data sources support the real-time replication approach or have delta enabled.

### Data Marketplace

So far, we have discussed the various data integration options with DWC for SAP and non-SAP systems, but how about data from other sources or the ecosystem? For that, SAP introduced the Data Marketplace for SAP DWC as its enterprise-grade data sharing and monetization platform.

Within the DWC tenant, you can access or purchase external data from other data providers and combine it with other internal and external data for reporting and analytics use cases. It provides self-service capabilities to avoid the need for long-lasting IT projects for data integration and simplifies how to choose data vendors based on the marketplace catalogs.

Any DWC customer can become a data provider to share and monetize their data assets with other companies, with a strong toolset to create, publish, license, and deliver their data products in an enterprise-grade fashion. This enables SAP customers to benefit from the growing ecosystems of data across various industries and business processes.

## Data modeling

**Data modeling** is a way to define the structure and semantics of data to gain insights from the data based on business requirements. For that, SAP DWC provides two different modeling layers that allow customers to leverage the benefits of business and technical data modeling:

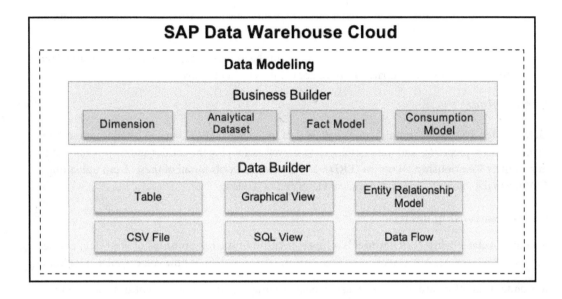

Figure 13.2 – Data Builder and Business Builder in data modeling

The data layer is for technical users, typically data engineers, who can use it to create models in a technical approach. In comparison, the business layer is where the business users can work independently from the technical users in a more business-centric way. With the data layer and business layers, technical users and business users can work together based on the same underlying data. *Figure 13.2* depicts the two modeling layers in DWC.

### Facts, measures, and dimensions

In data modeling and analytics scenarios, we often speak about the concepts of facts, measures, and dimensions. So, let's understand them. A fact usually indicates an occurrence or a transaction, such as the sales of a product. A fact can be composed of multiple measures, and most of these measures are quantitative, such as the price of a product or the number of units sold. Dimensions are attributes that have master data, such as a product that provides the context to understand and index the measures. Part of the data modeling approach is applying calculations and aggregations to the quantitative measures and linking them with the dimensions for analytical purposes.

In DWC, there are different types of measures, depending on the type of model:

- **Aggregation measures** are the default type and aggregate data (sum, average, count, max, and min).

- A **derived measure** refers to another measure. Here, you can define restrictions on available attributes.

- **Calculated measures** combine other measures with elementary arithmetic operations (addition, subtraction, multiplication, and division).

- There are also **count distinct measures** to count the unique occurrence of attributes and **fixed value measures** for comparisons or to apply further calculations.

### Data Builder

**Data Builder** is where the technical users will do data modeling in DWC, such as creating connections to data sources, preparing, and transforming data, as well as defining the entities and their relationships in an **Entity Relationship Diagram** (**ERD**). DWC provides tools for all of these, from uploading a CSV file to data flows to creating graphical views and SQL views.

### Entity-relationship models

An **entity-relationship** (**E/R**) **model** is a representation of the relationships of your data entities (tables and views). An E/R model doesn't contain any data but defines how you organize it logically.

It is quite straightforward to create an E/R model: we drag and drop the data entities and join them together in Data Builder. The created E/R models are available in the Space and other users can reuse them to create views.

### Data flows

One of the benefits of data modeling in DWC is that you can use a **data flow** to create the ETL steps in an easy-to-use way graphically. It allows you to combine both structured and semi-structured data from SAP and non-SAP systems, generic OData APIs, or just files. Different operators support data transformations, such as join, union, projection, or Python operators, which allow you to implement business logic in a script that can be embedded directly in the model. For example, you can apply sentiment analysis in Python using the pandas and NumPy libraries, and then use the result in the model and combine it with other attributes.

Once a data flow has been created and deployed, its execution can be monitored in the Data Integration Monitor. In addition, it can be scheduled to run at regular intervals to keep data updated. Once the execution is completed, the transformed data can be leveraged to create views or for business modeling in Business Builder.

### Graphical view and SQL view

In DWC, you can use a graphical interface or write SQL code to create a view. With the graphical view, you can simply drag and drop tables or other views from sources, join them, transform them, and specify measures in the output structure. If the relationship between entities has been defined in an E/R model, they will be joined automatically. If you are comfortable with SQLScript, you can always write the code to create views. A view will be saved in the repository of the Space first and runtime objects will be generated when it is deployed.

## Adding business information to views

When creating the views, it is a good practice to add the business information, so it is easier for others to make sense of the data. This enables the business users to perform business modeling in Business Builder, which we will discuss next. We call the business information the **semantic layer**.

The semantic layer is the information that's provided in business language to help others understand the data better; for example, adding a new business user-friendly view name or column name. Here is a list of the semantic usage types that can be configured for the tables and views:

- **Relational dataset**: The default type contains columns with no specific purpose for analytics.

- **Dimension**: Contains attributes with master data such as a product.

- **Analytical dataset**: The primary type for analytics; it contains one or more measures and attributes.

- **Text**: Enables multi-language support for master data. A Text view must be associated with a Dimension view.

You can also define the appropriate semantic type for each column that identifies that a column contains a quantity, a date, and geospatial or other types of information. This can be very useful in data analysis. You can only add semantic types to a column when the view or table it belongs to has the semantic usage set to Dimension or Analytical Dataset. While both views and tables can have semantic usage types, only views can be consumed in SAC or other BI tools. A view will only be available in SAC when it is exposed for consumption and has its semantic usage set to **Analytical Dataset** with at least one measure.

The facts, measures, and dimensions modeled in the data layer will be visible to the business users, who can use Business Builder to add even more business information to the models.

### *Business Builder*

Business Builder helps model the data in business terms and makes business users more independent from IT. Once data is made available by IT (for example, by creating connections), business users can create data models and collaborate with technical users or other business users based on a semantic view of the data. One of the advantages of DWC is that you can bring together the different parts of the organization with different skills to collaborate and create data models to address concrete business questions.

Using the tables and views from the data layer as the sources, business users can create the business entities in Business Builder. A business entity represents the business objects such as products or sales of products. **Dimensions** and **Analytical Datasets** are such business entities. Dimensions only contain the attributes that represent master data. An Analytical Dataset is a fact table that includes both the facts and attributes associated with foreign keys. While the associations can be predefined in the data layer and business users can focus more on the consumption models, business entities are independent of the data layer (including versioning) to allow business users to control and prepare their use cases. You can always enrich business entities with additional calculations.

A **fact model** groups the analytical datasets and dimensions together and is used to model complex scenarios that need to combine multiple facts and dimensions. Fact models can be nested and thus can be embedded and reused by other users in other models. **Consumption models** combine the business entities and fact models to create the outputs exposed for consumption, such as in SAC. A consumption model includes one or more perspectives, which is the final consumption unit containing the measures and attributes that can be visualized and analyzed by the analytics clients.

Finally, you will need to restrict access to part of the data in a business context; for example, managers can only access information of employees in their teams. This can be achieved by creating and assigning an **authorization scenario**. An authorization scenario helps filter data based on some criteria based on data access control, which defines and enforces the filtering by the criteria. You cannot create an authorization scenario on a consumption model, but you can reuse the authorization scenarios that have been assigned to the relevant business entities.

### Creating a hierarchy

You may need to organize your data with a proper hierarchical structure. This can be very helpful in many business scenarios. Two types of hierarchies are supported in DWC: parent-child hierarchies and level-based hierarchies. Hierarchies are modeled in Dimensions.

A common example of a parent-child hierarchy is to represent organizational structures, such as HR reporting lines. In this case, members in the hierarchy have the same attributes and it contains a *parent* attribute to describe the *self-joining* relationship. For example, immediate managers will be the parents of the employees, even though managers themselves are also employees. The limitation of a parent-child hierarchy is that each node must have a single parent, and data must be normalized to a tree-like structure, which can be very difficult in complex scenarios, such as a matrix organizational structure. Other constraints include that only one hierarchy is allowed in a Dimension, and the attributes that are used for parent keys cannot be composite keys.

A level-based hierarchy is used when your data contains one or multiple levels of aggregation. It is not recursive, and each hierarchy has a fixed number of levels in a fixed order. Typical examples of level-based hierarchies are time-based hierarchies (Year, Quarter, Month, Week, and Date) and location-based hierarchies (Region, Country, State, and City). You can navigate the hierarchy to drill up and drill down in analytics; each level contains the aggregated values for the levels below it.

## Data consumption

The consumption layer of DWC is created by integrating with SAC. SAC connects with DWC through remote connections to build stories on top of analytical datasets and perspectives exposed for consumption. You can also connect with third-party BI tools with your Space data to build visualizations.

### Working with SAC

To build stories and analytics applications with SAC, you can expose your DWC Space data through the live connections between SAC and DWC tenants.

Before release 2021.03, DWC offered an embedded version of SAC where DWC and SAC were run in the same tenant, and stories that were created in SAC were saved directly in the DWC Space. This is called *Space-aware connectivity*. There are limitations of embedded SAC; for example, it is limited to five user licenses. SAP recommends only using the embedded version for testing purposes. For tenants provisioned after 2021.03, customers will need to have two separate tenants – one for DWC and another for SAC.

Technically, a SAC tenant can connect to multiple DWC tenants as data sources and combine them with additional data to create stories. Any DWC tenant can be connected to any SAC tenant through a live connection. To consume data and models from DWC, it is important to expose them for consumption, which can be enabled in either Data Builder or Business Builder for the respective objects.

DWC and SAC share the same authentication mechanism and **Identity Provider (IdP)** settings. You can also link the DWC tenant with the SAC tenant through Tenant Links to enable the product switch to easily navigate between them on the UI.

There are certain product limitations of the live connections. Please check SAP Note 2032606 for more details at `https://launchpad.support.sap.com/#/notes/2832606`.

### Working with third-party BI tools

To connect a DWC tenant with third-party BI Tools such as tableau or Microsoft Power BI, an ODBC driver needs to be installed. The IP address of the tool needs to be added to the allow list in the DWC configuration. Since it is a SQL-based connection, a database user who has access to the Space schema needs to be created and objects for consumption in a third-party tool must be exposed in DWC. Once connected, you can use the DWC objects to create visualizations with your existing BI tools.

## Audit logging

**Audit logs** help you understand *who did what, where, and when*. It is important for your security, auditing, and compliance teams to monitor possible vulnerabilities or data misuse. In DWC, you can set up audit logging for both change operations and read accesses, which can be configured separately. It can be enabled at the Space level and the retention time can be configured from 7 days to a maximum of 10,000 days. The default retention time is 30 days. Based on your business requirements, you can determine your retention policy. Please be aware that audit logs also consume the storage capacity of your DWC tenant.

For individual database schemas such as Open SQL schemas created for database users, the audit logs need to be enabled separately. Please note that statements executed in SAP HANA Cloud, data lake through the wrapper procedures are not audited currently.

To view the audit logs, SAP recommends creating a dedicated Space for audit logs so that only users with access to this Space can see the logs. These logs are saved in the `AUDIT_LOG` view of the `DWC_AUDIT_READER` schema and the `ANALYSIS_AUDIT_LOG` view for database analysis users separately.

This wraps up our introduction to SAP DWC, where we focused on data integration and data modeling. Next, we will discuss SAC as the consumption layer of DWC and how it can be used for advanced analytics scenarios.

# SAP Analytics Cloud (SAC)

SAC is a SaaS offering for analytics that combines capabilities such as BI, enterprise planning, and predictive analytics into one product. SAC is the analytics layer and provides a consistent experience for all SAP applications through embedded analytics and enterprise analytics use cases.

## Connectivity

SAC can access data from cloud data sources or on-premise systems by providing two types of connectivity, online live connections, and batch-based data acquisitions. Live connections allow you to build stories and perform analytics with live data without any data replication. In data acquisitions, data is imported into SAC and its underlying HANA database first. You may be wondering what the right approach is for your specific use cases. Please refer to *Table 13.1*, which shows the criteria you must consider when choosing the right approach:

| Criteria | Live Connection | Data Acquisition |
| --- | --- | --- |
| Functional | Performance and product limitations may apply. No planning support on the live connection. Available for HANA, DWC, BW, BOE Universe, and S/4HANA. | Support analytics, planning, and predictive scenarios. Available for SAP cloud applications and third-party data sources. |
| Data Storage | Data stays in the source system and connects to SAC in real time. | SAC stores the model and data locally in its underlying HANA database. |
| Data Security and Privacy | Managed on the source system. This is preferred when full control of data is required, and data cannot leave the source system. | Security is added to the models within SAC, and data is fully encrypted and secured. |
| Data Volume | No theoretical limitations as the data is processed in the backend. However, it needs to apply adequate filtering and aggregation to limit the volume returning to the web browser. | Limitation in file sizes (< 200 MB for Excel files and < 2 GB for CSV files), row and column counts (< 2 B rows, < 100 columns in models, < 1,000 columns in datasets), and cell sizes. |

Table 13.1 – Live connections and data acquisition

## *Understanding live connections*

Unlike the live connection we discussed in HANA Cloud and DWC through the data federation at the HANA database level, the live connections between SAC and the data source systems are mainly browser-based. In this case, SAC only stores the metadata (for example, measures, column names, and filter values) for building the stories and queries. The browser, in turn, sends queries through a live connection to the source HANA database that executes the queries and returns the results to SAC to render the charts. None of the actual data or query results will be stored in SAC. All communication between the browser and SAC is encrypted, and all metadata persisted in SAC is fully encrypted.

In the live connection scenario, the browser must access SAC for metadata and the data source at the same time. The same-origin policy is a critical security mechanism that restricts how a resource in an origin can interact with resources in another origin, to reduce possible attach vectors to isolate and prevent potentially malicious documents. SAC supports a direct live connection by leveraging **Cross-Origin Resource Sharing** (**CORS**) as a mechanism (use additional HTTP headers) to connect with data sources such as HANA on-premise, SAP BW, and SAP S/4HANA. In these cases, CORS must be enabled at the data sources and the browser must accept third-party cookies and disable the popup blocker.

The most secure way to connect to an on-premise data source is through the SAP Cloud Connector by creating a secure tunnel between the data source and SAP BTP where SAC is hosted. It acts as a reverse proxy and the communications are always initiated by the SAP Cloud Connector, so there is no need to open any port in the firewall to the on-premise systems. The trust to SAP Cloud Connector is configured in SAC to a specific SAC subaccount in SAP BTP. All communications across the tunnel are secured based on **Transport Layer Security** (**TLS**) and can be monitored and audited within SAP Cloud Connector. You learned more about SAP Cloud Connector in *Chapter 4, Security and Connectivity*.

For cloud data sources such as SAP HANA Cloud and SAP DWC, there are dedicated connection types. For example, the *SAP HANA Cloud* connection type is highly recommended for live connections to HANA Cloud databases. For previous offerings of HANA in the cloud such as HANA 2.0 hosted in BTP, you can create a live connection using the SAP HANA Analytics Adaptor for Cloud Foundry. In embedded analytics scenarios where SAC is embedded in a cloud application such as SAP SuccessFactors Core HXM, the SAC OEM integration service is leveraged. The key responsibility of these adapters or integration services is to act as the proxy to execute queries in the data source system based on the SAP **Information Access Service** (**InA**) protocol, which defines queries using rich or complex semantics to perform multidimensional analytics, planning, and search data in HANA.

To provide a better user experience, **single sign-on** (**SSO**) should be enabled between SAC and the data source systems by using the SAML 2.0 protocol and have a common authentication based on the same IdP. For SAP applications, SAP **Identity Authentication Service** (**IAS**) is the default IdP, though it can also act as the proxy to delegate the authentication to another IdP of the customer's choosing.

*Figure 13.3* depicts the live connection options:

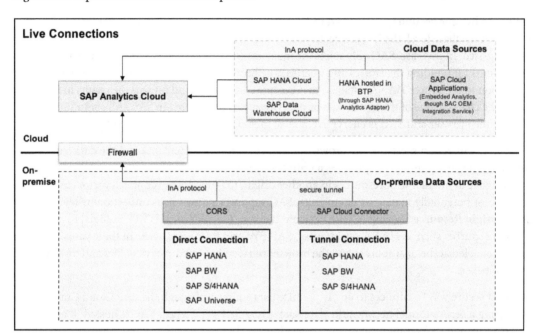

Figure 13.3 – SAC live connections overview

**Important Information**

To learn more about the limitations of live data connections, please check `https://help.sap.com/viewer/00f68c2e08b941f081002fd3691d86a7/release/en-US/6ac0d03d53f3454f83d41c6f51c2fc31.html`.

## Understanding data acquisition

If combining multiple data sources and blending data through live connections is not sufficient, for example, due to large data volume and high-performance requirements, then you should consider using the data acquisition approach to replicate data into SAC. Here, data is copied and stored in the underlying HANA database of SAC.

While the live connections mainly work for HANA-based systems and SAP Universe or Web Intelligence, you can replicate data from many more cloud and on-premise data sources. Most SAP cloud applications such as SAP SuccessFactors, SAP Concur, SAP Fieldglass, and Qualtrics provide data integrations with SAC through a common integration interface based on the OData protocol. SAC also supports integrations with Google Drive, Google Big Query, Salesforce, Dow Jones, and others through dedicated connectors. Additional non-SAP applications are supported through SAP Integration Suite Open Connectors.

For connectivity with on-premise data sources, such as live connections, SAP Cloud Connector is required to establish the secure tunnel and act as the reverse proxy. To connect with SAP BW, **SAP Business Planning and Consolidation for Microsoft (BPC MS)**, **SAP BusinessObjects Business Intelligence platform universe (UNX)**, and **SAP Enterprise Resource Planning (ERP)**, a SAC agent must be installed and configured. It is recommended to install an SAC agent and SAP Cloud Connector on the same server. *Figure 13.4* summarizes the options for data acquisition:

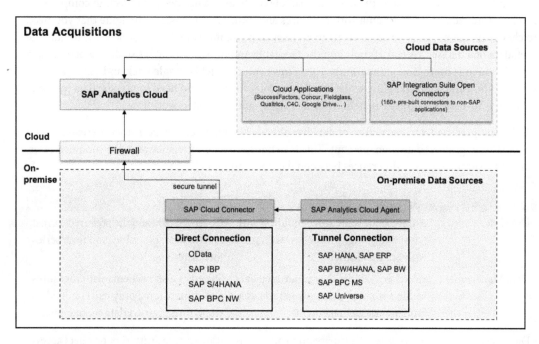

Figure 13.4 – SAC data acquisition overview

**Important information**

To learn more about the limitations of data acquisition, please refer to the official document at https://help.sap.com/viewer/00f68c2e08b941f081002fd3691d86a7/release/en-US/5f61b6509a5e4d499e8cb9685f32db73.html?q=sizing#loio5f61b6509a5e4d499e8cb9685f32db73__section_tuning.

# Data preparation

Before creating a story, you will need to prepare data. In SAC, preparing the acquired data can be done using either a dataset or a model. A dataset is not a new concept but has been used in Smart Predict behind the scenes before. The new data preparation experience called Smart Wrangling uses *datasets* directly within the scope of a story, instead of a model.

One of the advantages of using datasets is the reactivity to changes in a more efficient way. This is because the data structures of datasets and models are different. Datasets store data in a single table with a semantic structure defined by the metadata, so it is considered a lightweight object. In comparison, models store data in a star schema with measures and multiple dimensions. Imagine that you need to change the data type of an attribute from a dimension to a measure; SAC just needs to update the metadata of a dataset instead of updating the fact table and dimension tables such as when using a model, which is more time-consuming. This allows you to quickly toggle back and forth between story creation and data wrangling when building a story, so there is no need to prepare data perfectly upfront. SAC users can greatly benefit from this agility and integrated workflow.

Models are preferred if the structure of data has already been defined before a story is created and it supports fine-grained data management. This is better for data governance and planning use cases. *Table 13.2* summarizes the differences between datasets and models:

| | Dataset | Model |
| --- | --- | --- |
| Use Cases | Ad hoc data, agile story building with data wrangling, predictive scenarios with Smart Predict | Governed data and the preferred format for live data, planning, and time series forecast scenarios |
| Data Management | Stored as a table with separate metadata within a story or as a standalone dataset, limited data management | Stored as a star schema with measures and dimensions, only exists outside a story, fine-grained data management |
| Data Access | No row-level security and can access the dataset as a whole | Row-level security, supports data access control per the dimension value |

Table 13.2 – Datasets versus models

There are various tools you can use to edit the data in a dataset to clean, enrich, and transform the data into the desired structure. For example, you can change measures and dimensions, resolve data quality issues such as setting default values for missing data, add geo-enriched data with coordinates or areas such as countries and regions, define level-based hierarchies, update aggregation types for measures, and more. One of the cool features is the *Custom Expression Editor*, which allows you to implement complex transformations such as calculating a new column based on other columns. The custom logic is implemented in scripts with the support of operators for different data types.

From a business scenario perspective, there are two types of models – analytic models and planning models. Planning models are preconfigured to support the planning process, such as forecasting, and come with some default configurations and features such as categories for budget, plans and forecast, a date dimension, and additional auditing and security features. Analytics models are more flexible for general-purpose data analysis. Analytics models work with both live data and acquired data while planning models only work with acquired data.

In addition, depending on how the measures are structured, there are two types of models – the classic account model and the new model. Launched in the Q2/2021 QRC release of SAC, the new model is a significant change in how models are structured around the measures. It is based on the learnings from the Account model, which originated from the planning scenario. The new model enables greater flexibility and adds benefits in both analytics and planning scenarios in multiple areas:

- **A flexible model structure** that supports model configuration with measures, an account dimension, or both. This flexibility allows more accurate aggregation over measures and explicit data types (decimals and integers).

- **Improved calculations** on measures and numeric dimension properties. Calculated measures in models can be reused in stories and analytics applications.

- **Better data integration** with the measure-based model aligns better with other SAP systems such as S/4HANA and SAP BW. This means less transformation is required to import data from source systems into the target models.

- **Improved data wrangling** with a custom expression script, which acts like a dataset, is now available in the new models.

- **Multiple base currencies and conversion measures** in the models support planning on multiple currencies and allow you to see the results across dependent currencies.

The new model type offers more flexibility, and it is possible to convert from the classical account model into the new model with measures. To convert, the dependencies must be resolved (for example, if a model is used by stories), and currency conversion should be turned off. After the conversion, the data import/export jobs need to be updated so that they fit into the new target model. At the time of writing, models created from a CSV file or Excel file are based on the classic account model. *Figure 13.5* illustrates how to convert from a classic account model to a new model:

**Classic Account Model: Single measure with multiple accounts**

| Account | Customer ID | Product | SignedData |
| --- | --- | --- | --- |
| No. of License | 1 | Prod-1 | 100 |
| No. of License | 2 | Prod-2 | 200 |
| Opportunity Value | 1 | Prod-1 | 100,000.00 |
| Opportunity Value | 2 | Prod-2 | 200,000.00 |

**New Model: Multiple measures without account dimension**

| Customer ID | Product | No. of License | Opportunity Value |
| --- | --- | --- | --- |
| 1 | Prod-1 | 100 | 100,000.00 |
| 2 | Prod-2 | 200 | 200,000.00 |

Figure 13.5 – Classic account model and the new model

While SAC provides the necessary data modeling capabilities, more features are available in SAP DWC, as discussed earlier in this chapter. In that case, most data modeling is performed in DWC and exposed for SAC to consume via a live connection between SAC and DWC.

## Creating stories with Story Designer

Data visualization is a great tool for telling the stories behind data. It helps the consumers interpret and understand data at a faster pace and makes it easier to recognize patterns and identify exceptions. In SAC, a **Story** is a presentation-style document that uses visualizations to describe and analyze data.

There are many ways to visualize data, and choosing the right visualization can have a big impact on how easily the users will be able to consume the information. So, before starting with visualization, it is important to understand your audiences – for example, what story you want to tell, what questions should be answered, and what insights the data will give.

While the design aspect of a story can depend on many aspects and it is hard to compare which design or style is better, there is some general advice from SAP and the SAC community to consider:

- Start from the big picture to design the high-level summary pages first and then drill down into detailed pages for more insights.
- The main information should come first, without the need to scroll down the page. Group the related information to make it easier to compare and analyze.
- Use colors when appropriate, don't make a dashboard too colorful, and use the same color theme throughout the entire story.
- Use the best-fit charts for the data. For example, a pie chart is not recommended when there are too many values to present.
- Apply a standard checklist for all visualizations to check text alignment, chart sorting, ranking, font type and size, and more.
- Follow corporate brand design guidelines whenever applicable – for example, if the corporate has specified the color schemes, background colors, logo size, and placement.

It is not easy to keep all stories consistent in terms of colors, fonts, and corporate standards. This is where **story templates** can be considered. **SAP Analytics templates**, which are created by administrators, are the global templates saved in the default **Sample folder**, which is visible to all users who can create stories from a template. A story template defines not only the colors and formatting but also the page layout, background, default color, font and border, default table setting, input controls styling, and more.

### Story pages

A **story page** can be a blank canvas, a responsible page, or a grid for different kinds of use cases. Responsive pages allow you to create lanes to section the page into groups; widgets within a lane will stay together when the page is resized. You can run the device preview to see what the page will look like in different screen sizes and device types.

A canvas page is a flexible space where you can add charts, tables, geo maps, or other visualizations and apply styling either to individual objects or groups. A canvas page can be used to create a reporting layout by adding a header and footer. Grid pages are best for working with tabular data, just like Excel sheets. They are especially useful when working with numbers and formulas.

### Linked analysis and linked models

A **Story** often contains multiple charts or tables. Linked analytics enables the interactions between the different widgets, for example, by applying a filter or drilling through hierarchical data in one chart and seeing the update in linked charts. Linked analytics must be based on the same underlying model or across different models with linked dimensions.

When performing cross-model linked analysis, you must set up the link between models by defining the common dimensions. Once this link has been established, applying a filter to one model can influence the widgets based on the linked model. Filtering across models works for linked dimensions directly and other unlinked dimensions indirectly. For indirectly filtering on unlinked dimensions, even though it can achieve a similar filtering experience, it is usually performance intensive as technically, it will apply the filter on a model first and pass all the filtered values of the linked dimension to the model that doesn't have the dimension that the filter is based on. To optimize performance, link the dimensions directly whenever possible or link as few dimensions as possible if the dimension to be filtered cannot be linked. You can specify the Linked item set to apply the filtering and then drill through hierarchal data for all the charts in the same story, on the same page, or only for selective charts.

While linked analysis enables filtering across models, data blending is the process of adding a linked model to the primary model. This allows you to combine data from multiple models in a chart or table. For example, you can combine data from a BW live connection with imported data from an Excel spreadsheet. Both **linked analysis** and **linked models** start by defining the common dimensions to link the models. Once linked, the dimensions and measures from both models can be used in the visualizations.

In SAC, there are two types of data blending – browser-based blending and **Smart Data Integration** (**SDI**)-based blending. Browser-based blending doesn't require you to install anything. At the time of writing, you can blend data from a BW live connection with imported data, a HANA live connection with imported data, and a S/4HANA live connection with imported data. It is easier to start with browser-based blending, but there are limits in terms of data volume. For example, it supports up to 2 MB in dataset size for HANA live connection scenarios. SDI-based blending is recommended for larger datasets and supports more data sources. For this, you must install and configure the Data Provisioning Agent.

When blending the models, links between models only occur within the story; no new model is created. There are other restrictions in linked models – for example, geo maps are not supported, and blending across multiple live connections is not supported.

## Digital Boardroom

**Digital Boardroom**, which is built on SAC, is a presentation tool that combines stories with agenda items, to enable decision-makers to make collaborative and data-driven decisions based on real-time data. It integrates multiple data sources to produce a single source of truth and enables the drill-down analysis from aggregated insights to the line items. Besides this, decision-makers can adjust drivers and run simulations to see the impacts of a decision and predict the outcomes. Digital Boardroom is an add-on to SAC's existing use licenses.

# Creating analytics applications with Analytics Designer

Business users create stories in a self-service workflow using the various widgets and configurations with guided steps in the story design-time environment. However, the amount of customization is limited in stories.

In comparison, an analytics application typically contains some custom logic and requires more flexibility to present and interact with data, ranging from simple dashboards to highly customized and complex applications. For example, you can dynamically switch between different chart types at runtime.

Unlike stories designed for business users, analytics applications have more freedom to change the default behavior and usually require developer skills to implement custom logic with scripting. Stories and analytics applications are two different artifacts in SAC with corresponding design-time environments. However, stories and analytics applications are similar from a consumption perspective, with a similar look and feel, and share the same widgets and functionalities.

**Analytics Designer** is the dedicated low-code development environment for creating interactive analytics applications in SAC, which includes the capabilities to define data models, create and configure widgets, build UIs and layouts, and implement custom logic with the help of scripting through JavaScript-based APIs (**Analytics Designer API Reference Guide** at https://help.sap.com/doc/958d4c11261f42e992e8d01a4c0dde25/release/en-US/index.html).

An analytics application can be embedded with the support of bi-directional communication, which passes parameters through APIs so that they can interact between the embedding application and the embedded analytics application. This is extremely useful for *insight-to-action*-like scenarios, such as finding valuable insights from a dashboard to trigger actions through an OData call in a transactional system and seeing the outcome reflected in the same dashboard in real time. This helps achieve *close-the-loop* scenarios.

Analytics Designer completes SAC in addition to its BI, planning, and predictive capabilities and brings them together, and enables agile development by leveraging existing functionality and connectivity for more interactive use cases. Since it is built on top of SAC, you can create integrated planning applications, and use all the smart features such as Smart Insights and Smart Discovery in the analytics applications. R scripts can be involved to create a lot of different types of visualizations using libraries such as ggplot2. Furthermore, custom widgets can be created with a provided SDK; they can be set in the widget palette and work like the predefined widget. Creating a custom widget requires two files. First, there is a JSON file for metadata, which defines the ID, properties, events, and methods and specifies the location of the web component. The metadata file must be uploaded to the SAC tenant. The actual web component can be deployed remotely, and it is written in JavaScript. It contains the implementation as an HTML element.

To summarize, **Analytics Designer** extends the use cases beyond transitional analytics scenarios and supports sophisticated applications while leveraging the same design, concepts, and capabilities of SAC. There are many more things you can achieve with Analytics Designer. The developer handbook is one of the best resources for exploring and learning more about Analytics Designer: https://d.dam.sap.com/a/3Y16uka/SAPAnalyticsCloud_AnalyticsDesigner_ DeveloperHandbook.pdf.

## Content Network

**Business content** in SAC includes models, stories, and SAP Digital Boardroom presentations and they are providing the actual values for businesses to accelerate analytics content creation and data-driven workflows. The Content Network is where the business content is stored, managed, shared, and consumed. Content packages are organized by industries or LoBs. There are content packages from both SAP and third-party partners. Some third-party content is paid content; most of them also provide a trial option and customers can purchase the full version later through the SAP Store, which is the marketplace for SAP solutions or extensions from the partner ecosystem of SAP.

After importing the content package into your own SAC tenant, you will need to connect the content with your data. The business contents in the Content Network usually have two ways to connect with data – data acquisition or live connection. The contents that come with data acquisition are usually ready to run immediately with the sample data included that's facilitated by the models without additional effort. However, it is not recommended for productive use, which is required to import data from the actual data source or establish a live connection with the source system. The sample data should be cleared before you load the actual data. For content based on live data connectivity, no sample data is provided, so you will need to establish a connection with the data source to view the visualizations.

While there are many advantages to using the Content Network to import, export, and share content packages, it is always recommended to import and copy the content to a different folder to prevent any accidental loss of modifications and customizations during a re-import or a version update from the Content Network when the **Overwrite objects and data** option is selected. Content in Content Networks is forward-compatible, but there is no guarantee of backward compatibility.

For the latest information on published content in the Content Network and how to use it, please check out the *Content Network Release Information Guide* at https://help. sap.com/viewer/21868089d6ae4c5ab55f599c691726be/release/

en-US/975ca591bc45435b8ebe89a210757466.html and the *Content Package User Guide* at https://help.sap.com/viewer/42093f14b43c485fbe3adbbe81eff6c8/release/en-US.

## Embedded analytics

**Embedded analytics** allows you to analyze and visualize data directly in the source system without the need for complicated data preparational steps. The embedded SAC offers predefined dashboards, personalized data access, integrated role and screen variants of S4/HANA, and an intuitive ad hoc reporting capability for business users to gain insights from data. Besides this, with SAC as the analytics layer, it provides a consistent experience across SAP applications. At the time of writing, embedded analytics is available in S/4HANA Cloud, SuccessFactors, and Fieldglass solutions.

So, how does embedded analytics work technically? Let's take S/4HANA embedded analytics as an example. For each S4/HANA Cloud tenant, an SAC tenant is provisioned with it. SAC accesses the S/4HANA system through live access to ABAP CDS Views via underlying persistent data models and uses the transient queries generated from the CDS views. The relevant features, such as tenant provisioning, connectivity, and content life cycle management, are exposed through SAC APIs that are involved and fully managed by the embedding application, such as S/4HANA. The UI of SAC is embedded as iFrames in S/4HANA's Fiori-based UI, whereas SAC stories are integrated by a *wrapper application* that supports screen-variant savings, personalization, and intent-based navigations between analytical and transactional applications. Custom content is supported as you can create custom ABAP CDS Views and build stories and dashboards on top. Custom content can be exported and imported through Extensibility Inventory, which leverages **Analytics Content Network (ACN)** to move contents between tenants. The life cycle of analytical contents such as data models, KPI definitions, and preconfigured dashboards are integrated into the application life cycle management of the embedding application. Embedded analytics doesn't require an additional license as it is already included as part of the applicable licenses.

*Figure 13.6* provides a high-level overview of the integration architecture of the embedded analytics scenario. The following are the detailed steps for setting it up:

1. The SAC OEM tenant is provisioned together with the embedding application.

2. SAC and the embedding application must have a common authentication based on a shared IdP. SAC users are created via the identity service or SAC User and Team Provisioning API. Users are kept in sync between SAC and the embedding application.

3. Applications deliver predefined content, which is the metadata to describe data models, queries, and other analytical contents. Such contents will be provisioned into the SAC OEM tenant.

4. SAC accesses the application data through the SAC OEM integration service, which uses the live connection to access the underlying HANA database of the embedding application. The integration service provides a metadata adapter, runtime authentication and authorization, multi-tenancy handling, and an InA provider for runtime query metadata and data access.

5. **SAC UI** is embedded in the application UI through iFrames:

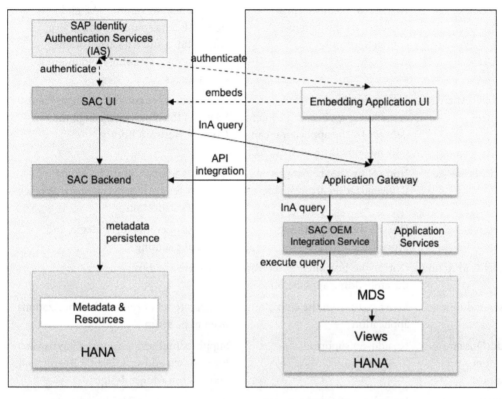

Figure 13.6 – Embedded analytics integration architecture

The integration service uses the **Core Schema Notation** (**CSN**) for the semantics of data structure. It supports the ad hoc data modeling tool Query Designer for end users, thus enabling self-service for business users in addition to predefined dashboards.

However, embedded analytics is exclusively bonded to the embedding application, meaning it cannot be used by other applications. If you are interested in business scenarios that will require data from multiple applications, you will need an enterprise SAC tenant. More differences between embedded analytics and enterprise analytics are shown in *Table 13.3*:

|  | Embedded Analytics | Enterprise Analytics |
|---|---|---|
| Data Sources | Restricted to embedding applications through live connections only | Can connect to various SAP and non-SAP data sources through live connections and data acquisitions; supports data blending from multiple data sources |
| Prebuilt Analytics Content | Prebuilt dashboard for the embedding application; content delivery by the application can only be done through SAC APIs | Comprehensive content packages from SAP and third parties through the Content Network library |
| Smart Features | None of the smart features or R-Visualization are available | Supports Search to Insight, Smart Insights, Smart Discovery, Smart Predict, and R-Visualization |
| Planning | Doesn't support planning processes | Supports operational, strategic, and financial planning |
| Insights to Action | Out-of-the-box integration with the embedding application | No out-of-the-box setup |
| User and Role | Reuse roles from the embedding application | A separate set of roles and authorizations need to be setup |
| Add-Ons and Custom App Support | No add-on support | Supports multidimensional analysis via Excel-based add-ons, Digital Boardroom, and custom widget design |
| License | Doesn't require any separate license | Requires separate SAC licenses |

Table 13.3 – Embedded analytics and enterprise analytics scenarios

## SAC APIs

SAC provides REST APIs to support the automation of administrative tasks such as user creation. Before using an API, you must create an OAuth client in the SAC tenant. In SAC, the following APIs are available:

- **OEM Tenant Management APIs**: These allow applications to create and manage SAC tenants and configure them, such as by adding a live connection, an OAuth client, or a trusted IdP. It also provides APIs for getting the quotas for each landscape and retrieving the logs. Multitenancy support for the application is facilitated by the OEM integration service with the support of the Tenant Configuration API when it processes the data and metadata by supplying the **tenant ID** context.

- **Open Story and Application URL APIs**: These allow applications to access a story and analytical application directly via a URL, which can be used for embedding SAC in the UI of your application as an iFrame control.

- **SAC Tenant APIs**: These allow applications to access information of the SAC tenant such as stories and metadata, users, groups, the permissions of SAC artifacts, and the User and Team provisioning **System for Cross-Domain Identity Management (SCIM)** API for managing users and teams programmatically for tasks such as creating users, assigning users to teams, enabling correct user setting for language, date, time, and number formats, updating SAML mapping for SSO, changing licenses, transporting users and teams between different tenants, and more.

- **Content Network APIs**: These allow you to manage analytical content through APIs, such as getting the list, details, and permissions of items in the Content Network, creating an import job, and getting the job's status.

- **Analytics Designer APIs**: These can be used to create interactive and custom-designed analytical applications as you can write scripts for interactions. For example, you can assign a script to a button's onClick event when the user selects it within a chart. Scripts are based on JavaScript and are available to almost all controls in SAC.

Most of these APIs have been published on SAP API Business Hub at https://api.sap.com/package/SAPAnalyticsCloud/rest.

## Smart features

SAC includes a variety of smart features for leveraging machine learning and natural language processing technology to help you explore data and gain insights from data. These smart features are called augmented analytics in SAC and range from using natural language to search and generate visualizations automatically, to making predictions and recommendations from historical data.

### Search to Insight

Search to Insight provides a Google-like interface for querying data using natural language directly from the Story. Users can ask questions and SAC will create the most appropriate visualizations for the questions. For example, you can ask questions about showing the top five sales by region. Follow-up questions are supported in the same business context; for example, you can run subsequent searches by specifying the product types or other dimensions, such as showing the sales by product for the last four quarters. While typing a question, auto-completion is supported for dimension names, dimension values, and measure names. Synonyms can be created for dimension and measure names and used in the query.

The generated charts are interactive, and you can also change the chart types. The charts of Search to Insight can be embedded into a Story directly by simply copying and pasting. This democratizes the story creation process by enabling the user to use natural language to build visualizations.

Search to Insight works with indexed data models either through data acquisition or live connection (limit to 5 million members for indexes based on live data models) and supports data sources such as SAP HANA, SAP S/4HANA, SAP Universe, SAP DWC, and SAP BW. Visualizations based on indexed data are determined by the date access rights of the users. At the time of writing, Search to Insight only supports querying questions in English.

### Smart Insights and Smart Discovery

**Smart Insights** and **Smart Discovery** are two advanced features in SAC that use ML/AI technologies to help users gain insights from the data. Smart Insights identifies the top contributors of a selected value or variance point, while Smart Discovery identifies the key influencers of a selected measure or dimension.

Smart Insights identifies the top contributors that have the highest contributions to the data points being analyzed – for example, what contributed most to revenue across the regions, such as North America. The generated insights are explained in natural language. We can deep dive into the generated result and investigate it further by running Smart Insights again for the North American region to understand the different sets of top contributors, such as product types, customer segments, and more. It doesn't only explain what top contributors are but also how they are calculated.

By using Smart Insights in combination with Variances, you can quickly identify the positive and negative influence factors behind the variance, such as those between actual and budget sales.

Smart Insights is a significant time-saver for business users looking for insights into a particular value; otherwise, they may have to investigate the members of each dimension to understand how they will contribute to the result. Smart Insights only works for a single data point or variance. It can be enabled by simply clicking a data point in a chart and using the right-click context menu, and then selecting the light bulb symbol to open the **Smart Insights** side panel.

In comparison, Smart Discovery works against a data model as an automated data exploration tool to identify key influencers and explore the key differences between the different attributes. It is especially useful for open-ended questions. Users can run the discovery against a measure or a dimension. Here, it will build regression models for measures to predict future outcomes and classification models for dimensions to segregate results into different groups.

During runtime, Smart Discovery will build and test multiple models and determine the best fit model based on accuracy and robustness to generate the results. It does so in the form of intuitive charts and correlations explained in natural language. It helps you discover the key influencing factors and understand the positive or native impacts of each influencer, how they are related to each other, and the results.

Smart Discovery helps users start analysis right away and gradually explore the key influencers in great detail. Besides this, it works nicely with Smart Insights, which provides more insights for a selected value.

*Table 13.4* summarizes the differences between Smart Insights and Smart Discovery:

| | Smart Insights | Smart Discovery |
|---|---|---|
| Features | Identifies the top contributors and various insights for the selected value or variance. They are visualized in the **Smart Insights** side panel, with different types of charts and dynamic text explanations. | Identifies key influencers for selected dimensions or measures and explores the relationship between different attributes. The results are presented in a generated story that covers key influencers, unexpected values, and simulations. |
| Use Case | Looks for insights for a particular value, performs deep-dive analysis, and explains surprising elements in data. An example of a use case is as follows:<br><br>• Understand what contributed most to the revenue for a county | Jump starts data exploration, understands what is relevant to a result and the complex relationships and outliners, and performs what-if-like simulations. An example of a use case is as follows:<br><br>• Discover how sales or marketing activities influence the revenue |
| Data Context | Single data point or variance | A data model with multiple dimensions and measures |

Table 13.4 – Smart Insights and Smart Discovery

### Smart Predict

**Smart Predict** is an advanced feature designed for a business analyst to leverage machine learning to answer business questions about future trends and make recommendations. The users are guided through the predictive workflows, and basic knowledge of statistics and machine learning is required. In this section, we will focus on Smart Predict, though SAC for planning includes a variety of features that help generate planning forecasts by analyzing the historical data while leveraging the same techniques. We will cover predictive planning later.

Three types of predictive scenarios can be created:

- **Classification** ranks the population and predicts the probability that an event will happen. For example, who is likely to buy a product based on buying history data?

- **Regression** finds the relationship between variables and estimates the value of a measure. For example, how much would a customer spend in my store?

- **Time Series Forecasting** predicts the values of a time-dependent measure. For example, what are the expected sales by products for the next few weeks?

The quality of data is important when building a predictive model; the training dataset must represent the business domain and the predictive goals. Among the variables, one of them is special – the target variable that you want to predict. For classification, the target variable is a categorical value while the target is a numeric value for a regression model. Variables that are highly correlated to the target variable are called leaker variables and they must be excluded to avoid something having a dominating influence on the results.

During the training process, Smart Predict assigns 75% of the dataset as the estimation dataset to build the predictive model; the remaining 25% is used for the validation dataset to calculate the performance of the model. For the prediction, the dataset must have the same structure as the training dataset. This means it must have the same number of variables and the same variable names and types as the training dataset.

Once the predictive model has been trained and run, you can evaluate the accuracy and robustness of the model by using performance indicators such as Prediction Power and Prediction Confidence, and built-in reports in SAC such as **Confusion Matrix**. We will discuss these later in this section. The predictive outputs can easily be stored and visualized in SAC stories, as well as used in other models such as a planning model.

Before we discuss each of the predictive scenarios, we'd like to share a little bit more background on how predictive analytics has been evolved in SAC. The model behind the prediction initially came to SAC from SAP's acquisition of a predictive analytics company called KXEN. KXEN's predictive models were based on an algorithm named Ridge Regression. Ridge Regression has been found to work well, unlike **Ordinary Least Square Regression (OLS)**, which overfits and tries too hard to fit all data points. However, it does assume the predictions will have a linear relationship with predictors.

**SAC Smart Predict** is now based on **Gradient Boosting**, which has made substantial improvements in the model performance. At the core of Gradient Boosting is a data structure called a tree. It uses a collection of trees, with a philosophy to iteratively build weak learners and then combining them will create accurate and robust predictions.

For example, if you take the dataset and fit the first tree first, and the first prediction is more distant from the truth and left with a residual (the difference between the predictions and actual values), then you can build another tree to explain the residual until you reach a point where most of the residuals have been explained or the maximum number of trees has been reached (this is limited to four levels to avoid overfitting and reduce model complexity). For structured datasets, Gradient Boosting has been proven to outperform the previous version of Smart Predict, which is why it has been chosen for the new predictive models in SAC.

## Classification

**Classification** is used to predict the probability that an event will happen. For example, it can help predict scenarios such as which customer is likely to churn or which employee may potentially leave the company. At the time of writing, SAC Smart Predict only supports binary cases in classification.

To rank a population and make a prediction, the quality of the data is important to build a predictive model. A good predictive model finds the right balance between accuracy and robustness, can predict correctly, and avoid overfitting, is robust, and can be trusted to predict new cases. The performance of a classification model is usually measured by two indicators:

- **Predictive power** measures the accuracy and quality of the model. It is the ratio between correct predictions and total cases, ranging between 0 and 1.

- **Prediction confidence** measures the robustness of the model and represents that the model can be used to predict new cases reliably. It can be increased by improving the training dataset.

The classification model also explains the influencers and how these variables are contributing to the target. The top ones are summarized on the **Influence Contributions** page, which allows the user to navigate and understand the relationship between different variables. For example, in the use case of whether a customer is likely to churn, you can analyze how the customer segments, industries, countries, and LoB may impact the results.

Other useful tools include Confusion Matrix and Profit Simulation, which allow you to choose a threshold on the percentage of the population to predict the results. For example, if you select 20% of your customers with a high probability of churn, what is the percentage of that 20% you are likely to keep if you can prioritize your customer success activities to retain these customers? This is very helpful, for example, if you have a limited budget and need to determine and find the balance between costs and outcomes. *Figure 13.7* depicts the predictive model performance metrics and top influencers for predicting whether a customer will churn:

Figure 13.7 – Customer churn classification

Underneath, a classification predictive model uses Gradient Boosting trees to combine multiple week learners in an iterative process. Each iteration includes three steps. First, it calculates the residual for each case of the estimation dataset (75% of the dataset, which is used for training purposes). Second, it splits the estimation dataset on each variable and calculates the decision trees that predict the residual best based on the accuracy of the tree. Finally, it selects the tree with the highest gain for the next iteration and calculates a predicted value. This process stops when one of the conditions is satisfied and the final model is the combination of all winning trees – the trees with the highest gains.

## Regression

**Regression** is used to predict the value of the target measure from historical data. For example, it is useful for answering questions about how much a customer will spend on a store, and how much revenue will be impacted by the new marketing campaign.

To predict, you will need the historical dataset, which represents the domain with a set of variables. For a regression model, the target variable must be numeric – a measure. In the example of a marketing campaign, the target variable can be the expected revenue resulting from the campaign based on other variables in the dataset such as promotions, country, customer type, and so on.

Regression in Smart Predict also relies on the Gradient Boosting technique to generate the best predictive model. The robustness of the regression model is also measured by prediction confidence. However, the quality of the regression model is measured by another indicator – the **Root Mean Square Error** (**RMSE**). The RMSE is calculated as the average of the square difference between the predicted and actual values for all cases of the validating dataset. The quality is better when the difference is smaller. RMSE is calculated with the following formula:

$$RMSE = \sqrt{\frac{\sum_{i=1}^{n}(P_i - A_i)^2}{n}}$$

Here, $n$ is the number of cases in the validation dataset, $P$ is the predicted value, and $A$ is the actual value of the case of the target.

The debrief information of a regression model includes two views. The overview page covers the performance indicator explained earlier, such as RMSE or prediction confidence, as well as the target statistics, and a summary of influence contributions. The **Influence Contributions** page lists the most important influencers, and how they positively or negatively influence the target. Knowing this will help users discover new insights and make better decisions. *Figure 13.8* shows an example of the overview page for predicting sales opportunities:

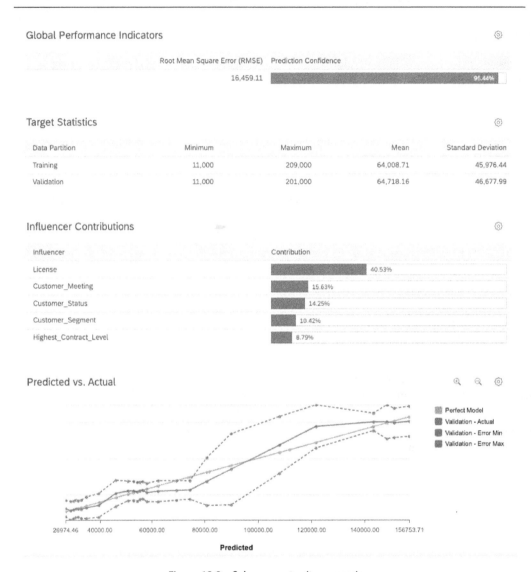

Figure 13.8 – Sales opportunity regression

### Time series forecasting

Time series models are used to forecast the future values of a time-dependent measure. For example, you can use time series forecasting to answer questions such as, what are the expected sales by products in the next few months?

For the dataset, it must have a time dimension and the values of the target variable in the past. The combination of the date and target variable is called a *signal* and will be analyzed by the predictive model. Depending on how far in the future you want to predict, typically, a *5:1* ratio is recommended for historical data and the prediction. For example, you can predict the next 2 months if 10 months of historical data is available. Here, the scale of the historical data and the prediction need to be the same. If the recorded historical data is more fine-grained, it is better to aggregate data in the unit of time you will need to predict. The other variables related to time are called candidate influencers – for example, the number of working days of a month, or specific events during the month such as holiday sales events. These candidate influencers are often domain-specific and have special meaning to detect certain components of signals, such as trends or cycles.

Technically, signals are broken down into four components:

- **Trends**: The first step is to determine the trend and the direction of the signal. The trend is either linear or quadratic for seasonal patterns. SAC Smart Predict tests eight trend models grouped into two groups:

  - Three stochastic methods that assume the forecast value will depend on the past values

  - Five deterministic methods that assume the forecast is independent of the past values and considers the candidate influencer variables

- **Cycles**: The second step is to determine the cycles, which represent the periodical and seasonal patterns. Cycles are computed by encoding the signal, either based on a period length or calendar events for seasonality. After that, it runs an iterative process for each of the eight detected trends to measure the links between the signal – the trend and the cycle – to see if it improves the forecast.

- **Fluctuation**: The third step is to determine the fluctuation of the signal after the trends and cycles have been extracted and use an auto-regression model to compute what is left on the signal.

- **Residual**: Finally, the remaining signals after trends, cycles, and fluctuation that are removed are considered *noise* – that is, random effects.

*Figure 13.9* depicts the aforementioned process:

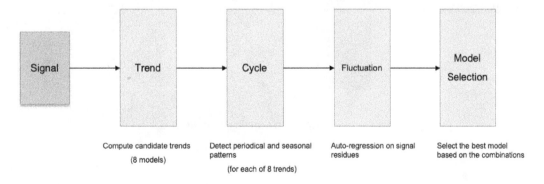

Figure 13.9 – Time series forecasting signal components

In the end, based on the determined components of the signal, **SAC Smart Predict** tries the combination of different models to find the best one, with the selected model whose residues are closest to white noise. To measure the performance of a model, the validation process compares the predicted values with the actual values based on a metric called **Horizon-Wide Mean Absolute Percentage Error (MAPE)**, which is used as the quality indicator. MAPE measures the accuracy by comparing how much the forecast is different from the actual value. Horizon-Wide MAPE computes several individual MAPEs and calculates the average based on the requested horizon – how far you want to predict. A Horizon-Wide MAPE is computed with the following formula:

$$\text{Horizon Wide MAPE (forecast, signal, H)} = \frac{1}{H}\sum_{h=1}^{H}(\frac{1}{N}\sum_{i=1}^{N}\left|\frac{(forecast_{i+h}^{h} - signal_{i+h})}{signal_{i+h}}\right|)$$

Here, *forecast* is the predicted value, *signal* is the actual value, *h* is the horizon (the number of periods in the future for prediction), and *n* is the number of items for the target variable.

If a predictive model has a Horizon-Wide MAPE near zero, it is a good model. Otherwise, you will need to apply your domain knowledge to determine the accuracy and check if it is applicable.

### Using the predictive model

Once you have trained the predictive model and you are satisfied with the quality of the model, you can apply the predictive model and save the output into a dataset. *Figure 13.10* shows how to apply a classification model based on the customer churn example we discussed previously:

Figure 13.10 – Applying a predictive model

Once the output dataset is available, you can use it directly in a story, or create a model on top of the dataset and use it in a planning story.

## Planning

For many companies, planning is one of the most critical and complex processes for their business operations and priorities. SAC offers full-fledged planning functionalities to support collaborative enterprise planning. This includes strategic and financial planning to set the overall direction at an aggregated level using planning assumptions, growth drives, profit and loss statements, balance sheets, and cash flow, as well as operational planning inside organizations such as sales, HR, and supplier chains and how they each impact the business results.

Planning in SAC is supported by a collaborative workflow. SAC addresses the collaboration challenges by providing collaborative and commenting functions. For example, you can create a planning calendar in SAC, where each task can be assigned to a planner that is responsible for it, and all the planners will be informed by the system of the assigned action items.

The Smart Predict features introduced previously can be used for predictive planning to create automated planning proposals that can be adjusted by experienced planners or enable planning with time series forecasting. SAC can disaggregate plan data to the raw data level, support distribution and spreading functions, or create advanced formulas using scripts.

Planning is all about connecting the various data from surrounding enterprise systems. For that, SAC can integrate master data and transactional data from SAP S/4HANA or populate the planning results back to S/4HANA. SAC can also integrate with SAP SuccessFactors for workforce planning in HR.

> **Important note**
>
> There are many more concepts, architectural considerations, and best practices about planning we cannot cover in this chapter. To learn more about planning with SAC, enroll in the open SAP course at `https://open.sap.com/courses/sac3`.

## System landscapes and content life cycle management

In SAC, depending on the business needs, multiple environments can be provisioned, such as Sandbox, Dev, QA, Test Preview, and Prod. All these environments are updated on a scheduled basis by SAP as a managed SaaS offering. Multiple factors determine the landscape architecture, such as the test strategy, choice of public or private edition, integration with on-premise systems, and the life cycle and change management of content between environments.

SAC offers the choice of public and private hosted editions. For the public edition, a tenant is provisioned in a shared HANA database with a schema per customer. For the private edition, there are some other shared infrastructure components, but the HANA database is dedicated. If your business requires you to manage encryption keys with the **Bring Your Own Key** (**BYOK**) feature, then note it is only available with the private edition. In that case, an SAP Data Custodian key management service tenant is required for each SAC private tenant. Performance testing is only permitted in the private edition, while penetration testing can be requested for both editions. To request penetration testing, follow the process described in KBA 3080379 at `https://launchpad.support.sap.com/#/notes/3080379`.

Just like HANA Cloud and DWC, SAC follows a **Quarterly Release Cycle** (**QRC**) schedule. Within the QRC, SAC organizes the releases in waves; each wave occurs every 2 weeks. For example, Wave 2022.02 is the second wave as part of 2022.Q1 QRC. Dev, QA, and Prod all follow the same release schedule so that content can be transported between them without having to worry about versioning. The test preview environment is only available in the private edition, which receives the quarterly release around ~1 month earlier. This provides some customers with the opportunity to validate the new release with existing productive content. However, it should not be used for development or production purposes. For example, you cannot transport content from the test preview to other environments for the first month when its version is not aligned. Technically, there is also the **Fast Track** option, which is updated for each wave. It can be used as a Sandbox environment. Sandbox can only be used for testing purposes. *Figure 13.11* summarizes the aforementioned release cycles for different environments:

| | 2022 | | | | | | | | | | | |
|---|---|---|---|---|---|---|---|---|---|---|---|---|
| | Jan. | Feb. | Mar. | Apr. | May | Jun. | Jul. | Aug. | Sep. | Oct. | Nov. | Dec. |
| Quarterly Release Cycle (Dev, QA, Prod) | | | Wave 2022.02 | | | Wave 2022.08 | | | Wave 2022.15 | | Wave 2022.21 | |
| Test Preview Release Cycle | Wave 2022.02 | | | Wave 2022.08 | | | | Wave 2022.15 | | | Wave 2022.21 | |
| Fast Track Release Cycle | 2022.02 2022.03 | 2022.04 2022.05 | 2022.06 2022.07 | 2022.08 2022.09 | 2022.10 2022.11 | 2022.12 2022.13 | 2022.14 2022.15 | 2022.16 2022.17 | 2022.18 2022.19 | 2022.20 2022.21 | 2022.22 2022.23 | 2022.24 2022.25 |

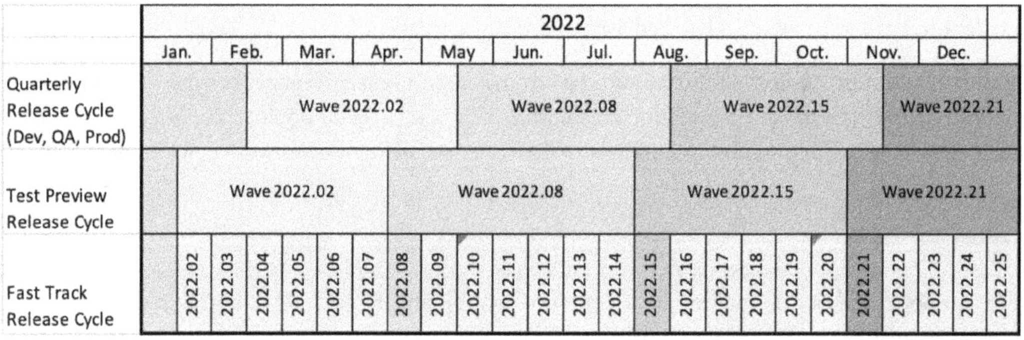

Figure 13.11 – SAC release cycles

Some of the best practices for content life cycle management include the following:

- Follow the same update release cycle for the Dev, QA, and Prod environments.
- Validate content with production data; for example, use the test preview environment to validate new releases.
- Use Fast Track to test upcoming new features and plan your projects ahead of time.
- Only create an object once and transport it to different environments to keep the same ID and its dependencies.

- Make sure the content namespace is consistent across different environments. SAC APIs will refer to this content namespace.

- Use the Content Network to transport objects between environments without exporting/importing them.

## Security concepts – users, roles, teams, and licenses

SAC organizes its security features around users, roles, teams, and licenses. A role can contain many users and a user can be in many roles. The role is the only place where you can define the application rights, such as `create`, `update`, or `delete` content types such as **models** or **stories**: a team can contain many users and a user can belong to many teams. Teams can be used as aggregators to group roles together; a user that belongs to a team inherits the rights that have been assigned to the roles of the team. Access rights to the folders in SAC are assigned by teams or users, not roles. For each project, SAC recommends that you create a project `Folder` and follow the same naming convention for the contents within the project folder.

Licenses are assigned to users through roles. The following license types are available; a single role can only consume one of the following license types:

- **Business Intelligence**: Named user

- **Planning Standard**: Named user; it includes a *Business Intelligence – named user* license

- **Planning Profession**: Named user; it includes a *Planning Standard – named user* license

In terms of BI, concurrent session licenses and Analytics Hub licenses that were previously available are no longer available for purchase. A single user can consume multiple licenses, but a user can only consume one of the BI licenses. For example, a Business Intelligence – concurrent session license cannot consume a planning license because the planning license includes the Business Intelligence – named user license.

The following are some general best practices for managing licenses with roles and teams:

- If you're not using a user provisioning solution, it is recommended that you use a SAML2 IdP to map users to teams:

  - Enable *dynamic user creation* in the SAC setup

  - Use the SAM2 *team* user attribute to map with SAC teams, and use teams to group roles together

- If you're using a user provisioning solution such as SAP Identity Provisioning, it is recommended that you create the users without any role. Instead, assign users to teams and assign roles to teams.

## Administration Cockpit

Starting from the *2022.Q1 QRC* release, the Administration Cockpit is available, which provides a consolidated view for all administrative tasks, including but not limited to authorization, dependencies, content sharing, usage analytics, tracing performance statistics, and many more. The Administration Cockpit itself is a SAC analytics application that is enabled by default in the system folder; users don't need to import it from the Content Network.

Technically, the Administration Cockpit includes two parts – the main application, SAC_ADMIN_ COCKPIT, and the fact sheets for detailed information. Together, they provide the following:

- A content summary for all content types in SAC such as folders, models, stories, applications, connections, dimensions, data actions, and more, grouped by general content or planning-related content.

- Authorization assignments of users, teams, and roles, as well as checking the teams without any user assignment, inactive users and users never used, and more.

- Sharing settings for folders, models, stories, and applications to understand who has access to a list of shared objects

- Allow you to understand the dependencies between objects and how models, connections, stories, and other objects are related to each other.

- Allow you to understand the usage of objects – for example, the top 10 used models, applications, and housekeeping help to identify objects that are not actively used.

- Tracing to show the error history and correlation, and the top 10 users with more errors.

- An end-to-end performance analysis tool based on the SAC_PERFORMANCE_TOOL analytics model, which shows page startup time and load time, the runtime distributions, backend processing statistics, network statistics, and frontend performance.

- Data action performance statistics and analysis based on the live data model, PLANNING_ DATA_ACTIONS, shows the number of users who have scheduled or triggered data actions, the number of models with data actions, and how they are triggered or executed, such as the scheduling, median duration to complete, number of failures, and so on.

- Fact sheets for detailed information about a particular user, role, team, analytics application, story, connection, folder, dataset, and more.

*Figure 13.12* shows the **Administration Cockpit** home page:

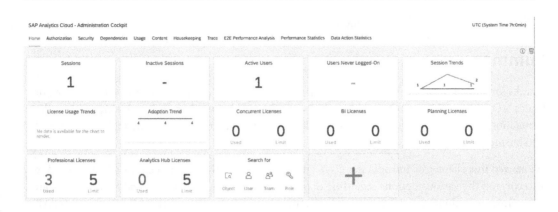

Figure 13.12 – The Administration Cockpit home page

The Administration Cockpit organizes the features mentioned earlier in the different tabs of the same application in SAC.

### Performance Benchmark

Starting from the *2022.Q2 QRC* release, SAC provides a Performance Benchmark to help customers understand and measure how performance can impact the user experience. It runs several scripts to calculate a normalized score of the client machine, or the network latency and bandwidth. Network performance impacting the speed of accessing SAC and downloading and uploading data can be negatively affected by network configurations such as VPC and firewall rules. Performance Benchmark can be accessed by going to **System | Performance | Benchmark Tool**. *Figure 13.13* shows an example of this:

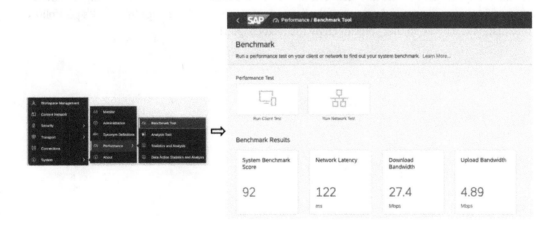

Figure 13.13 – Performance Benchmark

With this, we have a deeper understanding of SAC.

## Summary

Thanks for staying with me. This was probably one of the longest chapters as we covered two major topics – DWC and SAC. This is because they are related to each other and, together, serve as the foundation for providing the necessary capabilities to turn data into insights and actions integrated into business processes.

We started this chapter by introducing DWC, its use cases, and the key concepts, such as Space. We also covered the various options regarding data integration – both federation and replication from on-premise and cloud data sources – and explained how DWC works with SAP BW through SAP BW Bridge, which is important for customers who have existing investments in SAP BW. After that, we discussed the different modeling capabilities, which include Data Builder for technical users and Business Builder for business users. We wrapped up the DWC section by explaining how to consume content from DWC in SAC.

Regarding SAC, we discussed the connectivity it offers, which includes both live connections and data acquisitions, the differences between datasets and models in data preparation, creating visualizations with stories, and the more interactive analytics applications. We also talked about embedded analytics and how it is different from enterprise analytics, as well as the SAC APIs for tenant and content management. One of the coolest things about SAC is its smart capabilities, which include Search to Insight, Smart Insights, Smart Discovery, and Smart Prediction. We also talked about the different predictive scenarios in smart prediction. Finally, we discussed the system landscapes, content life cycle management, security concepts, and the Administration Cockpit, which provides a one-stop hub for all administrative tasks.

In the next chapter, based on the knowledge of the ML/AI capabilities we covered regarding the smart features of SAC, we will extend the scope of the broader AI strategy and offerings from SAP's portfolio. Before that, take a break so that you can enjoy the next chapter!

14

# SAP Intelligent Technologies

Today, many enterprises are increasingly leveraging intelligent technologies such as **Artificial Intelligence** (**AI**) as part of their business processes, to forecast demands, augment employee productivity, and improve customer experience. As a result, businesses can prepare for new situations or address existing challenges more intelligently and proactively. Ultimately, AI enables humans to focus on value-adding tasks and reduce human errors, especially for repetitive and manual tasks. AI can have significant impacts on all aspects of business processes.

In this chapter, we will discuss the different product and technology offerings in ML and AI covering data preparation, training, inference, and AI operations. The following topics will be covered:

- SAP HANA ML
- SAP AI Core and AI Launchpad
- SAP AI Business Services
- AI capabilities in SAP Data Intelligence and SAP Analytics Cloud
- SAP Conversational AI
- SAP Process Automation
- Intelligent Scenario Lifecycle Management for S/4HANA
- Data architecture for AI

Throughout this chapter, you will learn the differences between the preceding technologies and gain an understanding of how to apply them in your business processes. Let's get started!

## Overview of Intelligent Technologies

SAP Intelligent Technologies is a cornerstone of the Intelligent Enterprise strategy. SAP offers a full set of intelligent applications and services to help businesses with better decision-making based on data and intelligence. The intelligent technologies are embedded in SAP's intelligent suite applications to support and optimize business processes. They are also exposed as part of SAP BTP for customers and ecosystem partners to extend and create new solutions that are innovative and provide competitive differentiation. As depicted in *Figure 14.1*, SAP's intelligent offerings include the following:

- **HANA ML**: This contains in-database ML libraries and related tooling for AI modeling and algorithms, for structured and tabular data.

- **AI Core and AI Launchpad**: These are the foundation for AI runtime and the lifecycle management of AI scenarios. AI Core offers a robust environment for training and serving. AI Launchpad is a SaaS offering to operationalize and manage the lifecycle of AI models.

- **SAP AI Business Services**: They provide ready-to-use AI capabilities as reusable business services as part of SAP BTP that can help solve specific business problems in various business processes. These kinds of services are typically consumed as APIs as part of SAP API Business Hub.

- **SAP Data Intelligence**: This provides data integration, data governance, and features to create, deploy, and execute ML models.

- **SAP Analytics Cloud (SAC)**: This provides smart features for citizen data scientists and business users to perform classification, predication, and forecasting.

- **SAP Conversational AI**: This is a low-code/low-touch chatbot building platform, with capabilities to build, train, test, and manage intelligent AI-powered chatbots to simplify business tasks and workflows and improve the user experience.

- **SAP Process Automation**: This combines **Intelligent Robotic Process Automation (iRPA)** and workflow capabilities to automate repetitive processes and help users to focus on high-value tasks.

- **Embedded AI in SAP applications** enables customers to consume AI directly as part of the standard applications. In this way, AI is natively infused into the business processes in SAP's intelligent enterprise scenarios, with the support of AI clients such as ISLM for S/4HANA:

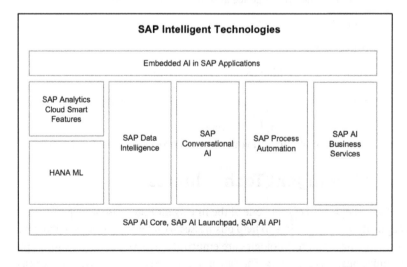

Figure 14.1: Overview of SAP Intelligent Technologies

SAP's AI strategy is to focus on infusing AI into applications as part of business processes. Tools cover areas such as AI design-time activities, data analysis, modeling, experiment tracking, data acquisition, production runtime, operations, and the lifecycle management of AI functionalities.

Next, we will discuss the aforementioned capabilities in more detail.

# HANA ML

SAP HANA contains in-database ML libraries and related tooling for AI modeling and algorithms, based on relational data. There are a few different ways to support ML use cases, with the built-in functions of the **Automated Predictive Library** (APL) and the **Predictive Analysis Library** (PAL) and Python and R clients for SAP HANA ML.

## APL and PAL

APL provides data mining capabilities based on the Automated Analytics engine of HANA through functions that run, by default, in the SAP HANA script server. APL functions provide the capabilities to develop predictive models, train the models, and run the models to answer business questions based on data stored in SAP HANA. PAL is another library that provides built-in algorithms and functions to leverage ML capabilities in HANA.

APL and PAL together provide a broad range of AI scenarios, such as Classification, Regression, Time Series Forecasting, Cluster Analysis, Association Analysis, Statistics, Social Network Analysis, Recommender System, and Miscellaneous. In addition, PAL provides algorithms for outlier detection scenarios and advanced features, such as a unified interface for classification and regression scenarios for easy consumption by providing the same procedure interface.

For metrics to qualify AI model performance, APL and PAL generate them as part of the standard output of model training and function runs. The metrics can be persisted and used for comparison. Most algorithms provide functions for automated model evaluation and parameter search and comparison for the section of different regression algorithms. APL also supports additional metrics such as Predictive Power and Prediction Confidence for model performance. For example, SAC uses the HANA ML capabilities for its smart features as mentioned in the previous chapter.

APL and PAL are the embedded AI engine in SAP HANA, designed for providing maximum performance by leveraging HANA's parallelization capabilities. As they are embedded in the database, both PAL and APL are invoked through SQL Scripts and expect the training dataset to be in a relational format from HANA data structures such as database tables, virtual structures such as calculation views, or remote data sources federated from other databases. Calls to APL and PAL could be SQLScript files and SAP HANA Stored Procedures. It can also be included in the table functions and calculation views. An important aspect of deployment is the integration with SAP applications to gain insights embedded in the business processes. One example is the **ABAP Managed Database Procedures** (AMDPs) that wrap SQLScript codes into standard ABAP syntax. SAP S/4HANA provides a framework for the integration of AI scenarios based on AMDPs called **Intelligent Scenario Lifecycle Management (ISLM)**. We will discuss it later in this chapter.

APL provides another option for deployment. Models can be extracted as JavaScript code snippets, thus having the flexibility to run in existing JavaScript engines in addition to HANA runtimes.

> **Important Note**
>
> For more details about the supported algorithms in APL and PAL, please find the developer guide of APL at `https://help.sap.com/docs/apl/7223667230cb471ea916200712a9c682/59b79cbb6beb4607875fa3fe116a8eef.html` and reference guide of PAL at `https://help.sap.com/docs/HANA_CLOUD_DATABASE/319d36de4fd64ac3afbf91b1fb3ce8de/c9eeed704f3f4ec39441434db8a874ad.html`.

Next, SAP HANA introduced native libraries for Python and R to enable data scientists to interact with HANA's built-in functions of APL and PAL for ease of consumption.

## Python and R ML clients for SAP HANA

Python and R are the most popular languages for data science. The goal of Python and R clients is to provide a similar experience for HANA ML just like any open source ML library while the actual execution is delegated to HANA, without the need for data transfer.

Python and R clients include the standard data manipulation operations based on the DataFrame features. SAP HANA DataFrame provides a way to view data in SAP HANA, such as native DataFrame in Python and R – however, all the operations, including data training and scoring, are translated into SQL statements, and executed on the database, resulting in faster performance. Depending on the use cases, the generated SQL statements can be captured into SQLScript or data model artifacts. SAP HANA DataFrame is only available while the connection to HANA is open via the `ConnectionContext` object. The following statement creates a simple SAP HANA DataFrame instance:

```
with ConnectionContext('address', port, 'user', 'password') as
c_context:
  dataframe = (c_context.table('TABLE1', schema='SCHEMA1').
select('COL1','COL2','COL2'))
```

SAP HANA DataFrame doesn't contain any data but provides a way to view data stored in HANA. If data manipulation and transformation with other datasets or use of other native libraries are required, you can convert SAP HANA DataFrame to a pandas DataFrame through the `collect()` function.

The library includes the modules and respective algorithms:

- `hana.ml.dataframe`: This represents the HANA data structure as a DataFrame.

- `hana_ml.algorithms.apl`: This package includes APL functions such as gradient boosting classification and regression, time series, and clustering algorithms.

- `hana_ml.algorithms.pal`: This package contains various algorithms of PAL for auto ML, classification, regression, clustering, exponential smoothing, association, time series forecasting, statistics, recommender systems, and miscellaneous algorithms, such as ABC Analysis, as well as model, pipeline, and metrics support.

- Other modules and packages such as exception and error handling, model storage, visualizer, spatial, graph, and text mining packages.

SAP HANA Cloud provides scalability and elasticity to manage resources and better scaling to support AI workloads. The algorithm libraries support multi-threading options to speed up training processes. To support the highest performance, HANA can be configured to hold ML models in the main memory if the use case requires it. Equally, the Python client provides the model storage that supports the versioning of models.

SAP HANA ML focuses on data scientist productivity and provides internal tooling and lifecycle management to support data preparation, model training, and evaluation. As HANA supports multi-mode data storage and processing, the ML libraries also tightly integrate with advanced capabilities such as the spatial and graph processing, and text mining of HANA. Consider SAP HANA ML libraries when HANA is the central data platform in your architecture. Within SAP, many products such as SAC, S/4HANA, and **Integrated Business Planning** (**IBP**) leverage HANA ML as the foundation of their intelligent capabilities. *Figure 14.2* summarizes the AI capabilities in SAP HANA:

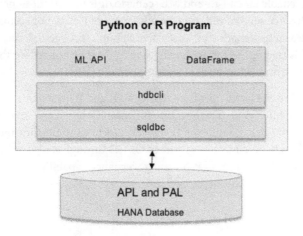

Figure 14.2: SAP HANA ML libraries

SAP HANA ML continues to bring more algorithms to improve the offerings for AI scenarios based on structured and tabular data in HANA. Next, we will talk about the ML/AI capabilities in SAP Data Intelligence.

## ML/AI in SAP Data Intelligence

SAP Data Intelligence is SAP's data management solution to provide complex orchestration scenarios, data cataloging, data quality, and metadata management. It brings together data management capabilities that were previously available in SAP Data Hub and integrates them with ML capabilities from other SAP solutions. In *Chapter 8*, we already discussed the data integration capabilities of SAP Data Intelligence – here, we will focus on the ML capabilities of SAP Data Intelligence.

When all your data is already structured and in SAP HANA or SAP Data Warehouse Cloud, the built-in ML libraries discussed earlier might be sufficient. However, in many use cases, data is located across multiple places, with a mix of unstructured and structured data such as IoT data. SAP Data Intelligence is recommended for use cases when multiple disparate data sources need to be consolidated or orchestration of data pipelines to additional ML environments is necessary. SAP Data Intelligence includes more than 200 operators for different kinds of tasks, such as Image Classification, **Optical Character Recognition** (**OCR**), and the ability to create custom operators for different requirements. In addition, it can perform data transformation and data cleaning, is able to apply data quality rules, and has the ability to script in Python, R, and HANA ML as mentioned earlier.

As part of the SAP Data Intelligence, ML Scenario Manager provides a single place to track all ML-related artifacts, such as datasets, notebooks, training runs, and pipelines. The Modeler provides a low-code interface to utilize the functions as part of APL and PAL without knowing how to do SQL Scripting. It is also possible to combine HANA ML with open source R and Python libraries in the same pipeline to enable an end-to-end ML scenario. It is important to note that models run on standard data intelligence servers will not take advantage of GPUs. For scenarios where GPU is required such as deep learning scenarios, an alternative solution is suggested, such as AI Core, which we will cover later in this chapter. SAP Data Intelligence can still be utilized for the pipelining of the data to a different training or serving environment supporting GPUs.

Deployment of models is done using operators that wrap R and Python code and make it reusable in any pipeline. SAP Data Intelligence's architecture is container-based and each operator runs in its own Docker container and can scale independently. Monitoring and pipeline metrics are available, and the pipelines can be scheduled to run as part of CI/CD through tools such as Git and Jenkins. *Figure 14.3* depicts the core data orchestration and governance capabilities and the support of ML and AI scenarios in SAP Data Intelligence:

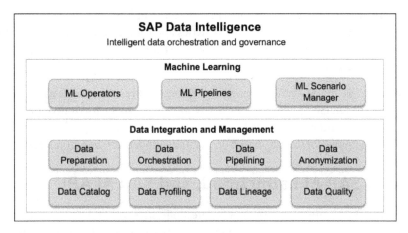

Figure 14.3: ML/AI support in SAP Data Intelligence

However, there are no specific MLOps lifecycle management tools available in SAP Data Intelligence, which we will discuss as part of AI Core. Before that, let's review the smart features available in SAC that we discussed in the last chapter.

## SAC smart features

SAC offers a set of smart features such as Smart Insights and Smart Predict, mainly for citizen data scientists and business users. We introduced the details of these capabilities in the last chapter, so here, we will briefly discuss what was not covered previously – the lifecycle and differences of predictive models, from data preparation to the operation of the models.

SAC supports two types of models – based on datasets or planning-enabled models. Datasets whether acquired or through live connection can be used as data sources to create any supported predictive scenarios. Planning-enabled models can be used for time series forecasting models.

SAC provides a simple way to create predictive models – underneath SAC, the predictive engine uses similar capabilities to the APL in SAP HANA. SAC doesn't offer the ability to parameterize the underlying algorithms on purpose to keep it simple.

To evaluate the quality of predictive models, the following metrics are made available in SAC, as shown in *Table 14.1*:

| Predictive Scenario | Accuracy | Robustness |
|---|---|---|
| Classification | Predictive Power | Prediction Confidence |
| Regression | **Root Mean Squared Error (RMSE)** | Prediction Confidence |
| Time Series Forecasting | **Mean Absolute Percentage Error (MAPE)** | |

Table 14.1: SAC Predictive Model Metrics

Predictive scenarios and predictive models are created, stored in SAC, and the consumption of the prediction is typically done in SAC stories and analytics applications for the end users. Predictive forecasts generated from planning-enabled models can be exported and written back to the source systems for further integration with specific business processes.

The lifecycle of predictive models is fully managed within SAC. Predictive models created based on datasets will need to be retained manually for classification, regression, and time series forecasting. However, time series forecasting models can be created on top of datasets or planning-enabled models and the refresh of time series forecasting based on planning models can be automated.

# SAP AI Core, SAP AI Launchpad, and SAP AI API

SAP AI Core and SAP AI Launchpad are the two latest offerings from SAP to provide the unified AI consumption and lifecycle management of all types of AI scenarios. AI scenarios can be realized through the AI runtimes provided by SAP AI Core or using any framework, such as TensorFlow. The management of operations of AI scenarios such as versioning, training, deployment, and serving is provided through AI Launchpad. Together, they provide similar and additional functionalities to the SAP Leonardo Machine Learning Foundation. Let's start by understanding SAP AI Core.

## SAP AI Core

SAP AI Core is SAP's AI runtime for ML and AI workloads with integration in SAP BTP to deploy AI scenarios at scale. Operationalizing AI scenarios, such as bringing an AI model developed by a data scientist to production, is not easy. SAP AI Core is the solution to productize AI for **Bring Your Own Model** (**BYOM**) scenarios. However, SAP AI Core is not intended for developing models – models can be created by leveraging any open source ML library and packaged as a Docker container. Once a model is built into a training workflow, SAP AI Core can execute and schedule the training, including the support of GPUs for parallelization.

Typically, datasets are provided via object stores such as AWS S3. SAP AI Core provides integration with all supported object stores for different hyperscalers. Unlike SAP Data Intelligence as a general data preparation tool, SAP AI Core offers limited capabilities and is only suitable for small and AI processing-focused data transformations. It is recommended to transform the dataset outside SAP AI Core to prepare it to train the AI models.

SAP AI Core offers the runtime environment to run AI scenarios, including capabilities such as multi-tenancy, auto-scaling, GPU support, and KFServing to standardize ML operations on top of Kubernetes. SAP AI Core leverages the standard Argo Workflows as the open source and container-native workflow engine, based on GitOps principles. Customers can create Argo workflows either by bringing their own models from experimental environments or promote training workflows within SAP AI Core. SAP AI Core supports multi-tenancy – each tenant can support multiple resource groups for the isolation of data and functions.

With a focus on the productization of AI scenarios, SAP AI Core collects and stores a wide range of metrics that can be configured, including the performance metrics of models and statistics on training jobs. Through the integration of the AI API, a standardized list of metrics is provided or can be further extended by customers specific to their scenarios. Monitoring of all key metrics is one of the main capabilities of SAP AI Core to enable operations. Through the integration, the metrics are available and can be analyzed in SAP AI Launchpad.

## SAP AI Launchpad

SAP AI Launchpad is the SaaS offering that provides a **user interface** (**UI**) for managing and operating AI scenarios across multiple deployments and instances of supported AI runtimes such as SAP AI Core or other third-party AI runtimes. SAP AI Launchpad also provides all the necessary information on metrics and artifacts and supports the full lifecycle of training, executing, and operating in AI scenarios across AI execution engines.

From an MLOps perspective, SAP AI Launchpad is envisioned as the tool for data scientists and ML engineers for all AI content development and productization across the SAP landscape. Customers can leverage SAP AI Launchpad to trigger jobs to deploy a model and productize existing training models in supported AI runtimes, including SAP AI Core.

SAP AI Launchpad is considered the single place to explore and manage the full lifecycle of AI scenarios within the SAP landscape, regardless of runtimes.

## SAP AI API

The lifecycle management of AI scenarios is standardized through a common set of APIs called SAP AI API. SAP AI Core and SAP AI Launchpad are also integrated through SAP AI API as the standard interface.

The AI API provides tools for managing the artifacts, workflows, and AI scenarios, such as the following:

- Register supported object stores such as AWS S3 and WebHDFS for storing training data and training models
- Create a Docker Registry secret to authorize the pull of docker images from your Docker Registry
- Create a configuration to specify the parameters (artifact references)
- Register an artifact for use in a configuration, such as a dataset or model
- Deploy a trained model and start to serve inference requests
- Manage training and execution metrics based on filtering conditions

SAP AI API is independent of the AI runtimes, whether it is in SAP HANA ML or leverages partner technologies such as the AI runtimes from **Amazon Web Services** (**AWS**), Microsoft Azure, and **Google Cloud Platform** (**GCP**).

> **Important Note**
>
> For more details about SAP AI API, please read the API reference at `https://help.sap.com/doc/2cefe221fddf410aab23dce890b5c603/CLOUD/en-US/index.html`.

To summarize, *Figure 14.4* depicts the integrations between SAP AI Core, SAP AI Launchpad, and SAP AI API:

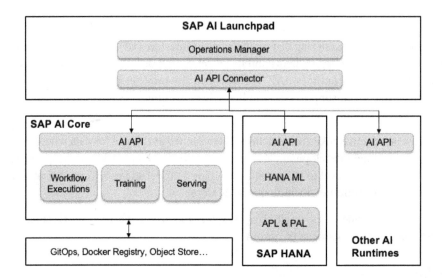

Figure 14.4: SAP AI Core, AI Launchpad, and AI API

Next, let's have a look at SAP AI Business Services, the simplest way to consume intelligent capabilities from SAP BTP.

## SAP AI Business Services

SAP offers differentiated business-centric AI services through SAP AI Business Services. SAP AI Business Services is not a single product but a set of reusable business services and applications that provide the capabilities to automate and optimize business processes based on learning from historic data. It solves some specific business problems such as processing documents and business entity recognition.

Most of the SAP AI Business Services are delivered as SaaS offerings with their own UIs or as ready-to-use APIs that can be integrated into existing business processes. By embedding SAP AI Business Services, some SAP applications such as S/4HANA provide out-of-box integrations that infuse intelligence as part of the business application. SAP customers and partners can use SAP AI Business Services for their specific scenario with ready-to-use AI algorithms in your business context through SAP BTP, based on their own data.

*Figure 14.5* summarizes the list of services in SAP AI Business Services. SAP will continue to offer new services through SAP BTP:

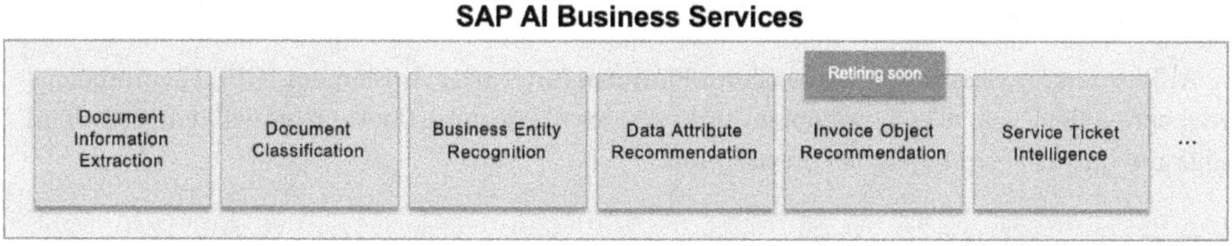

**SAP AI Business Services**

Figure 14.5: SAP AI Business Services

Here are some more details:

- **Document Information Extraction** to process a large number of business documents such as invoices and payments and extract information from header fields and line items as structured data. It allows you to use master data to enrich information and find the best match and create your own template for processing custom documents.

- **Document Classification** helps to classify and manage many documents with either pre-trained or custom classification models to improve overall document processing productivity. It supports various use cases such as contract management and invoice processing.

- **Business Entity Recognition** helps to detect and extract business entities from unstructured text. It supports both pre-trained models and allows users to create their own ML models to detect new types of entities. Business Entity Recognition is offered as an API-only service without a UI.

- **Data Attribute Recommendation** helps to match and classify master data, such as matching a point of sales information with a product category and adding missing numerical attributes in sales orders. Data Attribute Recommendation is also offered as an API-only service without a UI.

- **Invoice Object Recommendation** helps the accounts payable department to recommend or increase the accuracy in assigning **general ledger** (**G/L**) accounts and cost objects for incoming invoices without a purpose, in order to reduce the time taken to process and carry out repetitive manual tasks. Invoice Object Recommendation is also offered as an API-only service without UI. At the time of writing, Invoice Object Recommendation is marked as to be deprecated soon.

- **Service Ticket Intelligence** helps to classify service tickets into their categories and assign them to the right agent with recommended solutions or knowledge base articles to improve service response time and overall support productivity and efficiency. Service Ticket Intelligence is embedded in SAP Service Cloud or can be consumed as a REST-based API.

SAP AI Business Services provide ready-to-use AI models consumable through standard REST APIs, enabling developers to use AI services without the need for data science know-how. Most SAP AI

Business Services provide APIs for both training and inference – SAP also takes care of the deployment and ongoing operations of the models. Due to its simplicity and position to solve specific business problems, SAP AI Business Services is considered the starting point of the AI journey for your SAP landscape, all through easy-to-consume cloud offerings.

SAP AI Business Services is part of the **Cloud Platform Enterprise Agreement** (**CPEA**) commercial model of SAP BTP that allows customers and partners to consume the services with entitled cloud credits and only charged based on consumption.

## SAP Conversational AI

SAP **Conversational AI** (**CAI**) offers **Natural Language Processing** (**NLP**) capabilities to enable users to create intelligent chatbots to automate workflows. SAP CAI is the conversational AI layer of SAP BTP to help businesses to build bots through its low-code bot building platform and embed chatbot experiences into SAP applications to deliver a personalized experience and automate time-consuming and repetitive tasks.

As an enterprise conversational AI platform, SAP CAI provides the following capabilities:

- **Build the bot**: Give skills to the bot that include the trigger, requirements, and responses, and create the conversational flow with the Bot Builder tool

- **Train the bot**: Create intents and use expressions to teach the bot what it can understand and recognize from the users

- **Connect the bot**: Connect the bot to SAP solutions and various messaging platforms and integrate with a fallback channel to a human agent if required

- **Monitor the bot**: Understand how users interact with the bot, understand unaddressed requirements, and improve user experience

Originally acquired from Recast.AI, SAP CAI helps to enhance the NLP capabilities for SAP solutions by providing a conversational user experience for SAP customers. CAI is offered as a service in BTP and will continue to provide more integration and usage with other SAP solutions, such as the SAP SuccessFactors Human Experience Management suite.

## SAP Process Automation

There is an increasing demand for companies to enable their employees to focus on business-critical activities rather than manual and repetitive tasks. One approach is to upskill the workforce to leverage process automation tools to improve productivity and reduce cycle time. Think about the use cases such as automating repetitive tasks such as copying and pasting into a spreadsheet, high-volume process steps such as entering sales order data, changing purchase orders, the employee onboarding process, and leave request approval.

SAP Process Automation is an intelligent process automation platform that provides a low-code and no-code experience to users for building applications and process extensions. It combines the capabilities of SAP Workflow Management and SAP iRPA. It helps business users (aka Citizen Developers) to build automation for their business processes without the need to depend on the IT department. In this way, it unleashes the power to have a domain expert with process knowledge but not necessarily the developer skills to participate in simplifying and automating business processes.

SAP Process Automation is available as part of BTP's free tier and can be consumed through the CPEA or pay-as-you-go models. Once enabled in the BTP Cockpit, the SAP Process Automation application development workbench is the no-code environment to create, test, deploy and monitor the processes, with different skills such as automation, forms, and advanced workflows, as *Figure 14.6* shows:

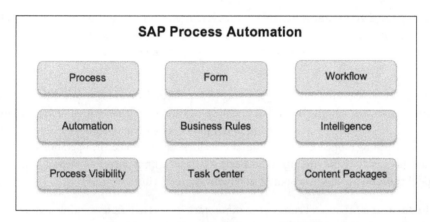

Figure 14.6: SAP Process Automation capabilities

As part of SAP Process Automation, the desktop agent is an on-premises component, with a setup program as a Windows MSI installer. The installer can be downloaded from SAP Software Center.

SAP Process Automation organizes the features in the following areas:

- **Lobby**: For creating and managing business process projects or action projects. A business project is a way to group tasks of business scenarios and it can consist of different skills such as automation, approval forms, or business rules. An action project is a place to encapsulate external APIs typically created by IT teams that allow business users to consume in a business process project.

- **Store**: The place to browse and use existing pre-packaged content curated by SAP, which includes templated automation, forms, actions, workflows, processes, and process visibility dashboards. All the content is versioned and free to use but SAP doesn't warrant the correctness

- **Monitor**: Allows business users to see how automation is performing through Process visibility dashboards. Users can create rich dashboards and collect events from automation jobs and workflows.

- **Setting**: Where to register and configure the desktop agents, backend settings such as a mail server or integration with SAP Cloud ALM, and configure API keys, destinations, and so on.

Now that we have covered the intelligent technologies offered through SAP BTP, let's have a look at how they are integrated with SAP applications such as SAP S/4HANA.

# Intelligent Scenario Lifecycle Management for S/4HANA

ISLM is the standardized framework for the lifecycle management and operation of intelligent scenarios in the context of SAP S4/HANA. ISLM acts as the central cockpit to operate ML in SAP S4/HANA and it cannot be used outside of it. An intelligent scenario is an ABAP representation of an ML-based use case.

The ISLM framework offers the necessary support to standardize the integration and consumption of intelligent scenarios for both embedded and side-by-side scenarios, which allows application developers for SAP S/4HANA to create scenarios and perform lifecycle operations including training, deploying, and activating models directly within the business applications. The operations of intelligent scenarios are supported by the Intelligent Scenario Management application. Depending on where the ML model runs, ISLM supports both of the following scenarios:

- **Embedded**: The ML model runs in the same stack as S/4HANA, leveraging SAP HANA ML capabilities such as the APL and PAL, and is consumed by the ABAP-based applications directly.

- **Side-by-side**: When the ML model runs in a separate stack such as SAP AI Core or through the consumption of SAP AI Business Services. The side-by-side scenarios have more flexibility to support advanced AI use cases by leveraging capabilities such as image recognition or deep learning based on neural networks

Through ISLM, an intelligent scenario of either type can be created. It provides the customers the possibility to perform prerequisite checks in the exploration phase and check whether the scenario will run successfully in their environment. An ML model can be trained and deployed for inference consumption; deployment is only applicable to side-by-side scenarios. To be consistent with the ABAP programming model, ISLM provides customers more control to specify the trained model to be activated and used in production, with the additional step of activation of an intelligent scenario. The inference result can be consumed through ABAP APIs for side-by-side scenarios and CDS views for embedded scenarios; batch inference requests can also be involved in the business applications. *Figure 14.7* depicts the architectural integration for the side-by-side scenario:

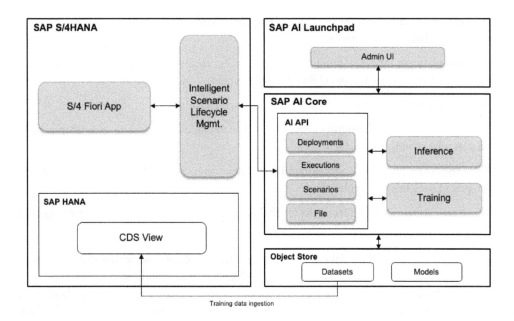

Figure 14.7: A side-by-side intelligent scenario in S/4HANA

The focus of ISLM is to support more scenario types for the diverse need of S/4HANA business applications and provide enhanced capabilities for metering, model comparison, and multi-model management. In the current scope, ISLM doesn't support data management capabilities. Depending on the scenario, it relies on HANA for embedded and can leverage a cloud object store or HANA data lake files for the side-by-side scenarios. ISLM also integrates with AI Launchpad for monitoring and metrics.

One of the key challenges in AI projects is how to handle the data – from data integration and transformation to data governance. Next, we will discuss the data architecture for AI that covers these aspects.

## Data architecture for AI

Data is an essential ingredient for any AI scenario. One of the key elements for the success of an AI project is the data architecture – how to bring data together, store and process it, bring the results back, and integrate the insights and actions back into the applications. The following are some of the typical challenges of the data architecture for AI:

- Data is located across different data sources based on different formats, systems, and structured and unstructured data types.
- Data integration and consolidation require a common data model.

- Replicating data involves how to address data privacy and data protection concerns, as well as other compliance requirements.

- The data platform provides data for the AI execution engine and also needs to address data ingestion, data storage, and data lifecycle management.

- AI requires metadata such as labeling for supervised learning.

- AI lifecycle events can be tightly coupled with the data lifecycle, such as an inference based on a live data change.

- The insights and AI-based recommendations need to be served by the data platform and integrated back into the applications.

- There are performance requirements for the initial load and event-based data integration for incremental changes.

In this section, we will describe the data architecture for AI. Most of the time, we have SAP AI Core as the AI execution engine, but SAP also supports other AI execution engines from partners, such as the relevant services from AWS, Azure, and GCP. HANA ML as described earlier provides in-database AI and doesn't necessarily require an extended data architecture. Thus, we will not discuss it further here.

The availability of data is critical for the success of AI projects, for both the design time and run time in the production phase.

During design time, for exploration and experimentation, data acquisition and access to training data is the first important step. Data integration tools such as SAP Data Intelligence can be leveraged to extract data from source systems, in batch or through events, as well as manage the lifecycle of data pipelines. In many use cases, access to and management of third-party datasets will be required. For that, the data architecture should be able to leverage scalable cloud storage such as object stores such as AWS S3. AI runtimes such as AI Core can work directly with object stores. Besides, content creation such as labeling can be labor-intensive and should be automated and coordinated as much as possible.

In production, the data architecture needs to support the severance, monitoring, and retention of the models. Data needs to be continuously available from various data sources including SAP applications to do the re-training and inference processes. A frequent challenge is how to make sure that data governance and compliance are ensured across heterogeneous data sources. A common approach for data governance and policy enforcement is required. It is important to trace the data lineage to understand where data is coming from and how it is processed, especially when data is transported and transformed over several stages, which is often required in modern AI use cases.

In the meantime, it is important to meet the non-functional requirements specific to business needs. Such requirements include but are not limited to multi-tenancy support to isolate the needs of different customers, the ability to monitor the data quality, and ensure consistency with training data. AI in production requires operational readiness. For that, SAP AI Launchpad can support lifecycle management in production as the central operational tool, which supports flexible AI runtime options including SAP AI Core.

Based on the design time needs and runtime requirements described previously, we can start to draw the data architecture diagram covering three major components that include a data platform, an AI platform, and business applications. We will describe the roles and responsibilities of each of them here in detail.

The data platform will be responsible for the following:

- Ingest and store data from SAP applications and third-party data sources
- Keep data up to date through streaming or delta loads from various data sources
- Expose data and make it consumable for AI runtimes
- Store and expose inference results and make them consumable for the applications and downstream consumers
- Store and manage the metadata such as domain models, labeling, connectivity, data cataloging, and data lineage
- Handle data privacy, data protection, and compliance requirements, such as data encryption at rest, data segregation, and audit logging
- Store the AI model and intermediate artifacts such as derived datasets and models

The AI platform will focus on the following responsibilities:

- Manage the AI scenarios and its lifecycle, such as training, deployments, and inference
- Manage the artifacts such as datasets and models as well as the intermediate artifacts
- Expose the AI lifecycle via AI APIs across different runtimes if necessary
- Provide capabilities for data anonymization, labeling, a data annotation workflow, and data quality management

While most of the heavy lifting is performed by the data platform and AI platform, the applications are still responsible for the following aspects:

- Provide and integrate data into the data platform by exposing API or data events
- Consume the inference results and integrate them back into the application for the end users
- Control the AI lifecycle using specific clients such as S/4HANA ISLM (optional)

This kind of data architecture is depicted in *Figure 14.8*, leveraging some of the offerings from SAP BTP described in this chapter and previous chapters:

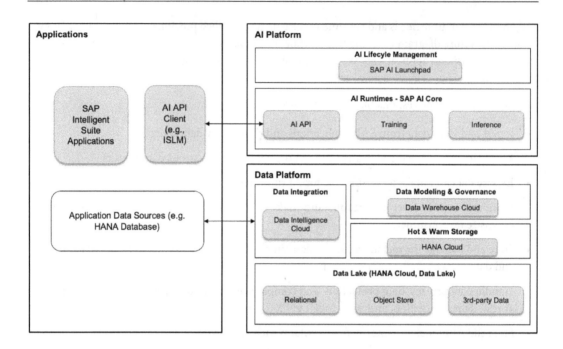

Figure 14.8: Data architecture for AI

In this data architecture, as part of the described *data platform*, the data lake provides the *cold storage* and the processing layer of relational data, object store support through HANA Cloud, the data lake, and HANA Cloud and data lake files. For HANA Cloud, the data lake is a disk-based relational database optimized for an OLAP workload and provides native integration with a cloud object store through HANA Cloud and data lake files, to leverage it as a cheaper data storage with **SQL on Files** capabilities. HANA Cloud as the in-memory HTAP database provides the *hot and warm storage* and processing of relational and multi-model data such as spatial, document, and graph data. HANA Cloud includes multi-tier storage, including in-memory and extended storage based on disks. SAP Data Warehouse Cloud focuses on the data modeling and governance of the data architecture and provides the semantic layer and data access governance. Besides this, SAP Data Intelligence provides the data integration and ingestion capabilities for extracting data from source systems and managing the lifecycle of data pipelines. Next, the AI platform comprised of SAP AI Core and SAP AI Launchpad is responsible for managing the AI scenarios across training, inference, monitoring, and the operational readiness of AI projects. Finally, applications are served as both the data sources and consumers in an AI scenario.

While this data architecture illustrates how different kinds of technologies can be put together to serve AI needs, regardless, it is not a necessary architecture for all kinds of use cases. Depending on the complexity and integration needs of your use cases, the data architecture can be dramatically simplified, and not all the mentioned technology components will be required. For example, SAP AI Core can directly consume data from a cloud object store bucket and manage the AI lifecycle directly together with SAP AI Launchpad. In the simplest scenario, you may even just call an API from SAP API Business Services without the need to worry about the operational complexity of AI models.

## Data Privacy and Protection

**Data Privacy and Protection** (DPP) in the handling of customer data in AI scenarios is a critical enterprise quality that must be prioritized in the data architecture. For an ML/AI use case, data that comes from different sources may contain **Personal Identifiable Information** (PII) and therefore must be handled properly.

When PII is involved, no human interaction will be allowed whether data is in a structured or unstructured format. This is applicable to data extraction and integration, the inspection of data, model training, and the deletion of data. Concretely, the data architecture needs to consider the following concepts and mechanisms to support DPP-compliant data processing:

- **Authorization management**: Only authorized data can be processed and the user's data authorization in the applications needs to be translated into the data authorization of replicated data. Authorization management is based on DPP purposes and can be achieved by providing the DPP context of the user from the leading source system to the data platform. For example, a manager should only see the salary information of members of their team.

- **Data anonymization**: Applying the anonymization function to translate a raw dataset into an anonymized dataset while preserving the necessary information for the AI use cases. HANA supports in-database anonymization or can be applied as part of the data pipeline for in-transit anonymization enabled by the K-Anonymity operator of Data Intelligence.

- **Data access and change logging**: If sensitive DPP data is stored, the data platform must provide read-access logging. Besides this, any change to personal data should be logged.

- **Data deletion**: Data is usually replicated to the data platform. If the data is erased in the source system when the retention period has expired or when requested by the user in the context of the **GDPR (General Data Protection Regulation)** in the EU, it also needs to be prorogated to delete the data replicated in the data platform.

# Summary

This chapter wrapped up the overall "*data to value*" offerings from SAP BTP. Throughout this chapter, we introduced a broader set of intelligent technologies, starting from the ML capabilities in SAP HANA through the APL and PAL. After that, we discussed the embedded ML/AI capabilities in SAP Analytics Cloud and how SAP Data Intelligence supports the orchestration and governance of AI scenarios.

We also briefly covered SAP CAI for supporting the digital assistance experience and SAP Process Automation for workflow automation to enable business users to automate repetitive tasks without the need to depend on the IT department.

Of course, SAP AI Core and SAP AI Launchpad are the core offerings to support advanced AI use cases such as deep learning, with SAP AI Core as the execution runtime and SAP AI Launchpad providing lifecycle management and monitoring operational AI scenarios.

Lastly, data is essential for any AI scenario. In this context, we explored what the typical challenges in data management for AI are, the core components of data architecture, the SAP technologies that can be used as part of the data architecture, and the guidance for supporting DPP requirements.

# Index

`Packt.com`

Subscribe to our online digital library for full access to over 7,000 books and videos, as well as industry leading tools to help you plan your personal development and advance your career. For more information, please visit our website.

## Why subscribe?

- Spend less time learning and more time coding with practical eBooks and Videos from over 4,000 industry professionals

- Improve your learning with Skill Plans built especially for you

- Get a free eBook or video every month

- Fully searchable for easy access to vital information

- Copy and paste, print, and bookmark content

Did you know that Packt offers eBook versions of every book published, with PDF and ePub files available? You can upgrade to the eBook version at `packt.com` and as a print book customer, you are entitled to a discount on the eBook copy. Get in touch with us at `customercare@packtpub.com` for more details.

At `www.packt.com`, you can also read a collection of free technical articles, sign up for a range of free newsletters, and receive exclusive discounts and offers on Packt books and eBooks.

# Other Books You May Enjoy

If you enjoyed this book, you may be interested in these other books by Packt:

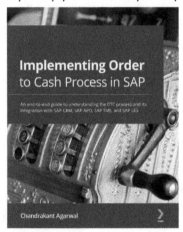

**Implementing Order to Cash Process in SAP**

Chandrakant Agarwal

ISBN: 978-1-801-07610-4

- Discover master data in different SAP environments
- Find out how different sales processes, such as quotations, contracts, and order management, work in SAP CRM
- Become well-versed with the steps involved in order fulfillment, such as basic and advanced ATP checks in SAP APO
- Get up and running with transportation requirement and planning and freight settlement with SAP TMS
- Explore warehouse management with SAP LES to ensure high transparency and predictability of processes
- Understand how to process customer invoicing with SAP ECC

**SAP Intelligent RPA for Developers**

Vishwas Madhuvarshi, Vijaya Kumar Ganugula

ISBN: 978-1-801-07919-8

- Understand RPA and the broad context that RPA operates in

- Explore the low-code, no-code, and pro-code capabilities offered by SAP Intelligent RPA 2.0

- Focus on bot development, testing, deployment, and configuration using SAP Intelligent RPA

- Get to grips with SAP Intelligent RPA 2.0 components and explore the product development roadmap

- Debug your project to identify the probable reasons for errors and remove existing and potential bugs

- Understand security within SAP Intelligent RPA, authorization, roles, and authentication

## Packt is searching for authors like you

If you're interested in becoming an author for Packt, please visit authors.packtpub.com and apply today. We have worked with thousands of developers and tech professionals, just like you, to help them share their insight with the global tech community. You can make a general application, apply for a specific hot topic that we are recruiting an author for, or submit your own idea.

## Share Your Thoughts

Now you've finished *Architecting Solutions with SAP Business Technology Platform*, we'd love to hear your thoughts! Scan the QR code below to go straight to the Amazon review page for this book and share your feedback or leave a review on the site that you purchased it from.

https://packt.link/r/1801075670

Your review is important to us and the tech community and will help us make sure we're delivering excellent quality content.

# Download a Free PDF copy of this book

Thanks for purchasing this book!

Do you like to read on the go but are unable to carry your print books everywhere?

Is your eBook purchase not compatible with the device of your choice?

Don't worry, now with every Packt book you get a DRM-free PDF version of that book at no cost.

Read anywhere, any place, on any device. Search, copy, and paste code from your favorite technical books directly into your application.

The perks don't stop there, you can get exclusive access to discounts, newsletters, and great free content in your inbox daily

Follow these simple steps to get the benefits:

1. Scan the QR code or visit the link below

https://packt.link/free-ebook/978-1-80107-567-1

2. Submit your proof of purchase
3. That's it! We'll send your free PDF and other benefits to your email directly